TOWARD A SOCIOLOGY OF THE TRACE

Toward a Sociology
of the Trace

· · · ·

Herman Gray and Macarena Gómez-Barris
Editors

MINNESOTA

University of Minnesota Press
Minneapolis
London

Portions of chapter 2 were previously published in Avery F. Gordon, "Methodologies of Imprisonment," *PMLA* 123 (2008); this essay originated as a contribution to the conference "The Collapse of Traditional Knowledge: Economy, Technology, Geopolitics" at Duke University in 2007. Chapter 6 appears in a slightly different form in Rebecca R. Scott, *Removing Mountains: Extracting Nature and Identity in the Appalachian Coalfields* (Minneapolis: University of Minnesota Press, 2010).

Published by the University of Minnesota Press
111 Third Avenue South, Suite 290
Minneapolis, MN 55401-2520
http://www.upress.umn.edu

Library of Congress Cataloging-in-Publication Data

Toward a sociology of the trace / [edited by] Herman Gray and Macarena Gómez-Barris, editors.
   p. cm.
Includes bibliographical references and index.
ISBN 978-0-8166-5597-7 (hc : alk. paper) — ISBN 978-0-8166-5598-4 (pb : alk. paper)
1. Culture. 2. Social inclusion. 3. Group identity. 4. National identity. 5. Memory. I. Gray, Herman. II. Gómez-Barris, Macarena.

HM621.T68 2010
306.01—dc22   2010027766

Printed in the United States of America on acid-free paper

The University of Minnesota is an equal-opportunity educator and employer.

18 17 16 15 14 13 12 11 10   10 9 8 7 6 5 4 3 2 1

Contents

Part III. Managing and Reconciling Memory

Traces in the Social World

Macarena Gómez-Barris and Herman Gray

A T SOME POINT in the process of writing about traces in social worlds, we began to work with the metaphor of rehearsal inspired by an exhibition of Francis Alys's work at the Hammer Museum in Los Angeles. At the time, the language of rehearsal and the symbolic image that it provoked for us was the closest we could get to capturing the spirit and challenge of our concerns, concerns that were neither neat nor clean nor easily expressed in words. What we sought to capture with this image of repetition, failure, new beginnings, disappointment, delay, and limits was the sense of messiness and contingency that defines our social worlds. This image of constantly starting over, of beginning again and again, also defined our process of working with a conception of culture that bore the traces, if you will, of a complex engagement with the social and cultural fields within which we locate this volume. We wanted to acknowledge our formation in the field of sociology and, at the same time, to critically engage with and draw on advances and insights from our active participation in the related interdisciplinary fields that also appear in the chapters in this volume. This presented us with the challenge of negotiating multiple fields, methods, theoretical insights, and intellectual advances that were legible in one area but too often suspect in another. For example, notions of discourse, representation, and traces, to take three somewhat controversial concepts, are often used differently in sociology, cultural studies, literature, and ethnic studies. Rather than produce a volume that reached consensus across fields (or even within fields) we elected to keep the tensions, sharpening and sometimes highlighting them for the insights they offered us and our contributors about working with scales, sites, and practices that constitute social worlds and the traces they register.

Eventually we dropped the reference to rehearsal; it proved too unwieldy and oblique, and while it perfectly described our process, it could not sustain the emphasis on trace that we sought. Nonetheless, the spirit of that initial impulse (and all the indeterminacy and messiness that it conjured) remains and, as our opening chapter suggests, continues to shape our thinking about the importance of interruption and beginning again in how social worlds are made, the importance of thinking about where the social resides, and how powerful the transactions that occur there are for comprehending the resilience of social subjects and their capacities for making social worlds despite what often seem to be daunting circumstances.

In the first chapter, we offer an account of the intellectual influences, methodological challenges, and the political stakes of the collection. Our aim is that the collection offers readers a way of working with the idea of culture that retains the commitment to the empirical without being reductionist and that engages related fields without being territorial. In the end, we aim to show how a flexible but grounded idea of culture—as practice, meaning, site, and process—can be useful for getting at the crucial importance of social traces for making sense of social worlds across a range of sites and situations.

We are well aware that investing so heavily in the centrality of culture and representation as a way of tracking the social dimension of traces may be messier, less than analytically precise, and less empirically exact than the certainty of language, images, and referents conventionally used to talk about "structures" in traditional disciplines like sociology or anthropology. We are more than willing to take this point, and as we indicate in our chapter, we do so because we think the nature of culture and the complex sites and transactions that take place under the sign of the social compel us to acknowledge (even occasionally use) the language of imprecision to signal the dense, imprecise, and often elusive nature of our endeavor to understand and describe social worlds.

This is precisely Avery Gordon's challenge. She asks us to imagine a new vocabulary with which to critically interrogate the modes and operations of domination whose rehearsal we want to understand and disrupt so that we can tell the stories "of the ones whose existence has been denied, abandoned, and forgotten" (Gordon, this volume). For Gordon, the contemporary zones of captivity that ensnare the worker, enemy, migrant, resident, and prisoner are the sites for the exercise of power and the production of subjects that circumscribe social life and social death through what she calls racialized statecraft. She argues that state-sanctioned racism works by coupling difference and power to produce vulnerability to premature death. In her chapter "The Prisoner's Curse," which is staged through Gordon's interrogation of and meditation on the suicides of three prisoners at Guantánamo Bay, Cuba, she announces the two major themes of the book: ritualized repetition—if you will—and the centrality of knowledge, power, and representation for modes of domination, including those that take place under conditions of permanent war. For Gordon, the relationship between slavery and imprisonment, and captivity and social death, is a central feature of the operations of power and knowledge under such conditions. Gordon's challenge in finding a new vocabulary is not only to account for these new forms of power-knowledge but also, following Foucault, to carve out a place for subjugated knowledges—in this case, the prisoner's curse of the chapter's title—that might form the basis of critical scholarship, with which to expose the secrets, selections, and rehearsals of power, as Gordon puts it, "that negates the dispossessions, disabilities, and dehumanizations experienced by those deemed inhuman or subhuman."

Cartographies of Belonging

Next we turn our attention to marginal and disposable subjects who are constituted and regulated through discursive strategies of policy discourse and legislation. The chapters concerned with the mapping, production, and meaning of belonging suggest that discursive strategies are used to culturally reimagine subjects and legally set the terms of subjection to the discourse of the cultural dominant. Helped along by media representations, sacrificial subjects circulate in the popular imagination (and are deployed by the state) to mark normative boundaries and regulate behavior. One of our claims is that forms of power-knowledge operate in neoliberal states through the proliferation or incitement to difference that works to secure the terms of national identity and produces new forms of inequality and difference more so than those traditionally marked by race or ethnicity.

The focus of Tanya McNeil's chapter, "A Nation of Families: The Codification and (Be)longings of Heteropatriarchy," is the production and deployment of social science knowledge about welfare mothers and gay, lesbian, and transgender families as a means of shoring up the institutions of families and marriage that are thought to be under assault. Key to this project of regulation is a conservative, neoliberal national government that has deployed social science, affect, and morality as forms of power-knowledge in the state project of building (and protecting) the institutions of family and marriage as the crucial site for reproducing the heteronormative nation. In McNeil's analysis, gay, lesbian, and transgender individuals and Latino, black, often-single, urban, and poor welfare mothers are the subjects of neoliberal state policies that recognize, and even claim, multicultural tolerance and diversity on issues of race and gender but do so within the terms of racial, gender, and sex orders organized according to racial privilege, patriarchy, and heteronormativity.

The operation of discursive strategies is also the subject of "Culture, Masculinity, and the Time after Race," Herman Gray's discussion of the deployment of culture as a regulatory discourse that produces appropriate subjects of the nation in what Gray ironically calls "the time after race," or the historical period after the American civil rights revolution and after the September 11 bombing of the World Trade Center in New York City. Gray considers how the concept of "culture" is used in public discourse as a response to the moral panics of a black youth culture that threatens the narrative of racial progress and color-blindness in the U.S. national imagination. Gray argues that the return of this form of knowledge, especially in the context of neoliberal national government, be read as a way of constructing normative (racial and masculine) ideals of citizenship through the marking and regulating of unruly black bodies.

Finally the theme of marginal and disposable subjects who are constituted and regulated through discursive strategies of policy discourse and legislation is powerfully illustrated in Akiko Naono's discussion of the discursive production of Japanese national subjects in the operation of juridical procedures. In "Producing Sacrificial Subjects for the Nation: Japan's War-related Redress Policy and the Endurance Doctrine," Naono examines rhetorical devices and narrative strategies that produce disposable national subjects while generating inequality among the citizen subjects and erasing colonial subjects from the space of the nation. She examines Japanese war-related redress policy in its relationship to the endurance doctrine, which claims that "all national subjects must equally accept and endure some loss of life, body, or assets in a state of national emergency, such as a time of war" (Naono, this volume). Furthermore, Naono argues that Japan continues to sustain a colonial project even in its postcolonial liberal democracy. For Naono, the discursive effect of Japanese colonial violence is inscribed, and therefore remains productive, in contemporary Japanese law and public policy, where juridical contests over the endurance doctrine constitute social subjects by producing new social inequalities.

Spectacles of Consumption

For several of our contributors, cultural practices like consumption and representation take place in the media, at parades and public celebrations, and through official memorials. These are active scenes of cultural production and *contestation* where social worlds are discursively imagined and emotionally felt, and they offer telling examples of the pivotal role of culture, representation, and feeling in constituting the social world. Constructions and representations of place and citizenship are the subjects of chapters that address these themes directly. In training their analytic focus on points of cultural struggle over competing definitions and representations of place, the contributors to this part show how dominant ideas about the national symbolic are constituted at the level of representation and meaning. Methodologically, these chapters illustrate the kinds of productive possibilities that result when complementary approaches and dialogic exchanges occur among different disciplines through problematics involving nature, the environment, and place.

In "Coal Heritage/Coal History: Progress, Tourism, and Mountaintop Removal," for example, Rebecca Scott argues that disputes over coal heritage memorials are both struggles about the past (i.e., the meaning of place) and contests about futures. That is, as new technologies of coal excavation (i.e., mountain top removal) are introduced, they bring changes in the regional economy, the deformation of the landscape, and, most significantly for Scott, cultural disputes over the identity and meaning of place. Scott details this struggle over the cultural meaning of place among energy companies, environmentalists, and union activists. She examines competing claims over whose story about the past should drive or define what we remember and how we experience the region as a place within the national narrative. As she shows, the stakes in these cultural disputes about memory and history are quite high and connected to the contemporary political economy of the region's development as a tourist site, as a business model of progress and economic expansion, and as a place of environmental consciousness.

Barbara Barnes is also concerned with the cultural role of writing and representation in the production of place and national identity. In contrast to Scott, Barnes's focus is on the frontier and the cultural production of contemporary representations of the frontier as empty. Utah is the stage for "Ecoadventures in the American West: Innocence, Conflict, and Nation Making in Emptied Landscapes," Barnes's account of the circulation of the eighteenth-century frontier myth of open space, rugged individualism, and mobile masculinity. For Barnes, the endurance of this cultural mythology is evident in the number and range of representational sites—historical texts, the western movie genre, oil paintings, television advertisements, and contemporary television spectacles—and cultural narratives through which the myth is recycled and enacted. But the endurance of this myth is enabled by its capacity to underwrite conceptions of the nation as a structure of feeling, a form of recognition and sense of knowledge that is emotionally felt as much as it is intellectually understood. Hence, her analytic focus is on strategies of representation in painting and cinema and the discourses of manifest destiny and white supremacy that invited, and even entitled, viewers and audiences to feel at home in a frontier emptied of traces of its original inhabitants. With her analysis of these representational strategies and the discourses that enable them, Barnes focuses her sites on Mark Burnett's *Eco-Challenge®* television spectacles from the 1980s. As was the case with Scott, Barnes argues that the disputes over the use of the land and its meaning to environmentalists, television executives, locals residents, and *Eco-Challenge®* participants are all central to understanding the contemporary televisual representation of the West as nature and place in the national imagination.

Managing and Reconciling Memory

As the chapters by Barnes and Scott show, the meaning of place in the social world of subjects is crafted out of the struggles over representations and the processes and social relations through which we find our place in those meanings. But just as powerful are the emotional feelings of attachment to place that are mobilized in representation (Hall 1997). A number of our contributors pay careful attention to the discursive production of emotional connection—anger, shame, guilt, pleasure, fear, and comfort—on which a felt sense of belonging is built.

In "Drinking the Nation and Making Masculinity: Tequila, Pancho Villa, and the U.S. Media," an examination of the role of masculinity in the production of U.S. and Mexican identities, Marie Sarita Gaytán considers the production of masculinity in Mexican and U.S. popular culture. In looking at the association of masculinity with tequila, banditry, and recklessness in the early part of the twentieth century, Gaytán shows that Mexico was constructed in the popular North American press, in cinema, and in the popular imagination as a place of fear, mystery, and vice. It should come as no surprise that these qualities evoked powerful anti-Mexican sentiments and feelings of loyalty and nationalism in the United States. In contemporary image culture, these same images have been rewritten as strategies to market Mexico to American tourists as a destination where purportedly any and everything goes. On the Mexican side of the border, national identity was crafted and solidified through disputes over what bodies and traditions could represent the national symbolic, given the internal histories and divisions within Mexico and Mexican history. Gaytán traces the discursive battles over national identity in corridos, novels, and cinema among genealogies that variously claim indigeniety, colonial Spain, and *mestizaje* as the constitutive elements for building a modern Mexican national identity. Most important, these notions of Mexican national identity are fashioned in opposition to U.S. national identity.

In a different register, with "Reinscribing Memory through the Other 9/11," Macarena Gómez-Barris anaylzes narratives by looking at two traumatic events (in Chile and the United States) that occurred on September 11. With these events as a backdrop, Gómez-Barris examines the transformation of exilic identities in relation to adopting national identities for Chilean intellectuals. She demonstrates the crucial role of memory and representation in crafting selves and attaching subjects to social worlds. In the examples of writer Isabel Allende and scholar Ariel Dorfman, Gómez-Barris examines the biographies and literary imaginations of each writer and traces the processes and the strategies of self-crafting through which these writers make and remake themselves as national subjects. By bringing her sociological training and interdisciplinary interests to bear on the process of self-writing, in this case with examples of autobiography and novels, Gómez-Barris shows in careful detail the historical context and representational strategies through which very different notions of belonging are realized, including notions of coming to terms with memories of terror and displacement in Chile and the cultural politics of difference in the United States.

Like Gómez-Barris, Sudarat Musikawong emphasizes memory as a key site of emotional work in connecting subjects to national formations. In foregrounding this aspect of both of these writers' interests, in part III we sharpen our concern with marginal, invisible, and excluded subjects, the social traces of those integral to the production of nations and national identities. In "Between Celebration and Mourning: Political Violence in Thailand in the 1970s," Musikawong looks at struggles around the memory and the memorialization of the popular protests against the government in Thailand and the violent massacres of 1972 and 1976 that ensued. Concerned with the question of how a state like Thailand builds tradition in the aftermath of social rupture through exclusion, selection, and incorporation, Musikawong shows how the selective fusion and celebration of single events with distinct histories work as discursive strategies through which to narrate and recast Thai history, in the process making new social subjects. This narrative retelling and fusing of two distinct events is also a discursive strategy by which undesirable social actors, in this case, communists, are confined to the margins of, if not eliminated from, the narrative altogether. Both discursive operations—the fusion of distinct events and the marginalization of key social actors—not only work to retell a national story but also work to build forms of identity and identification with a national symbolic that appeals to terms that seem distinctly Thai (e.g., the combination of royalty and democracy). From another vantage point, however, such discourses also regulate and manage political threats.

Finally, we end with some remarks from media studies scholar Sarah Banet-Weiser on the interdisciplinary implications of working with the idea of social traces and affect through the category of culture. In addition to considering the fertile possibilities for new research directions and collaborations across fields, Professor Banet-Weiser addresses the urgency and political implications of such work in terms of inequalities involving racism, immigration, gender, and other forms of difference.

In the end, while this emphasis is not especially new (with antecedents in social constructionism, cultural studies, and certain strains of poststructuralism), the conceptual promise of the social trace is that it enables us to approach anew some of the processes that our field may take for granted. Ours then is a provocation that urges the discipline of sociology, and within it that strain of sociology concerned with culture, to lend some of its considerable powers of investigation, contextualization, reasoning, and prestige to the pivotal role of absent presences in the production of subjects, the conduct of social relations, and the making of social worlds.

In this sense, the sociology of the trace and the examples we offer in this volume represent a bid to deepen sociology's claim on the social through the cultural, perhaps even returning to the foundational idea that practices, relations, and histories alone do not make us and our social world; ideas, memories, fantasies, and imaginings are just as important and thus the rightful province of the field (Lemert 2006).

Over twenty years ago, the fields of communication studies, sociology, anthropology, literature, and certain quarters of area studies experienced intellectual and scholarly ferment over how questions of culture, intellectual authority, and politics might impact various scholarly fields. The then-emergent field of cultural studies was identified as interloper who, as Stuart Hall put it in another context, came in like a thief in the night and crashed the party (Hall 1992). The lively debates and the studies in these fields challenged a generation of scholars with questions about power, domination, freedom, and the role of scholar in making and changing social worlds. Though some of those debates have not been settled and the entrenched disciplines have renewed their assertions regarding the place of science and objectivity to their objects of study, some have taken on board some of the most productive insights made by theorists of culture from other locations.

With the sociology of the trace, we are willing take on the role of interloper. Our aim is to invigorate debate in our field—to mix it up, so to speak—in a way that expands the terrain and includes both an analytic of power and culture that denaturalizes and disarticulates the coherence that culture and power too often represents (especially for the abject, marginal, and subjugated) as natural and inevitable. Herein we search for a different register of knowing, one where traces can also tell us something about the productive possibilities, dreams, and imaginations of those subjected to national and colonial projects. In this way we trace what was once there or what might have been had it not been for the ruse of heterogeneous forms of power that are often difficult, yet not impossible, to map.

Works Cited

Hall, Stuart. 1992. "Cultural Studies and Its Theoretical Legacies." In *Cultural Studies*, ed. Lawrence Grossberg, Cary Nelson, and Paula Treichler, 286–94. London: Routledge. Also in *Stuart Hall: Critical Dialogues in Cultural Studies*, ed. David Morley and Kuan-Hsing Chen, 262–75. New York: Routledge.

———. 1997. "The Work of Representation." In *Representation: Cultural Representations and Signifying Practices*, ed. Stuart Hall, 13–64. London: Sage/Open University.

Lemert, Charles. 2006. "Durkheim's Ghosts in the Culture of Sociologies." In his *Durkheim's Ghosts: Cultural Logics and Social Things*, 8–29. Cambridge: Cambridge University Press.

CHAPTER 1

Toward a Sociology of the Trace

Macarena Gómez-Barris and Herman Gray

THE BOMBING OF HIROSHIMA AND NAGASAKI at the end of World War II is one of the signature events of the failures of modernity, a limit event that produced unimaginable annihilation and incomprehensible social effects. The devastation wrought by the atomic bombings in Hiroshima and Nagasaki left both material and immaterial traces such as ash, debris, blindness, radiation and its effects, burning buildings, burning bodies, and a city and population that burned. In the aftermath, and for generations to come, government officials, medical workers, legal experts, journalists, and even *hibakusha*, or atomic-bomb survivors, though with different intentions, would incorporate calculations, numbers, and measurable data into their reports and narratives. References to the temperature of heat rays, the pressure of the blast, and the number of casualties became central to how the atomic bombing and its effects were narrated not only in the popular press and legal and medical realms but also in the narratives of survivors. As Lisa Yoneyama argues, witnesses began to incorporate medical and legal discourses into their testimonies, thereby internalizing the objectified governmental criteria and bureaucratic procedures without always realizing the personal alienation that such discourses produced (1999, 94).

The abstract categories and quantitative classifications of legal and medical discourses—for instance, one's proximity to the hypocenter—not only attempted to account for the traces of social suffering in the bomb's aftermath but also ended up inscribing knowledge and power into the memories of those who witnessed, lived through, and continued to live with atomic radiation. This produced a flattening of catastrophe. In contrast to this form of alienation, later survivors' efforts to narrativize the experience of disaster instead emphasized the singularity of experience; individual experiences could not be easily folded into social groupings of victimization and survival.[1] In ways that disavowed full apprehension, description, or cohesion, these more personal accounts expressed the effects of the atomic bombing that traversed the bodies, minds, and experiences of those who continued to suffer unimaginable horror.

Indeed, the figure of the survivor or the witness makes visible the crisis of representation of modernity. It is as Giorgio Agamben describes that "not even the survivor can bear witness completely, can speak his own lacuna" (1995, 39). In the case of Jewish Holocaust survivor Primo Levi that Agamben details, the problematic remains the inability of the witness to express the indescribable that has taken place, which occurs precisely in the gap of language where all narrativity falls short in the act and translation of limit events. The case of the witness *after* the atomic bombing or the Shoah brings to the foreground central concerns of this volume: If narrativization by the witness cannot approximate the experience of disaster, what do abstract social categories, statistical regularities, and coherent histories lay claim to and what do they hide? In other words, what methods and *epistēmēs* may better approximate those social worlds that are not attainable through more conventional means that discipline their objects? Do speech acts such as testimonials fill in what numbers may not possibly reveal? Can silence fill in what testimonials impossibly narrate? What archives remain? Where does one trace the effects of such disaster?[2]

The atomic bombing, and its condensation into scientific and legal discourses, is an extreme example of large-scale structural violence, its effects, and its imbrication with power. What about the contemporary era of technology and its intersections with operations of knowledge and power? Despite technologies that increase empirical measurement and methodological precision, something ineffable remains palpable in our social worlds, a kind of dis-ease. In the scientific debates about the genetic evidence of racial difference, knowledge about race and racial difference is located at the molecular and genetic levels (Duster 2006; Reardon 2005). Rather than at the level of the social and cultural constructions of race, genomics research has become the leading scientific site of knowledge production about racial identification. In this scientific discourse, the salient evidence of race that matters most to science is no longer outside the body, which was once considered the realm of history, economics, markets, structured inequalities, and cultural representations (American Sociological Association 2003; Duster 2006; Reardon 2005; Wellman 2007).

With the evidence of race located at the genetic level, the truth of race can only be authorized by scientific experts and members of a specific community, rather than by scholars in the humanities and social sciences. Conventional claims about the socially constructed nature of race and racial difference have neither gone silent nor been declared illegitimate. Cultural and social explanations continue to account for some aspects of what we know about the social world and how race operates within it. Nonetheless, from the vantage point of scientific authority, claims about the social construction of race no longer exist within the horizon of the social sciences; these fields are much too speculative and subject to conjecture.[3] Perhaps it is fair to say that the everyday experience and meaning of race might be seen or understood as an effect of this specific operation of power-knowledge. In other words, the scientific truth of race is produced in one register, while the lived experience of race operates in another.

As former American Sociological Association President Troy Duster sees it, the shift in the locus of expert knowledge and authority of race involves both matters of the social construction of reality and matters of politics and history (2006). Indeed, according to Duster, for social scientists to accept this discursive shift in the production of knowledge about race is already to have conceded too much intellectual and political ground. At the same time, the privileging of a conventional notion of archives, methods, sampling techniques, peer review processes, and the circulation of findings in prestigious journals and associations together underwrite the shift. National funding organizations in the United States, like the National Science Foundation, corporate foundations, and prestigious universities, also secure this shift professionally and symbolically through funding, scholarship, and institution building that elevate the genetics of race while consigning sociology and the social sciences to a subordinate position (Bourdieu 1993).

The flattening of experience in limit events and the contemporary scientific production of race as genetics are, for us, object lessons about why tracing a trace matters. As Duster makes clear, it is not just the question of where race resides, whether or not it exists, or on what rightful intellectual terrain it operates. The more productive and significant challenge is to interrogate the discursive operations through which one specific understanding of social life is produced but that comes to represent all others. Still in dispute, and therefore a rightful object of sociological analysis, is the issue of how this understanding and the knowledge on which it is based is configured in terms of power. What agents are involved, how they are differently positioned, and what interests are at stake in disputes over the "fact" of race (Duster 2006; Reardon 2005)? Of course, we extend such disputes to include the struggles over the meaning of citizenship, place, the environment, progress, nation, and family.

This book engages the discipline of sociology through an interdisciplinary perspective that points toward inscriptions, traces, the audible, the inaudible, cacophonies, incoherences, assemblages, translations, appearances, and hauntings as methodological necessities rather than those things that do not quite fit into orderly social categories. We are interested in archives of traces and inscriptions, things often absent from the purview of disciplinary knowledge, not simply because we do not have the tools to see them but because imprints of power do not easily slide into proscriptive categories that definitively and indefinitely measure social inequality. There is necessarily an excess in the collision between structural projects and social experience, and this excess, we contend, provides clues for how to study them. What we term in this volume as the "social trace" leaves few material and social historical registers.

For scholars working within humanities and cultural studies traditions on the topics of racialized and queer subjectivities, this has meant turning to new kinds of materials and archives, in some cases piecing together a variety of relational events, figures, and tropes in order to complicate canonical or disciplinary histories that have served to elide such subjects or simply render such subjects invisible in their overdetermination. Akira Lippit, for instance, describes Sigmund Freud's desire to make visible the human unconscious as an archive of the self that catalogs the material and immaterial traces of each subject (2005, 35). If the unconscious is indeed the record of everything that has ever happened to each individual, what might be its social equivalent? In fact, the modernist disciplinary impulse is, as Foucault reminds us, to provide an exhaustive catalog of the social experience through the delineation of specific forms of knowledge and power (1990). Part of what gives us purpose, indeed urgency, in this volume is to work against the elision of the social analyst who discerns, translates, makes clear, and makes transparent, endlessly cataloging social experiences in ways that render invisible social traces. Further, through formations of knowledge and power, subjects are often constituted and rendered in ways that reify, disdain, and flatten their social worlds and individual subjectivities in the desire for a resolution of impoverishment, victimization, and normalization.

Tracing Sociology

One of the defining features of American sociology is its investment in the veracity of empirical evidence. Social facts that can be measured, seen, and accounted for are privileged by the discipline because they can be tracked through quantitative and qualitative social methods that are founded upon the scientific method of observation, reality testing, and corroboration. Although more recently certain methodologies have come under some pressure, statistics and other quantitatively based approaches like surveys have long occupied the top position in a hierarchy of approvable methods within the discipline. And, within the "toolkit" of qualitative sociology, methods such as large sample interviews and comparative case studies have been conferred with the status of reliable over observations that are referred to as "mere impression," including some forms of ethnographic work, textual analysis, analysis of visual archives, or "listening closely" to the field. Because they pose problems of generalizability, systematicity, and a normative notion of rigor, these latter methods are thought to be unscientific and therefore suspect, when in fact they may be the only tenable way to approach social traces.

We propose a sociology of the trace as a way to attenuate the distance between observable social worlds and those things that are not easily found through methodologies that attempt to empirically account for social reality. If we were to trace a trace, how would we do it? Where would it lead us? What would be gained through this approach? How would we trace time and space, the agents, the debris of structural projects like privatization and deregulation, the coal mining industry, state violence, and welfare and its representation? What of those cast on the edge by dominant representations and practices that flatten the complexity of and ability to access their social lives? A sociology of the trace thinks about erasures of violence, bodies used by powerful interests, emptied lands filled with spectacle, and memory receptacles that bide time with promised futures as partial answers that prompt yet more questions.

Two points help us to explain how we, and the contributors to this volume, study social things. First, we take seriously the insight that social facts are not always constituted as such but, instead, may show up within a particular historical social moment as a kind of "effect" of processes that may indeed be evidenced in other ways (Lemert 2006). We can measure the failures of the stock market in points, but what about how neoliberalism's mismeasure decimates social dreams? Second, forms of power, including state power as well as the various forms of micropower that Foucault so eloquently delineates, leave social and cultural imprints (1990). Whether these imprints may be obvious and provide material evidence of power's whereabouts, such as a body with scars in the aftermath of a torture session, or whether the imprint of power is less evident, as in the normalization of states of exception, social science has often had difficulty describing, apprehending, and showing why social traces matter. How they matter and how we can study them is the focus of this volume and each individual contribution in it.

A sociology of the trace may be able to link two structures of thought: the epistemological and the social (Gordon 1997, 12). If we are to overcome the problem posed by the poststructural turn of universalizing truth claims but also acknowledge that indeed some semblance of "the real" exists, then we must find ways to enter into social fields with new methods of perceiving what is there, what is absent, what remains, and what simply cannot be known. Herein, we owe a debt to Avery Gordon's powerful work on ghosts and haunting that is an effort to acknowledge the complexity of social life by thinking through, in consecutive chapters, the absent figures in the archives of Freudian psychoanalysis, Argentine state terror, and transatlantic slavery. *Ghostly Matters* does many things, including repositioning the role of sociology as an effort to apprehend disappearing social worlds (1997). For our purposes, Gordon's work is important for us because it explores how much of social life, due to its inherent complexity, exceeds the limits of what can be observed, what is often described as "evidence" or "the empirical." In the practice of sociology in particular and social science in general, evidence and an overreliance on the empirical do become forms or techniques of governmentality and a means of social control through which subjection operates. With the work in this volume, we take up the challenge posed by Gordon as an exercise in how to apprehend disappeared social worlds, subjectivities, and experiences that may be outside of the purview of disciplinary knowledge that relies exclusively on empirical forms of knowing. Whereas Gordon looked to literary texts, narratives, and biographies for expressions and traces of ghostly presence, we look to expressive sites of imagination and experience for clues about how subjects are constituted in a social and cultural field (Bourdieu 1989, 1993).

Subject Work

The useful intermediary concept of "subject work" articulated by Jon Cruz helps us make visible what Gordon calls a sociology of haunting, or the search for sites of social life that are not easily perceivable but make their seething presence felt (1999). Using the concept of "subject work" to designate nineteenth-century American discourses and the institutional forms that targeted premodern subjects—slaves and old country immigrants—as sites of social transformation into modern national subjects, Cruz gives us a language by which to identify the strategies through which forms of attachment are realized and sustained. Within the cultural terrain, "belonging" operates in the very construction, negotiation, and materialization of the subject. Making subjects, or "subject work," is not simply a matter of designating the social worlds or units to which one belongs but showing how such attachment is secured, sustained, and consolidated through emotional work. At the level of culture and representation, appeals to sentiment make identity matter, and we attend to how such appeals indeed constitute social relations as the glue that attaches social actors to signs, discursive positions, and social collectivities and as specific technologies and operations of power-knowledge (Ahmed 2004; Foucault 1980). We identify a range of tactics and operations through which belonging is renegotiated or rehearsed through effective (and not-so-effective) appeals to sentiment by institutions and agents charged with subject work. Here we point specifically to organizations and institutions engaged in memory work, and its legitimation, through representation and discourse (e.g., museums, cinema, the state; De Certeau 1984).

The social sciences and the humanities have long theorized the intersection of power and culture. Antonio Gramsci's concept of hegemony, or the practice of producing consent to the rule of the powerful, identifies the processes by which large publics collude with practices and understandings that may indeed work against a particular social group's own interests and identifications. The making and unmaking of the social world is a mode of engaging disappearing social realities. Hence, power operates as much through the bodies of subjects as through the form and registers of their attachments to social worlds (1971).

Interdisciplinary Crossroads

How do we do justice to social realities in a time that uneasily celebrates interdisciplinarity and simultaneously secures its modernist academic project, both in disciplinary *epistēmē* and through its institutional commitments? What is the impact of critical theory in the humanities and social theory in the social sciences for either making epistemological claims or mobilizing empirical data as forms of inquiry? We start with such questions to ponder how poststructuralism, deconstruction, postmodern theories, and other such critical ontologies and vocabularies that sought to dislodge the pillars of the Western metaphysical referent unsettled the strict boundaries within and between classic humanities and social sciences (Derrida 1988).[4] Critiques from the quarters of postcolonialism, feminism, queer studies, and critical race studies continue to rethink, remap, and differently articulate what the metropole and dominant epistemologies considered marginal scholarly terrain or a passing referent.

Within an expanded intellectual frame of how subjects are constituted and formed within the social world, Foucault's work illuminates how new forms of rule and domination operate through bodies and subjects rather than on them, and where the art of government is realized through concerns with regulating populations and life (1990, 1980, 2003). Though each intellectual formation in the "posts" era had a nuanced genealogy from which it emerged, the critical collective project of undoing, of seeing modes of social realities anew, of providing different epistemological entrance points, and of breaking with continuities made an impact on disciplinary scholarship, however unacknowledged. This effect has also been propelled by the urgency of the humanities and social sciences to make disciplinary knowledge "relevant" within a changing social and economic landscape that has seen a decline in disciplines that emphasize critical readings and an increase in the desire for professional schools (business, law, and so forth). Scholarship from interdisciplinary fields like feminist, queer, ethnic, and cultural studies understand that epistemological positions, flexible methodologies, and critical approaches to hegemony is not an end in itself, limited merely to reproducing disciplinary fields, but offers a mode of inquiring about history, society, the past, the present, and the future in ways that critically address power inequalities foremost.[5] The expanded set of critical tools from this scholarship allows us to unpack, reassemble, redefine, and dig deeper into the archive and to come out the other side with a more complex view of people's relationship to and engagement with society throughout time.[6]

Our collective project emphasizes working with multiple methods, sites, scales, and locations (each of which involves multiple vantage points, entries, and so on), the boundaries of which are only circumscribed by the archive of social traces and the potentiality of arcs of possibilities. We are well aware of the material manifestation of social traces and interrupted futures through media spectacles of refugee encampments, war zones, hunger, famine, and disease and refuse answers that may reproduce rather than ameliorate grave social problems of the era. Charles Lemert suggests that these are the manifestations of the logic of social things produced and sustained through difference, the study of which has a long and distinguished history whether it was alienation in the case of Marx, collective representation in the case of Durkheim, rationality in the case of Weber, the unconscious in the case of Freud, or the color line in the case of Dubois; these thinkers were very much concerned, too, with the social impact of unseen and difficult-to-detect structuring forces on social life (Lemert 2006).

Contemporary writers are also, of course, concerned with the impact of social traces on the psychic and emotional life of social subjects and their worlds; this concern was, in some ways, predominant in the aftermath of World War II, where the rupture of modernity exposed the liberal underpinnings of modern subjectivity as central a obstacle. The coproduction of subjects and social worlds frame our concerns with the capacity of actors to act within limits. Our focus, then, is on the conditions of possibility within which social action and meaning is possible. Our theoretical challenge is to make sense of the coproduction of social subjects and social worlds, understanding what was once there or what might have been there had it not been for power's ruse.

Therefore, we raise not new questions but perhaps new methods that trace cultural forms to draw out the specificities located in both time and space. In this volume, our contributors analyze representations as disputed sites about the production and meaning of the social world through power-knowledge as existing in a dense set of global, national, and local transactions that characterize and make possible our social world. That is, given the primacy of affect, representation, consumption, and information technologies as rubrics through which our social worlds are structured and our participation in them secured, we suggest that culture is more important, not less. Our contributors examine social traces evidenced by actors sacrificed in the name of war, landscapes emptied in the name of progress, comfort promised in the name of security, and memories refashioned in the name of unity. These forces, processes, and relationships also reside in the cultural traces and struggles over how to name, memorialize, and narrate massacre, war, displacement, and deterritorialization.

While the role of representation, memory, knowledge, and identity in the production of everyday life is not a new concern for sociologists, what distinguishes our approach is the range of sites we explore, the role we give to culture and representation in that exploration, and the attention we pay to the social relations, cultural processes, and discursive techniques through which these productions are realized (Bourdieu 1989; Garfinkel 1967; Giddens 1991; Goffman 1959, 1963; Gramsci 1971; Habermas 1981, 1989; Spivak 1987). Through a sustained focus on culture and representation, we refuse the often dichotomizing separations between culture and social action, economy, and environment and the conception of them as determinant, causal, and antecedent to culture. We also reject the disciplinary claims on social objects that gesture either in the direction of generalizations associated with aesthetic objects or in the obduracy of the real as identified with the empirical (Gómez-Barris 2009). On this point, we join Lisa Lowe in advocating an approach to cultural production that navigates through the pitfalls of disciplinarity. For Lowe, the objective is to "situate different cultural forms in relation to shared social and historical processes, and to make active the dialectic that necessarily exists between those forms, because of their common imbrication in those processes [...] While specifying the differences between forms, this understanding of cultural production troubles both the strictly empirical foundations of social science and the universalizing tendencies of aesthetic discourse [...] In this sense, cultural forms of many kinds are important media in the formation of oppositional narratives and crucial to the imagination and rearticulation of new forms of political subjectivity, collectivity, and practice" (1997, 356).

Although they are partial and selective, in our view, the cultural forms that we examine are useful social sites of engagement for understanding social formations, subject work, conjunctures of social crisis, and struggles for social justice. As such, these are sites of contradiction that do not easily resolve into triumphant narratives or stories of outright structural oppression without attending to the subjects of these histories. Instead, the cultural forms we track, and the subjects' experiences we elaborate, imagine social and political possibilities and make present histories that might otherwise not come into view.

As part of a methodological landscape influenced by interdisciplinarity, our contributors telescope a range of sites that allow for a lateral movement of archives. With the archives that we assemble, our concern with tracking cultural sites and forms of power-knowledge presents us with an occasion to show how social worlds are culturally made. Thus, we emphasize discontinuities, lost traditions, disappeared subjects, ephemeral traces, and struggles over meaning. More specifically, in this volume, we explore how cultural struggles and the meanings that are contested work through different registers of feeling and sentiment, knowledge and understanding, and narrative and representation (Berlant 2004).

We are interested in representations as the points of articulation between discourses and social institutions; thus, we pay particular attention to the operations through which people take up positions, and we pay attention to what the meanings and practices of the marginalized and subjugated tell us about the degrees of play and uncertainty at the sites of discontinuity in any totality or social formation. It is this uncertainty that must be contained or fixed discursively to produce identity and belonging, and identification and allegiance.

The examples of cultural struggle collected in this volume show the small procedures that go into subject work and into the work of crafting selves (Kondo 1990, 1997; Ong 1999). What may seem like a rather eclectic grouping of cases, sites, and *forms* is, following Lowe (1997), quite a deliberate choice on our part of juxtapositions and uneasy articulations. These choices bring together our shared interests in representation with engagements in interdisciplinary fields. Since we examine culture and representation as sites of attachment and struggle, we ask across a variety of historical and empirical circumstances how is it that unities are forged, at what costs, and for whom? Subjects are constantly being called on emotionally to feel at home in narratives and memories that often do not feel so welcome. Reckoning with these traces and memories can expand the basis of our understandings and, in the process, tell us much about social worlds.

Notes

1. Yoneyama describes how the ability of survivors to relativize their own experiences as self-conscious political subjects that did not rely on "authoritative interpreters" (journalists, medical experts, researchers, and so forth) became an important way out of the representational impasse of internalization (1999, 95).

2. Perhaps additional archives, such as the visual images drawn, sketched, and painted by *hibakusha*, may differently render that which might not otherwise be seen in the shadow of the bomb (Naono 2002).

3. See especially Foucault's work (1990, 1980).

4. For spirited critiques of these intellectual interventions see among others, Terry Eagleton, *After Theory* (2003) and Walter Benn Michael, *The Shape of the Signifier* (2004).

5. If we think back to the foundational moments of modern scientific thought, say through Descartes as one critical juncture of Western philosophy, the notion of verifiability and reproducibility of the experiment is central to the emergence of the scientific method. Knowledge through Descartes was (1) never to accept anything for truth that is not clearly known to be such (the falsity of objectivity); (2) divide each of the difficulties under examination in as many parts as possible (the fracturing of knowledge, or compartmentalization); (3) begin with the simplest and then work step by step to the more complex (the classification of knowledge); and (4) make enumerations so complete and reviews so general that it may be assured that nothing is omitted (the test of reliability and generalization of knowledge). Indeed, the project of canonical sociology, especially since structural functionalism, continues to be informed by the scientific method.

6. Daphne Brooks's methodological reconstruction of performance archives is stellar in this regard (2006).

Works Cited

Agamben, Giorgio. 1995. *Homo Sacer: Sovereign Power and Bare Life*. Stanford, Calif.: Stanford University Press.

Ahmed, Sara. 2004. *Cultural Politics of Emotion*. Edinburgh: Edinburgh University Press.

American Sociological Association. 2003. *The Importance of Collecting Data and Doing Social Scientific Research on Race*. New York: American Sociological Association.

Benn Michael, Walter. 2004. *The Shape of the Signifier: 1967 to the End of History*. Princeton, N.J.: Princeton University Press.

Bourdieu, Pierre. 1993. *The Field of Cultural Production*. New York: Columbia University Press.

Brooks, Daphne A. 2006. *Bodies in Dissent: Spectacular Performances of Race and Freedom, 1850–1910*. Durham, N.C.: Duke University Press.

Cruz, Jon. 1999. *Culture on the Margins*. Princeton, N.J.: Princeton University Press.

De Certeau, Michel. 1984. *The Practice of Everyday Life*. Berkeley: University of California Press.

Derrida, Jacques. 1988. "The Original Discussion of Différance." In *Derrida and Différance*, ed. David Wood and Robert Bernasconi, 83–96. Evanston, Ill.: Northwestern University Press.

Duster, Troy. 2006. "Comparative Perspectives and Competing Explanations: Taking on the Newly Configured Reductionist Challenge to Sociology." *American Sociology Review* 71 (February): 1–15.

Eagleton, Terry. 2003. *After Theory*. New York: Basic Books.

Foucault, Michel. 1990. *The History of Sexuality*. Vol. 1, *An Introduction*. New York: Vintage.

————. 2003. *"Society Must Be Defended": Lectures at the College de France 1975–1976*. Ed. Mauro Bertani and Alessandro Fontana. New York: Picador.

Garfinkel, Harold. 1967. *Studies in Ethnomethodology*. Englewood Cliffs, N.J.: Prentice-Hall.

Giddens, Anthony. 1991. *Modernity and Self-Identity*. Cambridge, U.K.: Polity Press.

Goffman, Erving. 1959. *The Presentation of Self in Everyday Life*. New York: Doubleday.

————. 1963. *Stigma: Notes on the Management of Spoiled Identity*. New York: Touchstone.

Gordon, Avery F. 1997. *Ghostly Matters: Haunting and the Sociological Imagination*. Minneapolis: University of Minnesota Press.

Gómez-Barris, Macarena. 2009. *Where Memory Dwells: Culture and State Violence in Chile*. Berkeley: University of California Press.

Gramsci, Antonio. 1971. *Selections from the Prison Notebooks*. New York: International Publishers.

Habermas, Jürgen. 1981. *The Theory of Communicative Action*. Vol. 1, *Reason and the Rationalization of Society*. Boston: Beacon Press.

————. 1989. *The Structural Transformation of the Public Sphere*. Cambridge, Mass.: MIT Press.

Kondo, Dorinne. 1990. *Crafting Selves: Power, Gender, and Discourses of Identity in a Japanese Workplace*. Chicago: University of Chicago Press.

————. 1997. *About Face: Performing Race in Fashion and Theater*. London: Routledge.

Lemert, Charles. 2006. "Durkheim's Ghosts in the Culture of Sociologies." In his *Durkheim's Ghosts: Cultural Logics and Social Things*, 8–29. Cambridge: Cambridge University Press.

Lippit, Akira. 2005. *Atomic Light: Shadow Optics*. Minneapolis: University of Minnesota Press.

Lowe, Lisa. 1997. "Work, Immigration, Gender: New Subjects of Cultural Politic." In *The Politics of Culture in the Shadow of Capital*, ed. Lisa Lowe and David Lloyd, 354–74. Durham, N.C.: Duke University Press.

Naono, Akiko. 2002. "Embracing the Dead in the Bomb's Shadow: Journey through the Hiroshima Memoryscape." Unpublished PhD diss., University of California, Santa Cruz.

Ong, Aihwa. 1999. *Flexible Citizenship: The Cultural Logics of Transnationality*. Durham, N.C.: Duke University Press.

Reardon, Jennifer. 2005. *Race to the Finish: Identity and Governance in an Age of Genomics.* Princeton, N.J.: Princeton University Press.

Spivak, Gayatri Chakravorty. 1987. *In Other Worlds: Essays in Cultural Politics.* New York: Methuen.

Wellman, David. 2007. "Unconscious Racism, Social Cognition Theory and the Legal Intent Doctrine: The Neuron Fires This Time." In *Handbook of The Sociology of Racial and Ethnic Relations,* ed. Hernan Vera and Joe R. Feagin, 39–65. New York: Springer Science.

Yoneyama, Lisa. 1999. *Hiroshima Traces: Time, Space, and the Dialectic of Memory.* Berkeley: University of California Press.

· I ·

Cartographies of Belonging

CHAPTER 2

The Prisoner's Curse

Avery F. Gordon

The Stance of Undefeated Despair

This chapter emerges from my efforts to develop a conceptual vocabulary for linking the socioeconomic dynamics of accumulation, dispossession, and political power to the dialectic of social death and social life as these meet in the ontological and epistemological status of the prisoner. In trying to grasp the work imprisonment does to deliver state power to human life, I have been following, to use Ruth Wilson Gilmore's terms for defining racism, the "state-sanctioned," "fatal couplings of power and difference" that lead some groups of people to become "vulnerable" to "premature death" (2007, 28). Fate and fatality, life and death, are linked in complicated ways and nowhere more so than in the extent to which racism explains not just who becomes a prisoner—almost everywhere and at all times the poor, dissidents, and racial, ethnic, and religious minorities—but also what the prisoner becomes. Racism is not merely external to imprisonment, and prisoners are never only racial subjects (in the sense in which we commonly use that word). Imprisonment is a medium of racialized state-craft and prisoners are usually, and definitively in the United States, considered in law and in social practice an inferior race in and of themselves. The artifactual carving up of human differences into distinct groups whose worth is ranked hierarchically, the assignment of innate and ontological characteristics to these groups, and the othering, denigration, stigmatization, and the vulnerability to premature death that accompanies such a ranking—in short the state-sponsored coupling of difference and power—this regime of fate has been applied to the prisoner as a class. "The captive," Claude Meillassoux wrote in his 1975 book on *L'esclavage en Afrique précolonial,* "always appears [. . .] as marked by an indelible defect which weighs endlessly upon his destiny" (quoted in Patterson 1982, 38).

The destiny or fate of the prisoner in and of himself, and as his fate is bound up with those of us who are not yet captured, is what I address here in the interest of altering deadly fates and of promoting what John Berger calls "the stance of undefeated despair" (5). The *stance of undefeated despair* is that "familiarity [. . .] with every sort of rubble, including the rubble of words," (3) that grief over cruelty and injustice, which is "without fear, without resignation, without a sense of defeat," (4) and that "stance towards the world" (4), which is the basis for the carrying-on-regardless that the struggle for emancipation and happiness requires. The *stance of undefeated despair* is a position from which to carve out a livable life when everything is organized to prevent you from doing so, and it is a standpoint that guides political movements, including the movements to abolish slavery and prison (Berger 2006; Gordon 2006a).

The immediate scene for the meditations that follow is set around the June 2006 suicides of three prisoners of war held at the naval base in Guantánamo Bay, Cuba.

The Discourse of Struggle

"The discourse of struggle," Michel Foucault said to Gilles Deleuze in 1972, "is not opposed to the unconscious, but to the secretive. It may not seem like much," he continues, "but what if it turned out to be more than we expected? A whole series of misunderstandings relates to things that are 'hidden,' 'repressed,' and 'unsaid' [. . .] It is perhaps more difficult to unearth a secret than the unconscious" (Foucault 1977, 214). Later, Foucault famously brought the secretive and the unconscious together in his definition of subjugated knowledge. Subjected knowledge was both unconscious and secret, for it referred to, as he put it, "two things" (2003, 7). Subjugated knowledge named, on the one hand, what official knowledge repressed within its own terms, institutions, and archives—official knowledge's unconscious, we might say. "I am referring," Foucault wrote, "to historical contents that have been buried or masked in functional coherences or formal systematizations [. . .] blocks of historical knowledges that were present in the functional and systematic ensembles, but which were masked, and the critique was able to reveal their existence by using, obviously enough, the tools of scholarship" (2003, 7). Subjugated knowledge also names or refers to "something else [. . .] quite different": to marginalized and discredited knowledge from below and from outside the institutions of official knowledge production to "a whole series of knowledges that have been disqualified as nonconceptual [. . .] as insufficiently elaborated [. . .] naïve [. . .] hierarchically inferior [. . .] below the required level of erudition or scientificity" (2003, 7). These fugitive, outlaw, insurrectionary knowledges are not hidden in the institutions of official knowledge and are not derivative by-products of these institutions but are their disqualified secrets. In this sense, Foucault was right to say that the discourse of struggle is opposed to the secretive and to the disqualification and disappearance of fugitive insurrectionary knowledge from below with its "memory of combats" and its plans for the future.

Foucault sought the collaboration and equality of these two types of subjugated knowledge on the grounds that the appearance or arising, whether welcomed or not, of disqualified knowledge by subjugated peoples makes advances in scholarly critique possible (2003, 8). "Genealogy" is the name he gives to the "coupling together of buried scholarly knowledge" and unauthorized, unrecognized knowledge in the service of "de-subjugating" or decolonizing knowledge (2003, 10). It was his great belief that the collaboration between these two types of subjugated knowledge and between their makers would provide a "knowledge of struggles" and a set of "antisciences" with the "strength" and the "tactics" to fight what he called the "power-effects [. . .] of any discourse" (2007, 8–9). Foucault's argument for the necessity of a collaborative relationship in knowledge struggles was especially misunderstood, although he was neither the first nor the last to try to carve out a place for the radical intellectual, the radical professor in particular, in social and political movements, a job whose essential requirement is a practical, that is, operative, belief in the equality of the two types of subjugated knowledge. By equality, I do not mean sameness in either form or significance. By equality, I mean the distribution or redistribution of respect, authority, and right to representability or generalizability, which, among other things, entails the capacity to be something other than a local knowledge governed or interpreted by a putative superior (Gordon 2006a; Robinson 2007). By equality, I am referring to the standpoint that negates the dispossessions, disabilities, and dehumanizations experienced by those deemed inhuman or subhuman and treats their knowledge as autonomous (not merely derivative), authoritative, and necessary.

Needless to say, many scholars have not proved capable of or interested in occupying such an egalitarian standpoint in general. With prisoners, this standpoint is especially absent and troubled, since, as Jared Sexton and Elizabeth Lee forcefully point out, most of what passes as critical discourse today cedes first and foremost to the legitimacy of criminalization, the rule of law, and the morality of innocence (Gordon 2006b, 2008; Sexton and Lee 2006).

To launch or participate in a discourse of struggle on this terrain requires first the confiscation of the authority not only to speak of specific prison conditions and the institution of prison but also to speak of what Dylan Rodríguez calls the U.S. "prison regime," by which he means the forms of state power and statecraft that imprisonment "possesses" (2006, 43).[1] "An indispensable element of American statecraft" and form of "domestic warfare," the U.S. prison regime "sanctions and exercises dominion (absolute ownership and 'inner power') over its human captives, a total power that does not require formal political approval or ethical consent from the ostensible polity" but that does require legitimation as a "respectable," "commanding," "common-sensical" authority (2006, 44). In the *chattel logic* of the U.S. prison regime, the prisoner is "conceived as the fungible property of the state" (2006, 42) and thus cannot and is not permitted to speak for him or herself, since as property, he or she lacks civil integrity and is what Subcomandante Marcos calls a "Nobody" (Taibo and Marcos 2006). This obviously makes confiscating the authority to speak, much less organizing for the arrival of the "Time of Nobody," especially difficult and treacherous. The difficulty is compounded by the fact that, as most prisoners know—and it is a knowledge that can make you crazy because it is always denied as a lie, an exaggeration, and an obvious reflection of why you are a prisoner in the first place—it is "utterly" impossible to communicate with the "force," much less the people, holding you in subjugation.[2]

For war captives subject to the U.S. prison regime and prisoners held in supermaximum or security housing conditions, it is arguably the case that communication and representation, both aesthetically and politically, are not only impossible in the sense of futile but also, practically speaking, impermissible. Under this condition, where more recognizable modes of reading, writing, speaking, teaching, and organizing are unavailable, prisoners must use other means to confiscate the authority to represent themselves and to speak about the power under whose dominion they reside. With a few exceptions, prisoners everywhere have always had to invent creative means to live and act in prison. That body of subjugated knowledge, an exemplary history of the infrapolitical, is what the genre of prison literature teaches over and over again.[3] That body of subjugated knowledge is very often the subject of the self-organized instruction and teaching prisoners do with each other in prison.[4] That body of subjugated knowledge constitutes a radical methodology of imprisonment, a pedagogy of finding and making life where death and destruction dominate. The body of subjugated knowledge that shows and tells how to live in the space of death, dispossession, and disenfranchisement is what I call a methodology of imprisonment. It requires analytic awareness of the prison regime but is not reducible to it.

The more repressive are the conditions of imprisonment, the more inventive the means of political and aesthetic representation: prisoners are renowned for making all kinds of things out of the highly controlled residues of the prison, including remaking themselves. Under extremely repressive conditions, the confiscation of the authority to represent is also more dangerous, more risky, and the punishment for disobedience more severe, especially where the theft of authority is critically articulated and collective or grounded in solidarity with others. When communication is utterly impossible and other weapons and means are unavailable, the terrain of the discourse of struggle, which is always a struggle for life, becomes more and more bound up with death itself, since the degradation, the disposability of a permanently confined life in time and space, makes such a life not only taxing to bear but also exactly expendable. We see this at the military prison in Guantánamo Bay, Cuba.[5]

Where Here Is, Briefly

I don't know exactly what they did but they must have done something wrong to be here.

—Master at Arms Seaman Leif Kreizenbeck,
quoted by Carol J. Williams, "At Guantánamo"

As is well known, in 2001 following the attacks on the World Trade Center in New York City, thousands of men were captured by the United States and the Northern Alliance when the United States went to war against the Taliban and al-Qaeda in Afghanistan. Some of those captured were freed; some were and are still held in U.S. military prisons in Afghanistan and elsewhere. Starting in January 2002, large numbers were sent—forcibly shaved, hooded, wearing blackened goggles and orange jump suits, drugged, and shackled to the airplane bay floor in formations resembling the holds of slave ships—to an outdoor prison of wire cages named Camp

X-Ray situated on the U.S. naval base at Guantánamo Bay in southeastern Cuba. On January 11, 2009, worldwide protests celebrated the seven-year anniversary of the arrival of the first prisoners of war to Cuba.[6]

The Guantánamo naval base, the oldest U.S. off-shore military installation, sits on forty-five square miles of leased land that Cuba gave up in 1903 after the end of the Spanish American War in order to secure its nominal political independence from U.S. occupation. Under the complete jurisdiction and control of the United States, the base not only is considered U.S. territory in the legal sense but also is "self-sufficient, with approximately 7,000 military and civilian residents—an American enclave," as Michael Ratner puts it, "with all the residential, commercial and recreational trappings of a small U.S. city" (2005, 35). Ever since 1964, when Castro cut off its water and supply avenues, Guantánamo has had "its own [airfield] and schools, generate[d] its own power, provide[d] its own internal transportation, [and] supplie[d] its own water" (2005, 35).

And it has its own penal colony. From January to April 2002, prisoners were held in wire mesh cages with concrete floors and metal covers in what was called Camp X-Ray. By April 2002, the United States had built a new prison compound, Camp Delta, "referred to informally as 'the Wire,'" because it is surrounded by barbed-wire fencing (Center for Constitutional Rights 2006a). Camp Delta consisted initially of five euphemistically named camps, sometimes known by their numbers 1 through 5 or by other names, such as Camp Echo (an early isolation unit) or Camp Iguana (holding juveniles), designed to house two thousand prisoners in maximum security conditions over the long term. In October 2006, the new $38-million supermaximum solitary confinement unit, Camp 6, built by contractor Kellogg Brown and Root, a subsidiary of Halliburton, opened to house transfers from secret U.S. Central Intelligence Agency (CIA) prisons (fourteen at the time), the estimated one hundred "most dangerous" and disobedient prisoners, and what were expected to be a continual influx of prisoners from newly opened theaters (Iran, North Korea, parts of Africa, most immediately Somalia) in the permanent global security war known as the "War on Terror."[7] Because "there is no such thing as a medium security terrorist," according to Rear Admiral Harry Harris, Director of Operations for the U.S. Southern Command and Commander of the Joint Task Force Guantánamo, because there have been continual uprisings at the prison, and because "detainees have [. . .] demonstrated they have the will and the thought processes to do self-harm [. . .] if [. . .] liv[ing] in a communal [. . .] environment," most prisoners have been held in Camps 5 and 6, where they are locked down in solitary confinement twenty-three to twenty-four hours a day in windowless steel cells measuring seven by twelve feet (quoted in Williams 2006a, 12).[8]

The six facilities that make up Camp Delta are not the first prisons to be built on the naval base. In 1991, after Haitian President Jean-Bertrand Aristide was overthrown, Guantánamo was used as a detention camp for Haitians seeking refuge in the United States. Thousands of Haitian and Cuban migrants passed through the prison—more than forty-five thousand in 1994—but it was the incarceration in foul and rat-infested conditions, guarded by armed marines, encircled by razor wire, of over three hundred so-called migrant contaminants that made Guantánamo the "world's first camp for HIV-positive refugees" (Dayan 2003, 96).[9] And that also made Guantánamo the site for a set of legal contests and precedents concerning the right to asylum and protection from unwanted rendition (both of which the Haitians were denied) and the right of the U.S. state to indefinitely quarantine or detain designated "alien" or "illegal" individuals who have been presumptively and secretively declared to be a threat to security without criminal charges and without access to legal or due process (habeas corpus). By June 2008, the United States anticipated completion of a ten-thousand-person "refugee camp" on the island to be used "in the event of a sudden, major influx of refugees" posing a security threat to the United States. Although no immediate regional refugee crisis appears on the horizon, the United States is planning for a scenario on the scale of 1994 and 1995.[10]

As Colin Joan Dayan has written, "[t]he haunt of Guantánamo Bay where the spirits of persons lie dead" (2003, 96).

A Captive or Prisoner at the Very Least

The term "detainee" has been used almost exclusively to refer to people held for an indefinite period, without charge or trial, by US forces in Guantánamo Bay. The guards there, under pain of punishment, were required, as they told me, to refer to us all as "detainees," which sometimes got me upset and into a quarrel with them. I was a captive [. . .] or prisoner at the very least.

—Moazzem Begg, *Enemy Combatant*

Contemporary international laws of war are relatively recent, their principles established in the seventeenth and eighteenth centuries, the first actual codes written in the mid-nineteenth century, and the regulative Geneva Conventions operative today established after World War II. In earliest Western history, the question of the disposition of captives in war was simple: no prisoners were taken. The purpose of war was to destroy the armies of the enemy and weaken the state, kingdom, or tribe that they were appointed to defend. Captives were put to death, and soldiers were encouraged to kill women, children, and the elderly on the theory that in destroying the entire people or society, the military strength of the enemy would be seriously reduced in the present and the future. Complete destruction was the goal, and the norm, even for the Romans, who were nonetheless the first to perceive the economic value of prisoners or captives taken in war. This value lay in the fact that in being captured, they could be enslaved. As long as it held a mercenary or pecuniary interest for the captors, the prisoner of war might not be killed but have his death sentence commuted to slavery, a point to which I will return. Indeed the main route to enslavement has always been capture in war or through armed force, and this triangular and moneyed relationship between war, captivity, and enslavement repeats itself throughout history.[11]

The development of a protectable prisoner of war, the "accidental enemy" to use Jean Jacques Rousseau's phrasing, developed in tandem with the increasing regulation, eventually in law, of warfare. Francis Lieber prepared the first substantial body of regulations covering the treatment of prisoners of war for President Abraham Lincoln in 1863 at the close of the U.S. Civil War, when thousands of war captives were held by the remains of the union and confederate armies. But it was Rousseau who formulated their conceptual or philosophical foundation, notably in the section of *The Social Contract* that argues against slavery in general and against Grotius's argument for the right of nations to enslave war captives. Rousseau wrote, "The aim of war is the destruction of the enemy's state, in which one has the right to kill the defenders of the state, whom he encounters with arms in their hands; but as soon as they lay down their arms and surrender, they cease to be enemies; they become men and one has no longer the right to take their lives" (1762). The soldier, Rousseau noted, does not fight for himself, as he has neither the power nor the right to raise an army; he is a lowly servant of the state, and therefore of its ambitions, its authority, and its monopoly over the use of force. More to the point for Rousseau, individual combatants are only casually and "accidentally" enemies: "Individuals are enemies accidentally, not as men, nor even as citizens, but as soldiers," he wrote. The enemy soldier, then, is an accidental enemy, a temporary, situational condition not even created by him— a temporary, situational condition of forced conscription in which he rarely profits and in which the state has only a limited property interest despite its monopoly over the use of force. The moment the soldier lays down his arms or has them taken from him, Rousseau concludes, he ceases to be a soldier, an enemy, and becomes again "merely" a man. Thus, for Rousseau, the war captive has not only the right not to be enslaved; once he lays down his arms he is neither soldier nor enemy and is thus entitled to something more than a negative or even positive right, he's entitled to the restoration of fellowship the lifting of enemy status confers (*Instructions* 1863; Michaelsen and Shershow 2004; Rousseau 1762).

In the main, the history of the laws governing warfare and the treatment of captives taken in war has been progressively humanitarian: to minimize the violence and disruption of war and to draw boundaries and distinctions between legal or acceptable forms of warfare and those deemed excessive. Regardless of the actual treatment of prisoners of war in the post–World War II period, the ideal of the Geneva Conventions and their vision of a limited but regulated peace between established actors in the international state system supervised by the permanent members of the United Nations (UN) Security Council and their needs has remained virtually unchallenged, and the international human rights framework on which it is based has grown in significance and political presence, if not political authority. To be clear, the Geneva Conventions and the international laws of warfare have never presumed the abolition of war but only—and only in the best of cases—the hope that it could be avoided or minimized. However, it is arguably the case that, through the introduction of the enemy combatant, the United States intended to circumvent and reverse this modestly progressive course.

According to the U.S. government, the prisoners held captive at the naval base at Guantánamo Bay, Cuba, and in Afghanistan are not prisoners of war but are "unlawful enemy alien combatants."[12] The legal difference between a prisoner of war and an unlawful enemy alien combatant is that the former is entitled to protections set forth in the Geneva Conventions. The main protections include these five (*Geneva Conventions* 1949):[13] One, prisoners of war are to be removed from the combat zone and treated humanely, without loss of citizenship and civil rights. Prisoners of war are not civilly disabled. Two, because Henri Dunant, founder of the Red Cross, was closely involved in the development of the Geneva Conventions, which originated with a concern for the care of wounded and sick soldiers, representatives of neutral states and the International Committee of the Red Cross itself have the right to make official visits to prisons. Three, prisoners may be delivered to a neutral nation for custody, but they may not be deported en masse and at the end of hostilities, they must be released and sent home or repatriated without delay, unless they have been charged with specific crimes and are being held for trial or serving sentences imposed by legitimate judicial processes in which their due process was legally secured.[14] Four, when there's a question about whether a person arrested, captured, or kidnapped is a lawful or unlawful combatant, the Geneva Conventions require that the person be treated as a protected prisoner of war until status determination by competent tribunal can take place. The military hearings to determine status are to be governed by modern legal standards of due process and legalistic evidentiary standards. Finally, the protections given prisoners of war under the Geneva Conventions remain with them throughout their captivity and cannot be taken from them by the captor or bought or bargained or given up by the prisoners themselves.

A prisoner of war, then, is in principle at least protected by the international laws of warfare. An unlawful combatant is someone who is not entitled to or is denied protection by the Geneva Conventions. The phrase "unlawful combatant" does not appear in the third Geneva Convention as such. This Convention does describe categories of people who are entitled to prisoner-of-war status and people who are not, and, in fact, much of the administrative history of the prisoner of war and the Geneva Conventions' protocols are attempts to determine who is and who is not entitled to this status. In summary, those in regular armies and militias and in many cases— although these can be contested—in rebel and guerilla armies, including some members of armed wings of resistance movements, are considered lawful combatants. Civilians who accompany armed forces, such as war correspondents, supply contractors, and members of labor service units, are also entitled to prisoner-of-war status. Soldiers without uniforms, spies, mercenaries, pirates, some rebels, and child soldiers are not.

On September 18, 2001, the U.S. Congress invoked the War Powers Act and gave the president a broad and sweeping Authorization for Use of Military Force (AUMF) against nations, organizations, and persons involved in planning, authorizing, committing, harboring, or aiding the terrorist attacks on September 11 and to prevent any future acts of international terrorism against the United States (*Authorization* 2001). The authorization enabled force for past acts and the prevention of future ones—preemption—and President George W. Bush used that authority to issue an important Presidential Military Order: "Detention, Treatment, and Trial of Certain Non-Citizens in the War Against Terrorism" permitted the "detention" and possible trial for violations of the laws of war of members of al-Qaeda and anyone else who conspired or committed acts of international terrorism or who has as their aim to cause injury to or adverse effects on the United States, its citizens, its national security, its foreign policy, or its economy. The individuals held were not called prisoners or captives, but "detainees." The name it gave to these detainees was "illegal enemy alien combatants" (White House Office of the Press Secretary 2001) The U.S. military began holding individuals captured in Afghanistan and elsewhere under this military order and not under the terms of the Geneva Conventions, asserting that "none of the provisions of the Geneva Convention[s] relative to the treatment of prisoners of war apply to our conflict with al Qaeda in Afghanistan or elsewhere throughout the world because, among other reasons, Al Qaeda is not a High Contracting Party to Geneva"; that is to say, it is not a state (*Memorandum* 2002).[15] Al-Qaeda was something else.

What it became was more clearly defined in the National Security Strategy issued in 2002 (and then revised in 2006) when the United States officially declared permanent global war against the enemy of "terrorism." Although terrorism is defined as neither political regime, person, religion, ideology, nor state, the United States nonetheless knows its shapeshifting enemies without question (Bush 2006, 5). Because this is a general war against an elusive, cunning, and new enemy who most frequently takes the form of ordinary powerless people, the United States argued that the conventional rules of warfare do not apply. In this context, al-Qaeda was and is only a face or front, one that appears and disappears as the public's fears ebb and flow, in a war in which the soldier and the authority he or she serves or represents are one and the same; the soldier is not a defender of an enemy state per se, following orders from above, but rather a more horizontal participant. The recognizable format for this kind of war is the war for self-determination, national liberation, or civil war, and in 1977, Geneva did recognize these as warfare, loosening the state-to-state hostility requirement, although it should be noted that the United States refused to ratify Protocol I because President Reagan said that it confused terrorism with national liberation.[16] To be in a possible war of liberation against a legitimate and dominating state is to immediately trigger the state's old and still-effective power, particularly acute when dedicated to the rule of law, to advance, order, and suppress through criminalization. The tension between enemy and criminal has beset the invention of the alien enemy combatant from the start. In this context, al-Qaeda was merely a face or a front in a war in which there are no accidental enemies, no even limited peace to be made, and thus no fellowship to be restored. The illegal enemy alien is a permanent one and thus a fundamentally racialized enemy, since his enemy status forms a part of his very being. Neither fellowship nor innocence can ever be restored; such a being is only fit for death or enslavement or permanent captivity.

Using first the Presidential Military Edict and then the 2006 Military Commissions Act passed by Congress, the president as commander in chief of the U.S. Armed Forces declared—and thus perhaps we might not be mistaken in calling this a declaration of martial law—that he or those to whom he delegates such authority can capture wherever they are to be found, secretly classify, and imprison indefinitely without access to lawyers or courts or the law under conditions determined solely by the captor those illegal enemy alien combatants who are presumed to threaten the security of the United States. As is well known by now, the unlawful enemy alien combatant—the individuals seized and captured in the War on Terror—has neither the protection of international law nor the protection of U.S. Constitutional law: no First Amendment right of access to a court or to petition for writ of habeas corpus to challenge the legality of detention, no Fourth Amendment protection against unreasonable search and seizure, no Fifth Amendment right to a lawyer, and no Eighth Amendment protection against cruel and unusual punishment (Olshansky 2005, 179–225).[17] Thus was born the great new enemy in the global War on Terror—the unlawful enemy alien combatant—and, as we will see, a certain historical trajectory from actual death to social death closed.

An Awful and Horrible Scene

I do not plan to stop until either I die or we are respected. People will definitely die. Bobby Sands petitioned the British government to stop

the illegitimate internment of Irishmen without trial. He had the
courage of his convictions and he starved himself to death. Nobody
should believe for one moment that my brothers here have less courage.

—Binyam Mohammed, quoted by Audrey Gillan,
"Hunger Strikers Pledge to Die in Guantánamo"

On June 10, 2006, three of the approximately 460 to 480 prisoners of war then currently held incommunicado and indefinitely at the U.S. military prison in Guantánamo Bay hanged themselves in a conscious and coordinated act of rebellion.[18] This was the second mass suicide attempt at the prison; in August 2003, twenty-three prisoners tried to take their lives (Center for Constitutional Rights 2006a, 16; Worthington 2007, 269–80). None of them had been accused of a crime or had access to any judicial process, although they had been tortured, abused, and interrogated hundreds of times. Despite the fact that the United States refuses to call the captives "prisoners of war," Navy Rear Admiral Harry Harris claimed the suicides were acts of "asymmetrical warfare," a U.S. military term describing the combat tactics "insurgents" in the War on Terror use to fight militarily superior U.S. forces (Barnes and Williams 2006, A-1).

The commander was certainly correct about the disproportion, the asymmetry, but he misidentified the objective of the struggle the prisoners of war—who are not really prisoners of war but juridicially nonexistent yet spectrally real alien unlawful enemy combatants—were waging locked away under twenty-four-hour human and electronic surveillance without any shoes (and periodically without bed sheets) in a fortified island prison. The three prisoners had been confined as a disciplinary measure in an isolation area and, like hundreds of others, were on an ongoing hunger-to-the-death strike, violently force-fed by tubes against their will, to protest their criminalization and the punishment and prison regime to which they have been condemned by the fiat of the conquering U.S. Army. This may account for the prison authorities' characterization of them as "hostile toward [. . .] camp rules."[19]

There have been hunger strikes at the prison since it opened, sometimes with as many as two hundred people, or half the prisoners, striking at once. There have been waves of strikes—February and October 2002, in August 2003 preceding the mass suicide attempt, and then again in June and July of 2005 (Worthington 2007). From all accounts, and as Binyam Mohammed suggested in referring to Bobby Sands and the

Northern Irish prisoners (and some of these prisoners would have had the longstanding Turkish example in mind as well), the prisoners were successfully using the hunger strikes to organize themselves and to deepen their political consciousness and antagonisms. The hunger strikes were also getting some, albeit intermittent, international media attention and had intensified by August of 2005, when the force-feeding started. Force-feeding is an invasive and painful procedure; medical records and prisoner accounts show that, with the help of a new six-point restraint chair, force-feeding was being used as a weapon to abuse and torture prisoners and to force "compliance" among the rebellious. By January 2006, the majority of the eighty-four August 2005 hunger strikers had been force-fed into submission. By June 2006, only three of the original August 2005 group were still being force-fed in the restraint chairs (Annas 2006, 1377). Are these three the same prisoners who killed themselves? We do not know for certain. We do know that by 2006, twenty-five prisoners had officially tried to kill themselves forty-one times at the camp, but these figures exclude what U.S. military officials euphemistically call "self-harm incidents," of which the U.S. Department of Defense reports 350 (including 120 "hanging gestures") in 2003 alone (ACLU 2006). These numbers also, of course, do not include the large numbers who had been on the hunger-to-the-death strike.[20]

It took several days for the names of the three men who died and the photograph of one of them to be made public. Their names are Mani al Utaibi, Yasser al Zahrani, and Ali Abdullah Ahmed. It should be said that even though the Guantánamo Bay prisoners are the most well-known prisoners in the world, having garnered the consistent attention of several major newspapers, the UN, human- and legal-rights organizations, and some notable public officials, which is far more attention than most ordinary prisoners receive, few know their names. Their names have been a state secret, a mark of their dispossession. There had been an unofficial but publicly available list maintained by the British group Cageprisoners.com based on a groundbreaking 2004 report by United Press International (UPI) journalist John Daly. But it was not until May 2006—at the height of the largest organized revolt at the prison—that the U.S. Department of Defense first disclosed the names of the near eight hundred men from over forty countries who have been confined at Guantánamo, and only then in response to a lawsuit filed by the Associated Press, prompted in part by the hunger strike.

A Small Gift for You, the Names to Hold and Remember

Released

David Hicks
Gholam Ruhani
Abdul Aziz al Matrafi
Abdullah Ghulam Rasoul
Yaser Hamdi
Abdul Sattar
Abdul Sattar Safeezi
Shabidzada Usman
Fahed Mohamed al Qahtani
Zafar Iqbal
Zia Ul Shah
Jamal Muhammad al Deen
Muhammed Ijaz Khan
Mohammed Sayed
Shah Mohammed Alikhel
Mohammed Ishaq
Salah Hudin
Isa Khan
Feroz Abbasi
Majeed al Joudi
Asad Ullah
Abdullah Alhamiri
Zayd al Husayn al Ghamdi
Majid al Barayan
Isa al Murbati
Saud Dakhil al Mahayawi
Mohammed al Zayla
Abdullah Tabarak
Salim al Harbi
Musa al Wahab
Sultan al Uwaydha
Adel Kamel Haji
Murat Kurnaz
Mohammed al Juhani
Abdel Hadi Sebaii
Omar Rajab Amin
Yasim al Sulami
Abdulrazzaq al Sharekh
Khalid al Bawardi
Sadeq Ismail
Abdul Raham Houari

Mishal al Shedoky
Lahcen Ikassrien
Yusif Khalil Nur
Mishal Saad al Rashid
Najib Lahcini
Rukniddin Sharipov
Mehrabanb Fazrollah
Fahed al Harazi
Fahd al Shabrani
Walid Mohammed Ali
Rasul Kudayev
Yusef Nabied
Ilkham Batayev
Munir Bin Naseer
Shafiq Rasul
Asif Iqbal
Wahldof Abdul Mokit
Said Mohammed Ali Shah
Ibrahim al Sehli
Abdul Rahman Al Ghamdi
Mohammed al Utaybi
Tariq Aziz Khan
Hafiz Ehsan Saeed
Abdul Razaq
Mohammed Ashraf
Mohammed Irfan
Mohammed Khan Achezkai
Adnan al Saigh
Mohammed Raz
Jan Mohammed Barakzai
Abdul Rauf Aliza
Yusef al Rabiesh
Rhuhel Ahmed
Ali al Tayeea
Abdul Aziz Al Oshan
Sarfaraz Ahmed
Yousef al Shehri
Yamatolah Abulwance
Abdul Rahman Juma Kahm
Suleiman Shah
Rabel Khan

Salman Mohammed
Bijad al Atabi
Muhammad Hussein Ali
    Hassan
Janan Taus Khan
Fawaz al Zahrani
Salim al Shihri
Ibrahim al Shili
Toufig al Marwai
Faha Sultan
Abdul Salam al Shehri
Mohammed Ouzar
Ghaser Zaban Safollah
Ejaz Ahmad Khan
Tarik Mohammad
Mohammed Tariq
Salahuddin Ayubi
Hafiz Liaqat Mansoor
Said Saim Ali
Haseeb Ayub
Fazaldad
Mohammad Saghir
Mohammed Ilyas
Hamood Ullah Khan
Muhammed Kashif
    Khan
Mohammed Arshad Raza
Salim Hamdan
Said al Boujaadia
Mubarak Hashem
Mazin al Awfi
Khalid al Hubayshi
Said al Malki
Majid al Harbi
Abdullah al Noaimi
Mohammed Benmoujan
Mourad Benchellali
Ali al Tays
Imad Kanouni
Mehdi Ghezali
Ayman al Amrani

Ali Mohammed Nasir Mohammed
Redouane Khalid
Hassan Mujamma Rabai Said
Majid al Qurayshi
Fahd al Jutayli
Abdul Rahman Al Juaid
Majid al Shammari
Bandar al Jabri
Issam al Jayfi
Othman al Omairah
Turki al Asiri
Rashid Balkhair
Murtadha Maqram
Jabir al Fayfi
Saleh al Khathami
Ibrahim al Rubeish
Mohsin Moqbill
Mohammed al Futuri
Musa al Amri
Mohammed al Asadi
Ravil Gumarov
Said al Zahrani
Nasser al Mutairi
Abdullah al Yamani
Mishal al Harbi
Maroof Salehove
Shamil Khazhiyev
Faik Iqbal
Ruslan Ogidov
Mohammed al Qurashi
Fahd al Sharif
Jamil al Kabi
Abdul Aziz al Shammeri
Fahd al Fouzan
Abdullah al Ajmi
Ali Mohsen Salih
Umar al Kunduzi
Hani al Shulan
Anwar al Nurr
Salah al Balushi
Abdullah Kamel al Kandari

Mohammed Fenaitel al Daihani
Humud al Jad'an
Abdulhadi al Sharekh
Khalid al Zahrani
Khaled Ben Mustafa
Mohammed Laalami
Abdullah al Utaybi
Haji Hajaj al Sulami
Sheikh Salman al Khalifa
Kay Fiyatullah
Saleh al Oshan
Faris Muslim al Ansari
Nayif al Nukhaylan
Ahmed Adil
Juma al Dossari
Abdullah al Wafi al Harbi
Abdul Aziz al Baddah
Tariq al Harbi
Abdullah al Ghanimi
Hamed Abderrahman Ahmed
Abdul Rahman Al Hataybi
Mosa Zi Zemmori
Ibrahim al Nasir
Ziyad al Bahuth
Abdul Aziz al Nasir
Bader al Samiri
Akhdar Qasem Basit
Haji Mohammed Ayub
Abu Bakker Qasim
Mohammed al Qadir
Ziad al Jahdali
Sami El Leithi
Yuksel Celik Gogus
Abdulli Feghoul
Adel Abdul Hakim
Muhammed Mazouz
Mesut Sen
Ibrahim Shafir Sen
Salih Uyar
Abid Raza
Zahid Sultan
Khalil Rahman Hafez

Mohammed Ijaz
Ali Ahmed
Mohammed Ansar
Hanif Mohammed
Mullah Abdul Salam Zaeef
Adil Uqla Hassan al Nusayri
Sherghulab Mirmuhammed
Ezat Khan
Yarass Ali Must
Ghuladkhan
Rami al Taibi
Mohammed al Subaie
Khalid al Barakat
Slimane Hadj Abderrahmane
Nizar Sassi
Abdullah al Tayabi
Mohammed al Harbi
Jarallah al Marri
Majid al Frih
Saad al Bidna
Wasim al Omar
Khalid al Morghi
Bessam al Dubaikey
Said Ali al Farha
Mohammed al Qurbi
Abdullah al Rushaydan
Rashid al Qa'id
Sami al Haj
Said al Shaibani
Mohammadullah
Aziz Khan Zumarikourt
Ehssanullah
Abdullah Ghofoor
Abdul Hadi Sayed
Abdul Waheed
Nabu Abdul Ghani
Nassir Malang
Abdul Razaq
Abdul Rahman
Mohammed Sargidene
Abdullah Edmondada
Murtazah Abdul Rahman
Shaibjan Torjan

Shai Jahn Ghafoor
Mohammed Kakar
Sabit Layar
Hazrat Sangin Khan
Mohammed Yusif Yaqub
Amran Hawsawi
Abd al Hizani
Brahim Yadel
Sa'id al Shihri
Hassan Abdul Said
Nayif al Usaymi
Faizal al Nasir
Hani al Khalif
Khalid Al Ghatani
Abdul Maula
Juma Khan
Jihan Wali
Mohammed Nasim
Mohammed Sadiq Adam
Hamdullah
Mohammad Gul
Abib Sarajuddin
Gul Zaman
Khan Zaman
Jamal al Harith
Saddiq Ahmed Turkistani
Aryat Vakhitov
Abdul Hakim Bukhari
Haji Noorallah
Mohammed Rafiq
Fizaulla Rahman
Nasir al Subii
Redouane Chekhouri
Emdash Abdullah Turkash
Nawaf al Otaibi
Saleh al Zuba
Aminulla Amin
Khalid al Muri
Sultan al Anazi
Mamhud Sadik
Abdul Rahman Khowlan
Abdullah al Anazi
Israr Ul Haq
Ghanim al Harbi

Sultan Mohammed
Khirullah Akah
Abdul Karim
Abdulrahim Kerimbakiev
Ehssanullah
Mohammed Anwar
Ataullah Adam Gul
Yakub Abahanov
Mohamman Daoud
Abdullah Magrupov
Bacha Khan
Dawd Gul
Abdul Hanan
Mohammed Sharif
Tarek Dergoul
Mohammed al Harbi
Amanullah Alikozi
Noor Allah
Mohammed Omar
Mohammed Noman
Mohammed Abas
Nuri Mert
Sajin Urayman
Muhibullah
Wali Mohammed
Abdul Majid Muhammed
Abdullah Khan
Abu Sufian Bin Qumu
Moazzam Begg
Bader Zaman Bader
Abdul Rahim Muslim Dost
Ehsanullah Peerzai
Sohab Mahud Mohammed
Abdul Hakim Al Mousa
Adel al Zamel
Sa'ad al Azmi
Rustam Akhmyarov
Noor Ahmad
Saeed Abdur Rahman
Abdul Rahman Noorani
Ibrahim al Umar
Karama Khamisan
Brahim Benchekroun
Khalid al Asmar

Ahmed Errachidi
Qari Esmhatulla
Bakhtiar Bameri
Majid Mehmood
Noor Habib Ullah
Nematuallah Sahib Khan
  Alizai
Mahngur Alikhan
Nisar Rahmad
Padsha Wazir
Rostum Shah
Muhammed Naim Farooq
Ali Mohammed
Mohammed Akhber
Nathi Gul
Insanullah
Badshah Wali
Bismillah
Niaz Wali
Abdul-Karim Ergashev
Hamidullah
Mohammed Tahir
Mirza Muhammed
Mohammed Kabel
Azizullah Asekzai
Zaban al Shamaree
Haydar al Tamimi
Mushtaq Ali Patel
Jabir Al Qahtani
Usama Abu Kabir
Abdullah al Qahtani
Arkan al Karim
Khudaidad
Abdul Baqi
Haji Faiz Mohammed
Bismillah
Abdulnour Sameur
Lotfi Bin Swei Lagha
Mamdouh Habib
Ahmed Sulayman
Reda Fadel El-Weleli
Rashid al Uwaydah
Sadee Eideov
Hezbullah

Kari Mohammed Sarwar
Abdul Al Hameed Andarr
Abdullah Hekmat
Said Abassin
Zakirjan Asam
Alif Khan
Timur Ishmuradov
Mohammed Anwarkurd
Mohammed Wazir
Fawaz Mahdi
Din Mohammed Farhad
Mohammed al Ghazali
  Babikir
Jamal Kiyemba
Labed Ahmed
Mohammed Hussein
  Abdallah
Mustafa Hamlili
Mohammed al Amin
Salim Muhood Adem
Hassan Hamid
Hammad Gadallah
Rashid Ahmad
Hussain Mustafa
Ala Salim
Fethi Boucetta
Mustafa al Hassan
Amir Yacoub al Amir
Abdullah Bin Omar
Menhal al Henali
Omar Deghayes
Muhibullo Umarov
Ibrahim Fauzee
Mazharuddin
Abdughaffor Shirinov
Mohammed Saad Iqbal
  Madni
Abbas Al Naely
Ibrahim Zeidan
Shams Ullah
Haji Roohullah
Sabar Lal Melma
Qalandar Shah
Richard Belmar

Haji Osman Khan
Mohammed Haji Yousef
Noor Aslam
Abdul Salaam
Tila Mohammed Khan
Qadir Khandan
Naquibullah Shabeen
Mohammed Rasoul
Sultan Ahmad
Saghir Ahmed
Mohammed Akitar
Amin Ullah
Mohammed Nasim
Barak
Abdul Nasir
Nasrullah
Ismatullah
Rahmatullah Sangaryar
Parkhudin
Abdul Rahim
Zakkim Shah
Taj Mohammed
Jamil al Banna
Bisher al Rawi
Habib Rahman
Peta Muhammed
Mohabet Khan
Mohammed Khan
Abdul Samad
Asadullah Rahman
Naqib Ullah
Shardar Khan
Abdul Razzaq
Abdul Qudus
Mohammed Ismael Agha
Haji Naim Kuchi
Swar Khan
Mammar Ameur
Adel Hassan Hamad
Juma Din
Abdul Ghani
Said Amir Jan
Anwar Khan
Abdul Zahor

Abdullah Khan
Allah Nasir
Haji Shahzada
Hammidullah
Abdul Ghafour
Mohammed Quasam
Abdul Ahmad
Mohammed Nasim
Bismaullah
Abdul Wahab
Abdul Bagi
Rahmatullah
Hafizullah Shah
Baridad
Naserullah
Haji Bismullah
Akhtar Mohammed
Amanullah
Kushky Yar
Alif Mohammed
Mohibullah
Abdullah Wazir
Izatullah Nasrat Yar
Kako Kandahari
Haji Ghalib
Abdurahman Khadr
Haji Mohammed Wazir
Mirwais Hasan
Hafizullah Shabaz Khail
Abdul Matin
Shabir Ahmed
Mohammed Yacoub
Bashir Ahmad
Mohammed Irfan
Abdul Halim Sadiqi
Haji Nasrat Khan
Zahir Shah
Mohammed Akbar
Aminullah Tukhi
Feda Ahmed
Walid al Qadasi
Soufian al Hawari
Wisam Ahmed
Naibullah Darwaish

Gul Chaman,
Abdul Ghafaar
Sada Jan
Haji Mohammed Akhtiar
Nazar Gul Chaman
Habib Noor
Abdul Razaq Iktiar
    Mohammed

Azimullah
Sharbat Khan
Mahbub Rahman
Said Mohammed
Mohammed Aman
Kakai Khan
Abdullah Mujahid Haq
Mullah Jalil

Said Mohammed Ali Shah
Hukumra Khan
Mohammed Mussa
Binyam Mohamed
Mohammed Nechle
Mustafa Ait Idr
Boudella al Hajj
Martin Mubanga

Still Held

Abdul-Haq Wasiq
Mullah Norullah Noori
Mullah Mohammed Fazil
Othman Mohammed
Muaz Alawi
Mohammed al Ansi
Ahmed al Hikimi
Mahmoud al Mujahid
Faruq Ali Ahmed
Mohammed al Adahi
Idris Qader Idris
Ibrahim Idris
Abdul Malik Al Rahabi
Ali Hamza al Bahlul
Abdel Qadir al Mudafari
Majid Ahmad
Abdul Rahman Shalabi
Samir Moqbel
Mohammed Ghanim
Ali Ahmad al Rezehi
Ibrahim Sudan al Qosi
Mohammed al Qahtani
Mohammad Hanashi
Adham Ali Awad
Poolad Tsiradzho
Abdul al Saleh
Abdul Rahman Naser
Muktar al Warafi
Ghaleb al Bihani
Salem Ben Kend
Fayiz Suleiman
Adnan Farhan Abdul Latif
Khalid al Qadasi

Sharaf Masud
Abu Bakr Alahdal
Hisham Sliti
Tareq Baada
Salem Gherebi
Sharif Al Mishad
Mohammed Al Shumrani
Younis Chekhouri
Mahmoud Bin Atef
Khalid al Mutairi
Abdul Rahman Sulayman
Abdul Rahman
    Muhammad
Fawzi al Odah
Abdul Salih
Saeed Jarabh
Abdullah al Shabli
Khaled Qasim
Abdul Latif Nassir
Mohammed al Hamiri
Yasim Basardah
Mohammed Khenaina
Said Hatim
Riyad al Radai
Abdul Nasir al Tumani
Muieen Abdal Sattar
Djamel Ameziane
Ashraf Sultan
Mohammed al Tumani
Moammar Badawi Dokhan
Ahmed Yaslam Said Kuman
Mashur al Sabri
Ahmed Ajam

Ali Hussein Shaaban
Abu Omar al Hamawe
Maasoum Mouhammed
Abdul Rahim al Ginco
Jawad Sadkhan
Mustafa al Shamyri
Mohammed Bawazir,
Abdul Rahman al Zahri
Mohammed Haidel
Khalid al Dhuby
Salman al Rabie
Mohammed Khusruf
Riyad Nasseri
Yasin Ismail
Hassan Zumiri
Tariq El Sawah
Mahmud al Ali
Omar al Dayi
Walid Zaid
Fouad al Rabia
Faiz al Kandari
Abdul Khaliq al Baidhani
Haji Wali Mohammed
Jalal Bin Amer
Mohammed Sulaymon
    Barre
Zohair al Shorabi
Sabri al Qurashi
Hamoud al Wady
Saad al Azani
Zahir Bin Hamdoun
Jamal Mar'i
Abdul Aziz al Suadi

Khairullah Khairkhwa
Ayman Batarfi
Abdul Hamid al Ghizzawi,
Mohammad Tahar
Emad Hassan
Ghassan al Sharbi
Fayad Ahmed
Mohammed Tahamuttan
Abdelrazak Ali
Abdel Hakim
Fahmi Ahmed
Mohamed Salam
Ahmed Abdul Qader
Mohammed al Zarnuki
Ali Bin Ali Ahmed
Sufyian Barhoumi
Omar Abu Bakr
Jabran al Qahtani
Ravil Mingazov
Noor Uthman Muhammed
Ismael al Bakush
Mohammed al Zahrani
Jihad Diyab
Jamil Nassir
Abdul Zahir
Ahmed Ould Abdul Aziz
Mohamedou Ould Slahi
Awal Gul
Obaidullah
Omar Khadr
Ahmed Mohammed Al
Darbi
Mohammed Nabi Omari
Ayoub Murshid Ali Saleh
Bashir al Marwalah
Shawki Awad Balzuhair
Musab al Mudwani
Hail Aziz Ahmed Al
Maythali
Said Salih Said Nashir
Mohammed Hashim
Tawfiq al Bihani
Shawali Khan
Mohamed Jawad

Abdul Ghani
Sharifullah
Bostan Karim
Mohammed Mustafa Sohail
Omar al Rammah
Abdul Hafiz
Mohammed Kamin
Saifullah Paracha
Mohammed Zahir
Mohamed Rahim
Haji Hamidullah
Adil al Jazeeri
Sanad al Kazimi
Hassan Bin Attash
Abdu Ali Sharqawi
Abdul Rahim Ghulam
Rabbani
Mohammed Ghulam
Rabbani
Abdulsalam al Hela
Belkacem Bensayah
Mustafa al Hawsawi
Ahmed Khalfan Ghailani
Ramzi Bin al Shibh
Waleed Bin Attash
Abdul Rahim al Nashiri
Abu Faraj al Libi
Ammar al Baluchi
Riduan Isamuddin
Majid Khan
Modh Farik Bin Amin
Mohammed Bin Lep
Gouled Hassan Dourad
Khalid Sheikh Mohammed
Mohammed Abdul Malik
Abdul Hadi al Iraqi
Abdullahi Sudi Arale
Haroon al Afghani
Inayatullah
Muhammad Rahim
Cleared for Release
Shakhrukh Hamiduva
Fahed Ghazi
Abdullah al Yafi

Ridah al Yazidi
Sayf Bin Abdallah
Assem Matruq al Aasmi
Nag Mohammed
Arkin Mahmud
Adil Mabrouk Bin Hamida
Asim al Khalaqi
Said al Busayss
Ali Yahya al Raimi
Adel Hakimi
Said Al Qahtani
Ahmad Tourson
Nabil Hadjarab
Shaker Aamer
Hassan Anvar
Mohammed Bin Salem
Omar Abdulayev
Fadil Hintif
Mohammed El Gharani
Yusef Abbas
Bahtiyar Mahnut
Abdul Helil Mamut
Saidullah Khalik
Abdul Ghappar
Hajiakbar Abdulghupur
Abdullah
Abdulquadirakhun
Motai Saib
Dawut Abdurehim
Ahmed Belbacha
Farhi Said Bin Mohammed
Huzaifa Parhat
Ahmed Mohamed
Ayman al Shurafa
Kahlid Saad Mohammed
Adel Fattough Ali El Gazzar
Abdul Rahman al Qyati
Oybek Jabbarov
Ali Sher Hamidullah
Abdul Ourgy
Sulaiman al Nahdi
Mahrar al Quwari
Fehmi al Assani
Mansoor Qattaa

Salah al Zabe
Adel Noori
Ahmed Zaid Salim Zuhair
Kamalludin Kasimbekov
Mohammed Hassen

Abdul Aziz al Noofayaee
Abdul Rauf al Qassim
Abdulhadi Bin Hadiddi
Aziz Abdul Naji
Rafiq al Hami

Mohammed Abdul
  Rahman
Hussein Almerfedi
Sabir Lahmar
Lakhdar Boumediene

Dead

Yasser Talal al Zahrani
Abdul Rahman al Amri
Mani al Utaybi

Ali Abdullah Ahmed Al
  Salami
Abdul Razzaq Hekmati[21]

The Letter

It is unlikely that the letters the three men left will ever be available to the public, especially since U.S. authorities seized eleven hundred pounds of documents belonging to four hundred prisoners and their lawyers during the investigation into the suicides.[22] But we received one from Jumah Abdel Latif al Dossari, signed "Prisoner of deprivation," on October 14, 2005, when he wrote to his lawyer, Joshua Colangelo-Bryan and interpreter, Khaled, saying "farewell" and explaining why his lawyer would find him hanging in his cell, arm deeply cut but still alive:[23]

> In fact, I don't know where to begin . . . or how to begin [. . .] I feel very sorry for forcing you to see . . . It might be the first time in your life . . . to see a human being [. . .] dying in front of your eyes . . . I know it is an awful and horrible scene, but [. . . t]here was no other alternative to make our voice heard by the world from the depths of the detention centers [. . .] for the world to re-examine its standing and for the fair people of America to look again at the situation and try to have a moment of truth with themselves [. . .] The detainees are suffering from the bitterness of despair, the detention humiliation and the vanquish of slavery and suppression [. . .]
>
> Take some of my blood . . . take pieces of my death shrouds . . . take some of my remains . . . take pictures of my dead body when I am placed in my grave, lonely . . . send it to the world . . . [t]o make them carry the burden of guilt in front of the world for this soul that was wasted with no guilt it has ever done . . . [t]o make them all carry this burden in front of the future generations for this wasted soul that

has done no sin . . . [t]o make them carry this burden of guilt in front of history for this soul that was wasted with no reason . . . After this soul has suffered the worst by the hands of "the protectors of peace and the callers for democracy, freedom, equality and justice" [. . .]

At this moment, I see death looming in front of me while writing this letter . . . Death has a bad odor that cannot be smelled except by people who are going through the agony of death.[. . .] (Dossari 2006)

I will return to the curse Jumah al Dossari delivers in his letter; it is best to take that slowly in any event. For the moment, we need to focus on the vision of *death looming in front*, the terrain or the smell of the discourse of struggle, that is to say, the nature of the attempt to confiscate the authority of the prison regime. About, which there is more to say than that there is a long tradition of using the hunger–death strike of which prisoners almost everywhere are aware. Indeed, this knowledge is almost organic to being a prisoner, etched or tattooed, as it were, in the skin of the prison. So too do prisoners know that, stripped bare, literally, your body remains the most adaptable oppositional technology when communication is utterly impossible and other weapons unavailable. The relationship between captivity and death has deep roots: the degradation and the disposability of a permanently confined life in time and space make such a life not only taxing to bear but also expendable.

The Language of Death, an Idiom of Power

> *The very first time, it was like dying.[. . .] Capture, imprisonment, is the closest thing to being dead that one is likely to experience in his life.*
>
> —George Jackson, quoted in Yee, *The Melancholy History of Soledad Prison*

The language of death surrounds captivity, follows it, envelops it, and taunts it. *The very first time it was like dying.* We should not be misled by the way Jackson says it; it could be said a hundred other ways. It has been said a hundred other ways. The language of death that surrounds captivity is not metaphorical in the sense of an analogy: the very first time, it was *like* dying. The language of death is, to use Orlando Patterson's term, an "idiom of power," a symbolic and ritualistic representation (Patterson 1982, 17–34). But it begins as a literal substitution for the one enslaved.

For the enslaved? Bonded labor, penal servitude, debt bondage: worldwide, these are so historically entangled that there is a warrant, despite the danger of neglecting important differences, for speaking of the captive, the prisoner, and the slave in one breath. Certainly, in the United States, the significance of plantation slavery to the historical development of the prison system and to who (Black Americans) became and still most frequently becomes a prisoner is clear; the proximate relation between imprisonment and enslavement was legally enshrined in the U.S. Constitution's Thirteenth Amendment, which abolished slavery "except as punishment for crime duly convicted." After the formal abolition of slavery, the fundamental racial ontology of permanent slavery was transferred to the prisoner who, faced with the scientific legitimacy of criminal anthropology and bearing always the double burden of racialist ontology, became an inferior race in and of themselves. It remains the case today that slavery is constitutionally enabled in the United States, and any place subject to their jurisdiction, for prisoners and for prisoners only. I am using the word prisoner in the British sense of the accused—by state or crown—because the constitutional power is applied to the condition of imprisonment, and not to the convict. Conviction, in fact, is no longer necessary; captivity itself confers a legally binding judgment of preestablished criminal status. The prisoner and the prisoner of war who is not really a prisoner of war held in captivity and confinement by the United States are in fact and in law enslaved to the state, under its dominion, and subject to its absolute rule (Rodríguez 2006, 41). *The detainees are suffering,* Mr. Dossari wrote, *from the bitterness of despair, the detention humiliation and the vanquish of slavery and suppression* (2006). The detainees are suffering from what Orlando Patterson (1982) famously described as social death.

The language of death is an idiom of power, a symbolic and ritualistic representation. But for the one enslaved, it begins as a literal substitution. Slavery was almost always a substitute for the death that would otherwise befall the defeated enemy in war or the criminal awaiting execution or some other form of capital punishment. As Patterson parenthetically notes, the substitution was understood as the origin or the source of the slave's condition of powerlessness (1982, 5). This understanding entailed a double burden, for it both lent to the condition of enslavement the aura of salvation—saved from death—and inscribed in the ontology of the slave a permanent connection to the death sentence. Indeed, as Patterson writes, "The condition of slavery did not [. . .] erase the prospect

of death. Slavery was not a pardon; it was [. . .] a conditional commuta-
tion.[. . .] The master was essentially a ransomer," masquerading, one
should add, as a god (1982, 5). To give and take life: in exchange for com-
muting the death sentence—and the death sentence itself *is* the mark
of the captive's incapacity for exchange even on the most degraded or
unequal terms—the owner acquired the "slave's life" (1982, 5). Patterson rightly emphasizes the importance of what is acquired—not only
a property interest in a person or a person treated as a property object
but also the entire life (1982, 18–27). In exchange for avoiding immediate
death, what is taken from the captive is his past, his family, his culture,
his honor, his future, his very being. A priced but inestimable forfeiture,
in exchange for his life, he must give his life.

What of this exchange, then? Captured, stolen, confined, and transported, the captive is offered a life of externally imposed social negation.
In the words used by Judge Thomas Ruffin in an important 1892 case,
North Carolina v. Mann, that extended the right of a slave owner to wound
and kill his own slaves, the captive is offered a life "doomed in his own person and his posterity" (quoted in Patterson 1982, 3). Fate and fatality: the
enslaved will be granted no legitimately recognized existence independent
of the entity—state, corporation, crown, empire, temple, individual, and
so on—to whom he is absolutely subject, and who possesses a monopoly interest in him. A "nonperson," he is thoroughly dishonored, natally
alienated, separated from "all 'rights' or claims of birth," and treated as a
"genealogical isolate" with neither present nor future claims or obligations
to living and dead "blood relations" (1982, 5–7). "Ceas[ing] to belong in
his own right," the enslaved lose, in effect, birthright or a socially recognized place in the stream of time itself. This is fatal. This is the slave's fate.
It is as if he or she were never alive to begin with. As Claude Meillassoux
famously put it, "*The captive always appears therefore as marked by an original, indelible defect which weights endlessly upon his destiny. This is [. . .] a
kind of 'social death'. He can never be brought to life again as such.[. . . He] will
remain forever an unborn being (non-né)*" (quoted in Patterson 1982, 38).[24]
Perpetual slavery, permanent war.

How Ordinary People Should Relate to the Living Who Are Dead

According to Patterson, there are two apparitional modes of social death,
both very ancient and powerful stories or myths designed to account for

the presence of human nonpersons, what the Greeks called animated instruments, and what Ruth Gilmore calls inhuman humans, who are designed to account for their presence and to define the terms of marginality by which they will be incorporated into the society in which they live. The living dead or the inhuman human must be accounted for, their presence explained, and the terms of their exclusionary inclusion defined; without such an explanation, too many other uncontrollable and less degraded possibilities quickly arise. For Patterson, there are two representational modes—the intrusive and the extrusive—by which this occurs (Patterson 1982, 41).

In the intrusive mode, where capture in war is the principal method of enslavement, the slave is taken to be "the permanent enemy on the inside," the stranger, the foreigner, or the hostile alien (39). Patterson quotes a telling saying of the Bella Coola Indians of British Columbia: "No slaves [they say] came to earth with the first people" (39). In the extrusive mode, where criminality, poverty, misery, heresy, and rebelliousness are the principal conduits to enslavement, the slave is conceived as a fallen insider or as someone who might have or did in principle belong but has been "expelled" and now no longer belongs (41). The fallen insider has violated the social or legal terms of order; the fallen insider is an outlaw. Here, penality and enslavement are virtually indistinguishable: the slave is a criminal, and the criminal is a slave. In some cases, most notably ancient China, even the prisoner of war, who under most circumstances was considered a foreign outsider, was "legally and ideologically assimilated to the status of the internal criminal" (42). Here is Patterson's summary: "In the intrusive mode the slave was [. . .] someone who did not belong because he was an outsider, while in the extrusive mode the slave became an outsider because he did not (or no longer) belonged. In the intrusive mode, the slave was an external exile, an intruder; in the extrusive mode he was an internal exile, one who had been deprived of all claims of community. The one fell because he was the enemy, the other became the enemy because he had fallen" (44).

The idiom of social death speaks of the captive, but it only partially addresses him or her. The idiom of social death teaches, Patterson says, "how ordinary people should relate to the living who are dead" (1982, 45). The pedagogical function of the idiom of social death is crucial and has been a little misunderstood, in my view. Social death is too often presumed to be both a condition *exclusive* to the one so tainted and a condition that defines the *totality* of the slave or the prisoner in that it becomes him or her, so to speak. Social death is an externally imposed form of social negation; it has, in fact, quite real—awful and horrible—effects, and some captives do succumb to it, lose the capacity for social life, lose the capacity, as Gregory Frederick puts it, to "live in prison without allowing the evil of prison to live" in you (2001, 85). But, social death is rarely a complete achievement, either socially or ontologically, and it is emphatically not a singular but a relational idiom that speaks most intently and essentially to the not-yet-captured and to those ordinary people who need instruction in how to relate to the living who appear to be dead.

The Prehistoric

> *There's no denying that our social system is totally without tolerance; this accounts for its extreme fragility in all its aspects and also its need for a global form of repression.*
>
> —Gilles Deleuze to Michel Foucault, "Intellectuals and Power"

The application and maintenance of intensive subjugation—the attempt to impose absolute control and absolute powerlessness on others—is extremely difficult; it foments a fierce rage, resistance, revolt, escape, and refusal that must be constantly deflected and prevented. The exercise of coercive power in its various guises is formidable, and it is also fragile. (Since it is usually a tactical response to the superior's failure to achieve aims with other methods, in this sense, coercion is a sign of weakness and not strength, accounting, for example, in the present circumstances for why the U.S. state operates principally on emergency powers and on the incitement of the heightened alert. It simply cannot rule otherwise.) The exercise of coercive power draws attention to itself and, like all arrogances, is blinded in significant places by its own conceits and paranoid delusions. This is why imprisonment and enslavement are always accompanied by ferocious violence and military enforcements, if not permanent siege. Notwithstanding Foucault's distinction between punishment and discipline, captivity has always been a tortuous and deadly affair and grows only more so today where technically sophisticated weaponry, excessive force, and extreme deprivation define the warlike nature of the normal paradigmatic punishment regime the United States follows and promotes (Gordon 2008).

Powerful and fragile: the fragility of such a project is why enslavement and internment almost always involve despoiling rituals of initiation that strip the captive of the powers he or she brings onto himself—given name, clothing, hair, and ancestral protection—and replace them with the visual stigmata of captivity—shaved head, number, new name, new skin markings. The fragility of such a project is why, as Elsabeth Welskopf argued some time ago, if a society needs or wants to replenish its enslaved population, it is "necessary continually to repeat the original, violent act of transforming free man into slave" (Patterson 1982, 3). Welskopf called this repetition of originary violence "pre-history," and we might see it not only as a synonym for the social death sentence—to live as if you never were born—but also as a form of primitive accumulation. For though I have not discussed the motivation for enslavement and mass imprisonment, only its ontological symbolics, needless to say accumulation by dispossession, has been and is highly profitable, if also deeply parasitical.[25]

For the captive, brute force is usually enough to solicit, up to a point, obedience or to extract "compliance," the prison's favorite word; almost everything else is extremely painful, too, but supplemental. (It is crucial to remember that brute force—violence and torture—target not just an inert body but a psychologically complex living human being and is always accompanied by talk and proximate contact, in which are encoded elaborate narratives or ideologies.) But, the spectacle of coercion—the whip, the chain, the boots, the guns, and now the technology and machinery of "shock and awe"—exposes, at every turn, the very sacrificial and deformed terms of the freedoms, the rights, the peace, the wealth, and the rules of law being ostensibly upheld or protected or secured; the spectacle exposes what is in, to use Dossari's words, the hands of "the protectors of peace and the callers for democracy, freedom, equality and justice" (2006). The spectacle not only reveals it to the captive, who bears the imprint of the terms or the conditions on his body and spirit and who knows it and can speak of it better than most, but also reveals it for the rest of us to see, if we dare. The face of social death—the fallen enemy—helps to mask the general terms that underwrite apparent, routine, innocent social life by explaining the captive's status as intrinsic to his being, his actions, his failures, and his fate *doomed in his person and in posterity* and by justifying the prohibition against contact with him, with his mark, and with his word. The story of the fallen enemy is one way force is transformed into right and obedience into duty for the large segment of the population, not

rulers, not yet captured and not yet able to imagine themselves as capturable whose solidarity is required for the whole regime to operate in a
state of normalcy, its attendant pathologies and nervous disorders taken
as the wonders of progress. One of the main pedagogical functions of the
idiom of social death is to create an impassable breach: a breach of fate, a
breach of faith, and a breach of kinship between those who are and know
themselves to be capturable and those who are not yet able to imagine
themselves, ordinary as they may be, subject to such a death sentence.

In the Hem, Crossing and Cursing

And, so, for you, for us, this neat schema is offered: *the one fell because he
was the enemy, the other became the enemy because he had fallen.* Sometimes
it works the other way around. Sometimes they are one and the same. At
all times, they fall, but into where or what? The socially dead fall into the
hem, the brink, the verge, or a state of liminality. In social death, one lives
"on the margin between community and chaos, life and death, the sacred
and the secular" (Patterson 1982, 51), shadowing one's former self and "tee-
tering on the brink between life and death," as Mumia Abu-Jamal puts it
(1995, 3). Marked with an indelible defect, forced to endure a fatal alienation, wrenched out of the stream of time, and stranded in the reiterating
prehistorical, the living dead suffer miserably, and the injustice of their suf-
ferance, the distress, haunts those still standing and haunts the very justice
that can be meted out. The living dead are scary and it is no wonder. People unjustly rendered spectral are haunted, too, and they carry the rattling
chains, the demanding hungers, and all the rest around with them. They
are frightening, in this sense, because they are unrequited and unloved and
because they are the exploited and down-and-out porters of the nastiness
that created them in the first place.

  The socially dead have lost some of the special and dangerous capacities
they were said to have enjoyed in the past, such as slaying sleeping drag-
ons, assuming the power of the bear, giving supernatural offense, or having
immunity to pollution, fatigue, and pain. But they have acquired today an
extraordinary shapeshifting power. The fallen enemy—whether foreign
infidel or illegal criminal—is said to possess the power to frighten and
terrorize at will, without reason, without any special powers, and without
weapons, regardless of the strength of the opponent. Even when captured
and under the constant watchful eyes of the soldier or guard, this fallen

enemy is a source of such looming unending insecurity and danger that perpetual war has been declared against him and permanent incarceration his punishment for capture.[26] In explaining why Amnesty International was "reprehensible" and misguided ("trapped in a 20th century mindset") in condemning the American military prison "gulag," then-Vice President Dick Cheney explained that these prisoners were more "threatening to individual life and liberty" than "the actions of sovereign governments" (Lobe 2005). The notion that the captives in this "asymmetrical" perpetual War on Terror, driven by ideologies of order and counterinsurgency and by the need to quarantine the effects of global poverty, are more powerful than the mightiest and wealthiest military empire in the world is one phantom effect all abusive power relationships exhibit: the weaker is mistaken for the more powerful. This is surely a phantom effect (and one the threat of terrorism is designed to continually magnify), but it is no less real for the captive or for his keepers who are, one must say, possessed—bewitched, haunted, bedeviled, spooked—by living in a state of permanent terror of and war with their own inventions.

The repetition of the prehistorical, a blind siege, the enemy that is always close but seems to come from nowhere: all this talk, bordering on the gothic, about the dead and ghosts and sheer terror emanating from every closet, can make you forget that the mask of social death is worn by actual living people up to all kinds of stuff, including trying to get themselves out of prison. The mask of social death is not, however, the kind of performative mask you can just put on and take off. The mask of social death is more like a carrying card, a passport of sorts, for living in a state of liminality, for living in the hem. Indeed, an old capacity still retained by those with the taint of social death is that they can travel, cross the boundaries, and curse. I return now, at the end, to al Dossari's curse:

> Take some of my blood . . . take pieces of my death shrouds . . .
> take some of my remains . . . take pictures of my dead body when
> I am placed in my grave, so lonely . . . and send it to the world . . .
> To make them carry the burden of guilt in front of the world for
> this soul that was wasted with no guilt it has ever done . . . To make
> them all carry this burden in front of the future generations for
> this wasted soul that has done no sin . . . To make them carry this
> burden of guilt in front of history for this soul that was wasted with
> no reason. (2006)

Take Some of My Remains . . . Send It to the World . . . to Make Them Carry the Burden

A curse is a malediction, bad speech, conveying a current that might alter fate and might rechart or transform a destiny that had seemed to be traveling the other way: "The curse, if properly prepared and recited, will bring about the wish it expresses" (Scott 1992, 42). It is the learned language of the accursed themselves. It is an angry, demanding, sometimes vengeful language, registering the recalcitrance, the indifference, and the venality that prompted it. The curse is a reply to the death sentence, a stepping back into the stream of time, a demand on *the world in front of history*, and a hurling of a heavy burden carried back across to *them*. The curse confiscates the authority to speak in a context in which communication is utterly impossible. The curse is not so much a means of communicating as a means for insuring that, even if no one is listening, no one can forget.

Abdulla al Noaimi, a former prisoner at Guantánamo Bay, "Former Detainee No. 159" as he signs his name, issued a statement following the deaths of Mani al Utaibi, Yasser al Zahrani, and Ali Abdullah Ahmed. At the end of it, he writes, "The three people who did this, I know them very well. I was next to them while they were on hunger strike and they were on hunger strike till death. And if nothing happens about Guantánamo [. . .] there are more people who will do it, and I can tell you who they are. Finally, sorry to say this, but the whole world would say something if it was alive, but the world is dead" (al Noaimi 2006).

Here, then, is perhaps the blade and the burden of the curse. What you will learn and what, once you learn it, you will never forget is that your world is dead. The curse delivers to you a vision of your own deathly existence laid bare. It is a kind of remythologizing, remaking the illusion of reality, or reilluminating the making of reality not with a simple reversal— "You are really the dead one, not me"—but with a more delicate and deep cut—"I have brought you to the other side and you do not even know it yet. How will you cross back without me?"

The prisoner's curse, then, replies to the social death sentence in multiple voices. It asserts the lifeworld and life force, the anticipatory afterlife of the ones whose existence has been denied, abandoned, and forgotten. *I am not what you say I am.*[27] It demands to know what the captive has done to deserve the reduction in and deprivation of personhood to which he is subject. *How have I come to appear to you so indelicately, as nothing or nobody to whom a care should be shown or a harm can be done?* And it calls for reparation. *You will carry the burden of guilt in front of the world for me.* The prisoner's curse also declares that, contrary to appearances, the social death sentence obtains and belongs to the ones who maintain and enforce its brutal reality and gratuitous fictionality, the ones who negate, deny, and abandon their fellow human beings. Without fellowship, they possess and are possessed by social death. Prefaced by an unnecessary apology—"sorry to say this, but the world is dead"—the curse cuts away at the effort to create an impassable uncrossable border of fate, of faith, and of kinship separating—oh so barely—the captured from the not yet captured. The curse cries out: *It could be you, it might be you, don't you see?!* And it also holds out a gracious hand, despite the fact that it is "horrible and unfair" that the ones so troubled and burdened should have to do this too.[28] *Here, let me show you what remains unimaginable to you. Here, we will return somewhere else together. Here, together, we will hasten the arrival of the Time of Nobody.*

Notes

Portions of this chapter have been published in Avery F. Gordon, "Methodologies of Imprisonment," *PMLA* 123, no. 3 (2008). The first version of this chapter was occasioned by the invitation from Janice Radway and Wahneema Lubiano to participate in the conference "The Collapse of Traditional Knowledge: Economy, Technology, Geopolitics" at Duke University in January 2007.

1. Rodríguez's idea of possession is more complex than I am rendering it here, and it is important for the way it emphasizes imprisonment not as a simple tool of state power but as a power or force that makes the state what it is and also what it is not: "I am attempting to examine the ways in which *it is the prison regime that possesses and constitutes the state.* I am invoking a doubled meaning to the terms of 'possession': first, in the sense of a haunting intervention—the state's 'possession' by the sometimes ghostly and always haunting technologies of power and violence that emanate from the prison . . . ; and second, as a reference to the . . . undeniably massive political influence of the prison regime's designated agents and administrators on the broader architecture of the state" (2006, 43).

2. The "Time of Nobody" is from the wonderful and clever novel about the search for "The Bad and the Evil" (the content of which is patently obvious even though it means different things to different people), jointly written by Paco Ignacio Taibo II and Subcomandante Marcos (Taibo and Marcos 2006). On the impossibility, I am taking a line from Dylan Rodríguez's *Forced Passages*: "This

body of knowledge and truth [by radical prison intellectuals] is premised on the utter impossibility of dialogue and communication with the force—discursive, embodied, institutionalized—of one's own domination" (2006, 9). These particular prisoner intellectuals got the idea not only from their own experiences but also from the lessons of the Black radical tradition with which they were deeply engaged and attached.

3. The genre of prison literature would be unknown to scholars today without the seminal work of H. Bruce Franklin (1989) and Barbara Harlow (1992). On infrapolitics, see James C. Scott (1992) and Robin D. G. Kelley (1996).

4. See, for example, Mumia Abu-Jamal (2009), Allen Feldman (1991), George Jackson (1970), Govan Mbeki (1991), and Nawal el Saadawi (1994).

5. Given President Obama's election promises and the executive orders he issued immediately upon taking office, I expected that by the time this book went to press, it would be happily necessary to change the sentence's verb tense from the present—"we see today"—to the past—"we saw." Unfortunately, as of May 2010, the prison complex at Guantánamo remains open and the disposition of the prisoners still pending and uncertain. Regardless, it should be noted that the new military prison regime evident at Guantánamo is in place in Afghanistan and Iraq.

6. On January 22, 2009, President Obama signed an executive order stipulating that the prison would be shut down within the year. As of May 2010, the prison remains open.

7. In January 2008, camps 1 through 3 were closed. All the prisons at Guantánamo Bay are maximum- or supermaximum-security facilities. Press reports that describe Camp 4 as medium or minimum security are misleading; the regime of maximum-security imprisonment always permits the arbitrary granting and withdrawal of privileges.

8. Harris is currently vice admiral and since November 2009 he has been in command of the U.S. 6th Fleet and Striking Support Forces, NATO, in Italy. He also serves as deputy commander, U.S. Naval Forces, Africa.

9. See also the U.S. Navy's history of the station at Guantánamo Bay at https://www.cnic.navy.mil/Guantanamo/AboutGTMO/gtmohistgenera.

10. The news of the building of a refugee camp was first reported and set in the context of the earlier wave of imprisonment by Carol Rosenberg (2007); its June 2008 completion was reported by Robert Burns (2008).

11. According to the Center for Constitutional Rights, 86 percent of the Guantánamo prisoners "were arrested by either Pakistan or the Northern Alliance when the United States was paying large bounties for apprehension of suspected Al Qaeda or Taliban supporters. Following the 2002 U.S. invasion of Afghanistan, the practice of 'selling' foreign nationals arrested in or near Afghanistan to the U.S. military for thousands of dollars in bounty money was commonplace" (Center for Constitutional Rights 2006a, 8). The report contains a facsimile of

a Psychological Operations flyer offering "millions of dollars" distributed by the U.S. military forces in Afghanistan.

12. The case of Iraq has been more ambiguous. Iraqi prisoners are sometimes considered prisoners of war and at other times ordinary criminals, reflecting the constitutive indistinction between criminal and enemy in counterinsurgency warfare. On March 13, 2009, in response to queries for clarification from the federal judiciary, the U.S. Department of Justice filed documents indicating that it would no longer use the term "enemy combatant." It nonetheless retained the right to detain, without trial and anywhere in the world, anyone the United States deems to be providing "substantial" assistance to al-Qaeda and the Taliban. Tom Parker, Amnesty International's advocacy director for terrorism, counterterrorism, and human rights, told the *Washington Post*, "It's symbolically significant that he's dropped the term 'enemy combatant,' but the power to detain individuals within the 'indefinite detention without charge' paradigm remains substantially intact" (Wilber and Finn 2009, A06).

13. The subsequent protocols and other documents are also available online from the UN Office of the High Commissioner for Human Rights, http://www.ohchr.org/EN/Pages/WelcomePage.aspx.

14. One of the main principles essential to the entire history of the development of the idea of the protectable prisoner of war and elaborated in the various Hague and Geneva conventions is that the prisoner of war, unless charged specifically with a war crime and provided that he is neither spy nor mutineer (important qualifications), is not a criminal and so may not be punished as if he were one. This is absolutely crucial. There are no extant laws of war that treat war in and of itself as a crime. The question of what constitutes a legitimate act of war—when is war a war and not something else, like a revolution, uprising, armed struggle, mutiny, murder, crime, act of terrorism, and so on—is the main problematic that has dominated the history of the development of the rules governing warfare. This main problematic has been overwhelmingly characterized by an unrelenting effort to delegitimize and criminalize political opposition and social revolt from below. This was clear already in Lieber's codes. Although Geneva has expanded the definition of war beyond situations in which recognized states make formal declarations of war or commit unequivocal acts of hostility and territorial aggression, the protections Geneva offers are only activated in a legally recognized state of war. Where war is recognized in international law, it is not a crime, and the captives of such wars are not criminals. This is why the United States sought UN authorization for its invasion of Afghanistan and Iraq and also why, in a nutshell, Virginia Woolf famously said that if you want to know how to prevent war you need to oppose the tendency toward war, or the war for the preparation of war. (See Woolf 1938; Gordon n.d.)

15. The U.S. government did recognize that "the provisions of Geneva" do "apply to our present conflict with the Taliban," and also that the president had

the "authority under the Constitution to suspend Geneva as between the United States and Afghanistan." Although he claimed that he "decline[d] to exercise that authority at this time," President George W. Bush did nonetheless determine that "common Article 3 of Geneva does not apply to either al Qaeda or Taliban detainees" and that "the Taliban detainees are unlawful combatants and, therefore, do not qualify as prisoners of war under Article 4 of Geneva. I note that because Geneva does not apply to our conflict with al Qaeda, al Qaeda detainees also not qualify as prisoners of war" (*Memorandum for the Vice President. Subject: Humane Treatment of al Qaeda and Taliban Detainees* 2002).

16. The United States signed Protocol II but never ratified the 1977 amendments to the Geneva Conventions. Protocol I was rejected by then-President Ronald Reagan because it "would give special status to 'wars of national liberation,' an ill-defined concept" (1987). Reagan was specifically opposed to the Palestine Liberation Organization's pending claim for prisoner-of-war privileges (Meron 1998, chapter 8).

17. The question of U.S. law was considerably more complicated until the progressive thrust of the two key Supreme Court decisions in *Rasul v. Bush* and *Hamden v. Rumsfeld*, challenging the Guantánamo regime was voided with the passage of the Military Commissions Act (MCA) in October 2006. The MCA enhanced and legalized the Guantánamo regime in ways most do not understand, and it established a military court system where the military serve as judge and jury and only government-approved lawyers may appear; where the defendant has no right to see the evidence against him and can be tried without being present. The MCA permits the admission of evidence seized without legal warrants and under "duress" and, most tellingly, it forbids the invocation of Geneva as a source of rights before, during, and after trial. The MCA and the variety of totalitarian security laws—Patriot Act I and II, the Protect America Act of 2007—have been the object of considerable attention, and rightly so in the face of arbitrary arrest, indefinite imprisonment, conviction without trial, and unsupervised and enhanced executive authority (Center for Constitutional Rights 2006b).

18. Almost a year later, on May 30, 2007, a Saudi prisoner who was never permitted access to a lawyer—Abdul Rahman al-Amri—killed himself, according to the U.S. Southern Command, http://www.southcom.mil/appssc/news.php?storyId=41. A fifth prisoner, Yemeni Muhammad Salih, took his life on June 1, 2009, "Yemeni Detainee Dies in Apparent Suicide," *The Washington Post*, June 3, 2009, http://www.washingtonpost.com/wp-dyn/content/article/2009/06/02/AR2009060203930.html.

19. Navy Commander Robert Durand, spokesman for the prison, told the press that the three men "were hostile towards camp guards, defied camp rules and took part in protracted hunger strikes." Apparently, the men also refused to participate in the military tribunals (Williams 2006b).

20. Despite the force-feeding and the media blackout, the hunger strikes have continued at the prison. The last major news report was issued on February 9, 2009, by a U.S. military lawyer—Lt. Col. Yvonne Bradley of the Air Force—who told a British newspaper that "at least 50 people are on hunger strike, with 20 on the critical list" (Mackey 2009). A Center for Constitutional Rights report issued on February 23, 2009, confirms that most prisoners remain in isolation and that hunger strikes and force feeding continued (Center 2009). See also Andy Worthington's analysis of the prisoner weight records released by the Department of Defense in 2007 (2009). He shows that from January 2002 until February 2007, "one in ten of the total population [. . .] weighed, at some point, less than 112 pounds [. . .] and 20 of these prisoners weighed less than 98 pounds."

21. This list is a redacted and condensed version of what is arguably the most thorough database on the Guantánamo prisoners. It has been compiled by Andy Worthington and can be accessed in its entirety in four parts on his Web site, http://www.andyworthington.co.uk/guantanamo-the-definitive-prisoner-list-part-1. As of January 1, 2010, Worthington counts 772 prisoners held in total: 574 prisoners have been released (42 under President Obama), 5 are dead, 198 remain in custody, 60 of whom are cleared for release. His records for each prisoner includes name(s); internment serial number (ISN); status (released, cleared for release, still held, deceased); nationality; place of capture; their rendition and torture, where applicable; and links to chapters and articles by Worthington that detail the stories of over seven hundred of the prisoners. See also Worthington (2007). Cageprisoners.com, which published the first comprehensive list based on the initial report by John Daly in 2004 and supplemented by other reports in the Arabic language press and the *Washington Post*, also has an archive of photographs, interviews, and letters.

22. According to Agence France Presse, U.S. authorities seized over one thousand pounds of documents from lawyers and from over four hundred prisoners during the "investigation" into the suicides. *AFP Wire*, July 22, 2006. These documents, which included habeas documents, have yet to be returned, despite the court's restoration of the right of habeas petition in *Boumediene v. Bush* (2008).

23. Al Dossari was kept in solitary confinement from the end of 2003 until his release in July 2007. He tried to kill himself many times but never succeeded. The authorities treated him less as a troublemaker and more as a pathetically disturbed individual, who nonetheless required supervision and isolation. He transformed this letter into a poem entitled "Death Poem" (Falkoff 2007, 31).

24. Claude Meillassoux takes the phrase "social death" from his colleague Michel Izard.

25. Although the specific term "accumulation by dispossession" is now attributed to David Harvey (2003), it has an older origin not mentioned by Harvey, whose African and Black radical reference is more relevant to the problems of

imprisonment and militarism discussed here, although Harvey's discussion of Rosa Luxemburg is suggestive in our context, too. See for example, Beinart, Delius, and Trapido (1986) and the variety of groundbreaking work done on enclosures, primitive accumulation, and the commons by the contributors to *The Commoner* at http://www.commoner.org.uk.

26. For a thorough critique of the government's operating definition of terrorism in the War on Terror that focuses on the extent to which nonstate terrorism, as a form of irregular warfare, is a result of the absence of alternative avenues of political redress and thus must be addressed by creating these, see Record (2003).

27. About the prison rebellion at Attica, James Baldwin famously said, "People are often not what we think they are" (Freedom Archives 2001).

28. Fred Moten, personal correspondence with author, December 12, 2006.

Works Cited

Abu-Jamal, Mumia. 1995. *Live from Death Row*. New York: Avon Books.

———. 2009. *Jailhouse Lawyers: Prisoners Defending Prisoners v. The U.S.A.*, San Francisco: City Lights Books.

Al Noaimi, Abdulla. 2006. "Statement from Former Guantanamo Detainee, Abdullah Alnoaimi on Guantanamo Deaths." *CagePrisoners.com*, June 14. http://www.cageprisoners.com/articles.php?id=14460 (accessed May 20, 2008).

American Civil Liberties Union (ACLU). 2006. "Pentagon Documents Reveal Details of Suicide Attempts at Guantánamo (6/19/2006)." http://www.aclu.org/safefree/torture/25926prs20060619.html (accessed May 11, 2010).

Annas, George J. 2006. "Hunger Strikes at Guantánamo—Medical Ethics and Human Rights in a 'Legal Black Hole.'" *New England Journal of Medicine* 355 (13): 1377.

Authorization for Use of Military Force. Public Law 107-40, 107th Congress. (September 18, 2001). http://news.findlaw.com/wp/docs/terrorism/sjres23.es.html (accessed May 20, 2008).

Barnes, Julian E., and Carol J. Williams. 2006. "Guantánamo's First Suicides Pressure U.S." *Los Angeles Times*, June 11, A-1.

Begg, Moazzam. 2006.. *Enemy Combatant: My Imprisonment by the United States at Guantánamo*. London: The Free Press.

Beinart, William, Peter Delius, and Stanley Trapido, eds. 1986. *Putting a Plough to the Ground: Accumulation and Dispossession in Rural South Africa, 1850–1930*. Johannesburg: Ravan Press.

Berger, John. 2006. "Dispatches. Undefeated Despair." *Race & Class* 48 (1): 23–41.

Burns, Robert. 2008. "Joint Chiefs Chairman: Close Guantánamo." *Associated Press*, January 14.

Bush, George W. 2006. *The National Security Strategy of the United States of America* Washington, D.C.: The White House. http://www.whitehouse.gov/nsc/nss.pdf.

Center for Constitutional Rights. 2009. *Report: Current Conditions at Guantánamo. Still in Violation of the Law.* New York: Center for Constitutional Rights. http://ccrjustice.org/files/CCR_Report_Conditions_At_Guantanamo.pdf.

———. 2006a. *Report on Torture and Cruel, Inhuman, and Degrading Treatment of Prisoners at Guantánamo Bay, Cuba.* New York: Center for Constitutional Rights.

———. 2006b. "Report: The Military Commissions Act of 2006." New York: Center for Constitutional Rights. http://www.ccrjustice.org/learn-more/reports/report%3A-military-commissions-act-2006 (accessed May 11, 2010).

Dayan, Colin (Joan). 2003. "Servile Law." In *Cities without Citizens,* ed. Eduardo Cadava and Aaron Levy, 87–116. Philadelphia: Slought Books.

Al Dossari, Jumah. 2006. "Dying For You To Listen." *Cageprisoners.com.* March 16. http://www.cageprisoners.com/articles.php?id=12861 (accessed May 20, 2008).

Falkoff, Marc, ed. 2007. *Poems from Guantánamo: The Detainees Speak.* Iowa City: University of Iowa Press.

Feldman, Allen. 1991. *Formations of Violence: The Narrative of the Body and Political Terror in Northern Ireland.* Chicago: University of Chicago Press.

Foucault, Michel. 1977. "Intellectuals and Power: A Conversation between Michel Foucault and Gilles Deleuze." In *Language, Counter-Memory, Practice: Selected Essays and Interviews,* ed. Donald F. Bouchard. Trans. Donald F. Bouchard and Sherry Simon, 205–17. Ithaca, N.Y.: Cornell University Press.

———. 2003. *"Society Must Be Defended": Lectures at the Collège de France 1975–1976.* Ed. Mauro Bertani and Alesandro Fontana. Trans. David Macey. New York: Picador.

Franklin, H. Bruce. 1989. *Prison Literature in America: The Victim as Criminal and Artist.* New York: Oxford University Press.

Frederick, Gregory. 2001. "Prisoners are Citizens." *Monthly Review* 53 (3): 76–88.

Freedom Archives. 2001. *Prisons on Fire: George Jackson, Attica, and Black Liberation.* Audio CD. San Francisco: The Freedom Archives.

Gillan, Audrey. 2005. "Hunger Strikers Pledge to Die in Guantánamo," *Guardian,* September 9. http://www.guardian.co.uk/world/2005/sep/09/uk.guantanamo.

Gilmore, Ruth Wilson. 2007. *Golden Gulag: Prisons, Surplus, Crisis, and Opposition in Globalizing California.* Berkeley: University of California Press.

Gordon, Avery F. n.d. "Criminalizing the Enemy: From Prisoner of War to Enemy Combatant." unpublished manuscript.

———. 2006a. *Keeping Good Time: Reflections on Knowledge, Power, and People.* Boulder, Colo.: Paradigm Press.

———. 2006b. "Abu-Ghraib: Imprisonment and the War on Terror." *Race & Class* 48 (1): 42–59.

———. 2008. "The United States Military Prison: The Normalcy of Exceptional Brutality." In *The Violence of Incarceration,* ed. Phil Scraton and Jude McCullough, 164–86. London: Routledge.

Harlow, Barbara. 1992. *Barred: Women, Writing, and Political Detention*. Hanover, N.H.: Wesleyan University Press.

Harvey, David. 2003. *The New Imperialism*. Oxford: Oxford University Press.

Instructions for the Government of Armies of the United States in the Field (Lieber Code). 1863. International Committee of the Red Cross. http://www.icrc.org/ihl.nsf/73cb71d18dc43727412567390 03e6372/a25aa5871a04919bc12563cd002d6 5c5?OpenDocument (accessed May 20, 2008).

Jackson, George. 1970. *Soledad Brother: The Prison Letters of George Jackson*. New York: Bantam.

Kelley, Robin D. G. 1996. *Race Rebels: Culture, Politics, and the Black Working Class*. New York: Free Press.

Lobe, Jim. 2005. "Bush, Cheney Attack Amnesty International." *InterPress Service*, June 1. http://www.commondreams.org/headlines05/0601-01.htm.

Mackey, Robert. 2009. "Hunger Strikes Continue at Guantánamo." *New York Times*, February 10. http://thelede.blogs.nytimes.com/2009/02/10/hunger-strikes-continue-at-guantanamo (accessed May 11, 2010).

Mbeki, Govan. 1991. *Learning from Robben Island: Govan Mbeki's Prison Writings*. Athens: Ohio University Press.

Memorandum for the Vice President. Subject: Humane Treatment of al Qaeda and Taliban Detainees. 2002, February 7. http://en.wikisource.org/wiki/Humane_Treatment_of_al_Qaeda_and_Taliban_Detainees (accessed May 20, 2008).

Meron, Theodor. 1998. *War Crimes Law Comes of Age: Essays*. Oxford: Oxford University Press.

Michaelsen, Scott, and Scott Cutler Shershow. 2004. "The Guantánamo 'Black Hole': The Law of War and the Sovereign Exception." *Middle East Report Online*, January 11. http://www.merip.org/mero/mero011104.html (accessed May 20, 2008).

Olshanky, Barbara. 2005. "What Does It Mean to Be an 'Enemy Combatant'?" In *America's Disappeared: Secret Imprisonment, Detainees, and the "War on Terror,"* ed. Rachel Meeropol, 179–225. New York: Seven Stories Press.

Patterson, Orlando. 1982. *Slavery and Social Death: A Comparative Study*. Cambridge, Mass.: Harvard University Press.

Ratner, Michael. 2005. "The Guantánamo Prisoners." In *America's Disappeared: Secret Imprisonment, Detainees, and the "War on Terror,"* ed. Rachel Meeropol, 31–59. New York: Seven Stories Press.

Reagan, Ronald. 1987. "Message to the Senate Transmitting a Protocol to the 1949 Geneva Conventions," January 29. http://www.reagan.utexas.edu/archives/speeches/1987/012987b.htm (accessed May 11, 2010).

Record, Jeffrey. 2003. *Bounding the Global War on Terrorism*. Carlisle, Pa.: Strategic Studies Institute.

Robinson, Cedric J. 2007. *Forgeries of Memory and Meaning: Blacks and the Regimes of Race in American Theater and Film before World War II.* Chapel Hill: University of North Carolina Press.

Rodríguez, Dylan. 2006. *Forced Passages: Imprisoned Radical Intellectuals and the U.S. Prison Regime.* Minneapolis: University of Minnesota Press.

Rosenberg, Carol. 2007. "Military Expands Plan for Migrant Tent City." *Miami Herald*, October 19.

Rousseau, Jean Jacques. 1762. *The Social Contract.* Trans. G. D. H. Cole. http://www.constitution.org/jjr/socon.htm (accessed May 20, 2008).

Saadawi, Nawal el. 1994. *Memoirs from the Women's Prison.* Trans. Marilyn Booth. Berkeley: University of California Press.

Scott, James C. 1992. *Domination and the Arts of Resistance: Hidden Transcripts.* New Haven, Conn.: Yale University Press.

Sexton, Jared, and Elizabeth Lee. 2006. "Figuring the Prison: Prerequisites of Torture at Abu Ghraib." *Antipode* 38 (5): 1005–22.

Taibo, Paco Ignacio, II, and Subcommandante Marcos. 2006. *The Uncomfortable Dead (What's Missing Is Missing).* Trans. Carlos Lopez. New York: Akashic.

White House Office of the Press Secretary. 2001. *Detention, Treatment and Trial of Certain Non-Citizens in the War against Terrorism.* http://georgewbush-whitehouse.archives.gov/news/releases/2001/11/20011113-27.html (accessed May 20, 2008).

Wilber, Del Quentin, and Peter Finn. 2009. "U.S. Retires 'Enemy Combatant,' Keeps Broad Right to Detain." *Washington Post*, March 14, A06. http://www.washingtonpost.com/wp-dyn/content/article/2009/03/13/AR2009031302371.html (accessed May 11, 2010).

Williams, Carol J. 2006a. "At Guantánamo." *Los Angeles Times*, October 7, A12.

———. 2006b. "Details on Detainee Suicides Emerging." *Los Angeles Times*, June 12. http://articles.latimes.com/2006/jun/12/nation/na-gitmo12 (accessed May 1, 2010).

Woolf, Virginia. 1938. *Three Guineas.* London: Hogarth Press.

Worthington, Andy. 2009. "Guantánamo's Hidden History: Shocking Statistics of Starvation." Andy Worthington, June 10. http://www.andyworthington.co.uk/2009/06/10/guantanamos-hidden-history-shocking-statistics-of-starvation (accessed May 11, 2010).

———. 2007. *The Guantánamo Files: The Stories of the 774 Detainees in America's Illegal Prison.* London: Pluto Press

Yee, Min S. 1973. *The Melancholy History of Soledad Prison.* New York: Harper's Magazine Press.

CHAPTER 3

A Nation of Families

The Codification and (Be)longings of Heteropatriarchy

Tanya McNeill

IN 1970 MARRIED COUPLES made up 70.6 percent of U.S. households; in 2005 that number had dropped to 51.3 percent (U.S. Census Bureau n.d.).[1] This demographic shift has been accompanied by significant cultural, legal, and social shifts in when and how individuals form familial relationships. The U.S. government has responded to these changes by urging a return to heteropatriarchal, nuclear family formations.[2] Put differently, the nation not only codifies and upholds heteropatriarchal families as superior but also imagines that they are necessary for the good of the nation. (Some) heteropatriarchal families are (and produce) proper citizens; whiteness, as I will discuss later, plays a central role here as well. This has been most explicit in welfare policy and in legislative responses to the judicial support of same-sex marriage. In this chapter, I analyze the mobilization of *affects of belonging* in the production of the nation as heteropatriarchal. I examine federal policies and laws that uphold hegemonic heteropatriarchy, paying particular attention to their deployment of "the empirical," and juxtapose them with personal narratives about how individuals respond to the disruption of heteropatriarchal desires in familial spaces. These two sites demonstrate the extent to which heteropatriarchal imaginaries,[3] and the nation itself, are produced through discourse and social practice. Central to my argument is the contention that empirical ("rational") and affective ("emotional") ways of knowing are entangled.

It is conventionally, methodologically, and linguistically difficult to write about the empirical and the affective as operating in and through each other. They are generally seen to preclude each other. As Jennifer Harding and E. Deidre Pribram write, "Emotions have tended to be ignored or denigrated within Western philosophical and scientific traditions" (2004, 863). The sociological research mobilized by the media and by the state tends to present itself (and be characterized) as objective, empirical fact.[4] Empirical (particularly quantitative) sociological research is taken to be objective scientific fact, yet the knowledge produced through such research is always already entangled in cultural, political, and emotional structures—some external, material, and visible, some interior and liminal. The production and deployment of empirical knowledges are entangled in the liminal. Affective modes of knowing are coconstituted through structural arrangements of power. Identity and subjectivity are shaped in and through affective processes and material structures of power, both of which are constituted in and through each other. Affects of belonging are produced through coconstitutive processes that are shaped by the material and the psychic. As Sara Ahmed writes, "Normativity is comfortable for those who can inhabit it. The word 'comfort' suggests wellbeing and satisfaction, but it also suggests an ease and easiness [. . .] Of course, one [. . .] can be made uncomfortable by one's own comforts. To see heterosexuality as an ideal that one might or might not follow—or to be uncomfortable by the privileges one is given by inhabiting a heterosexual world—is a less comforting form of comfort. But comfort it remains and comfort is very hard to notice when one experiences it" (2004, 147).

Subjectivity then is produced through a coconstitutive relationship between material structures (e.g., heteropatriarchal arrangements of sexuality and gender) and interior (liminal, psychic) interactions with these structures.[5] Normalization and belonging (like deviance and exclusion) function, in part, through categorization (a rational product of Enlightenment thought). They are also profoundly affective processes, both at the individual level, where we grapple with identities, and at political, cultural, and social levels, where the larger processes of categorization take shape. As Ahmed suggests when she references her own shift of identity from heterosexual to queer, shifts in identification result in a changed awareness of the processes and effects of categorizations.

A story borrowed from ethnic studies scholar Rhacel Salazar Parreñas's *Children of Global Migration* further illustrates this and what I mean by affects of belonging. During her fieldwork in the Philippines, Parreñas, a biologically female, heterosexual woman, was consistently read as a male-to-female transsexual (MTF). This resulted in a great deal of difficulty in her everyday interactions: "The 'gender trouble' embodying my everyday life in the Philippines is not mirrored in any other country I have visited [...] Thus, I often left the Philippines to take a break from my gendered woes and seek the comfort of gender recognition that welcomed me in another country. To be categorically defined as a woman, with all its labels, stereotypes, and assumptions, became a welcome break from my gender ambiguity. Categorization, I learned from experience, brings comfort" (2005, 2).

I would suggest, however, that it is not "categorization" that brings Parreñas comfort, but categorization in a "normal" category—and one in which she feels at home; when she is misread as transgender, she is being categorized, but not in a way that brings comfort. One might just as readily say that categorization (as an MTF) brought her discomfort. I borrow Parreñas's story here because it evocatively explicates how affects of belonging operate. It also demonstrates some of the questions that guide this chapter's inquiry into the production of knowledge about the family and the empirical processes through which families are categorized. What kinds of technologies of categorization are produced through policy? To whom does categorization bring comfort? What kinds of categorization bring comfort? How do comfort and belonging operate to produce heteronormative citizenship? How does empirical evidence about the family—putatively removed from this realm of affect—produce and mobilize itself in and through affects of belonging?

While the family has, in many ways, always been central to the nation's imagining of itself, during the last decade of the twentieth century up through the present, the family has been discursively and legislatively identified as the bedrock of the nation. Moreover, "the family," so central to the national(ist) imagination, is not any family but a specific family form: heterosexual, married parents with productive, well-adjusted, successful children. Ideally, in this view, the family will have a breadwinner father and a stay-at-home mother or be able to purchase the labor a stay-at-home mother would provide. In 1996, the 104th Congress passed two laws that explicitly codified the heteronormativity of the nation.[6] The Personal Responsibility and Work Opportunity Reconciliation Act of 1996,[7] enacted in August of that year, opens with the Congressional "finding" that "[m]arriage is the foundation of a successful society." In the Defense of Marriage Act, enacted exactly one month later, Congress declared that only marriages between "one man and one woman as husband and wife" would be recognized by the federal government.[8] In 2002, the Bush administration's Department of Health and Human Services created the Healthy

Marriage Initiative (HMI), a program designed to educate people about the benefits of marriage and increase the number of healthy marriages. Taken together, these policies and laws codify and produce a heteropatriarchal national fantasy of compulsory heterosexuality.[9]

I understand heteropatriarchy as always coconstitutively organized in and through gender, sexuality, race, and class; more specifically, hegemonic heteropatriarchy in the United States is inextricable from white supremacist logic.[10] I argue that the epistemological and affective operations of the federal government's welfare policy, the HMI, and marriage policies naturalize hegemonic heteropatriarchy and reproduce the operation of white, heterosexual, and class privileges. I focus on how social science evidence is deployed in ways that reproduce the nation as heteronormative and national belonging as contingent on heteropatriarchal family forms. Sociology, I suggest, while complicit in these processes, also has the critical potential to expose them. The discipline's attention to the social construction of gender, race, and sexuality, as well as the tools sociology offers for understanding how large social processes (e.g., capitalism, racial formations) shape individuals' lives, could be more frequently brought to bear on heterosexuality and heteronormativity. The analysis I offer here, even as it critiques certain aspects of sociological knowledge formations, is simultaneously enabled by my training in a critical and politically engaged approach to sociological inquiry and a commitment to interdisciplinary methodologies; it is not, then, outside the discipline of sociology. Toward the end of this chapter, I juxtapose my discussion of policy with an analysis of personal narratives of the parents of lesbian, gay, bisexual, and transgendered (LGBT) individuals. Following M. Jacqui Alexander, I "stage an encounter" (1991, 143) between texts and do an intertextual reading that reveals relationships between the affective density of heteropatriarchal law and the operation of compulsory (procreative) heterosexuality within personal narratives of familial relations.

Theoretical Frames and Epistemological Interrogations

In *Aberrations in Black*, Roderick Ferguson contends that at the beginning of the twentieth century, although the sociology of race imagined itself to be "studying racial phenomena that were external to it," it in fact *produced* racial difference (2004, 19). Ferguson's analysis of sociological knowledge production is an important model for the kind of analysis this chapter attempts. His work also offers insight into the relationship between heteronormativity and whiteness; the regulation of race is not separable from the regulation of gender: "Canonical sociology [. . .] emerges out of Enlightenment claims to rationality and scientific objectivity. These claims entail an investment in heterosexual patriarchy as the appropriate standard for social relations and the signature of hegemonic whiteness" (Ferguson 2004, 18). Ferguson traces these epistemological processes through the sociology of race. I take up his contention about canonical sociology's role in the "racializ[ation] of heteropatriarchy through whiteness" (18) and his epistemological orientation toward the production of sociological knowledge in order to examine relationships between the sociology of family and federal policy. Both, I argue, are imbricated in the production of a "racialized heteropatriarchy." Ferguson thus demonstrates that scholarship is political even as its claims to objectivity obscure that fact. The putative rationality of both empirical evidence and law similarly obscures the imbrication of emotion and reason.

Following Lauren Berlant, I treat the site of politics as "a scene for the orchestration of public feelings" (2005, 47). Berlant further suggests that "feelings are not the opposite of thought [. . .] Nor are feelings less abstract than thought" (2005, 47). I am not positing feelings versus rationality or thought; rather I argue that feelings and rationality are entangled with each other.[11] Ahmed writes, in her discussion of emotions, rationality, and action, that "what is relegated to the margins is often, as we know from deconstruction, right at the centre of thought itself" (2004, 4). The evacuation of emotions from scientific thought does not demonstrate their difference from each other, but rather their coconstitutiveness. "Feelings" and "rationality" are commingled in the production of knowledge and policy. As Harding and Pribram (2004) suggest, "emotions [. . .] operate in the reproduction of subjectivity, culture and power relations" (864). This chapter endeavors to make visible the operation and production of affects of belonging in the knowledge production practices of social science and of the regulation of the family by the state. I do this by analyzing the affective rhetoric with which "empirical evidence" is deployed to justify and explain federal policy. I also explore the overlap between national affects of belonging and familial affects of belonging, both of which produce a heteropatriarchal understanding of the reproduction of the social, familial, and national. A critical sociology interested in social justice requires an epistemology attentive to the technologies of knowledge production in order to make visible the operations of hegemony.

There are two threads to the argument I make here about epistemology. First, I suggest that through positivist epistemologies, the social sciences have produced a huge body of knowledge about the *effects* of structural forces without attending to the mutually constitutive regimes of power that produce those effects (e.g., racism, heteronormativity, class disparities, and sexism). My analysis here is simultaneously about the deployment of the empirical (what I call the *epistemology of the empirical*) and about how some, though not all, sociological research (most often quantitative) both produces and mobilizes positivist knowledge.[12] Privilege is naturalized and often reproduced by the epistemology of the empirical, which presumes the possibility of objective, nonpolitical work even as it reproduces (quite politically) privilege. For example, as Judith Stacey and Timothy J. Biblarz argue, popular, political, and academic discourse are shaped by a powerful assumption that heterosexuality is preferable to queer sexualities; this, as they say, "inflict[s] some of the very disadvantages [such research] claims to discover" (2001, 179). Similarly, research findings that demonstrate that heterosexual, two-parent families "do better" are taken to mean something about the family form itself rather than the social conditions that make these families "more successful." The federal policy I examine in this chapter is legitimated through social science findings that nuclear families produce the best outcomes for adults and children (see, e.g., Waite and Gallagher 2000). This prolific line of research on the family has in some ways done little more than measure and find the results of transgenerational accumulations of privilege and oppression and report them as resulting from the family form itself rather than from the structural forces that have produced that form as most "successful." The epistemology of the empirical that undergirds the logic of the production of these knowledges also enables the state (and others) to legitimate the political as empirical by mobilizing what "research shows." Sociology's critical possibilities and the insights of poststructural epistemologies, which share many characteristics, have been underutilized in the production of knowledge about the family and, even when they are deployed, are not legible by the state. The concepts of institutionalized racism and sexism, for example, attempt to describe this process, but they are difficult to describe empirically and are rarely employed as methodologies.

Second, as I suggested previously, in order to understand how knowledge about family and marriage is produced, it is important to attend to how knowledge is produced through emotional registers, how policy and law can be technologies of affects, and how feelings themselves are ways of knowing. The apparent "objectivity" and rationality of the deployment of research masks the imbrication of affect and the empirical. Moreover, I argue, feelings, affects, and emotions are structural and social process-es imbricated in the operation of power. For example, Ann Cvetkovich (2003) has articulated racism and homophobia as trauma, and Gloria Anzaldúa (1990, xix) has suggested that racism produces posttraumatic stress disorder. If not being "normal" (i.e., being oppressed) is traumatic, the process of being "normal," of being recognized, or of inhabiting the space of privilege might also be productively understood through affect— as comfort, belonging, safety, and privilege. Conventional sociological methodologies are often ill equipped to adequately measure these effects, which are simultaneously material and psychic. By drawing on method-ologies more commonly used in the humanities, and theorizing how affect operates in and through the deployment of the empirical, I hope to con-tribute to a body of academic work that strives to make the production of privilege more visible. Affects of belonging are clearly not the only affects that attend and are produced in and through privilege; there is, nonethe-less, something to be learned about power by attending to these affects.

"Familial Politics": Families as Citizens

Family forms have always been in flux; they are historical and cultural products. Nonetheless, the dominant narrative of the family in the late twentieth-century United States is one of change and of an unprecedented "diversity" of families. This narrative, in most cases, refers to a decline in the statistical and cultural prevalence of the nuclear family form, particularly the man-as-breadwinner, woman-as-homemaker model. The narrative emphasizes changes ranging from women's entrance into the workforce (usually without indicating that women of color and poor white women had always worked) to the rise in single-parent families and increased divorce rates. This narrative also tends to collapse into passing references to the disparate histories of racial and ethnic groups subjected to racist U.S. policy whose experiences fall outside the narrative of the "modern fam-ily." This narrative does not generally identity the family as white; rather it describes the experience of white families as if this experience were uni-versal; the effects of slavery on family formation for African Americans or the effects of immigration regulation on family formation for Chinese and

Japanese Americans are footnoted as exceptions to the history of the family (see, e.g., Coontz 1992, 1997; Stacey 1990). Similarly, the ways in which white families benefited from historical and contemporary inequalities are often left unaddressed. For the most part, however, social science and public policy attention to the family in the late twentieth century focused on increased divorce rates, "out-of-wedlock births," single-mother families, and the feminization of poverty. In the past decade, there has also been increased attention to gay and lesbian families. Even as transformations in law, cultural representation, and social conventions make nonheteropatriarchal families more common and accepted, much social science research and federal policy and legislation has emphasized the negative effects of these families on family members (especially children) and on the nation (i.e., "community" or society).

Despite (or perhaps as a result of) the fact that "in 2005, married couples became a minority of all American households for the first time" (Roberts 2007),[13] hegemonic discourse, research, and policy of the twenty-first century continue to evoke a nostalgia of sorts for heteropatriarchal family forms. In fact, a consensus seems to have emerged—within social science research on the family and the federal government and among politicians, activists, and organizations across the mainstream political spectrum—that the nuclear family is the ideal family form and that the federal government ought to be doing more to support and promote it. This consensus is, of course, contested and often contradictory; while the gay and lesbian movement's position on same-sex marriage is, in many ways, heteronormative, its heteronormativity looks rather different from the heteropatriarchy of the religious Right or that of the lawmakers for whom same-sex marriage is a "threat" to heterosexuality. At the same time, there is a dense coherence around the social science "evidence" that demonstrates two-parent, married families as "better"—for the nation and for individuals in the family. This coherence naturalizes the nuclear family form and has manifested in legislation (e.g., the personal responsibility act) and policy (e.g., the HMI) that explicitly urges Americans—particularly poor Americans—to reproduce the nuclear family for their own good and for the good of the nation. Morality and financial security become conflated.

These developments are not without historical precedent. As Gwendolyn Mink (1995, 1998) has documented, racism and moral regulation have always been central to welfare programs for poor women and children; poverty has, for most of U.S. history, been treated by the welfare system as a product of poor morals. Laws regulating marriage and divorce in the United States have always been symbolically and legislatively linked to the nation's conception of itself (Cott 2000). Eugenic policies implemented on the state and federal level between the late-nineteenth and early to mid-twentieth centuries entailed the regulation of families and the discursive linkage of family to the strength of the nation. The federal government has explicitly encouraged (and even mandated) marriage in certain moments; for example, "efforts to reform the sexual practices and family patterns of former slaves became central" to the functions of the Freedmen's Bureau (Cott 2000, 85) in the years following the Civil War. These examples also demonstrate the extent to which the moral regulation of the family and marriage has strong roots in racism and in a presumptive moral supremacy of whites.

In present-day federal policy, and the empirical evidence it deploys, the family is produced as a site of comfort and safety, and the public–private mythology of the liberal state becomes reified. On the other hand, as Berlant (1997) suggests, this public–private mythology has, to some degree, collapsed in on itself as belonging to the family becomes a requirement for proper citizenship and as the family itself becomes a unit of citizenship: "[T]he intimate public sphere of the U.S. present tense renders citizenship as a condition of social membership produced by personal acts and values, especially acts originating or directed toward the family sphere" (Berlant 1997, 5). Building on Berlant's analysis, I examine how this "familial politics of the national future" (Berlant 1997, 1) has been integrated into federal law and policy. The family is the site for the literal, cultural, and epistemic reproduction of the nation. Moreover, only certain families can reproduce "appropriately"; the "appropriateness" of various family forms has varied historically but has, within the United States, operated in accordance with hegemonic (white, Christian, middle-class, heterosexual) value systems.

Social science epistemologies and state policies on family need, thus, to be understood within the context of neoliberalism: "The specific neoliberal spin on [. . . the] cultural project [of federal welfare programs] was the removal of explicitly racist, misogynist language and images, and the substitution of the language and values of *privatization* and *personal responsibility*" (Duggan 2003, 16; emphasis in original). For example, the personal responsibility act and the HMI both transfer resources from the public to the private sector. Private companies are given federal subsidies when they create "workfare" programs employing Temporary Assistance for Needy Family (TANF) recipients. Private companies and churches are given federal grants to provide marriage education programs, and "costs for care of children (and for the ill and the elderly, who are also often cared for by unpaid or low-paid women at home) [are transferred] from the public purse to the lowest paid women workers" (Duggan 2003, 17). Meanwhile, the heteropatriarchal family is charged with the production of citizens while nonheteropatriarchal families are found guilty of weakening their communities and, by extension, the nation. Empirical knowledge production serves to naturalize the operation of these neoliberal policies rather than see them as simultaneously produced by and productive of imbricated discourses about race, gender, sexuality, class, morality, and family. The epistemology of the empirical is also mobilized in and through affective epistemologies that link "findings" to "feelings."

The Personal Responsibility Act

The personal responsibility act obliterated the nation's guaranteed cash-assistance program for poor families. Aid to Families with Dependent Children (AFDC) was replaced with TANF, a much more restrictive, regulative, and time-limited benefits program. TANF's regulations include a five-year lifetime cap on welfare benefits and workfare programs—in which welfare recipients are required to work for private and public employers who often receive government incentives to hire them. The personal responsibility act also gave states the option to include intrusive personal requirements, ranging from penalties for having additional children to the requirement that mothers disclose the father of a child for whom they seek benefits so that the state can collect child support payments (which, in some cases, are kept by the state as repayment for welfare benefits). The personal responsibility act strongly emphasizes the benefits of marriage and the detriments of single-parent families (particularly those that result from "out-of-wedlock births") and contains financial incentives for states to increase marital rates and to decrease the birth rates of children of single women (though this last point was also tied to decreased abortion rates).

The personal responsibility act posits that the heteropatriarchal family is necessary for the "success" of the nation, while nonheteropatriarchal families are sources of a range of social and individual problems. The heteropatriarchal family is thus a site of national belonging. These points are framed as empirical "facts"; they operate, however, through the register of morality and affect and produce the naturalization of heteropatriarchal families. This is made most explicit in the first three of ten "findings" with which the act opens:

1. Marriage is the foundation of a successful society.
2. Marriage is an essential institution of a successful society which promotes the interests of children.
3. Promotion of responsible fatherhood and motherhood is integral to successful childrearing and the well-being of children (7).

In these opening "findings" marriage becomes equivalent to family, specifically to child rearing and to fatherhood and motherhood. While "the interests of children" are located as central to the success of society, responsibility for protecting those interests laid within the "private" institution of marriage. More to the point, the heteropatriarchal family is produced as the only appropriate—in legal and affective terms—family form. This is achieved within the body of the act largely by pathologizing single-parent families, the majority of which are actually single-mother families, which is not incidental.[14] This produces and naturalizes the heteropatriarchal family as a site of comfort, safety, and responsible citizenship.

The personal responsibility act explicitly describes single-parent families as the source of a range of social problems that constitute "a crisis in our Nation," according to the language of finding number ten (9). Six of the ten "findings" in the first section of the law refer to social science research on single-parent families, the findings of which describe the "negative consequences" of single-parent families. These, according to the act, include increased welfare costs, increased teen pregnancies, higher crime rates, increased juvenile crime, and increased abuse and neglect of children. The personal responsibility act also lists a range of effects on children of being raised in single-parent families, including poor physical health, low cognitive skills, low educational achievement, and poor mental health. The enumeration of these "negative consequences of raising children in single-parent homes" (8) explicitly suggests a causal relationship between single-parenthood and this range of "negative consequences," even though most social science research methods can really only demonstrate correlations, not causation. The epistemology of pathology with which the personal responsibility act justifies itself is rooted in the racist history of the U.S. welfare system.

While current welfare discourses are usually less explicitly racist than those of the past, even a cursory historical detour demonstrates the extent to which they are rooted in, and still circulate, racist claims. Daniel Patrick Moynihan's 1965 report for the U.S. Department of Labor, titled "The Negro Family: The Case For National Action" but generally referred to as "the Moynihan report," described poor African American families as "a tangle of pathologies" and blamed a myriad of social problems (e.g., matriarchy itself, the failure of youth, delinquency and crime, and alienation) on the prevalence of a "matriarchal" family structure—that is, single mothers— in poor, African American communities: "[T]he weakness of the family structure [...] will be found to be the principal source of most of the aberrant, inadequate, or antisocial behavior that [...] now serves to perpetuate the cycle of poverty and deprivation" (Moynihan 1965, chapter 4). This culture of pathology and poverty discourse resonated powerfully through decades of social policy. Poor, black single mothers were blamed for the social problems plaguing their low-income neighborhoods—and their nonheteronormative family structure was seen as evidence of their pathology. This discourse was recirculated through the 1980s and beyond—for example, in Ronald Reagan's deployment of the term "welfare queens," who were generally imagined and described as black even though, at that time, the majority of welfare recipients were white (Delgado 2000). The groundwork for the Right's neoliberal project was consolidated through the pathologization of black women, a process with deep historical roots. Black women's race, gender, and sexuality were and are taken to justify the continued dismantling of public supports (see, e.g., Lubiano 1992; Mink 1995, 1998; Roberts 1997): "The welfare queen is omnipresent in discussions about 'America's' present or future even when unnamed [...] urban crime, the public schools, the crack trade, teenage pregnancy are all narratives in which 'welfare queen' is writ large" (Lubiano 1992, 332–33). Here we might see the Moynihan report and subsequent policy and legislation on family and welfare benefits as performatives: citing Butler (1993, 20), Ahmed writes, "[P]erformativity relates to the way in which a signifier, rather than simply naming something that already exists, works to generate that which it apparently names" (2004, 92). Thus, when knowledge about particular categories of people is produced and deployed (as in empirical sociological work), a political and social "reality" is produced and subjects are constituted: "Categories [...] like 'welfare mother/queen,' are [...] like so many other social narratives and taxonomic social categories, part of the building blocks of 'reality' for many people [. . .] They even stand for threats to ideas about what the relationship of the family to the state ought to be" (Lubiano 1992, 331). The Moynihan report, Reagan's repetition of the phrase "welfare queens," and federal welfare and marriage policies are performative. They produce knowledge and social practices that presume and constitute certain (brown and black, unmarried, queer, and poor) subjects as deviant and pathological and certain (white, heterosexual, married, middle-class, and Christian) subjects as normal. The detailing of the deviant inscribes the normative.

In many ways, then, the personal responsibility act continues in the vein of the Moynihan report, blaming complex social problems on the individuals most negatively impacted by them rather than interrogating the structural, historical, and psychic forces at work. The personal responsibility act also draws on and produces moral and affective cultural assumptions about family that naturalize heteropatriarchal families. The putatively causal relationship between "bad" single-parent (read "single-mother") families and negative social outcomes produces the heteropatriarchal family as morally and affectively "good" and as reflecting the best of the nation. The heteropatriarchal family is understood within the logic of the personal responsibility act to produce happy, well-adjusted, intelligent, high-achieving children, free of histories of abuse and, most importantly, destined neither to grow up "dependent" on the government for welfare benefits nor to produce offspring with such proclivities. Within this (heteropatriarchal) imaginary, the successful nation is one made up of happy, heteronormative nuclear families. This move draws on normative affective assumptions of what a family is supposed to do for a child and for the nation. The cracks in the foundation of society are seen, by this logic, to reside within the nonheteropatriarchal family rather than to be endemic to, for example, capitalism or entangled within violent American histories of oppression and privilege.

The nostalgia for the era of the happy nuclear family of middle-class suburban America elides innumerable inequalities and violences, including the fact that only some (usually white) families ever embodied that norm and that they were able to do so only because of discriminatory social policies and practices (see, e.g., Lipsitz 1998). Moreover, even those families were generally rife with "dysfunction" and inequalities, as evidenced by the narratives and scholarship generated by middle-class, white feminists of the 1970s and 1980s (see, e.g., Friedan 1963; DuPlessis and

Snitow 1998). "Nostalgia" is often an articulation of loss of privileges on the part of subjects who used to be able to take their privilege for granted (Berlant 1997). The national nostalgia for "the good old days" when family mattered is, particularly in its form as federal policy, a nostalgia for (an imagined era) when "everyone knew his or her place" in the social order. This nostalgia and the normative affective assumptions about the family are entangled with the epistemology of the empirical; the "facts" are used to legitimate the benefits of "the good old days" even as affective assumptions are used to naturalize social arrangements that reproduce privilege.

The Healthy Marriage Initiative

The heteropatriarchal fantasy of the personal responsibility act takes a far more explicit turn in the early twenty-first century with the George W. Bush administration's HMI, launched in 2002 through the Administration for Children and Families (ACF). In this section, I analyze the discourses about marriage and family on the HMI's Web site.[15] This initiative funds educational programs that teach both about the *benefits* of marriage and how to have a "healthy marriage." The stated goal of the HMI is to increase the percentages of adults in healthy marriages, youth prepared for healthy marriages, and children being raised by "a mom and a dad" in a healthy marriage. The program also aims to "increase public awareness about the value of healthy marriages" (ACF 2005) Thus, in addition to marriage-skills education, the HMI funds public awareness campaigns and research on the benefits of healthy marriages.

The initiative also contains four specialized projects: the Hispanic Healthy Marriage Initiative (HHMI), the African American Healthy Marriage Initiative (AAHMI), the Asian and Pacific Islander Healthy Marriage and Family Strengthening Initiative (APIHMFSI), and the Native American Healthy Marriage Initiative (NAHMI). Information about both the HHMI and AAHMI was on the HMI Web site in 2005. These two initiatives focus more explicitly on fatherhood than the HMI does. The APIHMFSI and the NAHMI were both developed (and appeared on the Web site) well after the HHMI and the AAHMI did, and unlike the two latter programs, they do not have special logos. This suggests that they are less established than the HHMI and the AAHMI and that they are, in some ways, afterthoughts. This resonates with the invisibility of Native Americans and Asian Americans in many national conversations and debates about race. It reflects, for example, "the long and storied myth of the Asian American model minority" (Takaki 1999, 84). The existence of these four racially and ethnically marked initiatives renders the HMI both as "not racialized" and as "white." The explanations for the existence of these racialized initiatives focus on the "cultural difference" of these groups; this positions whiteness as the cultural norm against which "difference" is visible. While there are complex and contradictory discursive regimes operating here, these initiatives can be said to operate as racial projects: "*A racial project is simultaneously an interpretation, representation, or explanation of racial dynamics, and an effort to reorganize and redistribute resources along particular racial lines*" (Omi and Winant 1994, 56, emphasis in original). The racially marked initiatives produce a specific set of meanings about race and family and redistributes resources (i.e., federally funded services) according to racial categories. The emphasis on fatherhood simultaneously relies on and produces a discourse about Latino and African American men's inadequacies as fathers. The production of knowledge about racially homogeneous families implicitly assumes and upholds antimiscegenation discourses.

The deployments of race on the Web site also raise questions about whiteness. Is the Healthy Marriage Initiative itself "white," or is it that healthy marriages themselves are "white"?[16] Histories of immigration, labor, and welfare policy make it clear that throughout U.S. history, white families have been valued above others. As a range of scholars have documented, welfare, immigration, and labor policies, marriage and divorce law, segregation and desegregation policies, and the colonization and genocide of Native Americans operated in and through the regulation of the family, sexuality, race, class, and gender (see, e.g., Collins 1990; Espiritu 1997; Lipsitz 1998; Luibhéid 2000; Mink, 1995; Roberts 1997; Romano 2003; Smith 2005). Federal policies have worked discursively and materially to regulate the family in ways that produce the patriarchal family form, whiteness, and heterosexuality as "natural" and as central to the nation. Thus, we might indeed be able to understand a "healthy marriage" to be white, not in the sense that all white people have them, but in the sense that the idea of a healthy marriage is constituted in and through hegemonic whiteness (which is always constituted in and through class, heterosexuality, and normative gender).

Belying the consistent attention paid on the initiative's Web site to the fiscal security that marriage bestows, the ACF states that the Healthy Marriage Initiative programs are not solely targeted toward low-income families. Yet, the Web site makes it very clear that the initiative is fiscally and legislatively linked to TANF. President George W. Bush introduced the project in his February 2002 TANF reauthorization proposal (Bush 2002),[17] and the Healthy Marriage Initiative's Web site repeatedly cites the personal responsibility act as legitimation. In particular the Web site emphasizes that "[i]n order to encourage States to strengthen marriages, Congress stipulated that three of the four purposes of the Temporary Assistance for Needy Families (TANF) block grant to states be either directly or indirectly related to promote healthy marriages" (AFC 2006). The consistent referencing of TANF and of the personal responsibility act makes it clear that the goal is not simply healthy marriages, but the creation of families in which children are raised by a mother and a father (and preferably their biological parents). This is a moral goal, but it is couched in the empirical and framed through affects of belonging, and it produces heteropatriarchal families as always already essential to the nation.

When George W. Bush was in office, the "ACF Healthy Marriage Mission" on the ACF's Web site opened with a quote from then-President Bush: "To encourage marriage and promote the well-being of children, I have proposed a healthy marriage initiative to help couples develop the skills and knowledge to form and sustain healthy marriages. Research has shown that, on average, children raised in households headed by married parents fare better than children who grow up in other family structures [. . .] By supporting responsible child-rearing and strong families, my Administration is seeking to ensure that every child can grow up in a safe and loving home" (ACF 2005).

Like the personal responsibility act that preceded it, the Healthy Marriage Initiative conflates marriage and parenting and, in and through the epistemology of the empirical (i.e., with references to "findings" and "research"), claims the moral and affective superiority of heteropatriarchal families. Children in heteropatriarchal families "fare better," have a "better quality of life," and grow up in "safe and loving home[s]." Children who grow up in "other family structures," one can thus infer, do not; single-parent families, and gay and lesbian families are not "safe and loving" according to the Bush administration's logic. The normative becomes inscribed through affects of national and familial belonging and through a rose-colored image of the heteropatriarchal family as providing a "safe and loving home."

The Healthy Marriage Initiative Web site consistently emphasizes the benefits of marriage to children, men, and women and specifically suggests that the correlation between marital and financial stability are a result of marriage itself: "Helping couples form and sustain healthy marriages is not, in itself, an anti-poverty program. Employment is the main anti-poverty program. Research has shown, however, that stable marriages are associated with more stable employment and higher wages. Helping couples form and sustain healthy marriages should, therefore, be part of the overall strategy to help families become or remain economically self-sufficient. In addition, researchers have found that, on average, men, women, and children do better physically and emotionally in healthy marriages" (ACF 2005).

According to one of the sources[18] for this claim, married men are more productive at work than single men and get correspondingly higher reviews and salaries from their employers (Waite and Gallagher 2000, 97–109). As feminist scholars have argued for decades, however, the wage structure in the United States has consistently favored married men (see, e.g., Heidi Hartmann's [1997] discussion of the family wage). It is the entrenched nature of this wage structure, on both a material and an affective level, that I suspect is at work in this particular statistical fact; a critical sociology might more productively interrogate how and why this is so rather than reflecting it as evidence that marriage might help resolve poverty.

While the putative financial benefits of marriage are central to the Healthy Marriage Initiative's mission, emotional benefits are also highlighted by the Web site. The definition provided for a "healthy marriage" is drawn from the work of Jerry M. Lewis and John T. Gossett (1999): "There are at least two characteristics that all healthy marriages have in common. First, they are mutually enriching, and second, both spouses have a deep respect for each other. It is a mutually satisfying relationship that is beneficial to the husband, wife and children (if present). It is a relationship that is committed to ongoing growth, the use of effective communication skills and the use of successful conflict management skills" (ACF 2005).

This argument is tautological. Furthermore, the initiative operates through claims that marriage is a desirable institution, relying on the affective density that surrounds marriage in U.S. culture: "ACF believes that government policy should play a supporting role in helping people achieve their aspirations for a healthy marriage." (ACF 2005). Those with nonheteropatriarchal aspirations are rendered illegible by the state. Marriage and family are thus mobilized as "structures of feeling" (Williams 1985) even as the means to have a successful marriage is operationalized to a set of skills with which the government can provide its citizens.

Federal welfare and marriage policies rely, thus, on empirical evidence, the "rationality" and affective densities of which are coconstitutive. They also produce (and are the product of) a national imaginary that sees the heteropatriarchal family as the ideal unit of citizenship and the necessary site for the appropriate reproduction of society. The affective logic of these policies mobilizes the empirical to argue that that only children raised in heteropatriarchal families will grow up to be successful, happy, and well adjusted and to reproduce the nation with families of their own. What happens, then, when the heteropatriarchal fantasy fails? When "the family" fails to reproduce itself according to this logic? What is the relationship between public policy and private feelings? In the next section, I will examine texts written by and for parents of LGBT children; juxtaposing their narratives with state policy reveals the affective operation of hegemonic heteropatriarchy from a different angle.

"How will we be able to pretend that we don't care?": Disruptions of Familial (Be)longing(s)

The state's investment in the ideal of the heteropatriarchal family is reflected in the personal narratives[19] of heterosexual parents grappling with the disruption of heteropatriarchal gender order within familial spaces. This is not to say that one causes the other, but rather that the national fantasy of heterosexual bliss is also a personal fantasy; this, I suggest, is not evidence of the "naturalness" of heterosexuality, but rather evidence of its powerful (affective) hegemony. I specifically focus on the intensity of grief and loss articulated in these narratives; I see this as evidence of the affective density of compulsory procreative heterosexuality. These narratives also reveal the discomfort associated with not belonging and the extent to which cultural and social belonging is imbricated with heterosexuality. Heterosexual parents of LGBT children suddenly find their own belonging to be imperiled, and the affects of belonging, comfort, safety, and privilege that inhere in heterosexuality become more visible to them in ways that grieve them and sometimes politicize them. The state's articulations of what the ideal family is and should be shows up in these parental narratives, not as state productions, but as deeply *felt* desires for their children's lives. The texts assume that parents will react to a child's coming out with grief, loss, shock, anger, or some sense of betrayal. The books work to assure parents that these reactions are "normal" and to demonstrate that the LGBT children are also normal and that parents can move through their grief and shock to acceptance and love.

These narratives reveal the extent to which (hetero)sexuality, heteronormativity, and gender (normativity) structure familial expectations as well as experiences of belonging. Notably, many of the parents are reassured when their children conform to what Duggan (2003) has dubbed homonormativity. Thus, parents often express relief (and acceptance) when their LGBT children maintain long-term monogamous relationships and have children or express the desire to do so. In these cases, parents come to see their children as "normal" and "just like everyone else." For many of the parents whose stories appear in the texts I examined, grief is transformed into activism on behalf of their children (e.g., Bernstein 1995, 2–3).

In his first chapter, "Rethinking the Unthinkable," Bernstein presumes that parents will first feel "devastation and loss" (1995, 3) upon learning of their child(ren)'s sexuality, he also works to reassure his readers that their (homophobic) feelings are natural and can be overcome though involvement with Parents and Friends of Lesbians and Gays (PFLAG). Fairchild and Hayward's book includes the following description of Fairchild's son's coming out to her:

> "Mom, it's—well, it's . . . I'm homosexual."
> Everything in me shrieked NO! and my mind raced idiotically.
> You can't be! . . . if only Laura were pregnant . . . no grand-
> children. . . . awful! . . . can't be . . . what did I do wrong . . . NO!
> "Well," I said, at last, "it's not the end of the world, honey."
> But inside me, it was. (Fairchild and Hayward 1998, 4)

Like Bernstein, Fairchild and Hayward move on to normalize this reaction and to assure parents that their reactions are normal. Similarly, Griffen, Wirth, and Wirth open with the following words: "The moment when our children chose to tell us of their homosexuality was a moment of shock and pain. Our lives were placed on a different course [. . .] It was a moment that marked the beginning of a journey through a powerful grief" (Griffin, Wirth, and Wirth 1986, 1). These texts illustrate the affective density of compulsory heterosexuality and suggest that compulsory heterosexuality is perhaps really compulsory *procreative* heterosexuality. For readers who are struggling with their children's disclosures, these narratives offer comfort, validation, and support. They, in the language of psychotherapy, "normalize" these experiences. This "normalization" must also be understood in the Foucauldian sense (1975, 1990): it is a normalization that disciplines. I contend that the validation of their feelings inevitably and simultaneously validates the heteronormative social conditions that produce those feelings. The normalization of the grief and loss of the heteronormative ideal reinscribes that ideal and reveals the extent to which emotional investments are inseparable from hegemonic social conditions. The federal policies and practices, the epistemology of the empirical, and the affective density of the range of discourses that uphold the heteropatriarchal family as the (national) ideal are elements of the hegemonic social conditions that produce homophobia and heterosexuality as normal, natural, and desirable.

The fantasy and presumption of adulthood equating marriage and family (i.e., children) is passionately and tenaciously clung to by the parents in these narratives. This heterosexual wedding fantasy is extraordinarily powerful for parents, who are particularly grief stricken by the loss of the wedding-day fantasy and the expectation of grandchildren:

> We know several parents who respond to the big announcement with: 'We knew it all the time. We wanted you to tell us when you were ready.' But most of us feel shock, disbelief, even horror [...] Suddenly the son or daughter we thought we knew is a stranger with a secret life [...] It's hard to face the future knowing that the wedding everyone anticipated will never take place, that the babies will never come home to be petted and praised and shown off to relatives. Their cousins will get married, as well as their friends from school. How will we be able to pretend we don't care? (Fairchild and Hayward 1998, 6)

Even when parents recognize that the safety and comfort of heterosexuality may be more fairy-tale than reality, the idea that the heteropatriarchal family is key to happiness structures their expectations.

> I don't imagine many babies who have been born whose parents had no agenda for them, for better or worse. First babies in particular, usually arrive heavily burdened with expectations. I suspect that few parents, when presented with pink bundles by cooing nurses, have foreseen lesbianism as their daughters' sexual choice.

I certainly was no exception, and while I think I can honestly say that I have accepted that choice on the part of both my daughters, I have to admit that *I would wave a magic wand if I could and provide them with Prince Charmings, rose-covered cottages, and nuclear families, even in the face of all the statistics about divorce, wife-beating, and child abuse.* This is where I came from, and what I have, perhaps ignorantly imagined that I had in my own life. However, there is no magic wand, and my choice has been very clear: accept, learn, love. (Ferguson in Rafkin 2001, 88; emphasis added)

Like the federal policies discussed in the first part of this chapter, these narratives express a heteropatriarchal fantasy in which heterosexual marriage (and procreation) constitutes an "idyllic life."

The affective density of this heteropatriarchal image of family is so powerful that it elides the possibility of unhappiness in heterosexual relationships. For the authors (and imagined readers) of these texts, familial belonging is also predicated on heteropatriarchal fantasies. Just as the state imagines families as citizens, parents imagine their children's reproduction of their own lives (family, marriage, and children) as the successful trajectory of their children's lives and as the route to adulthood and proper citizenship. To imagine their children's lives otherwise requires work (e.g., purchasing and reading the books that this section analyzes).

The narratives these texts are personal navigations of the coming-out process; the pedagogical goal of the textual narratives is usually to validate the experiences of other parents: *I felt this grief too; your grief, loss, anger, fear, embarrassment are normal.* Ahmed writes, "Shame can [. . .] be experienced as *the affective cost of not following the scripts of normative existence*" (2004, 107; emphasis in original). This suggests that moments of shame tell us something about normativity—about, for example, the social structural arrangements of sexuality, gender, and family. This discourse of normalization is also visible in the emphasis on the normality of LGBT individuals. The parents' movement into acceptance usually comes (in these texts) through the realization that their child can still live a "normal" life: *I have come to realize that s/he is still the same person, still my beloved child.*

Ahmed also writes, "Shame may be restorative [. . .] *when the shamed other can 'show' that its failure to measure up to a social ideal is temporary*" (2004, 107; emphasis in original). In the texts I have analyzed here, parents come to reconcile their own dashed dreams for their children when they get to know their children's friends and lovers, come to realize that their children are "still the same," and, moreover, come to realize that their children can still have loving, monogamous, long-term relationships and produce grandchildren. There is little room in these texts for narratives in which the LGBT child does not end up being "normal" (homonormative).[20] The interruption of the (re)productive (and heteropatriarchal) imaginary is resolved by its reconstitution.[21]

Conclusion

Together the personal responsibility act and the Healthy Marriage Initiative posit the success of the nation and the citizenship of the family on the intimate lives of husbands, wives, and children. If a successful marriage is at the foundation a successful nation, then the citizen's duty becomes intimate and heteronormative: form a successful marriage. The affective density associated with marriage and family is mobilized by the federal government in ways that produce the heteronormativity of the nation—a heteronormativity entangled in histories of violent racism and the operations of power through class, gender, and sexuality. At the same time, the epistemological work of the empirical legitimates heteronormative moralities as fact and masks the affects of belonging that produce these dense entanglements. This investment in heteronormative and heteropatriarchal familial relations is also intensely felt by (many) heterosexual parents, and while this is not a causal relationship, the discourses are linked; their connections reveal the operation of hegemonic heteropatriarchy on multiple levels. The state articulates heteropatriarchal families as sites of comfort, belonging, and safety; parents faced with the disruption of that ideal when their children come out as lesbian, gay, bisexual, or transgendered articulate discomfort, shame, and grief—the effects of the loss of privilege and comfort. Much as Parreñas felt uncomfortable when her gender was miscategorized, these parents feel uncomfortable in the "wrong" category.

Empirical knowledge is used in affective ways by the state in its regulation of the family and its calls for a resurgence of heteropatriarchal family forms. This occurs, in part, because of the epistemology of the empirical, which is a central feature of both sociology as a discipline and of the operation of the modern democratic political state (both, not incidentally, products of the Enlightenment).[22] Books written by parents of LGBT children for other parents deploy empirical evidence to demonstrate that their children are "normal" (a term we need to understand within the context of the Foucauldian theory of disciplinarity). Foucault suggests that the rise of social sciences coincided with the state's interest in and control of populations and with individual's internalization of the state's disciplinary and normative tactics (1975, 1990). The affective rhetoric deployed by the state in its mobilization of empirical data and its linkage of family and nation, juxtaposed with the narratives of parental grief, demonstrates how affective ways of knowing are imbricated in hegemonic processes and in empirical knowledge production.

While the state operates hegemonically through co-optation and subsumption, a critical sociology that works to tease out the normative assumptions of what is natural and to analyze their historical, political, and cultural contingency has, at the very least, the potential to expose the operations of power and to find moments of rupture. A critical sociology might reveal the "contingent foundations" of knowledge production (Butler 1995), attend to the entanglement of affect and reason, and be self-reflexive about the politics inherent in knowledge production and in its relationship to the state's efforts to regulate and control citizenship. Neither the nation nor the family is "naturally" heteropatriarchal. They are produced as such, in part through affective means.

Notes

I am indebted to the colleagues, mentors, and friends who challenge and support me with their insights, questions, and provocations. I would like to thank Barbara Barnes, Marie Sarita Gaytan, NeEddra James, Rebecca Scott, Dana Takagi, and, most especially, Heather Turcotte for their comments on this piece. Macarena Gómez-Barris and Herman Gray also offered invaluable editorial comments.

1. The *New York Times* reports this number at 49.7 percent (Roberts 2006) and makes much of the fact that married couples became the minority in 2005 (Roberts 2007). Census materials I accessed suggest the 2005 number to be 51.3; either way, the change since 1970 is considerable.

2. M. Jacqui Alexander's (1997, 1994, 1991) work on the heteropatriarchal operations of the law and the state in Trinidad and Tobago and the Bahamas has greatly clarified my thinking in this chapter.

3. See Chrys Ingraham (1994), whose conceptualization of "the heterosexual imaginary" informs my use of the heteropatriarchal imaginary.

4. This is, of course, also a question of legibility. As Lisa Duggan suggests, there is a "language gap" (1994, 3) that makes a poststructuralist queer critique

illegible outside of academic discourse. This "language gap," which we can also think of as an epistemological gap, is not endemic to queer theory (critical race theory might be equally illegible), nor to the academy (radical activist discourses might be equally illegible outside of specific communities).

5. See also Butler (1990), Fanon (1968), and Scott (1999) for psychoanalytically informed analyses of this process.

6. I do not mean to suggest that the nation was not already codified or marked as heteropatriarchal or that there are not other sites in which one could and should explore this. Many other federal and state policies and laws contribute to the regulation and production of the heteropatriarchal family, including the tax code, the regulation of private property, as well as policies on sex education, out-of-wedlock births, and other reproductive health policies. Immigration and labor policy are also sites through which the family has been and continues to be regulated.

7. Henceforth referred to as the personal responsibility act.

8. Furthermore, the Defense of Marriage Act declares that no state (nor territory or possession of the United States nor Indian tribe) would be required to recognize the marriages of same-sex couples in the event that any entity legalized such unions. As of April 2010, forty-three states have either constitutional amendments, state laws explicitly restricting marriage rights and marriage recognition to opposite-sex couples, or both (National Conference of State Legislatures 2010). Some of these states do offer an approximation of state marital benefits through domestic-partnership legislation. Same-sex marriage is available in Connecticut, Iowa, Massachusetts, New Hampshire, Vermont, and the District of Columbia; same-sex marriages performed in other states are recognized in Maryland, New York, and Rhode Island. Five states (Massachusetts, New Jersey, New Mexico, New York, and Rhode Island) have neither laws nor amendments that ban same-sex marriage.

9. Here I draw on Rich's useful conceptualization of "compulsory heterosexuality" (1980). In "Compulsory Heterosexuality and Lesbian Existence," Rich critiques feminist analyses that treat heterosexuality as natural and lesbianism as "requiring explanation" (637). The term "compulsory heterosexuality" simply and powerfully describes the array of social, cultural, political, and psychological forces that presume heterosexuality as the only option.

10. R. W. Connell's analysis of hegemonic masculinity (1995) is instructive in thinking though how hegemonic heteropatriarchy functions. Connell defines hegemonic masculinity as "the configuration of gender practice which embodies the currently accepted answer to the problem of the legitimacy of patriarchy, which guarantees (or is taken to guarantee) the dominant position of men and the subordination of women" (77). Connell also argues that hegemonic masculinities exist in relationship to nonhegemonic masculinities and that heterosexuality is central to hegemonic masculinity. See also Kane (2006) for a discussion of hegemonic masculinity.

11. Thanks to Barbara Barnes for pushing me on this point.

12. There is a tension in this chapter among sociological methodologies, sociology as a disciplinary formation, and the conceptualization of an empirical epistemology. Clearly there is much sociological work (most of it qualitative in nature) that contradicts, or at least severely complicates, the findings mobilized in support of the retrenchment of heteropatriarchal familial relations (e.g., Gerson 1993; Hochschild 1989, 1997; Stacey 1990, 1996). There is also a body of literature in sociology that utilizes queer theory in its analysis of gender and family (e.g., Ingraham 1994; Mamo 2007; Sullivan 2004).

13. See note 1 for a note on this statistic.

14. According to the U.S. Census, in 2003 mothers headed 83 percent of single-parent families, while 17 percent were headed by fathers (Fields 2004, 8–9).

15. My analysis in this section is primarily of the HMI Web site content as it appeared between July 2005 and April 2006. I do comment on a few changes (including the development of two new programs). Most of the content that I comment on is still on the site, though some has been updated or replaced with the change of presidential administrations.

16. Thanks to Rebecca Scott for posing these questions and pushing me on this point.

17. Delays in the reauthorization of TANF by Congress meant that the initiative was funded through the Department of Health and Human Services (rather than through its own budget appropriation) until the Deficit Reduction Act of 2005 was signed into law in February 2006. This act reauthorized TANF and included $150 million per year from fiscal year 2006 through fiscal year 2010 for the Healthy Marriage Initiative (up to $50 million per year can be specifically used for "responsible fatherhood" programs).

18. Very little of the research mentioned on the Healthy Marriage Initiative's Web site is specifically cited. When I contacted the ACF to request more specific information, they gave me a list of relevant sources, but they do not seem to have an actual bibliography of sources for the specific claims on the Web site. Waite and Gallagher's book *The Case for Marriage* (2000) was one of the sources e-mailed to me, and the initiative does appear to draw many of its claims from it.

19. In this section, I examine four books written by parents of LGBT children for parents of LGBT children: *Straight Parents, Gay Children: Inspiring Families to Live Honestly and with Greater Understanding* (Bernstein 1995), *Now That You Know: A Parents' Guide to Understanding their Gay and Lesbian Children* (Fairchild and Hayward 1998), *Beyond Acceptance: Parents of Lesbian and Gays Talk about Their Experiences* (Griffin, Wirth, and Wirth 1986), and *Different Daughters: A Book by Mothers of Lesbians* (Rafkin 2001). While these books seem (and are) dated, the first three are (as of June 2007) recommended by the PFLAG Web site.

20. Jessica Fields (2001) makes a similar argument in her study of a support group for parents (and allies) of LGBT individuals.

21. Here, I am not asserting that queer critiques, queer identities, or oppositional discourses do not exist. This is an analysis of what these particular texts, when juxtaposed with the federal policies I examine in the early portions of this chapter, *signify* about family and normativity.

22. The illegibility of critical discourses (e.g., queer or critical race theories) is another effect of the epistemology of the empirical.

Works Cited

Administration of Children and Families. 2005. "Healthy Marriage Initiative." U.S. Department of Health and Human Services. http://www.acf.hhs.gov/healthy marriage (accessed July 22, 2005).

———. 2006. "Strengthening Marriages and Relationships." U.S. Department of Health and Human Services. http://www.acf.hhs.gov/healthymarriage (accessed March 31, 2006).

Ahmed, Sara. 2004. *The Cultural Politics of Emotion*. New York: Routledge.

Alexander, M. Jacqui. 1991. "Redrafting Morality: The Postcolonial State and the Sexual Offences Bill of Trinidad and Tobago." In *Third World Women and the Politics of Feminism*, ed. Chandra Talpade Mohanty, Ann Russo, and Lourdes Torres, 133–52. Bloomington: Indiana University Press.

———. 1994. "Not Just (Any) Body Can Be a Citizen: The Politics of Law, Sexuality, and Postcoloniality in Trinidad and Tobago and the Bahamas." *Feminist Review* 48:5–23.

———. 1997. "Erotic Autonomy as a Politics of Decolonization: An Anatomy of Feminist and State Practice in the Bahamas Tourist Economy." In *Feminist Genealogies, Colonial Legacies, Democratic Futures*, ed. M. Jacqui Alexander and Chandra Talpade Mohanty, 63–100. New York: Routledge.

Anzaldúa, Gloria. 1990. "Haciendo caras, una entrada." In *Making Face, Making Soul: Haciendo Caras*, ed. Gloria Anzaldúa, xv–xxviii. San Francisco: Aunt Lute Foundation Books.

Berlant, Lauren. 1997. *The Queen of America Goes to Washington City: Essays on Sex and Citizenship*. Durham, N.C.: Duke University Press.

———. 2005. "The Epistemology of State Emotion." In *Dissent in Dangerous Times*, ed. Austin Sarat. Ann Arbor: The University of Michigan Press.

Bernstein, Robert. 1995. *Straight Parents, Gay Children: Inspiring Families to Live Honestly and with Greater Understanding*. New York: Thunder's Mouth Press.

Butler, Judith. 1990. *Gender Trouble: Feminism and the Subversion of Identity*. New York: Routledge.

———. 1993. *Bodies That Matter: On the Discursive Limits of "Sex."* New York: Routledge.

————. 1995. "Contingent Foundations: Feminism and the Question of 'Post-modernism.'" In *Feminist Contentions: A Philosophical Exchange*, ed. Linda Nicholson, 35–58. New York: Routledge.

Bush, George W. 2002. "Working toward Independence." *President's Welfare Reform Agenda*, February 26, 2002. http://georgewbush-whitehouse.archives .gov/news/releases/2002/02/welfare-reform-announcement-book.html (accessed April 20, 2010)

Collins, Patricia Hill. 1990. *Black Feminist Thought: Knowledge, Consciousness, and the Politics of Empowerment*. New York: Routledge.

Connell, R. W. 1995. *Masculinities*. Berkeley: University of California Press.

Coontz, Stephanie. 1992. *The Way We Never Were: American Families and the Nostalgia Trap*. New York: Basic Books.

————. 1997. *The Way We Really Are: Coming to Terms with America's Changing Families*. New York: Basic Books.

Cott, Nancy. 2000. *Public Vows: A History of Marriage and the Nation*. Cambridge, Mass.: Harvard University Press.

Cvetkovich, Ann. 2003. *An Archive of Feelings: Trauma, Sexuality, and Lesbian Public Cultures*. Durham, N.C.: Duke University Press.

Delgado, Gary. 2000. "Racing the Welfare Debate." *Colorlines* 3. http://www.color lines.com/article.php?ID=71&p=1 (accessed April 19, 2010).

Duggan, Lisa. 2003. *The Twilight of Equality? Neoliberalism, Cultural Politics, and the Attack on Democracy*. Boston: Beacon Press.

DuPlessis, Rachel Blau, and Ann Snitow, eds. 1998. *The Feminist Memoir Project: Voices from Women's Liberation*. New York: Three Rivers Press.

Espiritu, Yen Le. 1997. *Asian American Women and Men: Labor, Laws, and Love*. Thousand Oaks, Calif.: Sage.

Fairchild, Betty, and Nancy Hayward. 1998. *Now That You Know: A Parents' Guide to Understanding Their Gay and Lesbian Children*. New York: Harcourt, Brace and Co. (Orig. pub. 1979.)

Fanon, Frantz. 1968. *Black Skin, White Masks*. New York: Grove Press.

Ferguson, Roderick A. 2004. *Aberrations in Black: Toward a Queer of Color Critique*. Minneapolis: University of Minnesota Press.

Fields, Jason. 2004. *America's Families and Living Arrangements: 2003*. Washington, D.C.: U.S. Census Bureau.

Fields, Jessica. 2001. "Normal Queers: Straight Parents Respond to Their Children's 'Coming Out.'" *Symbolic Interaction* 24 (2): 165–87.

Foucault, Michel. 1975. *Discipline and Punish: The Birth of the Prison*. New York: Random House.

————. 1990. *The History of Sexuality: An Introduction*. New York: Random House.

Friedan, Betty. 1963. *The Feminine Mystique*. New York: Dell Publishing Co.

Gerson, Kathleen. 1993. *No Man's Land: Men's Changing Commitments to Work and Family*. New York: Basic Books.

Griffen, Carolyn, Marian J. Wirth, and Arthur G. Wirth. 1986. *Beyond Acceptance: Parents of Lesbians and Gays Talk about Their Experiences.* New York: St. Martin's Press.

Harding, Jennifer, and E. Deidre Pribram. 2004. "Losing Our Cool? Following Williams and Grossberg on Emotions." *Cultural Studies* 18 (6): 863–83.

Hartmann, Heidi. 1997. "The Unhappy Marriage of Marxism and Feminism." In *The Second Wave: A Reader in Feminist Theory,* ed. Linda Nicholson 97–122. New York: Routledge. (Orig. pub. 1981.)

Hochschild, Arlie. 1997. *The Time Bind: When Work Becomes Home and Home Becomes Work.* New York: Metropolitan Books.

———. 1989. *The Second Shift: Working Parents and the Revolution at Home.* New York: Viking.

Ingraham, Chrys. 1994. "The Heterosexual Imaginary: Feminist Sociology and Theories of Gender." *Sociological Theory* 12 (2): 203–19.

Kane, Emily. 2006. "'No Way My Boys Are Going to Be Like That!' Parents' Reponses to Children's Gender Nonconformity." *Gender & Society* 20 (2): 149–76.

Lewis, Jerry M., and John T. Gossett. 1999. *Disarming the Past: How an Intimate Relationship Can Heal Old Wounds.* Phoenix, Ariz.: Zeig, Tucker & Co.

Lipsitz, George. 1998. *The Possessive Investment in Whiteness: How White People Profit from Identity Politics.* Philadelphia: Temple University Press.

Luibhéid, Eithne. 2002. *Entry Denied: Controlling Sexuality at the Border.* Minneapolis: University of Minnesota Press.

Lubiano, Wahneema. 1992. "Black Ladies, Welfare Queens, and State Minstrels: Ideological War by Narrative Means." In *Race-ing Justice, En-gendering Power: Essays on Anita Hill, Clarence Thomas, and the Construction of Social Reality,* ed. Toni Morrison, 223–363. New York: Pantheon Books.

Mamo, Laura. 2007. *Queering Reproduction: Achieving Pregnancy in the Age of Technoscience.* Durham, N.C.: Duke University Press.

Mink, Gwendolyn. 1995. *The Wages of Motherhood: Inequality in the Welfare State, 1917–1942.* Ithaca, N.Y.: Cornell University Press.

———. 1998. *Welfare's End.* Ithaca, N.Y.: Cornell University Press.

Moynihan, Daniel Patrick. 1965. "The Negro Family: The Case for National Action." *U.S. Department of Labor.* http://www.dol.gov/oasam/programs/history/webid-meynihan.htm (accessed April 19, 2010).

National Conference of State Legislatures. 2010. "Same Sex Marriage, Civil Unions and Domestic Partnerships." http://www.ncsl.org/programs/cyf/samesex.htm (accessed April 19, 2010).

Omi, Michael, and Howard Winant. 1994. *Racial Formation in the United States: From the 1960s to the 1980s.* New York: Routledge.

Parreñas, Rhacel Salazar. 2005. *Children of Global Migration: Transnational Families and Gendered Woes.* Stanford, Calif.: Stanford University Press.

Rafkin, Louise, ed. 2001. *Different Daughters: A Book by Mothers of Lesbians*. San Francisco: Cleis Press.

Rich, Adrienne. 1980. "Compulsory Heterosexuality and Lesbian Existence." *Signs* 5 (4): 631–60.

Roberts, Dorothy. 1997. *Killing the Black Body: Race, Reproduction, and the Meaning of Liberty*. New York: Pantheon Books.

Roberts, Sam. 2006. "It's Official: To Be Married Means to Be Outnumbered." *New York Times*, October 15. http://query.nytimes.com/gst/fullpage.html?res =9500E6D71130F936A25753C1A9609C8B63 (accessed July 10, 2007).

———. 2007. "51% of Women Are Now Living without Spouse." *New York Times*. January 16, A1. http://www.nytimes.com/2007/01/16/us/16census.html (accessed June 22, 2007).

Romano, Renee. 2003. *Race Mixing: Black–White Marriage in Postwar America*. Cambridge, Mass.: Harvard University Press.

Scott, Joan Wallach. 1999. *Gender and the Politics of History*. New York: Columbia University Press.

Smith, Andrea. 2005. *Conquest: Sexual Violence and American Indian Genocide*. Cambridge Mass.: South End Press.

Stacey, Judith. 1990. *Brave New Families: Stories of Domestic Upheaval in Late Twentieth Century America*. New York: Basic Books.

———. 1996. *In the Name of the Family: Rethinking Family Values in the Postmodern Age*. Boston: Beacon Press.

Stacey, Judith, and Timothy J. Biblarz. 2001 "(How) Does the Sexual Orientation of Parents Matter?" *American Sociological Review* 66 (2): 159–83.

Sullivan, Maureen. 2004. *The Family of Woman: Lesbian Mothers, Their Children, and the Undoing of Gender*. Berkeley: University of California Press.

Takaki, Ronald. 1999. "Race at the End of History." In *The Good Citizen*, ed. David Batstone and Eduaro Mendieta, 81–92. New York: Routledge.

U.S. Census Bureau. n.d. "Families and Living Arrangements in 2005." http:// www.census.gov/population/www/pop-profile/files/dynamic/FamiliesLA .pdf (accessed July 10, 2007).

U.S. Congress. 1996. *The Personal Responsibility and Work Opportunity Reconciliation Act*. 104th Cong. http://frwebgate.access.gpo.gov/cgi-bin/getdoc.cgi?dbname =104_cong_public_laws&docid=f:publ93.104.pdf (accessed May 11, 2010).

Waite, Linda, and Maggie Gallagher. 2000. *The Case for Marriage: Why Married People Are Happier, Healthier, and Better Off Financially*. New York: Doubleday.

Williams, Raymond. 1985. *Marxism and Literature*. New York: Oxford University Press.

CHAPTER 4

Culture, Masculinity, and the Time after Race

Herman Gray

If hip-hop had done nothing but put more money in the hands of Black artists and business managers than ever before, it would mark a milestone in American cultural history.

—Greg Tate, *Everything but the Burden*

Duke Ellington [. . .] remains jazz's grandmaster at projecting different kinds of masculinity through music, from almost parodically effete to unforgivingly tough.

—Ben Ratliff, *Coltrane*

NARRATIVES OF NATION ARE STRUCTURED by the logics of gender, sexuality, and race. In the case of the United States, the foundational myth of the nation as white and heteronormative has heretofore been produced through, among other things, representations and moral panics associated with the black body (Diawara 1993; Collins 2004; Jackson 2006). Today, black self-styled thugs, gangstas, and bad boys who prey on the weak and live outside of the law have produced a sort of moral panic among the agenda setters and moral entrepreneurs in the black middle class. Indeed, the representations of black people (many produced by black media organizations and black image makers) in the media and popular culture in the United States are extremely contradictory, often disappointing and frustrating, amounting to what Paul Gilroy calls booty performances as body politics, buffoonery as transgression, and cultural performance as real politics (Gilroy 1994; Smith-Shomade 2008).

Black masculinity is the site of active cultural work; it sets the terms for belonging to the national body in the wake of disputes over affirmative action, identity, and the welfare state. Black masculinity is also the pivot point or the site for the deployment—redeployment really—of "pathology" as the primary cultural explanation for what threatens the national body of the United States and the middle-class body of blackness. Black masculinities—both those spectacles of excess "as seen on TV" *and* those normative measures of the black middle class's fitness for membership in the national body—are crucial for recalibrating the terms for belonging to the nation (and "the black community") in the aftermath of the great movements for racial and social justice and the national trauma of September 11. Once again, black masculinity functions as an especially charged site of the competing and conflicting claims about threats to the nation, who belongs to the nation, the terms of belonging, and the fitness to belong.

In a global media environment, the struggle for representation is about not only access to visibility in the national imagination but also the relations of power that structure representations. Culture is a crucial site of critical analysis and insight; but just as it is often a battering ram of moral indictment, it is effective means of regulating and policing the boundaries of identity and nation.

I consider both of these uses of culture, but I consider especially the specific mobilization of culture as a means for setting the terms of black identity and belonging to the nation. I will dwell on the use of moral suspicion in this use of culture to mark certain bodies as abject, outside the nation and civil society, and therefore subject to moral regulation and social control. In this discourse, culture is the presumed locus of questionable cultural traits, and the media is responsible for circulating hyperreal representations of blackness and masculinity. This is not a discourse easily located along a liberal or conservative political continuum; rather it is appealed to by both and, thus, central to the project of nation making in the time after race.[1]

In this formulation, I am not so much in search of positive, even alternative, models with which to contest representations about which there is so much complaint by keepers of the moral gate of entry into the nation and the race; I also do not want to promote one notion of blackness over others. Rather, my aim is use the politics of representation as an analytic to identify discourses and social conditions where culture has been deployed and representations of blackness enlisted to shore up ideas of the nation and national identity and, more importantly, what it means to belong to the nation.

The attacks of September 11 and the shifts in the geocultural politics occasioned by the wars in Iraq and Afghanistan are the most obvious and perhaps the most profound events structuring the public conversation and conception of the nation and, within that conception, of masculinity, vulnerability, and security. In the United States, or at least in the context of a national narrative about new terror threats to the national body, there is an emerging common sense, or what Brown and others call whitewashing race. This new common sense, especially with the election of Barack Obama as president, goes something like this: on social divisions where questions of race and ethnicity (rather than class inequality) are concerned, the United States has moved, decidedly so, into a time after racism (perhaps even race), a time after the consolidation of civil rights, and, of course, the time after September 11, 2001 (Brown and others 2003).

Whatever vestiges of racial inequalities remain, so this common sense understanding goes, are expressions of defects in individual attitudes, moral character, and the persistence of a distinct (and abnormal) culture of poverty. In the face of the national crisis signaled by the global war on terror and the institutionalization of the national-security state, individual and cultural explanations for the persistence of questionable behavior or suspicious populations is especially powerful. In this context of such national crisis and anxiety, the cultural production and representation of aberrant forms of black masculinity (and, by extension, the fitness for citizenship) are especially rife and charged with meaning. The location of black masculinity, as a charged site of representation about the meaning of belonging to the nation, produces blackness and masculinity as a lens through which to (a) view an *earlier* social and historical time (long since passed) when race served as an impediment to equal rights, social justice, and individual liberty; and (b) quiet anxiety and suspicion about undetected and identified dangers in the midst of the national body. Middle-class representatives of heteronormative black masculinity serve as powerful emblems of black success and models of national belonging, as evidence of moving on, and as evidence of moving beyond the time of race and racial thinking. In the theme of this volume, black aberrant bodies represent the traces of a time that no longer exists.

If not race, then what? If not racial time, to paraphrase Flava Flav of Public Enemy, then what time is it? In this time after race and racism, confirmed by the election of the America's first black president and the consolidation of black middle-class participation the mainstream, how should one account for the lingering effects of black poverty, crime, violence, and disproportionate imprisonment? If these are not due to structural factors like national policy retrenchment, new racisms, or racial inequality, then what? Defects in character? Defects in culture?

How can blackness simultaneously signify racial progress and national security, and national inclusion and containment? In the discourse of color-blindness in the time after race, black masculinity quells an anxious masculinity threatened by the attacks of September 11 and an anxious whiteness threatened by immigration- and race-based public policy (and gender- and sexuality-based policy, as well) by providing the alibi both for color-blind public policy (i.e., there is no racism because we recognize and reward merit) and locating the *source of threats in "bad people" and not social conditions and social policy*. Threats to the national body posed by poor and working-class urban youths are paradoxical: both particular and pervasive, and dangerous and mainstream. This perceived threat is contained and managed most powerfully in the militarization of crime and the criminalization of black urban youths. Central to this operation is the role of culture and representation.

The Fire This Time: Yet Another Crisis of Black Males

On March 20, 2006, under the headline "Plight Deepens for Black Men, Studies Warn," the *New York Times* reported on three studies by social scientists at Columbia, Princeton, and Harvard that showed, as they put it, "that the huge pool of poorly educated black men are becoming ever more disconnected from the mainstream society, and to a far greater degree than comparable white or Hispanic men" (Eckholm 2006). This more-sobering picture came to the attention of researchers and, presumably, the press because, as they reported at the time, the economy did "great" over the last two decades and, by comparison, one segment of the black community, "low-skilled women, helped by public policy, latched onto it." While black women were getting a toehold on the economic-mobility ladder to the mainstream, black men were "falling further and further back" (Eckholm 2006). According to the *Times*, among some of the most alarming findings reported in the three studies were that black males are disproportionately represented in the drop-out rates in education, unemployment rates, and rates of prison incarceration. Here are the three most significant findings reported by the *Times*:

1. The share of young black men without jobs has climbed relentlessly, with only a slight pause during the economic peak of the late 1990s. In 2000, 65 percent of black male high school

dropouts in their twenties were jobless—that is, unable to find work, not seeking it, or incarcerated. By 2004, the share had grown to 72 percent, compared with 34 percent of whites and 19 percent of Hispanic dropouts. Even when high school graduates were included, half of black men in their twenties were jobless in 2005, up from 46 percent in 2000 (Eckholm 2006).

2. Incarceration rates climbed in the 1990s and reached historic highs in the past few years. In 1995, 16 percent of black men in their twenties who did not attend college were in jail or in prison; by 2004, 21 percent were incarcerated. By their midthirties, 60 percent of black men who had dropped out of school had spent time in prison (Eckholm 2006).

3. In the inner cities, more than half of all black men do not finish high school (Eckholm 2006).

The report continues with a shift from the broad statistical portrait of this dire circumstance to more intimate and personal stories of one of two men caught in this web of desperate poverty. These portraits were punctuated here and there with interview excerpts from the various authors of the studies. The piece concludes with some explicit policy prescriptions recommended by the various authors of the studies, including supporting parents, extra schooling for children, and teaching life skills (including parenting, conflict resolution, and character building) and job skills.

Impoverished Culture

A series of commentators and observers chose to weigh in on the implications of the study reported in the *New York Times*. I am less interested in the *New York Times* story or the empirical studies on which they report solely as evidence for the presence or absence of a crisis than I am in the responses the story generated among commentators in the press and by intellectuals on the conception of culture in their responses to the story. In other words, I want to draw attention to the specific way that the formulation and deployment of culture (as opposed to market forces, discrimination, public policy, or the state) operates as the site of remedial action for what ails black men. I want to critically examine the conception of culture and its purportedly causal role in these responses as it relates to broader assumptions about where the "problem lies" and the appropriate site of policy intervention. The responses to the *Times* story illustrate just how the implied link between culture and pathology continues to organize common sense notions, even intellectual (consensus) thinking, about poverty, marginality, and exclusion, perhaps even more so in what I am calling the time after race.

John McWhorter, of the Manhattan Institute, is unequivocal about culture as the site of black pathology. He claims that a "culture of alienation" maintains a deleterious effect on social and economic advancement for a sector of the poorest members of the black community (McWhorter 2005). For McWhorter, this culture of alienation—he calls it "therapeutic alienation"—took hold in the liberal counterculture of protest and in the welfare rights movement of the 1960s. Deepened and transferred intergenerationally, this culture of therapeutic alienation now finds contemporary expression in black popular culture—especially hip-hop, liberal Left academic discourse (social science in particular), and liberal public policy. According to McWhorter, these liberal discourses relieve blacks (especially the poor) of social and moral responsibility for their poverty, unemployment, and poor education while resorting to large and abstract explanations like deindustrialization, globalization, immigration, and transformations of the inner city to explain the enduring social ills facing black urban communities. Closer to the ground, blacks simply have to be held accountable for the individual and moral choices they make, and by this same tough-love approach, black academics and policy makers need to stop delivering only bad news, generate policies that end dependency, and create a culture of responsibility to replace a culture of alienation. McWhorter is not alone in challenging the liberal common sense about the role of culture in black poverty.

McWhorter's response to the report sits in contrast (though not as sharp as one might think) to a rather moderate group of news media commentators, including syndicated columnists Cynthia Tucker and Earl Ofari Hutchinson and Harvard sociologist Orlando Patterson. I want to consider both Tucker and Hutchinson quite briefly as instances of this (re)turn to culture as a causal factor in the crisis of black masculinity and then linger a bit longer on the comments of sociologist Orlando Patterson to show how his empirically grounded and theoretically sophisticated deployment of culture, like McWhorter's, produces an understanding of the contemporary condition of black men as pathological. But first, what about the turn to culture by liberal and progressive commentators?

Cynthia Tucker and Earl Hutchinson represent moderate to progressive voices on questions of social inequality—especially inequality based in gender, race, and class. Although Tucker expresses some concerns about the stranglehold of irresponsibility on the part of black male youths—they are offered jobs that they refuse to take, for example—she stays fairly close to the conventional liberal line that explains black male impoverishment in terms of the large "structural" categories including a dying manufacturing sector, global competition that drives the cost of American labor down, and immigrants as a ready source of cheap labor (Tucker 2006). She does think that the human-capital argument carries some weight—that is, that employers will not hire black youths, especially males, because these youths are defined mainly through the lens of a popular media that represents them as unreliable and incorrigible. The big point of her response to the report is that black men are increasingly being pushed out of the "mainstream."

Like Tucker, Hutchinson, a progressive voice, is a tireless advocate for black equality and social justice. While he explains the state of black men by targeting conservative and neoliberal social policies (welfare reform) and federal and state rollbacks in job training, he is not ready to absolve young black males of some responsibility for their steadily worsening condition. "It's true," he notes, "that many employers refuse to hire young black males due to racial fears and ignorance. It's also true that many young blacks feed that fear and ignorance by their own actions. The studies made only passing mention of that" (Hutchinson 2006). Hutchinson directly implicates *the culture* of young black men in their fate and their lack of options when he says "the explosion of gangsta rap and the spate of Hollywood violence-themed ghetto films have convinced even more Americans that the thug lifestyle is the black lifestyle. They have ghastly visions of boys-in-the-hoods heading for their neighborhoods next. No matter whether a young black is a Rhodes scholar, National Science medal winner or junior achievement candidate, they could be tagged as a gangster" (Hutchinson 2006). Unlike McWhorter, neither Tucker nor Hutchinson is convinced that structural problems of inequality, job availability, and discrimination have been completely eliminated. But like him, they (and more recently Bill Cosby and Alvin Poussaint) are increasingly alarmed at the "culture of black males" (what McWhorter calls a culture of alienation) that promotes behavior by black males that separate them from the mainstream, threatening its social stability and middle-class normative ideal.

For Harvard sociologist Orlando Patterson, several decades of social science evidence suggests that the black poor, and especially black male youths, are increasingly disconnected from the mainstream of society. Moreover, for Patterson (like McWhorter), liberal social science has been complicit in this worsening state of affairs if for no other reason than by insisting on conventional accounts (and public policies) that privilege structural explanations over cultural ones. Patterson seems least persuaded by the structural explanations (or evidence) that show racial disparities in schooling, chronic joblessness, and incarceration. That the economic boom, combined with welfare reform, in the 1990s worked for women underscores the salience of cultural explanations rather than structural ones in explaining black underachievement. He describes the 1990s as a period of economic expansion and effective welfare reform. For Patterson, the explanation for the disparities in black achievement does not rest with racial discrimination by whites, with the lack of available jobs in the economy, or even with a discriminatory criminal justice system. For him, the explanation for racial disparities is cultural, that is, a set of "[. . .] distinctive attitudes, values, and predispositions and the resulting behavior of its members" (Patterson 2006, 13). By privileging this notion of culture, Patterson is, of course, aware of the usual criticism made of such uses of culture as an explanation: (a) *it blames the victim*, to which he says such an argument is "utterly bogus. To hold someone responsible for his behavior is not to exclude a recognition of environmental factors that may have induced the problematic behavior in the first place"; (b) *cultural explanations are deterministic*, to which he replies that "people use their culture as a frame for understanding their social world, and as a resource to do much of what they want. The same cultural patterns can frame different kinds of behavior, and by failing to explore culture at any depth, analysts miss a great opportunity to re-frame attitudes in a way that encourages desirable behavior and outcomes"; (c) *cultural patterns are unchanging*, to which he claims "cultural patterns are often easier to change than the economic factors favored by policy analysts and American history offers numerous examples" (Patterson 2006).

Like Hutchinson and McWhorter, Patterson reserves some of his harshest criticisms for the commercial entertainment representations of black culture most often associated with black masculinity—hip-hop, ghetto-centric film cycles of the late 1990s, and, most significantly, the "cool-pose associated with the sub-cultural style of black youths." Again, on this point, Patterson is worth quoting directly: "[T]he important thing to note about the subculture that ensnares them [black men] is that it is *not disconnected* from the mainstream culture. To the contrary it has powerful support from some of America's largest corporations. Hip-hop, professional basketball and homeboy fashions are as American as apple pie [. . .] for young black men, however, that culture is all there is—or so they think. Sadly their complete engagement in this part of the American cultural mainstream, which they created and which feeds their pride and self respect, is a major factor in their disconnection from the socioeconomic mainstream" (Patterson 2006).

For Patterson, cultures are adaptable and changing *resources for making sense* of the social world and *connecting* its members to each other and their social world. For all the social analysts and commentators, black youth culture must adapt, move, and adjust. In this view, the so-called culture of the mainstream or the cultural dominant is always already homogenized, economically vital, and capable of effectively negotiating and managing all sorts of differences with which it is confronted. Despite Patterson's claims otherwise, this is a static notion of culture and, in the aftermath of September 11, one that maps onto an anxious national identity, which I want to argue is shored up by, among other things, this poorly adaptive black subculture (Duster 2007). But I also have another concern about this static conception of culture, with its view that culture functions as the inculcation of larger social values and norms in the individual. I take exception to this view because it does not recognize, or perhaps refuses to acknowledge, that, as Tanya McNeill shows in "A Nation of Families: The Codification and (Be)longings of Heteropatriarchy," in this volume, the welfare reforms—welfare to work, privatization of the public schools, inculcation of soft skills for welfare mothers, the employment of poor blacks, especially welfare mothers—are themselves operations of culture (and power). Moreover, these deployments of culture operate as technologies of social management and moral regulation (Gilroy 1994; McNeil, this volume). That is, they regulate by marking a normative ideal against which aberrant behavior is defined. They also regulate through the production of knowledge about aberrant behavior not so much in terms of the social science complicities that Patterson and McWhorter identify but through the production and deployment of knowledge about subjects (Ferguson 2003).

The policy mandates specified in the welfare reforms of more than a decade ago are themselves technologies of power, that is, cultural prescriptions and mechanisms of regulation that establish how appropriate subjects of the nation are to behave, to live, and even how to feel at home in the nation. As technologies of control, these prescriptions expose the historic distinction and separation of various segments of the population from the cultural dominant as well as the terms by which that cultural dominant enforces its terms and boundaries. In this discourse, black youth "behavior and culture" are emblematic sites of pathology. This formulation also figures a "mainstream" as the site of normative citizenship. But this is not a formulation conceived or deployed in homogeneous racial terms; difference is key here, but racial difference is not the difference that matters so much as differences in class, culture, behavior, aspirations, and environment.

This conception and deployment of culture ignores the cultural excesses, moral lapses, behavioral transgressions, cultural contests, and moral panics that were widespread in the decade that Patterson sees as central to the transformation of black urban-poor women. On the short list of such, one could include the first Iraq war, corporate corruption, culture wars, the use of violence in defense of antiabortion rights, increases in xenophobia and hostility to immigrants, religious intolerance and fundamentalism, record-high divorce rates, the attacks on the welfare state, and a general privatization of the public sphere. In this decade, race, gender, and sexuality were at the center of debates and policy initiatives aimed at reinscribing the heteronormative and patriarchal terms of the normative and national ideal. In other words, part of what happened in the move to reform welfare cannot be separated from many of the cultural debates and moral panics of the decade. Culture, moreover, is not just what happened to black youths and men or what they and only they do or do not do relative to the cultural dominant.

The "cool pose" is the cultural expression of black youth culture (and, in particular, masculinity) that seems to have the most deleterious effects on black youth identity. From the angle of the cultural dominant, the "cool pose" is especially pernicious, as measured by its symbolic strangeness and social distance from that cultural dominant. Moreover, black popular youth culture purportedly exerts such a powerful impact on youths, especially males, because it is the source of respect and self-expression.[2] Pumped up to the level of cultural excess and spectacle in film, music, television, video, and fashion, the cultural myth—of the real, violence, and what is cool—in which these practices are anchored find their way into the mainstream via global entertainment corporations that exploit young black youths addicted to the empty promise of fame, fortune, and respect.

The problem that these powerful media spectacles create for black publics is that these mediated fantasy worlds are the only worlds available to young black men. According to the discourse of culture narrated by our guides, though white male youths also compose the economic market consuming these images, they are somehow insulated from the mythos of the thug life proffered by the culture of cool. In short, white youths have options—not structural opportunities mind you, but cultural and personal resources that inoculate against such images, teaching them instead the virtues of responsibility, community, and citizenship. Or, at least, so this version of the story goes. Culture is accordingly an important factor for what happens (or does not happen) to black men, since it (and not structural opportunity) is the social impediment to mainstream access, mobility, and possibility.

Culture, Race, and Nation

With the publication of the previously mentioned reports about the worsening conditions of black men in the United States, can we draw any connection at all between the images that circulate in the media and popular culture, the explanations of impoverished cultures, and the relative lack of opportunity, advancement, and the general plight of black men? Many of the conservative and neoconservative commentators think so. How ought we to think about this relationship? Is it causal, as some would have it? Is it correlational? Do the images of black male success run ahead of the experiences recounted in the studies and news reports? Are the dismal figures about dropping out, incarceration, and unemployment, while alarming, simply missing the point? While empirically true, are the facts of the matter merely expressions of a marginalization and exclusion so profound and out of the "mainstream" mode of thinking that they simply are not to be believed?[3]

Twenty years ago, it was black women—especially out-of-wedlock teen mothers and immoral welfare cheats—who provided the rhetorical cover for reforming welfare, dismantling the welfare state, and privatizing much of the public sector. Black women were used to recalibrate the meaning of citizenship (i.e., work and self-sufficiency) and the terms (i.e., moral responsibility and intact families) of belonging to the nation for yet another instantiation of anxious white masculinity (threatened then by feminism and an emergent queerness). Evidence of lingering cultural impediments to economic advancement of the black poor was the intergenerational transfer of a culture of dependence that contrasted with the steady progress of the black middle class that was unencumbered by the fetters of culture and inculcated with the appropriate values. Again, the normative ideal regulates by establishing the boundaries and terms of belonging. The traditional scene of this sort of cultural work is the family; however, with the return of the family secured by the reinscription of patriarchy and heteronormativity in policies such as welfare to work, the personal responsibility act, and the Healthy Marriage Initiative, the primary scene of cultural pathology shifts once again to masculinity and the street. This binary world of black pathology and achievement continued to confound researchers—so much so that they (re)turned to culture as the most compelling explanation, and not just any notion of culture, but a pernicious and pathological culture whose causal force was unmistakable and whose object was easy for all to see. This time, however, it is black men who are actively managed through criminalization, containment, and imprisonment and whose "aberrant" behavior and disconnection from the mainstream is explained by way of cultural impediments to economic mobility and success.

I want to push this further and also suggest that this sort of cultural explanation continues the neoliberal project of restructuring the welfare state in the United States by eviscerating the public sphere; in this process, of course, black male bodies (and unruly ones, at that) are important precisely because they make visible the necessity of those operations that mark boundaries and manage threats. Constituting black youths in terms of a culture of pathology establishes the terms and demonstrates the necessity for rightful citizens and subjects of the nation to be vigilant and to be on the lookout for disposable subjects who threaten the nation.[4]

Let me develop this point. Thirty years ago, members of the then-emergent school of British cultural studies were concerned about the pivotal role of culture and the relationship between declining national formations and emergent subjects of former colonial regimes. Working in the cultural studies tradition, multiple generations of scholars conceived of culture as an active social practice and the site of power (Carby 1987; Gilroy 1987, 1994, 1993, 2000; Hall 1988, 1999; Hebdige 1979; Hoggart 1991; Mercer 1994; Morley 1980, 2000; Thompson 1986; Williams 1977; Willis 1977). They sought to understand the role of culture, gender, race, and colonialism in the making and remaking of Britain, and especially the conception of British national identity (like the American "mainstream") as always and already fixed and stable. They were interested in the specific ways that moral panics organized around newly liberated subjects of British colonialism, most especially black and Asian immigrants, signified danger to an English national identity hopelessly wed to a nostalgic image of itself as empire. Cultures, especially in their form as narratives of empire and nation, were central components in the manufacture and circulation of this nostalgic identity and the imagined threat to it represented by immigrants. On the question of race, nation, and culture, one of the important insights of this early instantiation of cultural studies was to show that British national identity was a powerful narrative that appealed to past glories of empire and nation that established Englishness, whiteness, racial purity, homogeneity, and civilization as equivalents. With wars of liberation and decolonialization, and with the return of the repressed from former colonies, this narrative came under increasing crisis, especially as the nation was forced to reimagine itself (Gilroy, 1987; Hall 1988; Hebdige 1979; Mercer 1994). This myth of Englishness required constant *renewal and revision* through nativist, nationalist, and racist responses. Culture and representation were central to this attempt to shore up the idea of the nation, since they were used to both identify transgressors of things British—identifying deficiencies and strengthening a tenuous hegemony—and to establish the terms of acceptability or belonging to the nation. As Raymond Williams showed long ago, the process of producing tradition through remembering and forgetting is very much a selective process, one where the boundaries of national culture and identity are aggressively drawn around tradition and a culture that is always and already understood as white, male, and colonial (1977).

The language of subculture, including terms like "mugging" and "gangs," was a staple of dominant media representations used to identify and produce threatening bodies. Hall and his colleagues show the powerful role of discourse and language in actively producing and winning national hegemonies (Hall 1978). These examples are helpful not so much as alibis for the predatorily violent behavior of some African American males youths or to evade the question of moral and individual responsibility. Rather, the insights of the British school of cultural studies show how representations of race and ethnicity are used to secure, in cultural terms, the dominant relations of power that serve as the basis for national fantasies. More important, their insights suggest how culture (as a proxy for national tradition) works at the level of representation and meaning to equate being British with being white (or, in the American case, with being middle class). They show how the claim to cultural tradition—the "mainstream," for example—is itself part of the cultural practice of constructing hegemonies.

In nationalist and racial discourses, talk about "mainstream" culture presumes that those positioned as outside the mainstream bear the burden of adaptation so as to reduce the threat to the nation and to secure the terms of belonging. This, of course, ignores the active way that the cultural dominant is racialized and that the very normativity of this cultural dominant is socially and historically produced and sustained by the very presence of those who are said to threaten and contaminate the national body.

Saskia Sassen has written that "legal status entails the specifics of whom the state recognizes as a citizen and the formal basis of rights and responsibilities of the individual in relation to the state. International law affirms that each state may determine who will be considered a citizen of the state" (Sassen 2002, 7). As an interpretive lens through which to return to the question of culture, national identity, and either perceived threats to the cultural dominant or forms of exclusion from it, what if we shift the scale and perspective of our examination from the national to that of the city (the global city, to be exact), and what if we widen our notion of citizenship to include both the formal relation to the state and the cultural notions of belonging and national identity?

Among the major structural and global trends that scholars of globalization have identified is the changing relations between citizenship and the state, expressed in one way by the shift at the national scale between entitlement and citizenship. Sassen tells the following story: From the nineteenth through the mid-twentieth century, the state was the means of safeguarding the well-being of its citizens—this happened at the national level and with the working class and the bourgeoisie. In the twenty-first century, the emerging pressure on the some welfare states from emerging neoliberal states resulted in states, like the United States and Britain, cutting back on this presumed social contract. As one might expect, formally, this rearticulation weakened the relation between the state and the poor, but it also made it harder and harder to secure the loyalty and allegiance of the poor, making it more difficult to socialize the young into citizenship and allegiance to the state (Sassen 2002). (Recall that sociologist Patterson and neoconservatives like McWhorter claim that the structural origins of this loosening are a subculture of the "cool pose" that blocks inculcation of mainstream values.)

Sassen's story shows how arguments about black males and masculinity continue to operate at the level of moral judgment, individual disposition, and cultural values rooted in nineteenth-century notions of citizenship. Such notions continue to assume the existence of a bundle of rights protected by the state and some connection to the welfare state. The moral panics about threats posed to the national body by poorly socialized subjects, new immigrant subjects, and subjects outside the nation periodically flare because all of these subjects fail to behave as traditional citizens of the nation. Given the dismantling of the welfare state, the emergence of new zones of migration and new subjects, globalization, the permanent global war on terror, and the basis of new contractual relations to neoliberal states, the problem of poor black males who are disconnected from the mainstream may be less a matter of inadequate cultural socialization and more matter of *disposability*. In the contemporary cultural and political economy of the United States, poorly educated, structurally disconnected black and Latino youths are, in short, disposable subjects.

Can the framework for interpreting the relationship between disposable subjects and the nation be productively understood as issues of belonging to the mainstream and to the nation (Hall 1999)? Given the dissolution of the welfare state and the disappearance of the social contract between the state and the poor, is there another way to understand the cultural practices, forms, and expressions of black masculinity that liberal and conservative commentators alike find so troublesome? Neoconservatives hold that the insularity of the disposable subject's culture is responsible for failing to provide black youths with the moral and social training and disposition to gain and hold membership in the mainstream. Yet as policing practices, media spectacles, and moral panics with respect to black youths show, the terms of participating in the mainstream (an expression, at the very least, of cultural citizenship) are produced, in part, by practices of labeling, isolation, and exclusion. The dismantling of the welfare state and the extension and consolidation (and, in some cases, failure) of the neoliberal project has produced both emergent and disposable subjects throughout the world, including women workers subjected to feminicide along the U.S.–Mexico border, children soldiers in Africa and Latin America, children of destitute and cutoff communities in India and Brazil, and unemployed black male youths in the United States (Fregoso 2003). These neoliberal projects also bring together and concentrate the leading sectors of global administrative and finance capital as well as the growing disadvantaged and stigmatized populations (Fregoso 2003; Sassen 2002). This scene of concentration is, of course, the global city.

In the case of neoliberal markets like the United States and Britain and global cities like New York and London, race is a key element in both fiscal and discursive restructuring. As Miriam Greenberg shows, in film and television images in the 1970s, New York was portrayed as a debt-ridden, decaying, dangerous, crime-saturated city (Greenberg 2006). In both its fiscal restructuring, New York City became a globally based administrative and financial center, and in its geographical transformation, areas like Times Square were remade by developers and international financiers. That is, Times Square was transformed from a zone of destitution to a family-friendly destination and playground for middle-class professionals and tourists. Populations of homeless and unemployed people were displaced, institutionalized, or jailed. As John Jackson shows, in Harlem the entrepreneurial zeal of street vendors was criminalized or confined to highly regulated zones designated by the city (Jackson 2001). This cluster of fiscal and geographic structural changes was accompanied by aggressive public relations campaigns designed to purge and rewrite the city's image as a dangerous place. Public relations campaigns like "The Big Apple" and "I Love New York" reached audiences in the city and the rest of the country with saturated coverage in the form of magazine and television advertisements, movie placements, and so on. This logic has, of course, accelerated in the wake of the tragedy of September 11 (Greenberg 2006).

Race, poverty, and youths in particular played a key role in the transformation of New York at several levels, most obviously in the spate of ghetto-centric films, music, dance, and style that first emerged from the city around this time. This cultural expression of blackness and *Latinidad* worked both as a sign of danger and dread (and therefore something to be aggressively managed by New York Mayors Koch and Giuliani, and the New York Police Department) and a source of titillation and desire (i.e., something that could easily be tamed, exploited, and made to service the project of restructuring; Jackson 2000; Watkins 2005). There is a counternarrative in all of this—one that has to do with black expressive culture as critique and as outrage and rejection of their disposability and confinement. As Jeff Chang shows, this is a cultural politics that uses music, graffiti, and bodies to express a sense of place and identity in the midst of large-scale and often-devastating social dislocation and transformation (Chang 2005; Rose 1994).

Black masculinity works not only in isolation to fuel moral panics about danger and security, both of which were important for remaking New York, but also to stage new alternative visibilities about blackness— middle-class professionals who represented a new generation of college-educated cultural entrepreneurs whose very success served to shore up arguments about the culture of dependency among the black poor more created by the welfare state (Wellman 2009).

Representation

Let me turn finally to questions of representation and the cultural politics that black masculinity provokes or activates with respect to the question of the national symbolic and cultural dominant. Much of the debate about representations of black masculinity in television, cinema, popular music, music videos, and video games has been a response to the concerns about the purported pathology, unruliness, disconnection, and overall crisis that these representations indicate about black lives. The vulnerability of a heteronormative patriarchy, where notions of blackness and belonging were assured after the civil rights revolution, found fortification in, of all places, black male youth culture. A multicultural and multiracial story of national identity could be told in which the normative boundaries of mobility and inclusion were marked by class distinctions where a black middle class with appropriate cultural capital could be constituted within (and by) the cultural dominant.

My point is that this logic of producing sameness within the national dominant is at work within blackness, but this time, its form is expressed differently—as social class, as culture, and as morality. That is, in a post-9/11 nation where the discourse of color-blindness and the recognition of difference have become common sense, it is no longer just racial or sexual difference that is threatening and thus must be regulated. (The threat has moved decidedly to other realms—like religious, immigration, and foreign policies.) The form in which difference is expressed and its proximity to the normative ideal of the cultural dominant are important. Under a multicultural regime of difference, it is not so much that all black men are threatening, but that black, poor, urban males who exhibit qualities of the gangsta or thug lifestyle are. Indeed, it is this distinction of difference that is most significant, since it is the capacity for just such a distinction that invites or permits a form of regulation even while disavowing that race matters. Patterson's version of culture is important to this operation, since it is culture that both explains the aberrant behavior of those outside of the cultural dominant and offers the explanatory lens through which to measure the distance that must be overcome to belong to the nation. In the post–civil rights, post-9/11 global world, for members of the black middle class, the meaning and terms of belonging to the nation connotes something entirely different from a mere generation ago.

The media is, of course, the central site for staging these representations. The film cycles of "new jack," gangsta, thuggery, and the hood based claims on gritty realism. Music videos, news, movies, and up-from-the-hood novels enjoyed considerable commercial success and, for a while, even some cultural intrigue. The defiant media expressions of a blackness and masculinity under siege effectively turned the threat into serious box office success that, in turn, morphed into some serious mainstream titillation, buffoonery, clowning, and minstrelsy. Or did it? Ice Cube, DMX, Nas, Kanye West, 50 Cent, and Jay-Z, with their various beefs about reputations, turf, possessions, and skills, became exemplars of a craftily contrived and marketed mainstream genre (which, of course, spawned lots of regional and local independents who made new claims on thuggery, realness, and authenticity).

Along with these artists–businessmen appeared a generation of young black music moguls with large bank accounts and diverse financial portfolios whose job it was to generate, market, and leverage these images of dangerous black men. Was the very masculinity that was under assault deeply ensconced within the mainstream even as it became the poster example that marked the boundaries of the nation? That is, since these conditions formed the new terrain of possibility the politics of blackness mobilized around the stability of gender, sexuality, and race no longer held. Indeed, these old forms of blackness are pressured by new marketing demands and niches that demand a different level and intensity of performance, one where to be real, authentic, and believed, one needs to let it all hang out. No closets here: the more, the better, and the more outrageous, the better—it makes for more effective television (e.g., *I Love New York, Hell Date, Ghettofabulous*). The once certainty of categories like authenticity and realness to describe conditions in the post-9/11 and post–civil rights United States seemed to give ground to the need for new terms and formulations to make sense of what seemed like (in some quarters, anyway) an unstable and indeterminate social world, or a (black) world literally gone mad.

These shifts in the logic of race and the representation of blackness, where difference and race are more, and not less, visible, operate on the terrains of media hypervisibility. This is the outrage to which moral entrepreneurs like Bill Cosby, liberal social scientists, conservative pundits, and others are responding (Wellman 2009). This is also the representation of blackness that increasingly populates American television, marking the terms of difference and belonging to the national body.

What makes these behaviors so vexing is that they expose the fragility of belonging to the nation, the terms of power, and the *traces* of damage that inequality structures and the pursuit the American Dream promises. These behaviors that so offend are explained by resorting to pathological notions of culture and character, a primary example of which are those stranded citizens and residents of New Orleans in the aftermath of hurricane Katrina who were blamed for their own beleaguered condition. What analytic conceptions of culture are up to the critical task of identifying new racism and critiquing a hostile neoliberalism that explains persistent poverty and structural inequality as simple matters of moral transgressions and character defects (Goldberg 2008; Lamont and Small 2008)?

I am suggesting a critical conception of culture that does not automatically return to the default position of defending patriarchy, embracing homophobia, and policing the boundaries of blackness in search for authenticating indicators of belonging and membership. Instead of categories, images, and discourses that consolidate and shore up identities, representations that continue only to do the work of correcting and opposing racist stereotypes, we require a conception of culture capable of expressing and interpreting the multiplicity and range of black selves in ways that force a reckoning with the complicities and hurts of exclusive and exclusionary notions of self, community, and belonging.

Notes

1. Signal moments that set the stage for what the phrase "the time after race" means include the global shifts in population flows; the appointment of Justice Clarence Thomas to the Supreme Court of the United States; the elimination of the welfare state, including the scaling back of the federal commitments to affirmative action; and the institutionalization of color-blindness as the dominant policy position on the issue of racial diversity, discrimination, and civil society. Together, these events signal the end of the civil rights era.

2. It is a way of being recognized and asserting self-possession that Greg Tate claims is, at the very least, necessary for self-determination: "[T]here is no self-determination," Tate says, "without 'self-possession.' And, 'self-possession' is the existential issue for Black Americans" (Tate 2003, 249).

3. In Isaac Julien's film *The Darker Side of Black* and in Paul Gilroy's *Against Race* (2000), Gilroy explicitly asks whether the contemporary culture of violence among blacks in the Caribbean, England, and the United States are surface expressions of deeply rooted psychological wounds inflicted in a culture of terror and animus, which periodically reappear to rupture and disrupt what seems to be the normal order of things.

4. These new citizens are required to be appropriately armed with the surveillance tools required of the emergent subject in a global economy.

Works Cited

Brown, Michael K., Martin Carnoy, Elliott Currie, Troy Duster, David B. Oppenheimer, Marjorie M. Shultz, and David Wellman. 2003. *Whitewashing Race: The Myth of a Color-blind Society*. Berkeley: University of California Press.

Carby, Hazel. 1987. *Reconstructing Womanhood: The Emergence of the Afro-American Woman Novelist*. New York: Oxford University Press.

Chang, Jeff. 2005. *Can't Stop, Won't Stop: A History of the Hip-Hop Generation*. New York: Picador.

Collins, Patricia Hill. 2004. *Black Sexual Politics: African Americans, Gender, and the New Racism*. New York: Routledge.

Diawara, Manthia. 1993. "Black American Cinema: The New Realism." In *Black American Cinema*, ed. M. Diawara, 3–25. New York: Routledge.

Duster, Troy. 2007. "How to Read a Noose." *The Chronicle of Higher Education: The Chronicle Review*, 54 (11): B24. http://chronicle.com/weekly/v54/i11/11b02401.htm (accessed March 20, 2008).

Eckholm, Erik. 2006. "Plight Deepens for Black Men, Studies Warn." *New York Times*, March 20. http://www.nytimescom/2006/03/20/national/20black men.html?_r=1&oref=slogin (accessed March 20, 2006).

Ferguson, Roderick. 2003. *Aberrations in Black: Toward a Queer of Color Critique*. Minneapolis: University of Minnesota Press.

Fregoso, Rosa Linda. 2003. "Toward A Planetary Civil Society." In her *meXicana Encounters: The Making of Social Identities on the Borderland*, 1–29. Berkeley: University of California Press.

Gilroy, Paul. 1987. *There Ain't No Black in the Union Jack: The Cultural Politics of Race and Nation*. London: Hutchinson.

———. 1993. *The Black Atlantic: Modernity and Double Consciousness*. Cambridge, Mass.: Harvard University Press.

————. 1994. "'After the Love Has Gone': Bio-Politics and Ethno-Poetics in the Black Public Sphere." *Public Culture: Study for Transnational Cultural Studies* 7 (1): 49–76.

————. 2000. *Against Race: Imagining Political Culture beyond the Color Line.* Cambridge, Mass: Harvard University Press.

Goldberg, David Theo. 2009. *The Threat of Race: Reflections on Racial Neoliberalism.* Malden, Mass.: Wiley-Blackwell.

Greenberg, Miriam. 2006. *Branding New York: Fiscal Crisis, Image Crisis, and the Rise of Urban Neoliberalism.* New York: Routledge.

Hall, Stuart. 1988. *The Hard Road to Renewal: Thatcherism and the Crisis of the Left.* New York: Verso.

————. 1999. "New Ethnicities." In *Black British Cultural Studies Reader,* ed. Houston A. Baker, Manthia Diawara, and Ruth H. Lindeborg, 163–73. Chicago: University of Chicago Press.

————. Chas Critcher, Tony Jefferson, John Clarke, and Brian Roberts. 1978. *Policing the Crisis: Mugging, the State, and Law and Order.* London: MacMillan.

Hebdige, Dick. 1979. *Subculture: The Meaning of Style.* New York: Routledge.

Hoggart, Richard. 1991. *The Uses of Literacy: Aspects of Working-class Life with Special Reference to Publications and Entertainments.* New Brunswick, N.J.: Transaction Publishers. (Orig. pub. 1961 as *The Uses of Literacy: Changing Patterns in English Mass Culture.* Boston: Beacon Press.)

Hutchinson, Earl Ofari. 2006. "Why Young Black Men Are Endangered." *Pacific News Service,* March 21. http://news.pacificnews.org/news/view_article.html ?article_id=232dde985085dfca4143f7b59f266689 (accessed March 30, 2006).

Jackson, John L. 2001. *Harlem World: Doing Race and Class in Contemporary Black America.* Chicago: University of Chicago Press.

Jackson, Ron L. 2006. *Scripting the Black Masculine Body: Identity, Discourse, and Racial Politics in Popular Media.* Albany, N.Y.: State University of New York Press.

Lamont, Michèle, and Marío Luis Small. 2008. "How Culture Matters: Enriching Our Understanding of Poverty." In *The Colors of Poverty: Why Racial and Ethnic Disparities Persist,* ed. Ann Lin and David Harris, 76–102. New York: Russell Sage Foundation.

McWhorter, John. 2005. *Winning the Race: Beyond the Crisis in Black American.* New York: Gotham Books.

Mercer, Kobena. 1994. *Welcome to the Jungle: New Positions in Black Cultural Studies.* London: Routledge.

Morley, David. 1980. *The Nationwide Audience: Structure and Decoding.* London: British Film Institute.

————. 2000. *Home Territories: Media, Mobility, and Identity.* New York: Routledge.

Patterson, Orlando. 2006. "A Poverty of the Mind." *New York Times*, March 26, 13. http://www.nytimes.com/2006/03/26/opinion/26patterson.html (accessed March 20, 2008).

Ratliff, Ben. 2007. *Coltrane: The Story of a Sound*. New York: Farrar, Straus and Giroux.

Rose, Tricia. 1994. *Black Noise: Rap Music and Black Culture in Contemporary America*. Middletown, Conn.: Wesleyan University Press.

Sassen, Saskia. 2002. "Repositioning of Citizenship: Emergent Subjects and Spaces for Politics." *Berkeley Journal of Sociology* 47:7.

Smith-Shomade, Barretta E. 2008. *Pimping Ain't Easy: Selling Black Entertainment Television*. New York: Routledge.

Tate, Greg, ed. 2003. *Everything but the Burden: What White People are Taking from Black Culture*. New York: Broadway Books.

Thompson, Edward P. 1986. *The Making of the English Working Class*. New York: Penguin Books.

Tucker, Cynthia. 2006. "Idle Black Men, Tragically Aren't Just a Stereotype." *Atlanta Journal-Constitution*, April 16, F6.

Watkins, S. Craig. 2005. *Hip Hop Matters: Politics, Popular Culture, and the Struggle for the Soul of a Movement*. Boston: Beacon Press.

Wellman, David. 2009. "Reconfiguring the Color Line: Racializing Inner-City Youth and Rearticulating Class Hierarchy in Black American." *Transforming Anthropology*. 17:131–46.

Williams, Raymond. 1977. *Marxism and Literature*. New York: Oxford University Press.

Willis, Paul. 1981. *Learning to Labor: How Working Class Kids Get Working Class Jobs*. New York: Columbia University Press. (Orig. pub. 1977.)

CHAPTER 5

Producing Sacrificial Subjects for the Nation

Japan's War-Related Redress Policy and the "Endurance Doctrine"

Akiko Naono

MORE THAN SIXTY YEARS HAVE PASSED since the end of World War II, but we are far from having settled war-related matters. In fact, we still witness eruptions of emotionally charged disputes and rage over how to remember the war. As little time is left for the survivors, new initiatives to achieve justice are being launched, especially around the "comfort women" issues. The demands for the Japanese government to offer an apology and compensation are officially being made by several countries, such as the "comfort women" resolution in the U.S. House of Representatives (H. Res. 121) in July 2007 and similar resolutions in the National Assembly of the Republic of Korea in October 2008 and the Legislative Yuan of Republic of China in November 2008. The government of Japan, however, has not responded favorably to those calls.

In fact, the Japanese government is infamous for having refused to compensate individual victims of the Asia–Pacific War (1931–45). It insists that all war-related matters have been settled through the San Francisco Peace Treaty of 1951 and other normalization treaties with victims' respective countries. Attempting to overturn this legal claim, many overseas victims began filing lawsuits in Japanese courts in the mid-1990s. While progressive citizens' groups, lawyers, intellectuals, and journalists in Japan have supported those victims' demands for redress, conservative nationalists have successfully mobilized public support in minimizing, if not denying, Japan's past "wrongdoing." Their success in the battle over how to remember the nation's past has been increasingly institutionalized in educational programs and national ceremonies.

Putting them as opposing forces, the redress efforts of the progressives and the patriotism of conservative nationalists are often characterized as either crossing or policing the national border. Common in these two positions, though, is an assumption of an already-existing national border materialized in the legal boundary of citizenship. However, if we turned to another discursive site of war memories, that of "endurance," then the boundary of citizenship does not coincide with the border separating those who are "honored" and those who are not for their "service" to the Japanese nation.

A close analysis of laws and policies relating to war redress makes it clear that all Japanese citizens who survived the war are not equally honored by the state in the form of rights to compensation. Indeed, the Japanese state's refusal to compensate individual war victims is not limited to non-Japanese citizens; the majority of the Japanese civilians that survived the war have received no compensation for war-related losses. It is only the veterans, former civilian employees of the military (*gunzoku*), and their bereaved families that have been entitled to state compensations. With few exceptions, civilians have been denied rights for compensation under what we shall call a "doctrine of endurance obligation" (the endurance doctrine). As it states, "all members of the nation [*kokumin*] are obligated to equally accept and endure some loss as a result of war. Whether you lost life, suffered bodily injury, or lost assets, you ought to endure it in such a state of national emergency."

In this chapter, I outline the logic of the Japanese state's "endurance doctrine" employed in judicial–legal and policy discourses toward its citizens and examine it in the context of overall war-redress policy and in comparison with the narrative of "precious sacrifice." I do so in an attempt to make visible tactics of governmentality, or the "conduct of conduct" (Foucault 1991, 88), in producing the nation, together with disciplinary power and the sovereign power of the state. In particular, I analyze rhetorical devices and narrative strategies in legal and policy statements as state speech acts that not only produce sacrificial, national subjects in subjection but also establish and legitimize the state's exclusive right to violence, especially as a right to mobilize the population to death while caring for the selected subjects. Taking court decision and policy as the discursive sites of what Homi Bhabha calls "writing the nation" (Bhabha 1991, 297), this chapter identifies the "resurgence of sovereignty in the midst of governmentality" (Butler 2004, 59).[1]

This analysis is also contextualized in a broader theoretical and political framework to mark continuity between oppressive and liberal democratic forms of the state in its exercise of power and, especially, to illuminate the coexistence of sovereign and governmental operations of power (see Agamben 2004; Butler 2004). It is not only the oppressive state but also the liberal democratic state that explicitly and implicitly coerces citizens not only to endure the suspension of civil liberty and rights but also to sacrifice their lives for the sake of the nation by employing the rhetoric of "national emergency." Furthermore, I argue that the state can, and does, continue its colonial project in supposedly postcolonial liberal democracy.

Postwar Redress Policy

War-related relief measures during the immediate postwar period in Japan were formulated and put into effect with the initiative of the U.S.-dominated occupation authority—the Supreme Command of Allied Powers (SCAP). The first and primary objective of the occupation in its early stage was to demilitarize Japan and build a democratic and peaceful nation (Dower 1993). To attain this goal, SCAP promoted an understanding that it was the military leaders, not the Japanese people or the emperor, who led the entire nation of Japan to ruins. Among their programs to pacify Japan was to distance the Japanese people from the militarist state, which resulted in encouraging them to regard themselves as "victims" of the oppressive state (Dower 1993; Yoshida 1995). Historian James Orr observes, "[W]ar victim consciousness was promoted by Allied psychological warfare agents and Occupation authorities to encourage alienation from the wartime state and its military" (Orr 2001, 7).

In the course of demilitarizing Japan, SCAP ordered the Japanese government to terminate the Public Officials' Pensions Act ("the pension act"), which promoted militarism by offering better military pension compared to civilian officers (Tanaka 1995). In addition, the pension act is based on the notion of class in relation to the emperor, an iconic figure embodying national polity: the higher the military rank, the more generous the benefits. Responding to the SCAP order, the pension act was amended in February 1946, resulting in the termination of pension benefits for former military officers (Kosei-sho Engo Kyoku 1978, 235–36). In September of the same year, the Public Assistance Act was enacted, which replaced all wartime relief measures for civilians and soldiers alike with "the principle of equity in social welfare services" (Orr 2001, 140). As a result, veterans received no more privileged aid than civilians, since the amount of support was determined on the basis of need. Substituted by the welfare measure under the Public Assistance Act, suffering caused by the war is translated into hardship in need of public assistance, as if it somehow resulted from their own doing, or at least not from state's (wrong)doing.

No efforts to provide special assistance and benefits to the veterans and bereaved families materialized during the occupation. Gradually, though, the "reverse course" of the occupational policy paved the way to reactivate the favorable treatment of veterans, where the objective shifted from democratization and demilitarization to economic reconstruction and rearmament under a U.S. policy of containment. The demands for supporting the veterans and bereaved families materialized immediately after Japan regained its sovereignty in late April 1952 in the form of the Assistance Act for the Wounded and Sick Retired Soldiers and Bereaved Families of Fallen Soldiers and Others ("the assistance act"). In the following year, the pension support for veterans and bereaved families was reactivated through the partial amendment of the Public Officials' Pension Act, which was put on hold at the early stage of the occupation.

Application of the assistance act of 1952 was initially limited to veterans, former civilian employees of the military, and their bereaved families. As politically organized demands increased, its application gradually extended to other groups in the 1950s, such as bereaved families of mobilized students (in 1958) and the civilians killed in the Battle of Okinawa (in 1957; Nihon Bengoshi Rengo Kai 1997, 115–17; Tanaka 1995, 102–9). The vast majority of civilian victims, however, have not, to this day, been eligible for any support under the assistance act. The government has insisted that it is only those who have had a "direct employment relationship with the state" that are eligible for measures under the act. Special state assistance is provided for the former employees of the state on the same principle as employer's liability.

In extending the assistance measure to Okinawan civilian victims, a great emphasis was placed on their "exceptional sacrifice" in the Battle of Okinawa, the only ground battle on the civilian front, where about 150,000 civilians (more than 25 percent of the entire population of the islands) were killed. They are eligible for state assistance only in return for proving their "service to the military operation" upon their application (Ishihara 2005). In other words, state assistance is granted only so far as the state recognized the applicant's active and willful participation in the battle as members of the Great Empire of Japan. Yet, as many Okinawan survivors of the war have testified, far from willing to sacrifice for the nation, they were forced to become the protective wall for the Japanese Imperial Army and were killed not just by American but also by the Japanese soldiers (Oe 1970; Okinawa Ken 1971, 1974).

In sum, compensation measures under the assistance act were extended only to those who authorized by the state as having made great sacrifices for the nation. In fact, upon its enactment, then Minister of Health and Welfare Yoshitake Keichi characterized the assistance act of 1952 as a "state obligation, not a favor, to the bereaved families of those who sacrificed their lives for the country" (Shugi-in 1952). The stated objective of the act is to support the veterans, former civilian employees of the military, and their bereaved families in "the spirit of state compensation" (Senshoubyosha senbotsusha izoku tou engoho 1952) State compensation in this sense is far from an acknowledgement of state responsibility for having caused the losses but rather a token in return for one's service to the nation as a free-willed citizen–subject ready to sacrifice his or her life.

As the government's finances improved with the economic growth of the 1960s, many additional benefits, mostly in the forms of condolence payments, were provided to the wounded veterans and parents and wives of fallen soldiers, who had already been eligible for state support under the assistance act of 1952 and the pension act. Of the other Japanese-civilian groups, only the following were given some state assistance under other redress programs: (1) Family members of unreturned migrants to Japan's former colonies and occupied lands who have been confirmed in terms of neither death nor whereabouts; and (2) repatriates who had lost their overseas assets. Both of these groups succeeded in securing some state support by effectively mobilizing themselves to lobby the Liberal Democratic Party (LDP), the leading conservative party. The government had to put an emphasis on their "exceptional sacrifice" to justify providing relief measures for these two groups (Kosei-sho Engo Kyoku 1978, 141–48), as no war-redress program was being instituted for the general civilian population, including those who had died or were severely injured by U.S. air-raid campaigns (Kosei-sho Engo Kyoku 1978, 216–34). The government maintained that civilians were to be aided by social welfare services, and thus no special relief program was necessary. In other words, civilian victims of war are not treated as distinct from the rest of the population in need of being cared for by the state, such as the poor and disabled.

After a new act (the Act on Payment of Special Grants to Repatriates and Other Persons) passed in 1967 that gave special payments to repatriates, the government announced an agreement with the LDP that the final resolution to the postwar settlements was solved with this act and no further war-redress program would be instituted. This decision was made even though a case was still under review in the Japanese Supreme Court. In the end, the judicial branch delivered a decision that legitimized the already-stated policy on which the executive branch and the leading party agreed.

With the decision in 1967, the vast majority of Japanese citizens would be left with no redress measure for war-related losses. Furthermore, a doctrine of endurance obligation would, in the 1980s and the following decades, be cited as the main rationale behind withholding state compensation for civilians in court cases and policy documentation.

State Policy toward *Hibakusha*

With the exception of the two groups of civilians mentioned in the previous section, *hibakusha,* or atomic-bomb survivors, occupy a unique position in Japan's war-redress policy because they are eligible for medical and other allowances under state relief measures. This exceptional status was not, however, initiated by the state but rather earned as a result of the political struggles of *hibakusha* with the support of minority parties, particularly the former Socialist Party of Japan and the Japanese Communist Party. Unlike the families of the unreturned and the repatriates, *hibakusha* organized themselves to make demands to the LDP-led national government for state compensation that is based on an acknowledgement that the *hibakusha's* suffering was caused as a result of the war, which is an act of the state.

Hibakusha began to organize themselves in the early 1950s, but it was not until the *Lucky Dragon* Incident of 1954 that they could inaugurate a nationwide movement to demand redress from the state. Antinuclear sentiments swept Japan after a crew member of a Japanese fishing boat (the *Lucky Dragon*) died as a result of exposure to a U.S. hydrogen bomb test. Positioning the *Lucky Dragon* Incident as the third Japanese nuclear tragedy, *hibakusha* of Hiroshima and Nagasaki were re-membered as the first and the second Japanese victims of nuclear weapons.[2] Having been energized by the widespread antinuclear movement, *hibakusha* formed the national organization Nihon Hibakusha Dantai Kyogi-kai (Nihon Hidan-kyo) in the summer of 1956.

State compensation provided to the victims of the *Lucky Dragon* Incident and the powerful antinuclear movement helped fuel the efforts of the *hibakusha*, the cities of Hiroshima and Nagasaki, and doctors' associations in both cities to demand the national government provide some relief measure for *hibakusha*. Their efforts were materialized in the form of the *Hibakusha* Medical Law ("the medical law") in March 1957, which did not go very far to free many *hibakusha* from the vicious circle of illness and poverty. *Hibakusha* continued to push the national government to institute compensation measures, and with a partial victory at a lower court in 1963 that urged the government to offer welfare allowances to *hibakusha*, the *Hibakusha* Special Measures Law (the special measures law) was enacted in 1968.

The stated objective of the medical law was to "maintain and improve *hibakusha*'s health with state-sponsored check-ups and medical assistance" (Nihon Hibakusha Dantai Kyogi-kai 2009, 61). The law was, according to the national government, instituted to address *hibakusha*'s "special health conditions" (61), or radiation-related sicknesses. The *Hibakusha* Special Measures Law aimed at "improv[ing] *hibakusha*'s well-being by providing special medical and other allowances to those under special health conditions caused by the harming effects of the atomic bomb" (65). Both of these laws, in other words, concern *hibakusha*'s "special" health conditions caused by radiation and are in no way a state compensatory measure based on an acknowledgement of war responsibility for having made them vulnerable to the U.S. attack in the first place. In fact, state support for *hibakusha* was categorized as a public health issue, and the national government continued to withhold any form of state compensation to *hibakusha*, since it would pave the way for other war victims to legally demand compensation (Naono 2008).

Attempts to Grant the State the Right to Withhold to *Hibakusha*'s Compensation

A significant verdict, not only for *hibakusha*, but also for all war victims, was found by the Japanese Supreme Court on March 30, 1978, in a case filed by Korean *hibakusha* Son Jin-do. Mr. Son had entered Japan "illegally" to receive medical treatment for his radiation-related sickness.[3] His condition deteriorated after he was put in prison, and he was transferred to a hospital in Fukuoka. Having been hospitalized, Mr. Son applied for a *hibakusha* health certificate, an official document that would recognize him as a *hibakusha* under the medical law of 1957. The certificate would make him eligible for health and related benefits under the two existing laws (i.e., the medical law of 1957 and the special measures law of 1968). Yet, he was denied the classification, which meant he would not be recognized as *hibakusha* by the Japanese government. Attempting to overturn the government's decision, Mr. Son filed a lawsuit in 1972. Beginning with a victory at the Fukuoka District Court in 1974, the Japanese Supreme Court in 1978 finalized victory for Mr. Son (Nakajima 1998).

The Supreme Court verdict was very significant because it acknowledged Japanese state responsibility for Mr. Son's radiation sickness, which the Court considered as having resulted from the war—an act of the state. The verdict stressed that the medical law of 1957 ought to be interpreted fundamentally as a form of state compensation, since it is a special measure instituted by the state—the primary actor responsible for having engaged in warfare—precisely to address radiation sickness—a special case of war-caused suffering. The court also pointed out that, unlike all other war-redress measures such as the assistance act of 1952, the *Hibakusha* Medical Law does not include any citizenship clause because it is not only a social welfare measure but also a form of state compensation. Mr. Son is, therefore, eligible for all benefits provided under the law, regardless of his nationality or his status as "an illegal immigrant." Significantly enough, the Supreme Court rejected the long-held government position that classified relief laws for *hibakusha* solely as social welfare programs and suggested that the medical law embodies a spirit of state compensation.

Also noteworthy of the verdict is the reference to the conditions of colonial and postcolonial history. Mr. Son was turned into a Japanese subject during the war but subsequently was stripped of his right to Japanese citizenship after the San Francisco Peace Treaty took effect in 1952.[4] Taking these historical conditions into consideration, the verdict claims, the Japanese state is morally obligated to grant Mr. Son the right to receive support under the medical law. Put differently, the verdict implicitly criticized the state for having mobilized colonial subjects for the war as "Japanese," exposed them to an atomic attack, and then abandoned them as "aliens" after the breakdown of the empire (Naono 2005).

The Supreme Court verdict pressured the national government to reconsider its policy toward *hibakusha*. Subsequently, in 1979, the minister of health and welfare appointed seven "experts," including former

Supreme Court Justice Tanaka Jiro, to review the existing laws and propose the basic principle of government policy toward *hibakusha*. The chair of the seven-member panel was former president of the University of Tokyo Kaya Seiji, who had initiated a petition that demanded the national government enact state-compensation measures for *hibakusha*. Another member had also signed the same petition. It was, therefore, expected that the final report of this seven-member "Panel to Discuss the Basic Issues of the Policy Regarding the Atomic Bomb Survivors" would provide legal rationale and political advocacy for state redress for *hibakusha*. The actual report announced on December 11, 1980, was, however, completely opposite of such expectation and was met with fury from *hibakusha*.

The panel's final report presents legally bounded arguments, since its aim was to offset the influence of Mr. Son's case. Directly referring to the 1978 Supreme Court verdict, the report acknowledges the two existing laws regarding *hibakusha* as "a compensatory measure in a broad sense, based on resultant responsibility of the state" (Nihon Hibakusha Dantai Kyogi-kai 2009, 98). It stresses, however, that the state bears legal responsibility neither for redress for having conducted wrongful war nor for having waived (Japanese) *hibakusha*'s rights to bring the U.S. government to justice through the signing of the San Francisco Peace Treaty.[5] In other words, the legality of the state's act was not an issue. The report implicitly suggests that the state is immune from any legal obligation to compensate *hibakusha*, since conducting the war was not an illegal action: atomic bomb–related damage was caused as a result of the Asia–Pacific War, which was, as far as the Japanese state is concerned, legitimate under the rule of law.

The responsibility of the state for having caused atomic bomb–related illness, the report affirms, extends only to *hibakusha*'s unique health problems, which are attributable to aftereffects of radiation. These problems are classified as "exceptional sacrifice," which would qualify for state compensation in legal terms. Having contained state responsibility for compensating *hibakusha* to their radiation sickness, the report successfully avoids attributing any legal accountability of the state to meet *hibakusha*'s demand for the redress of war-related damage. It, thus, prevents rights for state compensation from being extended to other war victims by marking *hibakusha*'s unique vulnerability to radiation-caused illness.

By denying benefits equivalent to those under the assistance act of 1952, the panel report reaffirms the national government's position that those who were not directly employed by the state would be illegible for state assistance under the act. The report further appeals to a principle of equity and citizenship under democracy to justify its denial of state compensation to *hibakusha*. The report argues that granting state compensation to *hibakusha* would violate the principle of equity among citizens because it would strain the fiscal budget and, in return, burden the taxpayers, including other Japanese war victims who are left without any state assistance. Positioning *hibakusha* and other Japanese war victims as citizens who are granted rights and privilege only in return for civic duty, the report erases the state's historical role in having caused their suffering in the first place. The report, in the end, asserts that relief to *hibakusha* ought to be administered as a welfare measure.

Overall, the panel report substantiates the state's position with legal arguments for dividing the population into those worthy and unworthy of compensation. The former are honored by the state for having sacrificed for the nation, while the latter are left to suffer from war-related loss. Civilians, the report blatantly declares, ought to endure suffering caused by the war: "In war, a state of emergency, where the fate of the nation is at stake, all members of the nation [*kokumin*] are obligated to equally accept and endure some loss in forms of life, body, and assets resulting from war as its "general price" (103–4).

Treating members of the nation as disposable at state's will, this "endurance doctrine" was severely criticized by the *hibakusha* organization as a "horrifying justification of war" (107). It was not, however, the first time this doctrine was employed as the rationale to deny the legal obligation of the state to compensate civilians' war-related losses. Indeed, the "endurance doctrine" presented in the panel's report is almost an exact citation of a Supreme Court verdict in 1968 that was issued by eleven judges, including Mr. Tanaka who drafted the panel report.

The "Endurance Doctrine" in Court Decisions

It was not only the panel formed under the executive branch of the government but also the judiciary branch that maintained unequal treatment of civilians, compared to the veterans, in war-redress policies. With few exceptions at lower courts, the judiciary branch has consistently ruled that the denial of civilian rights for state compensation for war-related loss is neither illegal nor unconstitutional. Many verdicts that employ the "endurance doctrine" lay out the argument as follows: first, the "endurance doctrine" is introduced as a normative statement; second, the postwar constitution is not considered applicable to war-related matters;[6] lastly, the matter is handed over to the legislative branch, where the court has assigned the task of deciding whether war-related civilian loss ought to be compensated.

The leading case of the "endurance doctrine" was established by the Japanese Supreme Court decision of November 1968. It was an appeal case by a Japanese repatriate couple whose assets in Canada were forfeited to the Canadian government as a result of the Japanese government allowing signatories of the San Francisco Peace Treaty to seize Japanese overseas assets as a form of reparation. Rulings in the lower courts had been divided regarding whether the state is legally obligated to compensate the loss caused by the signing of the peace treaty. As noted in the section "Postwar Redress Policy," the government and the leading political party in 1967, a year before this Japanese Supreme Court decision, announced that all war-related matters were settled with the enactment of the 1967 law that granted a special payment to the repatriates.

In 1968, the Japanese Supreme Court dismissed the appeal by presenting normative and legal rationales. First, the verdict justifies an extrajuridical (or more precisely, extraconstitutional) act of the state for having seized citizens' assets without consent on a basis that, as a defeated nation, such act was inevitable and ought to be accepted. The verdict then lays out a normative rationale for dismissing the case by citing an "endurance doctrine": "The previous war and the following occupation put our nation in a state of emergency, where the fate of the nation was at stake. Under such circumstance all members of the nation [*kokumin*], more or less, were forced to endure some loss in forms of life, body, or assets, and these loss had to be accepted and endured as the general cost of war by all members of the nation equally. Therefore, the loss of oversea assets, as a result of being appropriated [by the state] for reparation, must be accepted and endured as a general cost of war" (Saikosai Daihoutei 1968).

The verdict then continues with a legal rationale: "it is absolutely beyond the scope of the [postwar] constitution to consider state obligation to compensate this kind of [war-related] loss" (Saikosai Daihoutei 1968). Legally speaking, therefore, the Supreme Court paved the way out for the state from being obligated to compensate war-related loss for civilians by putting the matter beyond the reach of law. The Supreme Court combined legal and normative arguments to deny plaintiff's rights to compensation: not only was the postwar peace constitution never meant to settle war-related matters but also loss resulting from war must be endured by all national subjects in the first place.

The "endurance doctrine" was first issued in this asset loss case, but it was later extended to the realms of bodily injury and loss of life. The following five cases are among those cases denying plaintiffs' rights to state compensation for loss of life or injury by citing the "endurance doctrine": (1) a man who lost his wife and eight-year-old son in the Greater Tokyo air raid; (2) three survivors of the Nagoya air raid, which left them physically disabled; (3) Taiwanese veterans who fought in the war as members of the Japanese Imperial Army and Navy and their bereaved families; (4) Japanese civilians who were interned in Siberia as forced labor after Japan's defeat; and (5) Japanese orphans who were abandoned in mainland China after Japan's defeat.

In case 1, the man that lost his wife and son in the Greater Tokyo air raid brought a case to the Tokyo District Court. His right to state compensation was denied in the rulings both at the Tokyo District and High Courts in January and May 1980, respectively. In both rulings, the plaintiff's loss of family members was judged "within the reasonable limit of endurance obligation under public law" (Tokyo Chisai 1980). The verdict further characterized the death of the plaintiff's wife and son as "sacrifice or loss contributing to the nation's survival" (Tokyo Chisai 1980), and such loss "was burdened equally among all members of the nation in the course of war" (Tokyo Chisai 1980). With this case, human life is treated as an object equivalent to an asset that ought to be dedicated to the nation for its survival, so far as one belongs to the nation. While the plaintiff in case 1 did not appeal the case any further, the Nagoya air raid case (case 2) went all the way up to the Supreme Court, which dismissed the case in June 1987 by again citing the "endurance doctrine," turning the human body into an object to be dedicated for the nation.

The Japanese Supreme Court's 1992 verdict on the case filed by Taiwanese veterans and bereaved families (case 3) extended the doctrine of the endurance obligation to those formerly colonized who were forced to fight as the "subjects of the Japanese Empire" during the war. When the case was at the Tokyo District Court, the defendant—the Japanese state—cited the 1968 Supreme Court verdict. It further argued that it ought to be in the hands of law makers as the representative body of Japanese citizens to determine what redress measures are to be instituted and to whom they are extended. The court accepted the defendant's argument and closed the door to Japan's formerly colonized people to become eligible for compensation under the assistance act of 1952.

In March 1997, the Supreme Court dismissed the case filed by those Japanese who had been interned in Siberia as forced labor after Japan officially declared defeat (case 4). This case extended the doctrine of the endurance obligation to the war-related bodily loss caused after the war was over. In the last few years, in July 2005 and January 2006, the Osaka District Court and Kobe District Court, respectively, cited the logic of endurance obligation and dismissed the case filed by the Japanese orphans who had been abandoned in mainland China after the Japanese surrender (case 5).

Colonial Inequality and the "Endurance Doctrine"

The central rhetoric the "endurance doctrine" relies on is a law of equality: "*all* members of the nation are obligated to *equally* accept and endure some loss in terms of life, body, or assets in a state of national emergency." It positions its addressees as national subjects whose membership is guaranteed in return for the equally shared burden to sacrifice for the nation. In other words, if you want to belong to a nation, you must accept the assignment of sacrifice. By translating imposed suffering into consent to sacrifice, the doctrine performatively produces a nation as "a deep horizontal comradeship" (Anderson 1991, 7). The "endurance doctrine," therefore, functions as what Homi Bhabha calls nationalist pedagogy, which attempts to smooth over contradictions and resolve ambivalence inherent in the project of producing a nation.

Upon close examination, however, it becomes clear that the assumed equality in the "endurance doctrine" sharply contradicts the actual class and colonial inequality instituted through war-redress policy and citizenship laws. If the loss or damage resulting from the war was to be endured truly equally, then some program to distribute the burden of redress must be implemented, as was the case in Germany and Italy, since all "Japanese" did not suffer to the same degree from the war. Yet, under Japan's redress policy regarding the Asia–Pacific War, those with Japanese citizenship who were directly employed by the state receive privileged treatment, while civilians and formerly colonized individuals are left to endure their loss, suffering, and even death.

Furthermore, the "endurance doctrine" serves as a rhetorical device to not only justify but also create and perpetuate colonial inequality in war-redress policy. Formerly colonized people were forced to fight the war as Japanese national subjects, yet they were stripped of their rights for choosing their citizenship upon Japan's reentry to the international community as a sovereign nation in 1952. As a result, those formerly colonized individuals are denied access to state compensation guaranteed under existing laws for Japanese citizens, such as the assistance act of 1952, because these laws, except for relief programs for *hibakusha*, all restrict their application to Japanese citizens. Having been treated unequally through redress laws, formerly colonized veterans and bereaved families filed lawsuits in the Japanese courts, but as noted in the previous section, courts dismissed their cases by deploying the "endurance doctrine" and other applicable legal arguments. The "endurance doctrine" has not been imposed on the veterans with Japanese citizenship, yet it was forced upon the formerly colonized.

In order to explicate the narrative strategies of the "endurance doctrine" in producing colonial inequality, let us examine the temporality of its narrative structure and assignment of subject positions. In those court cases where the plaintiffs are Japanese citizens, such as cases 1, 2, 4, and 5 in the previous section, the subject before the law and the subject the doctrine addresses are both presented as "Japanese nationals" who had to suffer from and endure loss resulting from the war. In cases brought by formerly colonized people, such as case 3, however, the subject before law has already been stripped of Japanese citizenship and therefore cannot assume a subject position of the narrative's addressee, that is, Japanese nationals. Yet, the "endurance doctrine" forcefully positions the formerly colonized as its addressee, as exemplified in the case brought in 1991 by the Korean veterans who were convicted as "Degree B and Degree C War Criminals" in the Far Eastern Military Tribunal. The formerly colonized veterans demanded state compensation and official apology, but the Tokyo District Court in September 1996 dismissed their case by claiming that the plaintiffs were "Japanese" at the time of their imprisonment and execution, and, therefore, the damage they suffered is part of "war-caused loss which all Japanese nationals at the time were obligated to endure equally" (Tokyo Chisai 1996).

They were stripped of their rights for state assistance provided in postwar Japan, and yet they are forcefully included in the community of imposed endurance during, as well as after, the war. Although the obligation to endure is presented as a prerequisite for membership in the nation, that is, civic duty in return for civic rights, the formerly colonized, who are forced into fulfilling this obligation through the court's verdicts, are not granted the rights of the postwar Japanese. In fact, those colonized by Japan did not suffer in the same way or degree as the Japanese citizens during the war, and thus the logic of equality in the "endurance doctrine" would not hold even at the time of the Japanese Empire. Furthermore, given that the formerly colonized were excluded from the postwar redress policy, colonial inequality was not redressed but rather widened under the pretence of a supposedly postcolonial Japan.

Nationalist Pedagogy and Memories of Sacrifice

The effectiveness of the "endurance doctrine" to not only conceal but also institute class and colonial inequality in the name of equality cannot be attributed solely to state power, materialized as policy and law; it is also attributable to the doctrine's discursive power as nationalist pedagogy. As such, it performatively produces a nation as an "imagined community of horizontal comradeship" (Anderson 1991, 7), which supposedly is glued together by the *equally* shared obligation to accept the state's assignment of "sacrifice."

The discursive power of the "endurance doctrine" is complementary to another narrative device in the war-redress discourse: that of "precious sacrifice." It presents the war dead as "our fellow countrymen," that is, the "Japanese," who *willfully* sacrificed themselves for the nation. Unlike the "endurance doctrine," which employs the language of obligation, the narrative of "precious sacrifice" constructs sacrificial national subjects with a rhetorical appeal to aspiration. This narrative induces a sense of fraternity that, according to Benedict Anderson, enables its members to dedicate their lives to the nation (Anderson 1991, 7).

In order to delineate narrative strategies of "precious sacrifice" in mobilizing such affects, let us turn to the text of Ernest Renan. According to Renan, it is the combination of the memories of sacrifice and a will to sacrifice that constitutes a sense of solidarity, that is, a nation:

> A nation is a soul, a spiritual principle. Two things, which in truth are but one, constitute this soul or spiritual principle. One lies in the past, one in the present. One is the possession in common of a rich legacy of memories; the other is present-day consent, the

desire to live together, the will to perpetuate the value of the heritage that one has received in an undivided form [...] A nation is therefore a large-scale solidarity, *constituted by the feeling of the sacrifices that one has made in the past and of those that one is prepared to make in the future.* (Renan 1991, 19; emphasis added)

It is, Renan claims, not only the memories of glorious sacrifice but also "the fact of having suffered, enjoyed, and hoped *together*" that unites members of the nation, despite their difference in terms of race and language (Renan 1991, 19; emphasis added). In fact, it is "suffering in common," more than joy, that unifies; this is why, according to Renan, grief, more than triumph, becomes more important in national memory, as they "impose duties, and require a common effort" (Renan 1991, 19). War memories as a narrative of sacrifice, therefore, induce a strong sense of attachment to the nation.

Production of historical memories alone, however, is not sufficient for constructing a sense of solidarity; they must become a *shared* past for the national present. It is the "totalizing pedagogy" of a "will to nationhood," Homi Bhabha reads in Renan's text, that enables this unity between the past and present (Bhabha 1991, 310). This will to nationhood, Renan also asserts, must be perpetually affirmed by "a daily plebiscite" (Renan 1991, 19). Practice of daily plebiscite, however, could pose a threat to the unity of a national will, since, as Bhabha points out, it "reveals that strange temporality of disavowal implicit in the national memory" (Bhabha, 1991, 311). It is this "strange temporality of disavowal" of a plebiscite, or what Bhabha terms as "performative temporality" of a nation, that the nationalist pedagogy attempts to make void in the production of historical memory.

For war memories to serve the will to nationhood, they must, therefore, incite a sentiment of shared grief and not of divisive rage among members of the community that plebiscite may otherwise evoke. It is "another memory"—memory of forced sacrifice and betrayal—that introduces dissonance in the community that nationalist pedagogy tries to expunge from the site of writing a nation. This is why Renan underscores the importance of forgetting fratricide. "To be obliged to forget," Bhabha argues in reading Renan's text, "is not a question of historical memory; it is the construction of a discourse on society that *performs* the problematic totalization of the national will" (Bhabha 1991, 311; emphasis in original). Without an act of forgetting, a daily plebiscite might upset the continuous process of renewing the national will.

Now, let us turn back to the narrative of "precious sacrifice" in Japan's discourse of war and redress. The phrase "precious sacrifice of our fellow countrymen for the nation," identifies the war dead and the enunciatory subject of the narrative as members of the same community, Japan. Furthermore, the peace and prosperity of Japan is directly attributed to the deeds of the war dead, and therefore "we" of the national present, including those who were born long after the war, must respect and honor them. The pedagogical temporality of the narrative attributes the national present to the direct accumulative of the past—the deeds of the war dead—that provides a basis for the nation. Thus, a direct link is drawn between the subject of address—the war dead—and the subject of enunciation—"we." This linkage is strengthened powerfully by the rhetoric of "sacrifice," which fuels the affective bonds between them.

It is forgetting to remember memories of forced sacrifice and betrayal that enables interpellation of the war dead and the enunciatory subject of the narrative as national subjects. The war dead are honored not because they willfully sacrificed their lives for the nation: what they actually felt does not matter. They must be honored as "precious sacrifice," re-membering them as "we, the Japanese people," so that a will to nationhood is secured; otherwise, the national present may find unbridgeable difference among themselves and decide to break up as a community unified under the banner of the nation.

The narrative of "precious sacrifice" as nationalist pedagogy incites sentiments of love and loyalty to the nation through which the "very act of the narrative performance interpellates a growing circle of national subjects" (Bhabha 1991, 297). Because of the unpredictability of "a daily plebiscite," this narrative has to be continuously and extensively reproduced and circulated not only in the political discourse regarding war redress but also in sites of popular and public culture, such as films, comic books, memorials, and museum exhibits, so that a feeling of collective grief is iteratively evoked.

Memories of the Battle of Okinawa—memories of "fratricide"—pose a threat to the national will and thus must be put aside or erased from the site of writing a nation. As noted earlier in the chapter, to be eligible for state assistance under the assistance act of 1952, which was financially necessary for many Okinawans due to the poverty they suffered under U.S. occupation, they had to testify that they *willingly* cooperated with the Imperial Military of Japan and were not forced at gunpoint

(Ishihara 2005). Okinawa's compulsory mass suicide must be forgotten and instead remembered as consented and voluntary sacrifice to disable elements of "disavowal" in the nation's performative temporality.

Okinawan war memories, in fact, have been targeted in recent years by the conservative nationalists and the state. Conservative historical revisionists, exemplified by the Liberal History Group, have tried to rewrite memories of the Battle of Okinawa as a story of Japanese patriots who willfully died for the nation. As if to empower their efforts, the Ministry of Education, Culture, Sports, Science and Technology decided in early 2007 to delete from high school textbooks reference to the role of the Japanese military in inducing and coercing Okinawans to commit "mass suicides." This blatant and forceful attempt to erase Okinawa's colonial memories by way of censorship was, however, overturned by Okinawans' protests. Also on the judicial front, Nobel prize–winning novelist Oe Kenzaburo and his publisher Iwanami were sued on the grounds of "disparaging reputations" by a former major and the bereaved family of a former colonel, both of whom were characterized in Oe's *Okinawa Notes* as having been responsible for the military's ordering of "mass suicides" in the Tokashiki and Zamami Islands. The plaintiffs argued that the inhabitants of those islands chose death with lofty self-sacrifice spirit, and the plaintiffs contend that they did not deliver any military order to coerce "mass suicide." Oe and Iwanami won both at the Osaka District and High Courts on March 28, 2008, and November 1, 2008, respectively, and the case is now in the hands of the Supreme Court.

While these are an overt attempt to erase and rewrite memories of "fratricide," other memories of coerced sacrifice and betrayal are also tamed in the cultural sites of war remembrance. Narratives of "precious sacrifice" and endurance obligation are, in fact, effective cultural affective devices in turning memories of violence and betrayal into those of "suffering in common" and thereby producing sacrificial national subjects. Furthermore, present conditions of inequality created by the state's policy and law are justified, maintained, and even perpetuated by those narrative strategies. Privileged legal treatment of Japanese veterans and their bereaved families is explained and justified by the logic of "precious sacrifice," in that those who made great contribution to the national present must be honored and cared for. Those civilian victims and formerly colonized people who have been abandoned by the state are required to fulfill civic duty to endure loss resulting from the war.

Triangular Power and a State Speech Act

Narratives of "precious sacrifice" and endurance obligation complementarily function as nationalist pedagogy to smooth over contradictions in the project of constructing a nation. They are part of the tactics of governmentality that operate diffusely through popular and public cultural productions, policy, and laws so that the national present is safeguarded. They operate not solely as governmental power, however; they are among many institutional and discursive strategies and tactics, including court verdicts, laws, and policies, that make up the triangle of "sovereign-discipline-government" power. It produces docile and obedient subjects who either aspire to or are obliged to make sacrifice for the nation, divides the population into those worthy of being cared for by the state and those deemed unworthy of support, and erases the formerly colonized from the site of writing a nation while exposing them to postcolonial violence.

In our analysis, narratives composed at the legal and administrative levels are central to this triangular power. Law is, therefore, treated not simply as an instrument of the exercise of sovereignty. As Mitchell Dean points out, law's function in service to sovereign power is linked to sets of governmental and disciplinary power (Dean 1999, 118).

Let us at first take a traditional view on law and follow its logic to explicate the way in which legally authorized statements are used as tactics of governmentality. The "endurance doctrine" clearly conflicts with the primary principle of the most fundamental legal document: the Constitution of Japan. While the initial application of the "endurance doctrine" was limited to asset loss, it was extended to the realms of bodily injury and loss of life in the later verdicts. No logic in public law, where the "endurance doctrine" is initially developed, provides legally bounded rationale for extending the obligation to endure to cases of bodily injury or death. Furthermore, the doctrine presents conflict with the spirit of peace, democracy, and human rights embodied in the postwar constitution. The constitution assures the rights of the people to "life, liberty, and the pursuit of happiness" as the highest priority, as long as "it does not interfere with the public welfare" (Article 13). Moreover, reflecting upon the preface to the constitution[7] and Article 9,[8] both of which are emblematic of "peace constitution," the norms and values laid out in the constitution certainly give much higher priority to people's rights for life over state rights to prosecute war, where the bodies of the people are disposable at the state's hands.

In the "endurance doctrine," however, the rights of the state, conflated with public welfare in the name of a nation, are given absolute priority over life, rights, and welfare of the people. The doctrine ought not to be understood simply as a citation of the well-established law or norm. It is rather a state speech act, or discursive practice, that performatively and self-referentially (re)establishes and legitimizes state sovereign power— a right to take life of its subjects—through tactics of governmentality.

Crucial to this speech act is the rhetoric of national emergency, which functions to justify suspension of norms and values promised under liberal democracy, such as basic human rights and liberty. Significantly, it is in the name of law, declared by the highest judicial authority, that the "endurance doctrine" presents this rhetoric to not only deny legal obligation of the state to compensate war-related loss but also grant the state extralegal rights to take away the lives of the people at will. This resembles what Georgio Agamben calls a "state of exception," which "appears as the legal form of what cannot have legal form" (Agamben 2004, 1), because under such circumstance, the state's acts, even in a legal arena, are put beyond the reach of law. In a state of exception, the rule of law is suspended, and yet the force of law is still claimed by the state authority (Agamben 2004, 38–39).

By employing a rhetoric of national emergency, or a state of exception, the state can lawfully exercise its oppressive power, including the right to kill, even in a liberal democracy. Furthermore, unlike most other liberal democratic states, Japan is obligated to the peace constitution that binds the state from disposing of the lives of the people, except in cases of the death penalty, and from mobilizing them to death and killing others by renouncing war. Yet, following the norm produced through the "endurance doctrine," the Japanese state, even in its constitutional renunciation of war, legally retains a right to dispose of its subjects if a state of national emergency is declared, even though there is no emergency clause in the constitution.

This is, however, not unique to the case of Japan: suspension of law, in general, is justified in a state of emergency as a necessary means through which to defend the sovereignty of the nation. As Judith Butler forcefully argues, such was the case with the Bush administration's program of "indefinite detention" of those who are condemned or suspected to be "terrorists" (see Butler 2004, 51–98). Furthermore, even in an "ordinary" state, or in a case where laws do not need to be suspended with the language of emergency, the use of state violence is justified; it is through the monopoly of violence, a marked characteristic of the modern state, that rationalizes state violence as a "legal" act, while other forms of violence are condemned to be "illegal" and are subject to punishment by state apparatuses (Benjamin 1996). Legality and legitimacy of state violence is, therefore, self-referentially justified by the state's monopoly of violence.

The state's execution of power cannot, however, always be violent or repressive, even in an emergency situation. In a liberal democracy, the sovereign power of the state, including its use of violence, must be legitimized by the collective will of the people. It is precisely the notion of "consent" expressed through representative democracy that not only legitimizes but also mobilizes the population to participate in the execution of state violence, even to death. Here, the idea of a nation becomes critical, since it is precisely the discursive site where "consent among the people" is iteratively produced, felt, and embraced. This is the decisive arena in which narratives of endurance obligation and "precious sacrifice" as nationalist pedagogy translate forced sacrifice to civic duty as members of the community with the aspiration to dedicate themselves for the nation.

Indefinite National Emergency

Japanese war-redress policies and the "endurance doctrine," together with a narrative of "previous sacrifice," produce national subjects who make sacrifices for the sake of defending and maintaining the sovereignty of a nation, while colonial subjects are erased from the space of postcolonial Japan. The "endurance doctrine" imposed on Japanese civilians and formerly colonized individuals, by employing a rhetoric of national emergency, functions as a state speech act to reestablish the sovereign power of the state—a right to kill—by placing the matter beyond the reach of law. Governmentality establishes law as its tactic, rather than simply an instrument, of sovereign power. The idea of a nation, most effectively constructed through affective memories of shared sacrifice, functions as a tactic of governmentality: it produces sacrificial subjects by working through their "desires, aspirations, interests and beliefs" (Dean 1999, 11). Redress policies and war memories bring together sovereignty, disciplinarity, and governmentality and divide the population into those worthy of redress and honor and those that are simply disposable for the sake of the nation.

Sacrificial and disposable subjects for the nation are produced not only in the state of war but also in postwar Japan, which supposedly broke free from militaristic imperial rule and transitioned to a liberal democracy with a peace constitution.[9] Put another way, as we have analyzed the postwar Japanese war-redress policies and discourses, it is not just in a state of national emergency but during "ordinary and peaceful" times when law is suspended and the population is managed and disciplined in the name of emergency. The most recent illumination of such instance is the Act Concerning the Measures for Protection of the People in Armed Attack Situations, Etc. ("citizens' protection law") of 2004: it aims at preparing Japanese citizens in case of a military or terrorist attack and outlines their rights and duties in a state of emergency. The citizens' protection law supposedly completes the series of so-called war contingency laws, which were passed in 2003 under pressure posed by the Bush administration. These are the state strategies that prepare the population for the coming war, which clearly violates the principle of peace and human rights laid out in the Japanese constitution. In other words, these extraconstitutional measures are instituted as laws in the name of preparation for national emergency.

Japan is not alone in violating liberal democracy's promise of respecting law and democratic procedures; the Bush administration's war on terror most vividly illuminates how liberal democracy could be violent and oppressive through the use of not just sovereign power of the state but also disciplinary and governmental powers (see Butler 2004). According to Judith Butler, it is through the suspension of law, enabled by declaring a state of emergency, that a space is carved out for resurgence of oppressive sovereign power in the midst of governmentality (Butler 2004, 55). The state extends its extralegal exercise of sovereign power indefinitely with "the means by which the exceptional becomes established as a naturalized norm" (Butler 2004, 67). By evoking national emergency and sovereign rights for defense when "presented an imminent danger of attack" (U.S. National Security Council 2002), the Bush administration, therefore, created the Guantánamo Bay detention center and adopted the regimes of preemptive strikes, both of which are clear violations of legal norms of liberal democracy and international community. Furthermore, extralegal and extraconstitutional exercises of sovereign power in Japan and the United States are complementary to each other; the war contingency laws of Japan were instituted because they are considered the key to U.S. military strategies in the Asia–Pacific region and the world, while Japan is integrated into U.S. military operations in the United States' attempt to extend their global reach.

Mobilizing and coercing the population to "defend" the nation is not achieved simply through extralegal sovereign power; disciplinary power works on the individuals' bodies and subjectivities to produce docile and disciplined subjects, and the self-regulatory governmental power operates through the individuals' will and aspirations to construct sacrificial subjects. It is, therefore, much harder to counteract state violence executed not simply through sovereign power but in alliance with disciplinarity and governmentality, which "conducts our conduct" even in realms of thought and feeling. Despite such difficulty, it is precisely the efforts by those who are condemned to be disposable, including *hibakusha*, Japanese civilian victims, and the formerly colonized people, that articulate a possibility to jeopardize the ongoing projects of state violence and of the making of sacrificial national subjects.

Notes

1. Methodologically speaking, the present study follows the endeavors of critical legal studies and critical race theory, both of which take law and policy as discursive operations of power.

2. For critical analysis of nationalization of atomic bomb memories, see Laura Hein and Mark Selden (1997, particularly the chapter titled "Commemoration and Silence: Fifty Years of Remembering the Bomb in America and Japan"), Akiko Naono (2002), and Lisa Yoneyama (1999).

3. Mr. Son's attempt to make an entry to Japan was made after Japan had normalized its relationship with South Korea in 1965, but it was very difficult for Mr. Son to receive a visa to Japan, especially given his previous history of having "violated" the Foreigners Registration Act.

4. Due to the bureaucratic order issued on April 14 by the Japanese Agency of Judicial Affairs, those formerly colonized by the Japanese Empire would lose Japanese citizenship upon the effecting of the San Francisco Peace Treaty in 1952.

5. Non-Japanese *hibakusha*, such as Koreans, one could argue, could obtain legal rights to demand U.S. compensation for atomic bomb–related damage, since there is no treaty between the United States and South or North Korea to waive their rights.

6. In the context of lawsuits, Article 29, Clause 3 (state obligation to compensate private property for public use) of the constitution was particularly at issue (Constitution of Japan 1946b).

7. The preface begins, "We, the Japanese people, acting through our duly elected representatives in the National Diet, determined that we shall secure for

ourselves and our posterity the fruits of peaceful cooperation with all nations and the blessings of liberty throughout this land, and resolved that never again shall we be visited with the horrors of war through the action of government, do proclaim that sovereign power resides with the people and do firmly establish this Constitution" (Constitution of Japan 1946c).

8. Article 9 reads, "Aspiring sincerely to an international peace based on justice and order, the Japanese people forever renounce war as a sovereign right of the nation and the threat or use of force as means of settling international disputes. [...] In order to accomplish the aim of the preceding paragraph, land, sea, and air forces, as well as other war potential, will never be maintained. The right of belligerency of the state will not be recognized" (Constitution of Japan 1946a).

9. This continuity can also be pointed out in the "endurance doctrine" itself. After all, the origin of the "endurance doctrine" could be traced back to the Imperial Rescript, where Emperor Hirohito, referring to the destruction brought by the atom bombs, called on his subjects to "endure the unendurable," while suppressing his responsibility for having brought the "unendurable" in the first place.

Works Cited

Agamben, Giorgio. 2004. *State of Exception*. Chicago: University of Chicago Press.

Anderson, Benedict. 1991. *Imagined Communities: Reflections on the Origin and Spread of Nationalism*. Rev. ed. New York: Verso.

Benjamin, Walter. 1996. "Critique of Violence." In *Walter Benjamin: Selected Writings, volume 1 1913–1926*, ed. Marcus Bullock and Michael W. Jennings, 236–53. Cambridge, Mass.: Belknap Press.

Bhabha, Homi. 1991. "DissemiNation." In *Nation and Narration*, ed. Homi Bhabha, 291–322. London: Routledge.

Butler, Judith. 2004. *Precarious Life: The Powers of Mourning and Violence*. New York: Verso.

Constitution of Japan. 1946a. Article 9. http://www.ndl.go.jp/constitution/etc/j01.html#s2.

———. 1946b. Article 29, section 3. http://www.ndl.go.jp/constitution/etc/j01.html#s3.

———. 1946c. Preface. http://www.ndl.go.jp/constitution/etc/j01.html.

Dean, Mitchell. 1999. *Governmentality: Power and Rule in Modern Society*. New York: Sage.

Dower, John W. 1993. "Peace and Democracy in Two Systems: External Policy and Internal Conflict." In *Postwar Japan as History*, ed. Andrew Gordon, 3–33. Berkeley: University of California Press.

Foucault, Michel. 1991. "Governmentality." In *The Foucault Effect: Studies in Governmentality*, ed. Graham Burchell, Colin Gordon, and Peter Miller, 87–104. Chicago: University of Chicago Press.

Hein, Laura, and Mark Selden, eds. 1997. *Living with the Bomb: American and Japanese Cultural Conflicts in the Nuclear Age*. Armonk, N.Y.: M. E. Sharpe.

Ishihara, Masaiye. 2005. "Okinawa sen no zirenma" (The dilemma of the Battle of Okinawa). In *Okinawa wo heiwagaku suru* (Peace studies on Okinawa), ed. Masaiye Ishinara, Nakachi Hiroshi, and C. D. Lummis, 133–76. Kyoto: Horitsu Bunka Sha.

Kosei-sho Engo Kyoku (Japanese Ministry of Welfare, Division of Assistance). 1978. *Hikiage to engo 30 nen no ayumi* (Thirty years of assistance toward war victims). Tokyo: Kosei-sho.

Nakajima, Tatsumi. 1998. *Chosenjin hibakusha sonzindo saiban no kiroku* (Report on the court case of Korean atomic bomb survivor Son Jin-do). Tokyo: Zaikan Hibakusha Mondai Shimin Kaigi.

Naono, Akiko. 2005. "Shinimasen okuni no tameni" (We shall not die for the nation). *Impaction* 147: 85–89.

———. 2008. "Tsugunai naki kuni no hibakusha taisaku" (No state compensation for the atomic bomb survivors). In *Nagasaki kara heiwagaku suru* (Doing peace studies from Nagasaki), ed. Funakoe Kouichi and Takahashi Shinji, 64–76. Kyoto: Horitsu Bunka-sha.

Nihon Bengoshi Rengo Kai (Japan Federation of Bar Associations), ed. 1997. *Nihon no sengo hosho* (Japan's postwar redress). Tokyo: Akashi Shoten.

Nihon Hibakusha Dantai Kyogi-kai (Japan Confederation of Atomic and Hydrogen Bomb Sufferers Organization), ed. 2009. *Futatabi hibakusha wo tsukuru na: 1956–2006 Nihon hidankyo 50 nen shi* (No more *hibakusha*: 50 years of Hidankyo's history). Supplementary vol. Tokyo: Akebi Shobo.

Oe, Kenzaburo. 1970. *Okinawa Note*. Tokyo: Iwanami Shoten.

Okinawa, Ken. 1971. *Okinawa Kenshi*. Vol. 1. Naha: Okinawa Ken Kyoiku Iinkai.

———. 1974. *Okinawa Kenshi*. Vol. 2. Naha: Okinawa Ken Kyoiku Iinkai.

Orr, James. 2001. *The Victim as Hero: Ideologies of Peace and National Identity in Postwar Japan*. Honolulu: University of Hawai'i Press.

Renan, Ernest. 1991. "What Is a Nation?" In *Nation and Narration*, ed. Homi Bhabha, 291–322. London: Routledge.

Saikosai Daihoutei (Supreme Court of Japan). 1968. Showa 40 nen (o) 417 go (1965, o, number 417), Showa 40 nen 11 gatsu 27 nichi Daihoutei Hanketsu (November 27, 1968, Supreme Court verdict).

Senshoubyosha senbotsusha izoku tou engoho (Assistance Act for the Wounded and Sick Retired Soldiers and Bereaved Families of Fallen Soldiers and Others). 1952. April 30. http://www.houko.com/00/01/S27/127.HTM#s1.

Shugi-in (House of Representatives). 1952. 13th session, Kosei-Iinkai (Welfare Committee) 19th session, April 2. http://kokkai.ndl.go.jp/cgi-bin/KENSAKU/swk_dispdoc.cgi?SESSION=21864&SAVED_RID=4&PAGE=0&POS=0&TOTAL=0&SRV_ID=1&DOC_ID=12603&DPAGE=1&DTOTAL=1&DPOS=1&SORT_DIR=1&SORT_TYPE=0&MODE=1&DMY=28279.

Tanaka, Nobumasa. 1995. "Kokka wa izoku ni dou hosho shitaka" (How did the state compensate for the bereaved family?). In *Izoku to sengo* (The bereaved family in postwar Japan), ed. Tanaka Hiroshi and Hata Nagami, 81–146. Tokyo: Iwanami Shoten.

Tokyo Chisai (Tokyo District Court). 1980. Showa 54 nen (wa) 2367 go (1979, wa, number 2367), Showa 55 nen 1 gatsu 28 nichi hanketsu (January 28, 1980, Court verdict).

———. 1996. Heisei 3 nen (wa) 15964 go (1991, wa, number 15964), Heisei 8 nen 9 gatu 9 nichi minji 33 bu hanketsu (September 9, 1996, Court verdict).

U.S. Congress. House Resolution 121, 110th Cong. (July 30, 2007). http://frwebgate.access.gpo.gov/cgi-bin/getdoc.cgi?dbname=110_cong_bills&docid=f:hr121eh.txt.pdf.

U.S. National Security Council. 2002. *National Security Strategy.* http://georgewbush-whitehouse.archives.gov/nsc/nss/2002/index.html.

Yoshida, Yutaka. 1995. *Nihonjin no senso kan* (The Japanese view on the war). Tokyo: Iwanami Shoten.

Yoneyama, Lisa. 1999. *Hiroshima Traces: Time, Space and the Dialectics of Memory.* Berkeley: University of California Press.

· II ·

Spectacles of Consumption

CHAPTER 6

Coal Heritage/Coal History

Progress, Tourism, and Mountaintop Removal

Rebecca R. Scott

Fire in the hole! Fire in the hole!

—Unnamed U.S. soldier in Iraq, blowing up a car
suspected of belonging to insurgents, "The Baghdad Bomb Squad"

I N THE LATE NINETEENTH CENTURY, the growing national demand
for coal brought new interest in the Appalachian Mountains. In what
some West Virginia coalfield activists call the great land grab, powerful corporations "acquired" large amounts of land and mineral rights in the area
(Gaventa 1980, 53). Since then, the place has been defined as a coalfield and
termed by some an interior resource colony (Lewis, Johnson, and Askins
1978). Today, the surface mining technique of mountaintop removal is
transforming Appalachian landscapes and communities. Unlike traditional
underground methods, which leave the topography relatively unaltered,
mountaintop removal starts from above. In a mountaintop mine, underground explosives loosen the rocks and soil above the coal seam. Workers
then use giant earthmoving equipment to remove the "overburden" and
mine the coal. Literally deconstructing the landscape, the technique calls
into question the meaning of mountains, mining, and the place itself.

To some, these changes represent economic progress, but environmental activists and other concerned citizens argue that this extensive
resource extraction is incompatible with nearby communities and ways
of life. Where some see only coal, overburden, and money to be made,
others see the ghosts of the mountains and traces of history. The politics
of mountaintop removal uncovers the uneven roots of America's postindustrial economy, unearthing questions about the meaning and direction
of the American nation and Appalachia's place within it. In the national

media, images of Appalachian poverty and environmental devastation periodically recur, disrupting national progress narratives. Appalachian differences unsettle notions of a uniform American modernity (Stewart 1996). These images often evoke scale-bending comparisons to the so-called Third World in a spatial politics that reasserts difference and conflict into abstract national space. The question of how Appalachia fits into America also haunts coalfield communities; are the sacrifices endured by the region evidence of their exclusion or of their belonging?

Appalachia is a strange place: as a marginalized region, it is excluded from the American mainstream; at the same time, it represents for many the "heartland," or the "real America." The billions of tons of coal taken from the mountains have cost the lives of countless workers and caused untold damage to the environment. In that sense, the Appalachian coalfields are a national sacrifice zone (Kuletz 1998). Simultaneously, however, Appalachia has served as a screen for the projection of some powerful elements of the national symbolic. In historical and literary accounts, it has been a location for an individualistic, quintessentially American struggle against nature. The region has been imagined as a cultural reservoir of "unadulterated" Anglo-Saxon cultural heritage, a source of true patriotism, and a site of degeneration (Batteau 1990; Foster 1988; McNeil 1989). These contradictions run right through the region, marking it as an uncanny place where the American paradigm of economic development is haunted by the specter of failed progress, precisely in the "heart" of American national space.

This chapter maps two accounts of coalfield history that reflect and attempt to manage these contradictions. These accounts emerged from ethnographic fieldwork I conducted in southern West Virginia in 2004, but my mapping of these stories extends beyond that time and place to a wider archive that includes relevant media sources. The divergences in these accounts remind us that popular memory is a political practice; the "past–present relation" is the object of this practice (Johnson and Dawson 1982, 211). The first account is the coal heritage movement, represented here by my reading of two tourist sites, the Bituminous Coal Heritage Museum in Madison, West Virginia, and the Exhibition Coal Mine in Beckley, West Virginia, and regional development plans related to coal heritage tourism. The second is a historical preservationist movement focused on protecting the site of the 1921 Battle of Blair Mountain from mountaintop removal. As a countermemory, this effort is represented here by my interpretation of the perspective of the activists involved and the institutional framework they are using. Both of these projects are invested in the preservation of the material traces of memory. For the heritage movement, everyday artifacts of coal camp life come to represent disappearing communities and lifeworlds. For the "save Blair Mountain" movement,[1] the potential destruction of the battlefield by mountaintop removal indexes a long history of more or less figurative bulldozing of mountain communities in the name of outside interests. Both of these visions of the coalfield past interweave "nostalgia and critical memory" (Baker 1999, 265) in order to tell a particular story. As Doreen Massey notes, "[T]he definition of any particular locality will [. . .] reflect the question at issue" (Massey 1994, 139). These two representations of the past are involved in competing scale-making projects concerned with the meaning, memory, and future of Appalachia as a place, and in terms of its belonging to an abstract national space (Lefebvre 1991; Smith 2004). These divergences are also reflected in the institutional frameworks that support each of these accounts of the past: the National Register of Historic Places (NRHP) and the National Heritage Areas (NHA) program.

A Contentious History

From the beginning, coal mining in West Virginia has been characterized by a struggle between the desire of coalfield residents for self-determination and the profit imperative of the industry. The policies of the state and federal governments have largely determined the conditions of this struggle. Worker safety was not a major concern for coal companies in the days before the federal government enforced workplace standards, but even after workers' rights were legally recognized, conditions underground were harrowing. In those "hand-loading" days, mining was a labor-intensive industry. The billions of tons of coal that left the mountains to fuel the national industrial economy were extracted by the intense, painful, repetitive, dangerous physical labor of hundreds of thousands of men (Corbin 1981; Eller 1982).

In those early days, as now, Appalachian regional identity was characterized by a contradiction. During World War I, President Woodrow Wilson exempted coal miners from the draft because of what they contributed to the war, declaring, "Scarcity of coal is the most serious danger that confronts us" (Wooten 1918, 361). Like soldiers at war, miners risked dying in cave-ins or explosions, losing limbs, or being poisoned by gas, and the coal they produced literally fueled the war effort. In 1918, the *United Mine Workers Journal* described the death of thirteen miners in an explosion in these terms: "These local boys died in the interests of democracy, they were exerting their manpower in the production of coal with which to help win the war" (quoted in Shogan 2004, 50–51). In this sense, mining coal was an expression of citizenship and an essential service to the nation. Not long afterward, however, Appalachian cultural marginalization asserted a spatial discipline on the disorder of industrial capitalism (Smith 1992). During the mine wars of the 1920s, national newspapers announced coal miners' essential difference, referring to unionizing miners as "strike feudists," for example (Batteau 1990, 111). Portraying miners as "Primitive Mountaineers" and "sixteenth century fauna" reaffirmed that this violence stemmed from the region's peculiarities, not from a national class struggle (112). Meanwhile, at the urging of the industry, West Virginia established a state police force to aid private mine guards in maintaining order in the coalfields (Williams 2002, 261). The workers had no real voice in state or federal politics. It was not until the 1930s that either the mainstream national press or the federal government recognized the miners' struggle as a "serious matter" (Batteau 1990, 119).

In the postwar period, a so-called coal boom led to a population boom, and communities thrived. Year after year, the industry employed up to a hundred thousand workers, and by this point, the union was a significant force in determining the conditions of production. Although the workforce was reduced by about half after the initial mechanization of mining in the late 1950s, frequent strikes continued up through the 1980s. In 1982, almost fifty-four thousand miners were employed by the coal industry in West Virginia, but the number has declined to around eighteen thousand today (West Virginia Coal Association 2006, 14). These changes have affected miners' bodies, working lives, and communities in positive and negative ways. The work became physically easier, with machines like the continuous miner, mechanized loaders, and conveyor belts. Workplace regulations and safety equipment saved lives. Mechanization of underground mining increased the incidence of silicosis, or black lung, because the equipment pulverized the coal more effectively than the earlier hand methods. Surface mining was initially unregulated, and these "shoot and shove" mines left scars all over the landscape, sparking an environmental movement that forced the federal government to intervene (Montrie 2003). As the demand for labor shrank with mechanization, communities were scattered in a widespread out-migration. McDowell County, once known as the "Billion-Dollar Coalfield," is now legendary for its poverty;

in 2000, almost 40 percent of children in McDowell County were living below the federal poverty line (U.S. Census Bureau 2000).

In recent years, the mechanization of underground mining and the increasing prevalence of surface mining, and mountaintop removal in particular, have further reduced the demand for labor, weakening the union, and allowing some companies to avoid union-mandated labor practices. For example, Massey Energy Company, the fourth-largest coal-producing company in the United States, and the largest in West Virginia, cuts its labor costs by using two twelve-hour shifts instead of the previously standard three eight-hour shifts (Nyden 2005). In the rush for profit, worker safety has also suffered. In January 2006, the deaths of twelve miners in International Coal Group's Sago mine in Tallmansville, West Virginia, along with three subsequent deaths the same month, focused public attention on the chronically inadequate enforcement of mine safety laws, especially in nonunion mines. Despite a push for better safety rules and enforcement after Sago, twenty-nine miners were killed in April 2010 in an explosion caused by faulty ventilation at Massey Energy's Upper Big Branch mine in Montcoal, West Virginia (Ward 2010).

These deaths are grim evidence that the hardship and struggle of coal mining is not a thing of the past. Massey Energy has actively worked to break the union in West Virginia. More that 98 percent of its employees are "union-free" (Massey Energy Company 2008). Massey has also been responsible for some of the worst environmental disasters in recent memory (Sever 2003; Shnayerson 2008, 49–50). Workers no longer have job security, which makes it difficult to report safety violations, and are unprotected in the length of their workday, as Massey takes over bankrupt mines and reopens them as nonunion operations (Nyden 2005). The increasing prevalence of nonunion mines represents a significant shift in mining culture toward disregarding workers' rights and safety in favor of profits.

Coalfield communities have shrunk with the increased mechanization of mining, but the effects of mining on those that remained seem to have increased. More mechanized underground mining methods increase the risks of subsidence, which occurs when intensive underground mining destabilizes the earth above the mine, destroying water wells and structures on the ground. In particular, mountaintop removal makes it possible for a workforce of 50 to be as productive, if not more productive, as 150 when they are underground, but it literally transforms the landscape, destroying forests, aquifers, and the headwaters of streams. A working mountaintop mine makes nearby communities uninhabitable, creates new flood hazards, and generates other unpredictable environmental risks. Mountaintop removal is worlds away from the underground coal mining of the coal-boom era. Instead of company towns, it builds empty space and destroys communities. Instead of generating "coal culture," it erodes the cultural specificity of the mountains.

The uncertainty of the coalfields' future has elicited an increasing interest in the preservation of its past. The Bituminous Coal Heritage Museum in Madison, West Virginia, displays artifacts representing these disappearing cultures of coal. These ordinary objects become souvenirs of a lost world, as mechanization severs mine labor from its landscape (Stewart 1984). "Coal heritage" offers people a way to grasp this rapidly disappearing "coal culture," but it is shaped by cultural, economic, and political forces that encourage selective forgetting (Connerton 2006). Indeed, heritage cannot properly be termed history at all; rather it is "a publicly instituted structuring of consciousness" that "functions by excluding traditions it cannot incorporate" (Bommes and Wright 1982, 266). Reflecting the interests of some of its financial and institutional backers, the "coal heritage story" locates coal-mining culture within a narrative of American technological and social progress. This liberal progress narrative is part of the habitus of American modernity, and it inhabits and shapes the coal heritage story without being spoken (Bourdieu 1998). The genre of heritage works via a compelling simplicity (Berlant 2008). Coal heritage substitutes a national allegory of development for the messy regional history of coal (Baker 1999, 264).

Meanwhile, a few people up on Blair Mountain, located only a few miles from Madison, have been scouring the forest for material evidence of a battle that took place there during the early twentieth-century mine wars (Savage 1990; Shogan 2004). They aim to get the battlefield, and the mountain, placed on the National Register of Historical Places. Their search for evidence is fueled, in part, by the desire to save Blair Mountain from destruction—if coal companies are permitted, they will blast away much of the mountain to access the coal beneath. All material evidence of this episode in American labor history, including the very land where it happened, is in danger of being erased by mountaintop removal. Although this countermemory is institutionalized in popular and labor histories, it also gains traction through anecdote, myth, and private remembrances (Johnson and Dawson 1982, 210). The save Blair Mountain movement represents the eruption of critical memory against the grain; blasted and unsettled by mountaintop removal, Blair Mountain is literally the "unquiet earth" (Giardina 1994).

These two projects are oddly disconnected, despite their apparent affinity. Working under the aegis of local governments, the coal industry, and other businesses, coal heritage writes West Virginia history into a national story of progress, culminating in a cleaned-up, postindustrial economy, complete with the ultramodern mining technique of mountaintop removal. In this narrative, coalfield hardships represent a necessary sacrifice for the national interest. But according to the save Blair Mountain movement, mountaintop removal is simply the latest form of hyperexploitation of a historically marginalized place. Their preservation activism is as much a fight for self-determination as it is for the environment and in their view, it fits perfectly within the history of American labor activism that the Battle of Blair Mountain symbolizes. For these activists, their project is part of a historical struggle for coalfield residents to claim the rights of full American citizenship, including the right to equality in difference. In their insistence on remembering the conflict between local and national interests, the save Blair Mountain movement mobilizes a spatial politics of difference against the push of national homogeneity.

In the United States, national identity, racial identity, and class distinctions have historically been maintained through hegemonic standards in material culture (Heneghan 2003; Moskowitz 2004). As Marie Sarita Gaytán demonstrates in "Drinking the Nation and Making Masculinity: Tequila, Pancho Villa, and the U.S. Media," consumption is a way to express both belonging and difference (this volume). Even prior to the ascendancy of coal, the distinctive material culture of Appalachia and its distance from the market economy were mobilized in the region's marginalization and have been taken to indicate backwardness and poverty rather than an alternative way of life (Precourt 1983; Semple 1989). In particular, since the rise of the industry, images of coal camp life are associated with a degree of hardship, degradation, and exploitation that does not conform to ideals of American national identity (see Light and Light 2006). But as Akiko Naono makes clear in "Producing Sacrificial Subjects for the Nation: Japan's War-Related Redress Policy and the Endurance Doctrine" (this volume), national belonging can also be compelled or performed through discourses of sacrifice for the nation. When the environmental and social damage caused by mining is read through a nostalgic lens of sacrifice for the nation, Appalachia's marginal status as a natural resource colony ironically provides coalfield communities a way to claim a core national identity. The hardships of mining can be read as evidence of their patriotic devotion to America and their central role in the national economy.

Heritage and History

The nostalgic face of coal heritage is frequently out of sync with the complex unfolding history of the coal industry in southern West Virginia. The violence and inequality of historical struggles and contemporary conflicts become very hard to represent in the nostalgic context of coal heritage (Bommes and Wright 1982; Levin 2007). The plantation tours of the American South offer an example of this heritage logic. The tours usually reproduce a racist, white-centered story of pre–Civil War plantation life, including slavery. Those few plantation sites that attempt to represent slavery and plantation reality in an antiracist way struggle to do so while pursuing their main mission, which is to present a nostalgic view of white "plantation heritage" for mostly white tourists (Eichstedt and Small 2002). Thus, while the save Blair Mountain movement struggles to preserve the history of a significant event in labor history, the coal heritage movement "writes the revolution as a well-passed aberration" (Baker 1999, 264). Coal heritage boosters commodify heroic stories of the sacrifices of early coal mining, along with images of a mountain and frontier culture, as part of an attempt to refigure an industrial wasteland into a postindustrial space of entertainment, nostalgia, and consumption (Bommes and Wright 1982; Zukin 1991). But the conflicting interests within the coal heritage movement highlight the disjunctures between the experience of people displaced by economic and environmental upheaval, people increasingly marginalized in the national economy, and the national progress narrative that shapes the coal heritage story.

My reading of these sites and their institutional locations draws on the examples of Annie E. Coombes and Liliane Weissberg, who, in two very different contexts, elucidate the tensions inherent in preserving the memory of historical oppression and resistance from within a social and cultural formation shaped by that oppression (Coombes 2003; Weissberg 1999). Weissberg writes of the conflicts arising in Germany over representations of the Nazi Holocaust that highlight the struggle to balance the requirement to remember past horror with the need to define the present community in some bearable form. This struggle is even more pronounced in the case of the democratic South Africa, where the divisive legacy of apartheid remains embodied in national memorials and museums. These museums and memorials have become focal points in struggles around the representation of the nation, its past, and its citizens. In both cases, cultural memory is shown to be a conversation and a compromise between different agencies, audiences, and forms. Visitors with different perspectives read museum displays differently, while the designers of these repositories of memory shape their work with an anticipation of their audience. Like Coombes and Weissberg, I want to understand the stakes involved in these different memories and representations of the coalfield past and, in light of current environmental and social transformations in the coalfields, their implications for Appalachia's future. For a region constituted by marginalization and conflict, cultural memory is an object of struggle in competing efforts to define the place and the terms of action.

Two Sites in Coal Heritage

There is a general movement in West Virginia to begin thinking of the "postcoal" economy. Even as the mountains come down, tourism is a key part of this postcoal economic vision. Winding roads through mountainous terrain in the heart of the coalfields are reconfigured as a Coal Heritage Trail; eleven counties in southern West Virginia have been named the National Coal Heritage Area (National Heritage Areas 2007; National Scenic Byways Program 2007). Local economic boosters optimistically hope that rechristening the roads and offering maps and tourist information online will bring the curious to the area to spend their money.

The Bituminous Coal Heritage Museum in Madison, West Virginia, was created as an entertainment for Boone County's annual Coal Festival. Clearly, the major purpose of the collection, for the donors, is to honor the memory of coal miners. It offers miners and their families a place to put the memorabilia of their working lives, a public place where their work can be recognized as important. Lunch buckets, different kinds of helmets, tools, union wage agreements, newspapers, chits, and scrip, when removed from someone's attic or closet and placed in a public setting, become more than personal keepsakes; they represent a lifestyle and a community. Many items are marked by cards noting who donated or loaned them. This embeds the museum in local social networks; these names are likely to be familiar to many visitors to the museum. At the same time, the "metonymic power" (Coombes 2003, 88) of this collection writes certain people and perspectives out of the commodified past of "coal heritage." Their embeddedness in the past and in existing social networks serves here to authenticate the museum itself (Stewart 1984, 151).

The displays are loosely organized around several themes: the early "hand-loading" era of underground mining, the union era (which itself increasingly seems to be a relic of the past), and developments in mining equipment, especially safety equipment. These groupings allow the museum displays to be read as reflecting "progress." However, overall the museum has a memorial-like aspect, with the sacrifices of miners being a major presence. This underlying affect of mourning suggests the breakdown of the progress narrative. One display case is labeled "Memorial Section," and includes bullets from the Battle of Blair Mountain. White flags, each with the black silhouette of a helmeted miner, hang from the ceiling, commemorating the annual festivals. A large placard bearing the names of West Virginia miners killed at work in recent years is prominently displayed in front of the entrance. In the fall of 2004, this sign listed ten deaths from 2003 and six from 2004, but in any given year, it is not unusual for ten miners to die at work in West Virginia. If the placard is still present at the museum, it most likely notes that 2006 was a really bad year, with a total of twenty-five deaths, and that 2010 has already witnessed record fatalities due to the disaster in April at Montcoal, West Virginia (West Virginia Office of Miners' Health, Safety and Training 2009; Ward 2010.)

The only other display to address current mining practices is a poster entitled "Boone County's Coal Heritage," where sepia-toned pictures of past mining operations are placed next to a picture of a dragline, the giant earthmover used in mountaintop removal. In the lower left-hand corner, the poster reports, "Surface mines, like Hobet's large mountaintop removal mine, produce one-third of the county's coal. With its huge 180 ton bucket dragline (living room sized) removing the rocks above the coals, Hobet mines five seams." The short text emphasizes the impressive technology of mountaintop removal and minimizes its destructiveness by referring to the mountain that is removed as "the rocks above the coals." This brief mention of mountaintop removal establishes underground mining as the unmarked subject of "coal heritage." Indeed, mountaintop removal is a constitutive force in coal heritage; its massive impersonal technology, which renders workers obsolete and communities uninhabitable, makes history of the artifacts documenting the lives of miners and mining communities. But this poster, with the picture of a dragline next to the title "Boone County's Coal

Heritage," reveals the hollowness of the term. The vast amount of coal being taken out of the area on a daily basis hardly seems like "heritage"; indeed, coal production levels are as high as they have ever been. On one level, the dragline might represent a technological rescue from the hardships of the early mining days. But the small, quiet presence of the dragline also reveals a new kind of sacrifice demanded of Appalachia.

Many of the donated objects contribute to an atmosphere of mourning, which enhances the memorial-like aspect of the museum. In two instances, mining-related objects are juxtaposed with references to World War II. The first example is an exhibit titled "Coal Camp Exhibit: Typical Boone County Home Furnishings in the 1930's and 1940's," in which a copy of the *Charleston Gazette*, with a headline announcing the bombing of Pearl Harbor, has been placed on a small homemade-quilt-covered bed, along with a local paper and a copy of the *Saturday Evening Post* from the same era.[2] (See Figure 6.1.)

In a display case across the room, a reproduction of a letter from a dying father and son, trapped by a mine explosion in Tennessee in 1902, is placed next to a newspaper with a headline marking the end of World War II: "Japs Bow to Terms." This quietly distressing display creates an affective link between the nationalist sacrifices of war and the sacrifices of coal

Figure 6.1. Exhibit from the Coal Heritage Museum, Madison, West Virginia titled "Coal Camp Exhibit: Typical Boone County Home Furnishings in the 1930's and 1940's." Photograph by the author.

miners and, at the same time, recenters coal miners in a civilizational racial discourse as American national subjects. (See Figure 6.2.)

Although there is no historical rationale for the association of these particular items in the museum, in the past, the link between mining and war was overt, as when miners were excused from the draft, as was mentioned previously. Indeed, this slippage between mining and war is currently reflected in the national arena by the use of the iconic cry of the underground miner, "Fire in the hole!" in military operations and war games.

A reproduction of a painting that is displayed in the museum underlines this articulation. The painting, titled *The Price of Freedom*, shows an older white heterosexual couple standing solemnly before a coffin draped with an American flag and surrounded by helmeted soldiers. (See Figure 6.3.)

It has no direct connection with coal heritage, but the inclusion of this image in the museum reiterates the articulations between mining and militarism, sacrifice and American national identity. As a repository of what some individuals in the community find important, the museum's collection entangles the patriotic grief evoked by the mourning parents

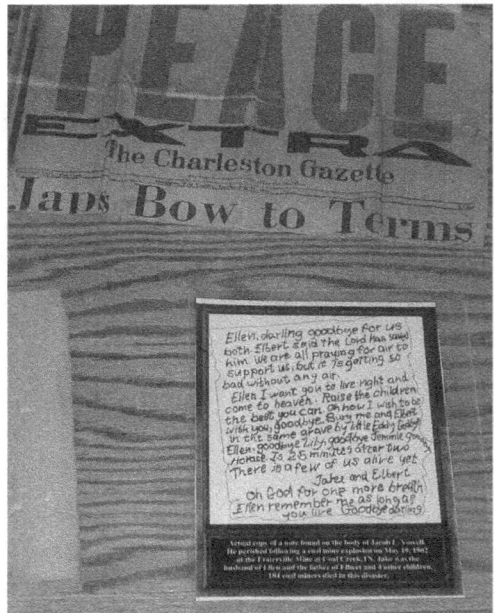

Figure 6.2. Vitrine display at the Coal Heritage Museum of the Charleston Gazette headline marking the end of World War II, with a note from a dying miner from 1902. Photograph by the author.

Figure 6.3. The Price of Freedom *by Robert Prichard, an artist from Madison, West Virginia. Courtesy of Patty Viera and the Coal Heritage Museum.*

in *The Price of Freedom* with the tragedy of miners' deaths underground. Through its emphasis of these linkages, the museum centers the "coal heritage story" on the *national* identity of the coalfields and articulates coal heritage through a discourse of masculine sacrifice. This patriotic lens diffuses the critical connections that can be made between the sacrifices of the past and the politics of mountaintop removal.

The Beckley Exhibition Coal Mine is located off a major interstate highway through the coalfields. A state park has been constructed around the mine, with several original coal camp buildings from different locations that have been moved to the spot in a recreation of some of the features of a company town. These include a large white-frame supervisor's house with a wrap-around porch, a one-room schoolhouse, a church, and two examples of miners' dwellings (a one-room "shack" for a single miner, and a three-room company house for a miner with a family). The Youth Museum of Southern West Virginia, featuring a "Mountain Homestead," is located beside the church. The "Mountain Homestead" is a recreation of "a typical settlement on the Appalachian frontier" and consists of a simulated homestead from the nineteenth century, including a barn, a woodshed, a workshop, other outbuildings, and a log house filled with rustic antiques (Youth Museum of Southern West Virginia Inc. 2007).

The spatial association in the state park of the "Mountain Homestead," the Exhibition Coal Mine, and the recreated coal camp conforms to an unspoken narrative of national development. The museum's Web site specifies that this homestead represents life in Appalachia in the late-nineteenth century, when Fredrick Jackson Turner was lamenting the closing of the (western) frontier. The naming of this late nineteenth-century Appalachian homeplace as a "settlement on the Appalachian frontier" accomplishes several things. It reiterates the logic of Appalachian marginalization; as a backward place, Appalachia always represents America's past, and, therefore, the Appalachian homeplace is culturally anterior to its actual date in history. At the same time, it locates the frontier as a quintessentially American place and process. The park's spatial association of the homeplace and the mine eternalizes and naturalizes an American frontier-like relationship to the land and natural resources, as embodied in the communities of geographic expansion and industrial resource extraction that are represented (Tsing 2005). As Barbara Barnes demonstrates in "Ecoadventures in the American West: Innocence, Conflict, and Nation Making in Emptied Landscapes" (this volume), these abstracted sites represent a traveling set of relationships between people and land that are essential to American national identity.

Inside the gift shop, there is an exhibit of old photos, domestic antiques, and old coal-mining equipment. The shop offers Appalachian arts and crafts and souvenirs, like replicas of old mountain cookbooks. The mine itself is an actual former mine, which operated from around 1890 to 1910. My fellow visitors, the tour guide, and I boarded a small train that begins under a shelter and then winds its way into the mine. The tour guide during my visit was a white retired coal miner, who recounted the harrowing conditions that pertained while the mine was being worked. He described how the miners, working only with hand tools and dynamite, drilled holes and loaded shot in a thirty-six-inch seam (i.e., the roof was thirty-six inches high) while lying on their sides or stomachs and scurried out of their holes as fast as they could to avoid getting caught in the blast. Then they used shovels to load the coal on cars.

The mine was well lit for the tour, but our guide momentarily turned off all the lights to demonstrate how dark it could be underground. He gave detailed explanations of all the equipment and answered questions from members of the small tour group about innovations in mining technology through the twentieth century, like the continuous miner, which uses rotating blades to mine the coal. He discussed concurrent developments in safety equipment, like rock dusters, which coat the coalface with limestone dust in order to prevent the pulverized coal from exploding. He also told a story about when the first women miners were hired in a mine where he used to work. He explained that miners usually relieved themselves in the "outtakes," or empty finished places in the mine, since the darkness provided a kind of privacy; it was so dark you could easily see anyone approaching by the light on their hat. But when "women came into the mines in 1972," the company was forced to provide portable toilets. (He did not explain the reasoning behind this requirement.) The men miners scoffed and said, "If you're going to use them, you'd better clean them." But, our guide continued, "I came out of here [the mines] in '88 and I never seen one with the plastic off." The women had evidently decided not to use the portable toilets either. As the guide explained, "Well, it's dark in the mines." We all laughed.

This "all cats are grey in the dark" tale was part of a tour narrative that emphasized the extreme working conditions that miners endure. It invited us to imagine conditions in which people (even women) might have to relieve themselves in a dark hole underground. His lengthy focus on the mining techniques that were used when the exhibition mine was in operation provided a dramatic background for a subsequent story of progress in mining technology throughout the twentieth century. In the context of this story, the presence of women in the masculine-coded mine indicates both the increasing liberalization of American society and the development of mining technology. Constructing mining as "naturally" masculine, this story erases the fact that, around the world and throughout history, women have worked and continue to work as miners, with or without mechanization (Hinton, Viega, and Beinhoff 2003; Moore 1996). This narrative naturalizes progress and elides the political struggles that have led to the enforcement of worker protection laws and affirmative action and that have spurred the development of mining technology.

This narrative of continual progress throughout the twentieth century provides a cultural context in which mountaintop removal becomes simply another step in an inevitable march of technological innovation. Viewed from the context of the lifeworld of the early twentieth-century underground miner, technological innovation in mining does doubtlessly benefit working people. But the popular narrative of capital-driven technological progress as represented in the mine tour is an overgeneralization of this benefit. Because technological innovation has improved people's lives in some cases, it cannot be assumed always to do so or to do so unequivocally. This progress narrative forestalls consideration of the physical, social, and environmental costs of increased productivity and mechanization.

The Coal Heritage Museum and the Beckley Exhibition Coal Mine reiterate the commonsense understanding of the "coalfields" as a place defined by coal and glide over the politics of this designation through nostalgic allegories of the hardships of coal camp life. These sites freely mix symbols of national identity with images of coal-mining sacrifice, telling a particular story about Appalachia's place in America. The headline announcing the attack on Pearl Harbor, for instance, is placed on a small, homemade-quilt-covered cot. The mine supervisor's house and the three-room coal camp house provide class-specific domestic contexts for the male-centered work life of the mine. In the three-room miner's house, for example, the kitchen table is set with colorful tin cups and plates, as if awaiting a father's arrival for dinner. These heritage sites offer representations of the national symbolic and affective domesticity that locate the practice of coal mining, and the history of the coal industry, in the context of a gendered and racialized American national identity (Berlant 1997).

Coal History

A look at the history of coal-mining activism in West Virginia creates a different sense of nostalgia. In one of the first battles of the West Virginia mine wars, striking miners and their families from Paint Creek and Cabin Creek, which are today surrounded by a vast spread of mountaintop mines, were thrown out of their company houses and forced to spend the winter in tents in the forest, where they were vulnerable to the weather and to armed attacks. During this time, the coalfields were like an occupied zone, where workers and their families were kept in line by a coterie of private mine guards, state police, and federal troops. In 1921, enraged union miners gathered to march on Logan and Mingo Counties in an effort to install the union by force. The sheriff of Logan, Don Chafin, was a friend of the coal industry and deputized the "better citizens" of Logan to defend the antiunion stronghold of Logan County. Union miners came from all over, some using guns and uniforms left over from military service. The Battle of Blair Mountain was bloody, and in the end, federal troops were called in to restore order. This battle is one of the most violent episodes in

American labor history (Corbin 1981; Savage 1990; Shogan 2004). Stories of these battles evoke nostalgia for times of solidarity and mass action and still animate the labor movement, in the form of union songs and quotes from labor leader Mary Harris "Mother" Jones.

In 1999, environmental activists sued the West Virginia Department of Environmental Protection for failing to enforce elements of the Clean Water Act that required a "buffer zone" between mine activity and streams. Responding to the suit, Arch Coal closed its Daltex mine on Blair Mountain, one of the largest mountaintop-removal mining operations in history. Subsequently, the Bush administration altered the Clean Water Act to permit mining in and around streams (Warrick 2004). With Blair Mountain again at risk, some environmental activists changed their focus on Blair to historical preservation. They collected and mapped artifacts from the battle, and they presented their case repeatedly to the West Virginia Archives and History Commission, which in 2005 made the decision in 2005 to recommend that the area be added to the NRHP (Dao 2005).

Many of the individuals involved in this effort have strong ties to Blair Mountain and to the battle. Bill,[3] who is a white environmental activist deeply involved in efforts to stop mountaintop removal, is fighting to preserve his family homeplace on Blair. Near his house is a creek that his mother saw run red with blood during the battle. Shawn, a white man who has been responsible for much of the legwork and archival research establishing the historical value of the area, lives at the base of the mountain and has family members who fought on Blair. For these men, the place, the physical site of the battle, is an essential piece of the area's history that must be preserved to honor the memory of the miners who fought for the union. They refuse to sacrifice the land to the corporate or national interest; rather, they insist on the right of coalfield residents to determine their future and on the inherent value of their communities. In an interview,[4] Bill argued that mountain communities' reliance on water wells is not an indication of historical backwardness or "Third World" poverty; rather, it represents an alternative and equally valid way of life. He actively contested the national progress narrative, exclaiming sarcastically, "Mining companies sink creeks, ruin wells, and put people on city water [...] That's economic development! That's improvement!"[5]

Shortly after the environmental lawsuit and the closure of the Daltex mine, the Blair Mountain Historical Organization held a reenactment of the "Miners' March" from Marmet to Blair, which preceded the Battle of

Blair Mountain. From the marchers' perspective, they were honoring coal miners and their heritage, and indeed, the Heritage Museum does house some bullets from the battle. But as a "symbolic transaction" (Coombes 2003, 14), the commemoration failed to create new constituencies around coal heritage. The marchers were pelted with eggs and physically assaulted by laid-off mountaintop removal miners holding a counterdemonstration. This symbolic transaction may have faltered around the definition of locality; is the community embodied in a place or is its existence tied to its economic function? This distinction reduces to two incompatible versions of the place; where the industry sees only labor or obstacles to production, the save Blair Mountain movement claims that mountain communities have intrinsic worth, regardless of their economic role.

Newspaper articles about these conflicts frequently refer to the issue as a new battle for Blair (Dao 2005; Janofsky 1998). I argue, however, that this is not a new battle but a continuation of the battle that was begun in the early twentieth-century mine wars about who controls the place and how the community will be defined. The sides of the battle have been reconfigured, however, as the United Mine Workers withdrew its initial support for having the battle site named to the NRHP. These shifting sides indicate the unbounded, situational spatial politics of defining universal and particular (Massey 1994, 154–65). The save Blair Mountain movement insists on local self-determination against a homogenizing economic logic that would push them from their homes and permanently alter their ways of life. As during the mine wars, the fight today is over what place coalfield communities have in the American nation, what kind of rights they have in their homes and property, and what level of citizenship they can claim. For the save Blair Mountain movement, as well as other coalfield activists, this history of struggle is also part of coal heritage. Whether as workers or as stakeholders in mineral-rich land, the ability of coalfield residents to control the fate of their physical environment as full citizens of a democracy has always been problematic in a nation that depends on the exploitation of their labor and their land.

The National Register of Historical Places and National Heritage Areas

Another way to approach these stories is to take a look at the federal institutions that support the different projects. In 2005, Blair Mountain was recommended for inclusion in the NRHP. After finally being placed on the list in 2009, the place was delisted 274 days later (Nyden 2010). Why is this listing such an object of contention? The NRHP is under the control of the National Park Service of the Federal Department of the Interior, which has a say over what can be done with the places listed there. The register's Web site states that federal intervention in property owners' business is unlikely, with one important exception: "consideration of historic values in the decision to issue a surface mining permit where coal is located in accordance with the Surface Mining Control Act of 1977" (National Register of Historic Places 2006).

As soon as the listing became a possibility, the coal companies and the land corporations were up in arms. The *New York Times* quoted the vice-president of Dingess–Rum Properties Inc., the land corporation that leases the land to the coal companies: "We are going to resist vigorously any attempts to take away our property rights. We have a right to exercise our lawful and legal right to mine coal, remove timber and drill oil and gas wells on our property" (Dao 2005). The activists are equally clear about what the potential listing means, as one of the preservationists put it in the *New York Times*: "This is a breakthrough nomination in terms of taking a chink out of the power of coal companies to dominate our land" (Dao 2005). In this case, federal oversight of the land actually increases the self-determination of the residents. According to Shawn, the final decision on whether the place is listed is decided by a vote of all the landowners affected, whether their property is thousands of acres or only half an acre, effectively negating the overwhelming dominance of coal.[6] However, this vote count has become controversial (Nyden 2010).

But if having the Blair Mountain battleground listed on the NRHP would entail this small but potentially significant degree of federal oversight on private property, the same cannot be said for the NHA. In 1996, eleven counties in the southern West Virginia coalfields were designated the National Coal Heritage Area (NCHA). The goals and mission of the NHAs are quite different from the mission of the NRHP; the emphasis in the heritage areas is on local control:

> National Heritage Area designation recognizes the coalfields of southern West Virginia as a treasure of national importance. This designation provides an opportunity to tell the story of the southern West Virginia coal mines to visitors from outside the region as well

as local residents. Because it is a project that stresses partnerships, land ownership and land use decisions remain at the local level. At the same time, southern West Virginia will gain new prominence on national tourist maps. Because it is a project for which the National Park Service provides technical assistance, the region is included in materials used to describe sites around the country—sites important to the history of our nation. As a plan takes shape and is implemented, the heritage area will become a much-needed focal point for the revitalization of southern West Virginia, encouraging residents to embrace their heritage with a new sense of pride and ownership. (National Coal Heritage Area 2006)

This statement includes several of the most important things to know about the NCHA. It is a campaign for the representation of West Virginia on a national level. The NCHA is part of an effort to "revitalize" southern West Virginia and allow residents to feel "pride" in their "heritage." By constructing the history of coal mining as "national heritage," the coal heritage movement centers West Virginia in American national history and naturalizes its status as a sacrifice zone. Significantly, heritage preservation relies on private property (Bommes and Wright 1982, 273). Thus, coal heritage is part of a series of new "partnership" initiatives in the coalfields that at least partly eschew federal or state government authority in favor of private control. The statement's emphasis on local control of the NCHA reveals part of the irony and subtle (or not-so-subtle) proindustry agenda of the heritage movement. In an area where two thirds of the land are owned or controlled by corporations (Appalachian Land Ownership Task Force 1983, 27), what can it mean to say "land ownership and land use decisions remain at the local level"?

The Strategic Management Action Plan (SMAP; Parsons, Brinckerhoff, Quade & Douglas Inc. 2001) of the NCHA reveals more about the contradictory goals of the coal heritage movement, as it suggests ways to implement the program. The SMAP includes repeated references to nationally held stereotypes about West Virginia and the coal industry and the necessity of an opportunity to more accurately represent the region and the industry in the national arena. The SMAP begins, "The [NCHA] encompasses hundreds of square miles of rugged industrial landscape where hard-working miners of all races labored to extract and transport the coal which shaped modern America." It continues, "The coalfield story is a uniquely American story which is expressed in the customs, communities and stories of this remarkable region" (i). However, the authors see stereotypes as an obstacle in the way of the NCHA's goal of attracting tourists to the area: "The coal heritage story, while important and compelling, has marketing challenges related to regional stereotypes and also to stereotypes about mining that provoke negative images" (42).

At the heart of the NCHA management plan is the hope that tourism will become an important industry in southern West Virginia. The SMAP puts it this way: "Unlike 'rust-belt' industrial districts and the downtown cores of older industrial cities, the coalfields have never benefited from a countermovement [to deindustrialization and population loss]—'gentrification'—that has converted obsolete structures and districts to the uses of service- and information-oriented industries and of consumers who search for touches of 'authenticity' amid the standardized offerings of a global economy. Tourism is one of the service industries that gentrification has served, and the National Coal Heritage Area represents an attempt to capture some of its benefits for southern West Virginia" (9).

This fervent hope to jump on the postindustrial–postmodern bandwagon is unfortunately mired in the realities of coalfield geography, however, because for one thing, the area is not yet industrially obsolete—coal production is as high as ever. The presence of the active coal industry in the heritage area is problematic for the NCHA's plans, as is the real "heritage" of coal mining. The SMAP laments, "Coal extraction, processing, and transportation has left [sic] visible impacts on the landscape. Population loss, depressed economic conditions and uneven waste disposal practices have compounded negative visual impacts. As a result, blight and clutter is [sic] commonplace" (95).

As a marginalized region, the area is stigmatized in the national media, popular culture, and scholarship and bears the physical and environmental effects of serving as an interior resource colony, as the SMAP notes. But at the same time, the processes of this economic and cultural marginalization are generative of "coal heritage" and the very regional identity that the NCHA celebrates. The authors acknowledge that tourists are reluctant to plan vacations to West Virginia because of "Appalachian stereotypes" that "perpetuate distorted and inaccurate perceptions of the region and its people" (60). However, according to the SMAP, those enterprises that succeed in attracting tourists do so on the basis of these stereotypes. For instance, when praising the successes of the coalfield all-terrain vehicle trail system, the authors state, "[the] Hatfield–McCoy Trail System [. . .] enjoys one of the few imprimaturs [sic] recognized by tourists and associated with West Virginia. The famous feud elicits curiosity even today" (74).

The SMAP includes plans for overcoming these obstacles in order to take advantage of the "compelling" story of coal heritage. Many of the major goals of the heritage movement hinge on the reimaging of the region in the national arena as an attractive and safe place to visit, no longer viewed through the distorting lens of Appalachian regional marginalization. As the authors state, "The NCHA provides the opportunity for the region's story in all of its dramatic and complex aspects to be told in an authentic and historically accurate manner" (60). The authors repeatedly claim core national status for the coalfields: "Eventually the NCHA may be able to take advantage of international visitors, who now show interest in getting away from their traditional destinations (major cities, national parks and Florida) and experiencing more of the real America" (64).

National Heritage Areas and Mountaintop Removal

The authors' claim that the NCHA is "the real America" needs to be backed up by successfully conforming to certain hegemonic American standards. One key to achieving the NCHA's goal of becoming a tourist destination, as recommended by the SMAP, is to improve local infrastructure: "A great deal of the viability of the NCHA, particularly interpretation opportunities and visitor services in core counties, depends on improvements to the transportation system" (59). Local roads are noted to be twisty, steep, narrow, and dangerous. One such road, Route 10 through Logan County, is by local reports one of the most dangerous roads in the nation. But the danger is not inherent in the road: it is the presence of overweight and speeding coal trucks that actually make it deadly (Ohio Valley Environmental Coalition 2007).

Two huge road projects in southern West Virginia have recently attempted to take advantage of the coal industry in the ways that its supporters have repeatedly suggested (Scott 2007; see U.S. Senate 2002, 21–23). The King Coal Highway and the Coalfields Expressway involve allowing companies to mine multiple seams of coal (according to some environmentalists, without a proper permit) and then prepare the post-mining surface for road building. These planned four-lane, limited-access highways are supposed to invigorate the depressed economies of the coalfields. These roads are a key part of a project to revitalize the economy of McDowell County, one of the most economically depressed places in the United States, with an industrial park and a new federal prison planned near their interchange. But environmental activists argue that these roads are primarily being constructed for the convenience of the coal industry, allowing access to remote areas for mountaintop mining, and making the transportation of coal easier (Chafin 2005).

For coal heritage boosters, these roads are part of a vision of the future in which the reimagined coalfields will become an international tourist attraction, and downtrodden coalfield communities will become "visitor experience zones." Relics of the company-town days are important elements of this visitor experience, and the SMAP urges their protection (Parsons, Brinckerhoff, Quade & Douglas Inc. 2001, 92). But one of the most valuable resources of the NCHA is, in fact, Blair Mountain. As the SMAP states, "[T]he site of the 1921 Battle of Blair Mountain [is] the only site in the region deemed to be of national significance according to established preservation criteria" (50). Despite the danger it poses to this valuable site, mountaintop removal cannot become an issue: "*The NCHA cannot and should not become mired in the politics of mountaintop removal.* However, if it is to be a successful progenitor of the post-coal economy of southern West Virginia, the NCHA must be a strong advocate for preserving and interpreting the physical and cultural remains of the coal boom era" (59; emphasis added).

The apparent contradiction of preserving coal heritage sites while not opposing mountaintop removal is addressed at another point in the SMAP. According to a study they cite, "[it] is the stories and culture of this area, rather than the sites, which are most important" (National Park Service 1991, 1). The SMAP goes on to conclude, "Public Law 100-699 [which established the NHAs] seems to have recognized this in giving 'cultural values' equal standing with historic and natural resources in its directives to the Park Service" (Parsons, Brinckerhoff, Quade & Douglas Inc. 2001, 55).

From an institutional perspective, then, the NCHA is concerned with "local" control but not with questioning the status quo. The NCHA wants to conserve coal heritage resources but, in the end, emphasizes the relative importance of "cultural values" over actual sites that may be destroyed through the continued activity of the coal industry. This reflects the divergence of the NCHA, which is an economic development initiative, from the desire of coalfield residents to remember their history and preserve their communities. Meaning, emotions, and cultural memory are rooted in objects and places (Stallybrass 1999; Sturken 2004). But individual and community memories are simply another resource for the coal heritage movement in its economic development form. The NCHA's concern with culture and local control is ironically antidemocratic and tied to the interests of coal boosters who see mountaintop removal as a way to modernize and rationalize the coalfield economy (see U.S. Senate 2002, 21–23).

According to the SMAP, almost any element of coal-mining life can be stripped of its local meaning and become fodder for commodification. Regarding the struggles for unionization, the authors comment, "Stories of these battles and how they helped shape history and the union movement could be told [in visitor experience zones] through recorded interviews, exhibits, and reenactments." (Parsons, Brinckerhoff, Quade & Douglas Inc. 2001, 30). But this is not the only topic of potential interest to tourists: "Another important, although less dramatic, battle, was the effort to protect miners as they worked through stronger mine safety and health legislation. The depiction of this effort could be reinforced through linkages with the mine disaster database now being developed by the National Mine Health and Safety Academy in Beckley, and the National Coal Miners' Memorial being planned in Nellis" (Parsons, Brinckerhoff, Quade & Douglas Inc. 2001, 30).

Unfortunately, this element of coal heritage has also slipped loose from its temporal categorization. Recent mine disasters have revealed that the battle for miners' safety is far from over. Nothing reveals the contradictions of coal heritage more clearly than this attempt to present what is actually an ongoing struggle for workplace safety in an antilabor atmosphere as a past event that can be educationally and entertainingly viewed by tourists.

The NCHA SMAP represents an uncomfortable compromise between local economic boosters, who envision and hope for a postcoal economy based on tourism, and the economic imperative of rapid, continuing extraction of coal by the coal industry. Whatever economic development can be generated by tourism must happen in the interstitial spaces of coal production as required by the industry, which still holds the economy hostage by virtue of owning two thirds of the land and having underdeveloped the region over the course of one hundred years of dominance. At the same time, the coal industry's continued operations in the area are destroying the natural features that have actually been West Virginia's most successful tourist draw and, most undemocratically, are permanently altering the future of the remaining coalfield communities postcoal.

"Coal heritage," as told by the coal heritage movement (if it has any substantive meaning at all), refers to a historical period when working people in coalfield communities had a small share in the industry's profits. Those coalfield residents invested in preserving the material traces of their communities, whether in the form of collected artifacts or in the landscape itself, are trying to hold on to distinctive ways of life that happened, and are still happening, in a particular place. But the NCHA's investment is in having the region reimagined as a safe, average part of modern America— as the SMAP suggests, as, part of the homogenized "global economy," with some remnants of an interesting and authentic past to engage tourists (Parsons, Brinckerhoff, Quade & Douglas Inc. 2001, 9). Despite the ongoing extraction of coal, the holders of this vision want West Virginia included with the rest of America in the so-called postindustrial era. This is a vision of a region that would offer plenty of safe, folksy chain restaurants, staffed by locals fluent in interpreting "coal culture" and Appalachian stereotypes like the Hatfield–McCoy feud for tourists. Hillbilly jokes and images are welcome on restaurant place mats, as long as the "blight and clutter" associated with them have been cleaned up outside. In the rationalized economy envisioned by the coal heritage movement and other coal industry supporters, these bits of local specificity are to be contained in commodifiable locations, allowing the area in general to be safely Americanized to attract the curious but fearful tourists whose sensibilities may be offended by "negative images." This is a vision of a "postmodern" economy to be sure, selling a commodified version of the coal cultures that economic exploitation has generated to visitors who must be protected from the real effects of historical and ongoing coal production.

Appalachia is a place caught in contradictions of geographic scale; it is an "all-American" region with "Third World" problems. For the last century, it has been a national sacrifice zone, where the coal industry has pushed the limits of the possible in its efforts to feed the national appetite for energy and meet its own profit imperative by extracting coal. This natural resource extraction has been a bloody, messy process involving the sacrifice of countless workers' lives and health and, increasingly, the landscape itself. The two accounts of history that I have presented here illustrate how the past constructs and inhabits the future. For the save Blair Mountain movement, stories of past labor activism offer hope for

the salvation of the landscape and the mountain communities it has shel-
tered. The coal heritage movement, however, blends Appalachian history
into the national through discourses of sacrifice and development. In this
account, the patriotic sacrifices of miners constitute the terms for Appalachia's membership in the American nation. As an economic development
project, however, coal heritage ironically commodifies local memory into
a new resource for extraction.

Notes

1. "The coal heritage movement" is my phrase for various heritage tourism
boosters and other people who have contributed to heritage tourism sites. The
"save Blair Mountain" movement is my term for a group of associated activists
and organizations all working to preserve Blair Mountain. There are many organizations fighting mountaintop removal in the Appalachian coalfields, and it is
beyond the scope of this chapter to thoroughly describe their efforts. For more
information, see the network's Friends of Blair Mountain at http://friendsofblair
mountain.org (which was formed after this research was conducted) or Friends of
the Mountains at http://www.friendsofthemountains.org.

2. Interestingly, this display parallels one in the Oregon Nikkei Legacy Center, where the internment of people of Japanese descent during World War II is
commemorated with a similar cot and newspaper, which in that case is dotted
with preserved flies to evoke the unhygienic conditions in the camp (Anna Tsing,
personal communication, October 6, 2005, in Santa Cruz, CA).

3. Bill and Shawn's names have been changed.

4. Interview took place August 12, 2004, in Logan, West Virginia.

5. Ibid.

6. Interview took place October 3, 2004, in Blair, West Virginia.

Works Cited

Appalachian Land Ownership Task Force. 1983. *Who Owns Appalachia? Landown-
    ership and Its Impacts.* Lexington: University Press of Kentucky.
Baker, Houston, Jr. 1999. "Critical Memory and the Black Public Sphere." In *Cul-
    tural Memory and the Construction of Identity,* ed. Dan Ben-Amos and Liliane
    Weissberg, 264–96. Detroit, Mich.: Wayne State University Press.
Batteau, Allen. 1990. *The Invention of Appalachia.* Tucson, Ariz.: University of Tuc-
    son Press.
Berlant, Lauren. 1997. *The Queen of America Goes to Washington City.* Durham,
    N.C.: Duke University Press.

———. 2008. *The Female Complaint*. Durham, N.C.: Duke University Press.

Bommes, Michael, and Patrick Wright. 1982. "'Charms of Residence': The Public and the Past." In *Making Histories: Studies in History-writing and Politics*, ed. Richard Johnson, Gregor McLennan, Bill Schwartz, and David Sutton, 253–301. Minneapolis: University of Minnesota Press.

Bourdieu, Pierre. 1998. *Outline of a Theory of Practice*. New York: Cambridge University Press.

Chafin, Barbara. 2005. "Mountaintop Removal in Mingo County—Without a Permit!" *Winds of Change: The Newsletter of the Ohio Valley Environmental Coalition*, May 15–16.

Corbin, David. 1981. *Life, Work, and Rebellion in the Coal Fields*. Urbana: University of Illinois Press.

Connerton, Paul. 2006. "Cultural Memory." In *Handbook of Material Culture*, ed. Chris Tilley, Webb Keane, Susanne Kuchler, Mike Rowlands, and Patricia Spyer, 315–24. Thousand Oaks, Calif.: Sage.

Coombes, Annie E. 2003. *History after Apartheid: Visual Culture and Public Memory in a Democratic South Africa*. Durham, N.C.: Duke University Press.

Dao, James. 2005. "A New Campaign to Preserve an Old Mining Battlefield." *New York Times*, May 15. http://travel.nytimes.com/2005/05/15/national/15blair.html (accessed January 15, 2006).

Eichstedt, Jennifer, and Stephen Small. 2002. *Representations of Slavery: Race and Ideology in Southern Plantation Museums*. Washington, D.C.: Smithsonian Institution Press.

Eller, Ronald D. 1982. *Miners, Millhands, and Mountaineers: Industrialization of the Appalachian South, 1880–1930*. Knoxville: University of Tennessee Press.

Foster, Stephen William. 1988. *The Past Is Another Country: Representation, Historical Consciousness and Resistance in the Blue Ridge*. Berkeley: University of California Press.

Gaventa, John. 1980. *Power and Powerlessness: Quiescence and Rebellion in an Appalachian Valley*. Urbana: University of Illinois Press.

Giardina, Denise. 1994. *The Unquiet Earth*. New York: Ballantine Books.

Heneghan, Bridget T. 2003. *Whitewashing America: Material Culture and Race in the Antebellum Imagination*. Jackson: University Press of Mississippi.

Hinton, Jennifer J., Marcello M. Viega, and Christian Beinhoff. 2003. "Women and Artisanal Mining: Gender Roles and the Road Ahead." In *The Socio-Economic Impacts of Artisanal and Small-Scale Mining in Developing Countries*, ed. Gavin M. Hilson, 161–203. Exton, Penn.: A. A. Balkema.

Janofsky, Michael. 1998. "As Hills Fill Hollows, Some West Virginians Are Fighting King Coal." *New York Times*, May 7, late edition, A10.

Johnson, Richard, and Graham Dawson. 1982. "Popular Memory: Theory, Politics, Method." In *Making Histories: Studies in History-writing and Politics*, ed.

Richard Johnson, Gregor McLennan, Bill Schwartz, and David Sutton, 205–52. Minneapolis: University of Minnesota Press.

Kuletz, Valerie L. 1998. *The Tainted Desert: Environmental and Social Ruin in the American West*. New York: Routledge.

Lefebvre, Henri. 1991. *The Production of Space*. Cambridge, Mass.: Blackwell.

Levin, Amy. 2007. "Nostalgia as Epistemology." In *Defining Memory: Local Museums and the Construction of History in America's Changing Communities*, ed. Amy Levin, 93–96. Lanham, Md.: Altamira Press.

Lewis, Helen Matthews, Linda Johnson, and Donald Askins. 1978. *Colonialism in Modern America: The Appalachian Case*. Boone, N.C.: Appalachian Consortium Press.

Light, Ken, and Melanie Light. 2006. *Coal Hollow: Photographs and Oral Histories*. Berkeley: University of California Press.

Massey, Doreen. 1994. *Space, Place, and Gender*. Minneapolis: University of Minnesota Press.

Massey Energy Company. 2008. *Annual Report*. U.S. Securities and Exchange Commission. http://www.sec.gov/Archives/edgar/data/37748/000003774809000005/form10k123108.htm (accessed February 11, 2009).

McNeil, William K. 1989. *Appalachian Images in Folk and Popular Culture*. Ann Arbor: University of Michigan Research Press.

Moore, Marat. 1996. *Women in the Mines: Stories of Life and Work*. Twayne's Oral History Series. New York: Twayne Publishers.

Montrie, Chad. 2003. *To Save the Land and People: A History of Opposition to Surface Coal Mining in Appalachia*. Chapel Hill: University of North Carolina Press.

Moskowitz, Marina. 2004. *Standard of Living: The Measure of the Middle Class in Modern America*. Baltimore, Md.: The Johns Hopkins University Press.

National Coal Heritage Area (NCHA). 2006. "Welcome to the National Coal Heritage Area!" http://www.coalheritage.org/moreabout.html (accessed February 2, 2006).

National Heritage Areas (NHA). 2007. "National Coal Heritage Area." http://www.cr.nps.gov/heritageareas/AREAS/NCOAL.HTM (accessed January 5, 2006).

National Park Service. 1991. "Reconnaissance Study of Coal Mining Heritage and Related Resources in Southern West Virginia." Unpublished report. Mid-Atlantic Regional Office, Division of Park and Resource Planning. Philadelphia, P.A.

National Register of Historic Places (NRHP). 2006. "What Are the Results of Listing?" http://www.cr.nps.gov/nr/results.htm (accessed February 1, 2006).

National Scenic Byways Program (NSBP). 2007. "Coal Heritage Trail." http://www.byways.org/explore/byways/10346 (accessed January 5, 2006).

Nyden, Paul J. 2005. "Miners Arrested Near Massey Plant: UMW Protests Loss of Pensions, Health Care and Union Jobs." *Charleston Gazette*, February 25, 1A.

———. 2010. "Group Appealing Blair Mountain's Removal from Historic Register." *Charleston Gazette*, January 16. http://www.wvgazette.com/Life/201001160391 (accessed April 20, 2010).

Ohio Valley Environmental Coalition (OHVEC). 2007. "Coal Truck Facts the Industry Is Trying to Ignore." http://www.ohvec.org/issues/overweight_coal_trucks/sb583_fact.html (accessed May 30, 2007).

Palmer, Mark. 2005. "The Baghdad Bomb Squad." *Wired* 13 (11), November. http://www.wired.com/wired/archive/13.11/bomb.html (accessed April 7, 2010).

Parsons Brinckerhoff Quade & Douglas Inc. 2001. "Strategic Management Action Plan." Unpublished report. http://www.coalheritage.org (accessed January 26, 2006).

Precourt, Walter. 1983. "The Image of Appalachian Poverty." In *Appalachia and America*, ed. Allan Batteau, 86–110. Lexington: University of Kentucky Press.

Savage, Lon. 1990. *Thunder in the Mountains: The West Virginia Mine War, 1920–21.* Pittsburgh, Penn.: University of Pittsburgh Press.

Scott, Rebecca R. 2007. "Dependent Masculinity and Political Culture in Pro-Mountaintop Removal Discourse: Or, How I Learned to Stop Worrying and Love the Dragline." *Feminist Studies* 33 (3): 484–509.

Semple, Ellen Churchill. 1989. "The Anglo-Saxons of the Kentucky Mountains." In *Appalachian Images in Folk and Popular Culture*, ed. William K. McNeil, 145–74. Ann Arbor: University of Michigan Research Press. (Orig. pub. 1901. *Geographical Journal* 17 [June]: 588–623.)

Sever, Megan. 2003. "Settlement Reached on Coal Slurry Spill." *Geotimes.org*, October 20. http://www.geotimes.org/oct03/WebExtra101703.html (accessed January 23, 2007).

Shnayerson, Michael. 2008. *Coal River: How a Few Brave Americans Took on a Powerful Company—and the Federal Government—to Save the Land They Love.* New York: Farrar, Straus and Giroux.

Shogan, Robert. 2004. *The Battle of Blair Mountain: The Story of America's Largest Labor Uprising.* Boulder, Colo.: Westview Press.

Smith, Neil. 1992. "Contours of a Spatialized Politics: Homeless Vehicles and the Production of Geographical Scale." *Social Text* 33:54–81.

———. 2004. "Scale Bending and the Fate of the National." In *Scale and Geographic Inquiry*, ed. Eric Sheppard and Robert B. McMaster, 192–212. Malden, Mass.: Blackwell.

Stallybrass, Peter. 1999. "Worn Worlds: Clothes, Mourning and the Life of Things." In *Cultural Memory and the Construction of Identity*, ed. Dan Ben-Amos and Liliane Weissberg 27–44. Detroit, Mich.: Wayne State University Press.

Stewart, Kathleen. 1996. *A Space on the Side of the Road: Cultural Poetics in an "Other" America.* Princeton, N.J.: Princeton University Press.

Stewart, Susan. 1984. *On Longing: Narratives of the Miniature, the Gigantic, the Souvenir, the Collection*. Baltimore, Md.: The Johns Hopkins University Press.

Sturken, Marita. 2004. "The Aesthetics of Absence: Rebuilding Ground Zero." *American Ethnologist* 31 (3): 311–25.

Tsing, Anna. 2005. *Friction: An Ethnography of Global Connection*. Princeton, N.J.: Princeton University Press.

U.S. Census Bureau. 2000. "U.S. Census Online Database." http://www.census.gov.

U.S. Senate. 2002. Subcommittee on Clean Air, Wetlands, and Climate Change, Committee on Environment and Public Works. *Clean Water Act: Review of Proposed Revisions to Section 404 Definitions of "Fill" and "Dredged Fill."* 107th Cong., 2nd sess. June 6.

Ward, Ken, Jr. 2010. "Last Four Upper Big Branch Miners Found Dead." *Charleston Gazette*, April 9. http://wvgazette.com/News/montcoal/201004090857 (accessed April 19, 2010).

Warrick, Joby. 2004. "Appalachia Is Paying Price for White House Rule Change." *Washington Post*, August 16, A1.

Weissberg, Liliane. 1999. "Memory Confined." In *Cultural Memory and the Construction of Identity*, ed. Dan Ben-Amos and LilianeWeissberg, 45–76. Detroit, Mich.: Wayne State University Press.

West Virginia Coal Association (WVCA). 2006. "Coal Facts 2006." Charleston, WV: West Virginia Coal Association.

West Virginia Office of Miners' Health, Safety and Training. 2009. "Summary of Fatal Mining Accidents 1997–2009." http://www.wvminesafety.org/fatal97.htm (accessed January 28, 2009).

Williams, John Alexander. 2002. *Appalachia: A History*. Chapel Hill: University of North Carolina Press.

Wooten, Paul. 1918. "Fuel Administration Working Hard to Increase Production." *Mining Congress Journal* 4 (9): 361.

Youth Museum of Southern West Virginia Inc. 2007. "Youth Museum Overview." http://www.beckleymine.com/ym/ym-overview.cfm (accessed May 12, 2007).

Zukin, Sharon. 1991. *Landscapes of Power: From Detroit to Disney World*. Berkeley: University of California Press.

CHAPTER 7

Ecoadventures in the American West

Innocence, Conflict, and Nation Making in Emptied Landscapes

Barbara A. Barnes

> *Eastward I go only by force, but westward I go free [. . .] I believe that the forest which I see in the western horizon stretches uninterruptedly toward the setting sun, and there are no towns nor cities in it of enough consequence to disturb me [. . .] that way the nation is moving, and I may say that mankind progress from east to west.*
>
> —Henry David Thoreau, "Walking"

"We have the space we need to fulfill our every dream"

The week of July 4, 2004, *U.S. News and World Report* ran a special issue, "Defining America: Why the United States Is Unique." At the time, national discussions of the war in Iraq retained a generally triumphant tone, and this national news magazine marked the independence holiday by reiterating notions of U.S. exceptionalism. The special section included eleven short articles, many of which referenced the well-preserved idea that "American exceptionalism" originated from the presence of frontier wilderness, which shaped the character of the nation and its citizens. These claims are punctuated by an uncannily familiar image situated in the center of the first page: a stock black-and-white photograph of a man wearing cowboy garb (chaps, boots, ten-gallon hat, neckerchief) standing on the ledge of a canyon vista. His back is to the camera, and his body is oriented just right of the center of the image but is turned toward the left (the cartographical west). The caption reads, "A cowboy looks down over the Grand Canyon: We have the space we need to fulfill our every dream" (Barone 2004, 38).

The image calls up frontier mythologies for an intended patriotic American audience and, by extension, the dreams, promises, and (for some) nightmares associated with the imagined open spaces of the American West. Indeed, the idea of an empty and vast frontier, naturalized by more than a century of repetitive representation in stories and images, has long presented a narrative of U.S. national identity that ensures individual freedom, abundant opportunity, and innocent mobility toward a better future and a better self—for those able to see themselves as part of the national project and the nation's right to expansion.

In this chapter, I explore the sustained nation-making impact of adventure spectacles in nationally coded "wilderness" spaces that have been symbolically emptied through their repetitive representation as empty and the ways adventure stories fit snuggly into accepted histories of the birth and growth of the nation and its subjects. Familiar and oft-repeated mythic stories of heroic white men traipsing through frontier wilderness in pursuit of noble causes have provided extraordinarily durable symbols of a "shared" national past that promises equal access to the freedoms and opportunities that the frontier (and, hence, the nation) promised.

Although criticisms are by now common of the ways these stories cruelly erase the lives, pasts, and presents of the people and places that come to be called frontier wilderness, they remain persuasive. Their public appeal appeared to increase at the end of the twentieth century, when "wilderness adventure" (realized through so-called adventure travel and adventure sports) became a much sought-after commodity that promised authentic experience, discovery, and even "first contact" with people and places imagined as isolated and remote at a moment when it seemed that modernity had found (and "ruined") every place. This recreational and representational shift was enabled by several historical factors such as recreational gear innovations, communications technologies that allowed outdoor feats to be captured and circulated to a curious public, and remote destinations around the world becoming accessible to wealthy travelers through globalization processes. Stories, images, and practices of outdoor adventure thus proliferated in media and recreational practices, not only in the United States, but also in various locations around the world. Importantly, the images, advertising, and narratives associated with this trend required, and still require, that outdoor settings be shown as empty backdrops for human adventurers. Nonetheless, historical contentions over the meanings of life, place, and landscape occasionally erupt to spoil the coherence of such heroic narratives.

I focus here on a moment in 1995 when enduring conflicts over land use in the southeast corner of Utah came to a head upon the introduction of an outdoor endurance sporting event called expedition adventure racing to U.S. territory and television. Expedition adventure races are international, multisport, multiday events in which mixed-gender teams of three to five cover as much as five hundred miles of "wild" terrain in five to ten days with very little rest. The particular event I consider here was called Eco-Challenge®: The Expedition Race™.[1] It was produced by Mark Burnett (who went on to become the executive producer of successful reality-based television shows including *Survivor* and *The Apprentice*), with television coverage by MTV. It was the first in a series of nine annual competitions with corresponding television programs (all produced by Burnett) that took athletes and viewers to "wilderness" locations throughout the world, from Utah to the Fiji Islands, with annual broadcasts that aired on various basic cable channels (i.e., ESPN, Discovery, USA Network).

The location of the 1995 event—southeastern Utah—is a remote region with a landscape that has come to visually stand in for the nation's frontier. Its distinctive burnt-orange cliffs, canyons, and buttes have been repetitively rendered as frontier space since the late nineteenth century in landscape paintings, Hollywood westerns, and advertising for everything from sport utility vehicles to Marlboro cigarettes. These desert landscapes have thus come to signify a national shared past based in myths of open spaces that guarantee laissez-faire freedoms and the nation's benevolent expansion. The controversy surrounding the 1995 Eco-Challenge® was ignited by local environmental activists, who, by the 1990s, had become powerfully organized and achieved political clout both locally and nationally. Their alarm over the proposed event was motivated by their fears that land they considered sacred and fragile would be misused and receive the wrong kind of publicity if a long-distance cross-country sports competition was held there and broadcast on MTV.

In the following discussion, I argue that representations of "real" landscapes must be symbolically emptied to make compelling backdrops for nationally coded adventure narratives. The nostalgic view of pristine wilderness and the creation of wild spaces as open playgrounds in televised adventure-sport images ignore the contentious histories and social relations of people, plants, animals, rocks, and soil. This matters because it mimics the kind of innocent conquest narratives that justified the United States' nineteenth-century imperial expansion.

Stories of unencumbered travel into emptied "wilderness" spaces implicitly work to articulate idealized "American" national identities and symbolically support historically entrenched rationales for the nation's benevolently boundless expansion. Because it was introduced into an already volatile political situation, the Eco-Challenge® in southern Utah brought some of the contradictions inherent in nation-making frontier narratives to the surface. In other words, in the situation I describe here, mythic notions of frontier space were reimagined through late twentieth-century adventure discourses that collided with varying views of the land and its tangled histories of empire and conflict, even as these tangled histories were erased both in the Eco-Challenge® and the environmentalists' representations.

I begin by considering the power of frontier symbolism in nation-making narratives; I then tell the intertwined stories of adventure racing, late twentieth-century conflicts in southern Utah, and the 1995 Eco-Challenge®. In the end, I consider whether mobility and the human–landscape nexus might be reimagined in ways that retain the intimate relationship between the promises of democracy in the United States and its imagined open spaces but refuse innocence and ignorance by remembering the social histories and agencies of nature and place.

Making the Nation in Emptied Lands

Underlying my analysis is the premise that modern nations are not statically bounded entities but political–cultural constructions continually in process and in need of constant, often-violent maintenance. In large part, this maintenance is carried out symbolically, as many scholars have argued, including some of the other the authors in this volume (Anderson 1991; Berlant 1991, 1997; Cronon 1996; Eley 1996; Gray 2005; Kaplan 2002; McClintock 1995; Stoler 1995). Since the United States' national boundaries had to be cobbled together to exclude American Indians and African Americans, but include select European colonizers and immigrants who did not already share a national history, language, or culture, symbols that produce shared national memories have been particularly useful in calming disparity and producing a singular national identity (Berlant 1991; Sears 1989).[2] Of course, any unified notion of national identity must deny large portions of history.

One particularly powerful story in the symbolic making of the United States and its boundaries of belonging is that of its innocent expansion into the Western frontier. I take the idea of the frontier as an example of what

Lauren Berlant has termed the "national symbolic"—a particularly useful conceptual framework for understanding elements of popular culture as political–cultural sites in which identities and notions of national belonging are formed symbolically. Through discursive practices within national spaces, as well as according to the laws of birthright and naturalized citizenship, individual subjects come to see themselves as holding a collective history and thus gain a sense of belonging in the nation. This powerful symbolic function is communicated through the nation's "traditional icons, its metaphors, its heroes, its rituals, and its narratives" (Berlant 1991, 20). Additionally, through the national symbolic, "the historical nation aspires to achieve the inevitability of the status of natural law, a birthright. This pseudo-genetic condition not only affects profoundly the citizen's subjective experience of her/his political rights, but also of civil life, private life, the life of the body itself" (22). Berlant's conceptual attention to the subjective experience of public rights, everyday life, and the body are particularly important to the questions I explore here, especially in terms of exploring the emotional attachments subjects form to nationally symbolic landscapes (e.g., Price 2004; Tuan 1974).

The frontier, or the "American West," operates as such a powerful and enduring national symbol because it is an idea—rather than a specific place or time—that has been produced and reproduced in stories, histories, and visual renderings (e.g., Hausladen 2003; Limerick 1987; Matsumoto and Allmendinger 1999; White, Limerick, and Grossman 1994). In the latter decades of the twentieth century, television was the primary conduit of national symbols—including the idea of the frontier, which was circulated in advertising, western specials and serials, and in adventure sports coverage of the 1990s. Because it is viewed in an intimate space (the home), and projects a sense of liveness (i.e., feelings among viewers that they are watching and participating in the event as it happens), television is a particularly effective medium for evoking a sense of proximity to reality and emotional involvement (Doanne 1990; Feuer 1983). This quality makes television a particularly effective medium for producing a sense of belonging—in the imaged community of the nation—through the creation of a shared experience of watching, and shared emotional reactions, within political environments in which emotions or feeling states are central pathways to national participation (Anderson 1991; Gray 2005; Sturken 1997; Williams 1974). Drawing on familiar frontier tropes and exploiting the immediateness of electronic media, televised adventure spectacles such as the Eco-Challenge®, instantly communicate images of nationally coded bodies in wild spaces and can evoke powerful visceral and emotional responses in television audiences. When television representations explicitly invoke the nation, as international sports competitions do, they reproduce an embodied national fantasy, a mass national audience, and normalizing notions of belonging and citizen bodies (Sturken 1997; Banet-Weiser 1999; Berlant 1997). In the case I study here, the normalized national body mirrors the historically iconic citizen: masculine, mobile, mostly white, self-sufficient, and fearless.

The Event: "An expedition with a stopwatch"

I begin my discussion of a late twentieth-century sporting event—and the late twentieth-century controversy over landscape that it instigated in the United States—with the most frequently told story of expedition adventure racing's origins (at least among U.S.-based adventure racers and media). As is the case with most origin stories, there are alternatives (e.g., Paterson and Gurney 1999), and the stories that rise to the top through repetition point to the desires of the storytellers, as they shape the past according to the power relations of the present (Foucault 1997; Haraway 1989). The tale usually begins with a French radio journalist named Gerard Fusil, known for his coverage of outdoor endurance events such as the Whitbread Round the World Race and the Paris–Dakar rally, and the race he invented called the "Raid Gauloise." As the story goes, Fusil was in Argentina in 1987, covering the Whitbread, when he "got the idea to organize an adventure competition for people who would use only physical and mental strength and no mechanics. The idea was to do it in the Tierra de Fuego and let people progress like the Indian Patagons living there a few centuries ago" (Fusil 2001, 15). Journalist Martin Dugard, who covered the Raid Gauloise for *Runner's World* magazine, explained Fusil's motivation this way:

> Noting that the Whitbread was an emulation of the expeditions of great colonial mariners, like Magellan and Drake . . . he conceived of a similar expedition-based race, but taking place on land [. . .] A race in which the team dynamic that drove colonial expeditions to either mutiny or success could be emulated in the same extreme, uncharted circumstances. A race in which the competitors would be self-sufficient, but for the safe harbor of refueling points. A race, thought the man who grew up idealizing an uncle who made his

living as an African bush pilot [. . .] to stir the imagination and
bring a sense of romance to competitive sports. (Dugard 2000, 12)

Together with his wife, Nelly, Fusil thus created a multiday team endurance race, which covered several hundred kilometers and required several
"disciplines," or modes of travel (all human powered), to complete, drew
on corporate sponsorship for funding, and incorporated media coverage.
The Fusils also stipulated that all Raid Gauloise teams have at least one
woman.[3] Adding to the "adventure," the event was staged in exoticized
locations far removed from continental Europe (e.g., Jordon, Madagascar,
Nepal, New Zealand). Additionally, no route of travel was specified, and
the exact course was kept secret until immediately before the race. Each
team thus had to decide on the best route in between designated check-
points where they had their "passports" (or "Raid-Books") stamped.

Although the blatant use of colonial tropes seemed anachronistic for
the late twentieth-century postcolonial moment, adventure racing was, of
course, a product of its time. It easily picked up on the growing interest
in worldwide "adventure" travel, extreme sports, and their media representations. These contemporary forms of recreation and entertainment
were enabled by global (if uneven) flows of capital, culture, and bodies,
the technologies that allowed these flows, and the neoliberal political and
economic environments mobilized by the Reagan and Thatcher regimes
in the 1980s. Adventure racing brought the contemporary cultural appeal
of outdoor adventure together with neoliberal discourses of self-help and
self-sufficiency, personal endurance, and flexibility in unpredictable environments (See Barnes 2009; Martin 1994). Such environments created the
conditions of possibility for a kind of self-knowledge and self-governing that
valued technologically savvy citizens governed, in part, through appeals
to freedom, choice, and the cultural enticements to make calculative, self-
managing choices on their own behalf (Ong 2005; Rose 1999). Enabled
by this *epistēmē*, adventure racing presented itself as a training ground for
success in late twentieth-century life.

From its inception, then, adventure racing was both a sporting event
and a media spectacle, staged within intertwining narratives of empire and
personal growth. In two autobiographies, Burnett casts himself as a creative
maverick with a potent entrepreneurial drive, whose entry into adventure
racing, and into American television, began in 1982. Upon finishing a stint as
a paratrooper for Britain's Royal Air Force, he was on his way from England

to an unspecified Central American location to work as a "military advisor" for England's Special Air Service (SAS) when, on a planned layover in Los Angeles, he decided to stay to seek his "American Dream" (noticeably missing from his account is how he was able to stay in the United States; Burnett 2001, 2005). As he tells the story, Burnett was introduced to adventure racing in the early 1990s through a *Los Angeles Times* reporter's account of his own experiences competing in the Raid Gauloise and stumbling upon contemporary market research "showing that the three dominant themes of the nineties would be the environment, extreme sports, and self-actualization through challenge. [As he saw it,] no other format combined all three like expedition racing" (Burnett 2001, 42).

He competed in the Raid Gauloise himself, bought the North American rights to the race from Fusil in 1992, and created the Eco-Challenge® by duplicating the Raid Gauloise form almost verbatim,[4] but with a vision of his "American" production as bigger, slicker, and more spectacular: "American racers would expect flawless execution. Also, any TV company that financed me would expect American-quality production. I planned to produce an efficient *Eco-Challenge®* and more than double the number of film crews covering the race.... I intended to produce a dynamic show about racers questing after this Holy Grail. I wanted Eco to be more epic, more dramatic, more bombastic—a David Lean film come to life" (Burnett 2001, 63).

His reference to David Lean in this story is telling. Burnett approached the production of the Eco-Challenge® as an imperial spectacle in unapologetic terms. Lean, of course, made his reputation directing epic historical films such as *Lawrence of Arabia* (1962) and *A Passage to India* (1984), films in which the landscapes were depicted in Orientalist terms as integral elements of colonial conquest narratives (Said 1994). In *Lawrence of Arabia*, for instance, long shots of the vast "Arabian" desert enable the main character's heroic military and personal mobility. These emptied landscapes depict distant colonial locations as inherently dangerous when faced by colonial adventurers who then are shown to tame them in complex and gendered ways (Shohat and Stam 1994). Lean's trademark wide-angle views of immense and ominous lands suggest both possibility and danger for the well-intentioned European bodies moving through them.

Burnett apparently intended to produce a similarly epic spectacle for the first *Eco-Challenge®* using the southern Utah desert. In each case, the story is set—and filmed—in a real place, emptied of any evidence of people, progress, or conflicts that might contradict the story being put forth.[5] In both cases, the narrative relies on producing close connections between emptied landscapes, colonial narratives, mobile bodies, and visual spectacle. Indeed, adventure narratives typically rely on conventions of representation developed through eighteenth- and nineteenth-century European exploration narratives (Pratt 1992). Following these conventions, scenes of deserts, forests, or mountains as the settings for outdoor adventures allege the local specificity that provides an air of authenticity for the experiences and knowledges shown (e.g., a southern Utah experience must qualitatively differ from a Saharan experience). At the same time, these adventure settings could be anywhere, or everywhere, and thus become fittingly flexible spectacles for national, colonial, and personal discovery.

Burnett masterfully marshals such landscape tropes. As anyone who has seen the *Eco-Challenge®*, *Survivor*, or even *The Apprentice* surely recognizes, part of Burnett's genius as a producer is his skill for creating drama in "real" places while emptying them of their historical specificity, their complicated social power relations, their troubles, and the ways of life that sustain the communities who live there, even while selectively invoking historical icons and conventions of genre for quick narrative and emotional associations. The 1995 *Eco-Challenge®*, for instance, called up images of explorers, cowboys, and Indians in the narratives that were fashioned for both the racers and the television audience. A memo distributed by Burnett's production company, Eco-Challenge Lifestyles Inc., to athletes registered for the 1995 race read,

> Utah is a rugged land of contrasts—majestic towers, great rivers, deep canyons, snow covered peaks, and vast rocky plains. Centuries ago the Anasazi Indians hunted, farmed and recorded their passings on rocks in these lands.
>
> More recently, cowboys searched the twisted canyons for their half-wild stray cattle, and an adventurer named John Wesley Powell made an incredible voyage of discovery mapping these lands where few had traveled and even fewer had returned. It is with these thoughts in mind that you *Eco-Challengers* will race (Burnett 1994).

Despite its "domestic" location, the U.S. Southwest was exoticized through Eco-Challenge Lifestyles Inc.'s effort to portray local landscapes, animals, and people in fantastic style and thereby to intensify the potential sense of thrill for both athletes and viewers. References to ancient inhabitants along with legendary explorers and ranching tales created southern Utah as a place outside of history (the "more recently" clause doing little to situate the place and its stories) and promoted the competition as an adventure through a mythic past as imagined for present and future selves. At the same time, references to John Wesley Powell, the Anasazi, and the unique geography situate the race solidly in the American West, and within nation-making frontier legends. Indeed, the very red-desert landscape in which Burnett had chosen to stage his race was a landscape that had come to stand in for the West largely through its repetitive representation as such, perhaps most notably in Hollywood westerns, but beginning with nineteenth-century landscape paintings, as famously rendered by Thomas Moran (1837–1926).

A Visually Inviting Frontier

Moran was just one member of a school of American landscape painters, including Albert Bierstadt (1830–1902), Frederic Church (1826–1900), and Winslow Homer (1836–1910), who visually depicted the nation's "exceptional" open spaces. When paintings and sketches by these artists were mass produced and distributed in books, magazines, and advertising, the spaces represented were produced as racially coded tourist destinations for patriotic Americans.

Moran's work was especially instrumental in advertising the West as landscape that represented the nation's aspirations and as empty wilderness that symbolized the nation's identity. His epic seven-by-twelve-foot landscapes—*Grand Canyon of the Yellowstone* (1872) and *The Chasm of the Colorado* (1873–74)—figured prominently in the creation of Yellowstone and the Grand Canyon as national parks. Each painting was imagined as a realistic representation, painted after Moran visited and personally observed each place. *Chasm,* for example, was created when Moran accompanied John Wesley Powell on the 1873 scientific exploration of the length of the Colorado River. Nonetheless, these paintings were ideological depictions of fantasy space. That is to say, the scenes painted by Moran do not actually exist—both in terms of the views presented, and in terms of the implied emptiness of the land. Clearly, the territories that would become national parks were not empty when painted by Moran (or any other "American" artist) but were, and continue to be, inhabited and widely used. At the time it was observed by Moran, the Grand Canyon was (and is) a region used by the Navajo, Hopi, Paiute, and Havasupai societies (to name just a few), but his canyonscapes are nonetheless endless and untouched, waiting for discovery.

Moran's work was hung in the U.S. Capitol, displayed at World's Fairs, widely distributed throughout the nation in popular magazines, and used as illustrations for Powell's own account of his expedition. Perhaps more importantly, the Atchison, Topeka and Santa Fe Railroad, in collaboration with the Fred Harvey Company, reproduced Moran's Grand Canyon landscapes through chromolithograph and distributed them by the thousands to hotels, schools, offices, and homes across the nation during the 1890s (Barringer 2002; Neumann 2002; Shaffer 2001; Weigle 1992). The name of the railroad was not imprinted on the framed prints, but they presented the canyon as a romantically inviting and uniquely American landscape (Figure 7.1). These images encouraged nationalistic associations with the scenery of the

Figure 7.1. Thomas Moran (American, 1837–1926), Grand Canyon of Arizona from Hermit Rim Road, *c. 1912. Color lithograph, 80.6 × 106 cm. © The Cleveland Museum of Art, Gift of Dr. Gerard and Phyllis Seltzer in honor of Phyllis Stone 1996.305. This image was reproduced as a print by the Atchison, Topeka and Santa Fe Railroad and was displayed in railway stations in the eastern United States to promote train travel to the Grand Canyon.*

Southwest even as they documented a "widespread sentimentalism for a 'vanishing' frontier" (Spence 1999, 4).[6]

As Foucault has shown, discourses are enabled by historical conditions of possibility, and the timing of the popularity of Moran's paintings (the late-nineteenth and early twentieth century) is significant (Foucault 1970, 1972). As national territory expanded and shifted through processes of industrialization, urbanization, and imperial ventures, boundaries of belonging were threatened. Increased immigration (mostly from Southern and Eastern Europe), colonial contact with racial "others" (including American Indians, Hawaiians, and Filipinos), and the increased mobility of freedmen and women intensified fears of racial tarnishing, while the growth of urbanization was perceived to feminize the nation's (white) masculine bodies. The presence of wilderness spaces and the possibilities of wilderness experiences were seen as a remedy for these problems that could create the kind of masculine bodies the nation needed as it sought to secure its Anglo identity and build an overseas empire (Bederman 1995; Roosevelt 1888, 1899).

Conveniently, the frontier simultaneously began to be firmly associated with emptiness, as the idea of the American West transitioned from "Indian wilderness" to wilderness as space devoid of all human dwelling and activity (Cronon 1996; Haynes 2003; Nash 2001; Spence 1999). According to historian Mark David Spence, around the 1860s, wilderness spaces were redefined as empty by redefining American Indians as foreigners to be removed rather than as part of the wilderness itself (Spence 1999). When the national park system was manufactured beginning in 1872, existing inhabitants were savagely forced from these spaces in order to create "untouched" wilderness. The vision of wilderness depicted in the landscape paintings—pristine and alluring to white middle-class travelers—was thus made by violently emptying it of its social and natural history and its human inhabitants. Lacking humans, wilderness could be seen in romantic terms as space where white men could have pure experiences of God and nature and, thus, escape the pressures, restraints, and feminizing influences of civilization, while gaining strength, renewal, and freedom.

After 1925, cultural (re)productions of the American nation-making myth of a vast frontier wilderness, and its related legacy of American Anglo-Saxon mobility, included Hollywood westerns. Perhaps most famously, John Ford frequently filmed on location in Southwestern landscapes. His films are especially associated with Monument Valley (spanning the border of southeast Utah and northeast Arizona, within the Navajo Nation), but he also repeatedly returned to the Colorado River valleys near the town of Moab in southeastern Utah.[7] More recently, red-rock Western desert landscapes have been used in the "Marlboro Man" advertising campaign (begun in 1954) and in advertisements for sport utility vehicles.[8] Each of these examples, and Moran's work, uses the same geographic location as the setting for reiterations of mythic frontier narratives. Setting these narratives in "real" landscapes with powerfully symbolic resonances in national memory enables the narratives to take on the urgency, emotional importance, and the tinge of truth, even while reproducing fantasy.

In similar fashion, the 1995 MTV broadcast of *Eco-Challenge*® exploits the frontier imagery already associated with the landscape of the place. It begins with a silhouetted cowboy on horseback in the desert at twilight, riding indirectly toward the camera, a crescent moon adorning the sky— an opening image that clearly references conventions of the western film genre. Bringing the image quickly into the present, the image cuts to a group of human bodies standing in silhouette on a diagonally framed ridge top alongside their horses and then to silhouetted athletes running against a purple sky background. The connection seems clear—these athletes are cast as modern-day western heroes. After a brief montage of the vast sandy landscape, a menacing snake, rappel ropes descending from sheer cliffs, and mountain bikes on dirt roads, the scene shifts to the beginning of the race itself, with aerial camera images of the athletes on horseback galloping across an open range dotted with sagebrush. This performance is captured in epic style by cameras in helicopters, and the magisterial wide-angle views are rapidly cut with brief, close shots of athletes struggling to tame their horses. The western landscape of southern Utah is thus again emptied and made visually available for the presentation of a staged epic journey. Unsurprisingly, this representation had to hide evidence of civilization and conflict—in this case, primarily highways and protestors.

The Place "where God put the West"

The location that Mark Burnett chose for the 1995 Eco-Challenge® is among the most remote spots in the lower forty-eight United States.[9] It falls within a region called the Colorado Plateau (in geological terms) and "America's Redrock Wilderness" (in public relations terms). It encompasses 130,000 square miles centered on the Four Corners region and includes the Grand Canyon, Monument Valley, and the town of Moab, Utah, which became known as a mountain-biking Mecca during the 1990s. This is a place where people can get lost, not only because of the dearth of towns and cities, but also because of the hundreds of deep-slot canyons where bodies can disappear from view.[10] The desolation of the place has historically been part of its appeal, as it is seen to ensure individual freedom and absence of witnesses and thus lack of state oversight. This is precisely why it appealed to the Mormons who wanted to establish a state of their own, "outlaws" such as Butch Cassidy and the Sundance Kid who hid in the labyrinthine canyons, extractive industries that prospect for uranium, oil, and gas, and the military who used it for nuclear-weapons testing. The sparse population and abundance of stunning vistas, cliffs, rivers, and slickrock are also why it appeals to wilderness advocates and adventure-sports enthusiasts.

Despite its sparse human presence, however, the Colorado Plateau has long been a disputed landscape with an intense modern history of contention over who owns the land, who should have access to it, and how it should be used. Although the place promises freedom, various notions of freedom tend to clash (e.g., the freedom of miners to build roads and the freedom of environmentalists to preserve road-free areas). Indeed, contention has been such an integral part of the landscape that a brief modern history of the place can be sketched in terms of its conflicts; each group involved in each successive and overlapping fray believed in their right to the land and that their way of using the land was right.

Situated near the confluence of the Colorado and Green Rivers flowing through the desert, the spot that would become the town of Moab provided a prime location for human settlement, and in 1855, Brigham Young sent Mormon contingents south to explore and colonize this region that had belonged to Mexico less than one decade earlier. The first waves of Mormons were easily expelled by Ute Indians, but over time and amid continuing skirmishes, white settlers began setting up tiny ranches and farms. This white immigration and settlement eventually led to increased pressure on the Utes from military forces, poverty, and widespread starvation, and by 1869 most had moved to the Uintah Reservation, set aside by President Lincoln in 1861 (in a sage brush desert to the north, less rich in aesthetically pleasing promontories and mineral resources; Delaney 1974; Firmage 1996). Throughout the twentieth century, the region was variously used by farmers, miners, ranchers, hikers, and sightseers, while portions were preserved as national parks.[11] In the 1950s, uranium was discovered near the town of Moab, and initially fueled by cold war militarization, a mining boom-and-bust cycle began that lasted into the 1980s.

The aesthetic beauty of the Colorado Plateau gained attention from the budding national environmental movements in the 1960s, and this was enabled by a number of factors, including the 1963 completion of the controversial Glenn Canyon Dam, which created Lake Powell (Porter and Brower 1963). The writings of Edward Abbey,[12] beginning with *Desert Solitaire* (1968; a polemic meditation on the meaning of wilderness and modernity based on Abbey's time as a seasonal park ranger in Arches National Park in southeast Utah), were also instrumental in redefining the region as a bastion of wilderness and a refuge from the decadence of modernity.

Relatedly, the Southern Utah Wilderness Alliance (SUWA), was formed in the early 1980s (c. 1983) in reaction to uncontrolled road building and prospecting. Its founders were largely relative "newcomers" to southern Utah: young, educated white men and women who had been drawn to the region for a range of reasons, including jobs in the mines and Abbey's books. This contingent of activists sought the legal protection of the Colorado Plateau wilderness for no other reason than its beauty—a stance utterly at odds with prevalent notions among Mormon ranchers and farmers that land is to be used productively, and resentment brewed against the interlopers. Quarrels between ranchers and environmental activists became so fierce that when SUWA was created in 1983, ranchers in the small town of Escalante hung the organization's three primary founders in effigy.[13]

In all likelihood, it was not simply the founding of SUWA that angered the ranchers; rather, shifting regulations in the meaning and management of public land had already intensified passions and threatened feelings of ownership when major land-management legislation was passed in 1976 (Roush 1995). The Federal Land Policy and Management Act (FLPMA), passed by Congress in 1976, shifted federal land management from wide-scale private use and ownership to public oversight. It also charged the Bureau of Land Management (BLM) with the administration of the land's "multiple uses" (e.g., ranching, resource extraction, recreation, and wilderness protection). Indeed, the passage of the FLPMA threatened an established way of life, undergirded by frontier values and a laissez-faire attitude toward land and private property, so fundamental to U.S. national identity: "In this [Lockean] tradition, that government is best which governs least. The right to life, liberty and the pursuit of happiness includes the individual's right to appropriate wealth from nature" (Roush 1995, 2).

However unhappy it made ranchers and farmers, the FLMPA opened up new avenues for legal protection of some of the land as "wilderness"[14] because it required the BLM to inventory all roadless areas of at least five thousand acres for possible designation and preservation as wilderness, and these parcels of land became known as Wilderness Study Areas (WSAs). The building of new roads was prohibited while the government conducted its inventory and until the lands were "released" from WSA designation. Nonetheless, in a 2005 interview, one man who had been employed by the uranium mines in the 1970s told me that the oil and gas companies exploring for uranium continued to bulldoze roads after the passage of the FLMPA in an attempt to create access to as many potential mine sites as possible.[15] The continued creation of roads precluded the possibility that some areas could qualify as wilderness, and unsurprisingly, the WSAs became central sites of contention among miners, loggers, developers, and environmentalists.

The closing of the uranium mines, when they became unprofitable in the mid-1980s, did not ease disputes as much as it simply changed the players because it coincided with the mass production of mountain bikes and the economic desperation of the economic shift (Ringholz 2002). After photographs of bikes on slickrock[16] were published in *National Geographic* and *Outside* magazine declared Moab its "favorite mountain biking spot" in 1989, the area began to gather international attention as a destination for outdoor play, and its fate was sealed (Williams 1994). Alongside mountain biking, river trips on the Colorado, rock climbing, and off-road driving also drove the unanticipated spike in tourism to the region.

Although this emergent form of tourism presented the possibility of economic salvation for the tiny town, when hordes of mountain bikers descended on Moab in the early 1990s, many residents felt cursed by this apparent success. Indeed, the rate of tourist visits quickly exceeded the town's resources. During Easter weekend 1991, for instance, Moab's population of four thousand swelled by 50 percent, as two thousand mountain bikers arrived for the first annual Fat Tire Festival. In addition, the new contingent of Lycra-clad mountain bikers fit uneasily with the local culture and stirred feelings of resentment. The new tourists were much different from those who had traveled as families or in group tours to the national parks in earlier decades; they were highly individualistic, highly mobile, and difficult to manage. In addition, it seemed to some that mountain bikers flaunted their relative wealth in the faces of those who were struggling just to hold on. As an environmental activist from the region explained to me, "There was always this negative reaction to the 'Lycra crowd,' as they call them. They were clearly more educated, had generally higher paying jobs, came from the city [. . .] Do you know what I'm saying? It's a cultural attitude as well."[17]

Adding insult to injury, developers rolled into town, buying up real estate devalued by the collapsed mining industry, and built motels and resorts that were corporately managed in absentia; it was certainly understandable that the town's earlier inhabitants felt some bitterness. Even environmentalists were taken by surprise at the potential environmental detriment of outdoor tourism. While it initially seemed preferable to cattle ranching, uranium mining, and gas and oil exploration, it came quickly to be viewed by many as a primary threat to the very existence of the landscape they hoped to protect. Thus the contours of a complex and multisided conflict were set in place.

Regardless of deep disagreements over the correct and responsible use of the land, however, its heritage as frontier seemed to shape all sides of the debate, as various groups engaged with and promoted its mythic emptiness. Environmental activists strove to represent the landscape in romantic terms as pristine, picturesque, untouched by human development, and therefore worthy of wilderness protection. Local businesses and the travel council wanted to push the idea of a wide-open natural playground (albeit with nearby amenities) for people with the disposable income to spend on travel, guides, and copious amounts of outdoor sports gear. Mining, oil, and gas companies (which included Gulf Oil, Standard Oil of New Jersey, and Union Carbide Corporation) would surely have benefited if the region remained largely unknown and ignored. In order to present a narrative of adventure, *Eco-Challenge®* producers needed to show the land as wild and uninhabited. Each approach perpetuated a national fantasy of innocent frontier mobility, subtly shaped by an expansionist ethos and an assumption that individual pursuits and closely guarded individualistic freedoms were, in fact, harmless, that is, no one else's business. As one self-aware environmental advocate explained,

> Mostly it's all about me-me-me. You know, all the newcomers, with their different uses, including us. The hikers, and the mountain

bikers are basically trying to protect a piece of the backcountry for our use to be there twenty years from now. And the miners, who you know, were raised here, farm here: their me-me-me is "I want the right to sell my alfalfa fields so that I can retire nicely." Twenty-five years ago, it was speculation on mining claims, and that expectation is still there [. . .] that "it's my right." And that's partly an American, or at least a western, philosophical [influence]: "it's my right to make money off public land"; "It's my right to have my use protected and I don't want anybody else coming in." We're all basically being selfish, and it becomes a competition; a political contest to see whose use is going to win out.[18]

By 1994, when Burnett and his partner Brian Terkelson proposed the Eco-Challenge® to local officials, disagreements over how this area of southern Utah should be used (or not) had thus reached a new intensity.

"Desert, not Disneyland": The Battle over *Eco-Challenge*®

With such a long history of contention, and such a long series of very real threats to the desert and various ways of life within it, why did Burnett's little race become such a fierce point of conflict? In part, it was the convergence of the historical, economic, and technological conditions described previously. In part, it was fueled by a "paradox of visibility": the increasing national and international visibility of the region increased the stakes of competing claims over the meanings of the landscape and, thus, over how it should be represented.

Mark Burnett stepped into this contentious situation with a naïve belief in the mythology associated with the emptiness of the romantic West, and according to his own accounts, he was stunned and confused by the opposition to his event, especially from environmentalists, to whom he thought his race would have particular appeal. He saw *Eco-Challenge*® as an economic boon for the state and believed that the television spectacle would provide a needed advertisement for outdoor recreation. The state and local chambers of commerce and the Utah Department of Community and Economic Development felt similarly. Burnett was also courted by Utah Governor Mike Leavitt, who accompanied Burnett in a private plane to view the state's deserts and pledged his support for the production. Unfortunately for Burnett, since the vast majority of land in the region (approximately 80 percent) is owned by the federal government and managed by the BLM and the U.S. National Park Service, his partnership with the governor had no bearing on the permitting process, which became particularly costly and complicated because of the intense resistance he encountered.

Yet it was precisely the potential advertisement for the "wrong" kind of land use that worried the SUWA and other opponents of the event, who already distrusted commercial enterprises and Hollywood interests for their ability to disregard laws and regulations. In other words, they were anxious about the event itself but were perhaps more worried that broadcasting a large athletic event like the Eco-Challenge® on television "would undercut efforts to encourage minimum impact recreation, sending the unfortunate message to a national audience that southern Utah is nothing but a red rock fun house. It would attract more recreational use to areas already at capacity, harm soils, and displace wildlife" (Southern Utah Wilderness Alliance 1995, 12).

SUWA spelled out their specific concerns in newsletters and on Internet news groups. They expected that the helicopters used to gain elevated camera images of the athletes and the landscape would disturb the endangered peregrine falcons that lived along the racecourse. They also expected the athletes to disturb bighorn sheep in the midst of lambing season and impact Anasazi archeological sites. Along with the BLM, SUWA was worried about the potential damage to delicate living soil structures known as cryptobiotic or cryptogamic soils, understood to provide a kind of structural support for the desert itself. These soil structures, formed out of algae, lichens, mosses, fungi, and bacteria, are seen to stabilize the sand against wind and rain erosion. Discourses advocating protection of the desert had begun in the 1980s to center on the deep, if subtle, damage being done to the land itself by marauding hordes of mountain bikers in the backcountry, and cryptobiotic soils became a symbol of the ways that too many people—and their toys—could destroy the very survival of the physical place. Of course, cows had been grazing on the desert lands and walking over cryptobiotic organisms for decades, but the hordes of new-style tourists came to be seen as more threatening to the desert than even the cows (Stiles 1999).

It only added to the dismay of race opponents that the television program would air on the still relatively new MTV, a venue perceived as likely to entice exactly the *wrong* type of people to the fragile desert environment.

As an editorial in the nationally distributed *Backpacker* magazine argued, *Eco-Challenge®* simply did not belong in the canyon country, and any kind of environmental message on MTV would be lost in the mix: "The organizers call this an environment-friendly event [. . .] But keep in mind that the primary television sponsor is MTV—music television, home to loud, overdone, and in-your-face video sensationalism. (That's when it's being tame)" (Viehman 1995, 8). Representing the land as an amusement park for teenagers and twentysomethings left no room for the kind of quiet and transcendental communion with the sublime that *Backpacking* understood to be more appropriate for the place.

These specific complaints were actually symptomatic of an often less clearly articulated, but larger, anxiety about the contaminating influence of corporate capitalist presence in a public outdoor space that many understood as sacred. Along with its association with MTV, *Eco-Challenge®* came in with corporate sponsorship from companies such as Hi-Tec athletic shoes and diet supplement company MET-Rx and, thus, seemed to support a growing and insidious brand of privatization in public lands.

Nonetheless, supporters of the event tried to validate their good intentions by arguing that the MTV event would serve the public good because viewers would be introduced to a lesson in correct citizenship, and this message could potentially reach those most in need of such lessons. Brian Terkelsen, Mark Burnett's right-hand man in the race organization, told the *Salt Lake Tribune* that since most of MTV's viewers are "inner city youth, [they] would benefit from exposure to environmental sensitivity and race participants displaying hard work, teamwork and compassion" (Gorrell 1994, D4). The idea that physical lessons in civic life can be learned through outdoor sport extend back to late nineteenth-century anxieties about the loss of the nation's frontier, when outdoor sport boosters, including Theodore Roosevelt, argued that surviving the dangers of nature could produce the kinds of citizen and soldier bodies the nation needed at the time (Roosevelt 1890). In the late twentieth century, programs such as Outward Bound (which provides opportunities for urban Americans to experience wilderness) and urban sporting programs extended these arguments. As C. L. Cole has shown, the privately operated urban programs of the 1990s characterized sport as able to transform inner city "at-risk" youth into productive adult citizens (Cole 1996). Terkelson's justification of the Eco-Challenge® thus evoked a clichéd and racialized discourse of social uplift, which in this case could be enacted through watching televisual images of teams of motivated white people caring for the environment and challenging themselves in nature.

Throughout the fray, however, very little attention was paid to the bodies that would actually be represented on MTV. The field of competitors was made up of approximately sixty teams of five, hailing mostly from the United States (although, according to my interviews, none were from Utah), but also from France, New Zealand, South Africa, Canada, and the United Kingdom. Rather than being made up of teenage boys pursuing gravity-induced thrills, most competitors were white people, mostly men, in their thirties and forties. One of the "characters" followed in the loosely constructed narrative was seventy-two-year-old Helen Kline—a compelling story, but not the demographic targeted by most MTV advertisers.[19]

The competitors were aware that there was environmental opposition to the race, but for the most part, they were as confused as Burnett by the hostility. In prerace footage, some claimed their event could cause no more harm than existing recreational uses of the backcountry. Again, however, it was not only the bodies in the desert but also the nationally broadcast spectacle that concerned environmentalists and the BLM, and attempts to regulate the event focused on both bodies and televisual representations. Of course, the ways that camera images are presented and the ways they are read have been neither manageable nor necessarily logically connected. Camera images can, and do, display as much as they conceal, and they can and do instill desire and evoke fantasy in excess of any intent in the image's production (Sturken 1997).

The Permit: Regulating Bodies and Images?

The FLMPA requires that producers of large-scale organized recreational events on public land must obtain permits from the BLM, who conducts an environmental assessment, and in the case of very new or very large events liable to generate a significant amount of impact, controversy, or interest, the BLM holds a public comment period. The local BLM office in Price, Utah, had never seen anything like the event proposed by Burnett and Terkelson and was certainly not prepared for the tenor of the opposition; they received over one thousand comment letters, more than on any other issue to date. Following procedure as usual, one lone employee was assigned to the environmental assessment and coordination of all the permits for movement across the variously categorized lands (e.g., BLM, national park, state park) of the three-hundred-mile race. Unsurprisingly, that one employee found herself utterly overwhelmed by the event, the corporate engine behind it, and the wave of opposition. I spoke with a person who was employed in the Price office in 1995, and she explained to me that "this was the first race [. . .] you see this on TV so much [now]. This was the first time this was done. We had no idea what extreme sports was here. You know, we do *backpacking*! [. . .] We didn't have ropes between our canyons and these free-rappels like that [referring to the extensive ropes section of the race]. We didn't have any knowledge of what could be. You know, we're here in a small community. These things don't happen here [laughter]!"[20]

Of course, *Eco-Challenge®* did receive their permit; the smallness of the place and its economic exigencies ensured that outcome. But the BLM made several changes and restrictions. For example, rather than allow the racers to find their routes across the desert, the BLM stipulated that the course follow existing roads and trails, steered the race away from WSAs, and even marked off-trail areas containing fragile cryptobiotic soils (thereby removing some of the "adventure" by removing some of the freedom for teams to find their own route).

Moreover, the BLM made several stipulations upon how southern Utah could be represented. Centrally, in order to protect specific spots from overuse, they asked *Eco-Challenge®* to eliminate any reference to specific locations and prohibited them from showing maps of the course in the television production. The producers were further required to incorporate a minimum-impact message into the program and to produce public service announcements with environmental messages for MTV. When I asked a BLM employee what she thought of the MTV broadcast, she acknowledged the futility of trying to allow, but control, the representation: "We were very, very upset because they promised to do these public service announcements about the environment, and we didn't think they did a very good job [. . . But] MTV is not the greatest medium to talk about environmental sensitivity in the desert and all [. . .] it could have been done better, but that wasn't the idea. It wasn't to do an environmental education show!"[21]

There was, however, one point in the MTV broadcast when the environmental controversy actually surfaced into the narrative, and it coincided with the closest thing to a low-impact message in the program. One stipulation made by the BLM in the permit was that teams carry out all waste, including human waste. Indeed, the BLM had reason to be concerned about human waste. Garbage and other kinds of waste left by the growing numbers of mountain bikers, river runners, and climbers camped out on BLM land had become an overwhelming problem and created some disgusting situations near popular trailheads and along the Colorado River. Yet it seemed somewhat inconsistent to some of the racers that they had to carry out their own waste while they traveled through areas scattered with cow dung. At one point in the broadcast, Burnett pointed theatrically and humorlessly to a plastic bag filled with something dark and, in an irritated tone, said, "They brought their human waste out. The whole team went in one bag. It doesn't look very nice, but they're just following the ecological rules. The land is not being hurt at all" (Byrnes and Sears 1995). Burnett's tone and his insistence that the land was actually remaining untouched while approximately three hundred athletes, support crews, and camera crews traveled across it point to the cynicism with which he approached the environmental concerns of the communities and the requirements to spread a low-impact message in his broadcast.

Moreover, the problems produced where human bodies and cow bodies came together in this desert event corporeally challenged the notion that self-sufficient travelers were racing through a pristine wilderness. The main source of physical distress during the race was diarrhea and dehydration due to the lack of clean water along the course. The BLM employee told me "People were becoming dehydrated because they would look at their maps and see springs, so they would not carry sufficient water, thinking they could refill along the way. What they didn't realize, is that the springs around here are all "cowed-out" [and therefore, filled with bacteria and Giardia parasites]"[22]

She further said she drove along the course to supply water to teams that had run out because she did not want to see them die, a very real possibility with dehydration and heat. In the broadcast, cases of severe dehydration were exploited for their dramatic effect. Those who passed out or became critically ill because of it were able to provide tears and stories of physical and mental tribulation to move the narrative of adventure along, while the reason for the dehydration—polluted water—was never mentioned. The imagery crafted for television was consistent with prevailing frontier mythology, but not with the desert, its people, or its history.

Indeed, the attempt to manage how the desert landscape was represented—and even how it might be received—was certainly an impossible

charge that left both *Eco-Challenge®* and the BLM in an awkward situation. This was made clear in the way Burnett's language flip-flopped when
he spoke to the press. As an article in the *Los Angeles Times* put it, "faced
with the delicate task of promoting the race while downplaying its effects
on the land, the man behind it [. . .] Mark Burnett, refers to the race alter-
nately as 'a *Ben Hur* type of production' and as a 'low-impact, spiritual
experience with the power of nature'" (Clifford 1995, 3).

In the end, and despite the permit's stipulations, race producers did
whatever was necessary to get dramatic television footage in certain key
spots. As a case in point, of all the sports, locations, and traumas that made
up the Utah *Eco-Challenge®* television show, the "ropes" section was set
apart as a highlight and it became a major site of conflict. As a BLM representative explained it,

> [I] went out late one night with Brian [Terkelsen], and [. . .] they
> didn't tell us they were going to do this, but they had this 500-foot
> rappel on this incredible slick rock, and this TV camera on a huge
> bar that swung out to take these pictures of the free-rappelling.
> And then, they had a couple of Tyrolean [Traverses] for them to go
> across. It was a real spider web of ropes. But they got a lot of people
> mad because they put the anchors [to secure the ropes] into the
> route where the Wilderness Study Area was. And then at the very
> end, they rappelled down into an [Anasazi] archeological site. That
> was a real point of contention [. . .] And they'd change things [. . .]
> If it wasn't good for the TV set-up, they would change it so it would
> be good. They weren't interested in their contestants, they were
> interested in great shots [. . .] They weren't interested in the bound-
> ary of the WSA or not WSA, or the fact that we said no anchors. If
> they needed a solid anchor there, they'd drill it.[23]

Certainly, humans dangling from three-thousand-foot sandstone cliffs
provide reliably dramatic television images and are crucial for creating
a sense of excitement in long-distance events like the Eco-Challenge®
(see Figure 7.2).

Most of any long-distance event like an adventure race is composed
simply of people moving from one point to another. Following conventions of adventure and travel literature, these visually boring sections
need to be hidden in the final cut and exciting promontory images strung

Figure 7.2. Bureau of Land Management photograph of Eco-Challenge® rappel with television camera equipment in 1995.

together by narration, individual stories, scenic landscape shots, and emotional music. Thus *Eco-Challenge®* needed the ropes section, along with the means of filming it, and in order to do this, they had to ignore the stipulations of the permit. Predictably, the ropes section became a symbol for the opposition because it demonstrated how a company with corporate connections, motivated by publicity and willfully ignorant of local debates and values, can and will do anything to get the "best shot."

Nonetheless, environmental activists attempted to insert their criticisms of the dangers of corporate recreation into the camera images by staging a protest at the race start with signs and banners that read,

"DESERT NOT DISNEYLAND," and "Wild Places are not for Races." One intrepid protestor climbed out onto the ledge of the cliff at the top of the ropes section and hung a banner denouncing corporate greed. Unsurprisingly, this protestor was arrested, and all protests were easily edited out of the final production, in which the land was ultimately represented as almost entirely empty and uncontested.

Did *Eco-Challenge*® Matter?

In 2004, when I interviewed people who were directly involved with various aspects of the 1995 Eco-Challenge® in southern Utah, including those organizations that either protested or managed it, many of them seemed puzzled at my interest. While some remained opposed passionately to the event and others like it, many had only vague memories of it, and some had never heard of it. After all, the event had occurred a decade earlier, and in the years since, adventure races and similar events such as twenty-four-hour mountain bike races had become common in southern Utah. At the same time, the use of all-terrain vehicles for recreation had escalated, and this was the primary concern of most of the folks with whom I spoke; in contrast, the Eco-Challenge® seemed almost quaint.

In fact, the MTV broadcast of the 1995 Eco-Challenge® went off with hardly a notice. It was a ninety-minute special that, in the end, fell far short of Burnett's vision of an epic production. The producers drew on the fragmented and dynamic MTV style, using frequent jump cuts between close-up and landscape, and the narrative was consequently subsumed under the visual and aural style. In many ways, the MTV production felt like music videos strung together to create a loose narrative of the competition; most of the show consisted of popular rock music playing over scenes of people walking, riding, and rafting through the southern Utah desert. There was very little backstory of the athletes or teams, aside from a handful of segments in which telegenic female competitors were interviewed, and segments focused on individual tribulations. The host of the program, professional surfer Peter King, appeared frequently in between segments that were sometimes broken by a change in "discipline" (e.g., mountain biking, ropes) and sometimes broken by stories of suffering—dehydration, sleep deprivation, and extreme temperatures. The flippant tone struck by King's narration and the style of the program contradicted any meaningful associations with epic journeys with which the program seemed to have begun. In the end, neither Burnett nor MTV was all too happy with the final product and Burnett quickly moved his ecospectacle—first to the Discovery Channel, then to the USA Network. The MTV broadcast hardly made a cultural ripple. But this event was, of course, only the beginning.[24]

Frustrated with the hassles caused by protestors and permitting processes, Burnett took his race, designed to appeal to an American market, out of the United States and into ever more distant locations with ever more foreign-seeming names and landscapes.[25] Regardless of where the race was staged, he continued to utilize and intensify frontier tropes, visually opening the world to American viewers' dreams of fulfillment through encounters with pristine and primitive places. In many ways, *Eco-Challenge*®, as the forerunner of *Survivor*, brought the entire globe to late twentieth-century "American" television, producing it as symbolically available for colonial dreams, freedom of mobility, and life-affirming recreation (especially for very fit, mostly white bodies from the overdeveloped world). As in *Survivor*, Burnett's army of camera crews, editing teams, and production teams were effectively able, under his artistic vision, to transform sites of local residences, government regulations, and historical tensions into landscapes of urgency and self-actualization (compare Tsing 2001).

Concluding Thoughts

I have sought to show how a remote corner of the Southwest United States has been repeatedly emptied and made wild in order to fulfill the aspirations and protect the nation-making dreams of personal freedom for a few. Images of the landscape as boundless and transcendently empty, which became a hallmark of American landscape painting early in the nineteenth century, served to advertise the promises of the nation's expansion as they invited the nation's subjects to participate in that expansion (Aikin 2000; Barringer 2002). Televisual representations of robust adventure athletes reproduced the chimerical emptied spaces and mobile bodies of frontier narratives through a late twentieth-century lens, which venerates neoliberal individualism and global mobility (see also Barnes 2009).

In the end, however, does it matter that culturally compelling adventure narratives continue to rely on colonial and frontier tropes that empty landscapes and wilderness spaces for their narrative and emotional effects? I have argued in this chapter that it does matter because of the nationally symbolic value of the empty frontier, which has long been seen to ensure individual freedom and pure democracy, even while it has enabled a severe form of oversight, that is, the visual and (brutally) material emptying of frontier spaces in order to protect an exclusive (and elusive) promise of freedom. The tensions that erupted over the 1995 Eco-Challenge® were at least partially rooted in problematic, proprietary, and racialized notions of territory, untenable imaginings of wilderness as uninhabited and empty, and related contradictory views of freedom, all profoundly shaped by the enduring significance of frontier mythologies.

If U.S. national identity can continue to be produced and reproduced through a narrative nexus of frontier landscapes and mobile subjects that requires existing inhabitants and contested claims over land and life be erased, the nation can continue to see itself as exceptional and benevolent in its expansion. When productions conform to frontier tropes (which admittedly enable instant recognition and narrative power), they also invoke the innocent mobility associated with nation-making frontier narratives. Historian Patricia Nelson Limerick has shown how *innocence* was a persistent value of white America that undergirded the westward expansion, and I contend that it remains a powerful national value in expansionist actions of the United States and its subjects, including global economic, trade, military, and travel practices (Limerick 1987). Images of innocent mobility in wilderness spaces are able, in effect, to transcend fraught histories of colonial expansion, as the adventurers are represented as the "good" kind of traveler, able to travel without harming landscapes or cultures. Indeed, what could be more innocent than recreation in apparently empty spaces?

At the same time, if "frontier wilderness" is going to continue to operate as a powerful metaphor through which nationally specific notions of democracy and freedom are envisioned, could it be figured as more than a backdrop for human ambition; as a space or entity that, like democracy, has deep and troubling histories that require both contention and diversity? Some scholars and poets have already called for this sort of reimagination of nature. For example, Gloria Anzaldúa, William Cronon, Donna Haraway, José David Saldívar, and Terry Tempest Willams have offered inspired reimaginings of the necessarily fraught histories of people, nations, and nature. Terry Tempest Williams lives in, and writes from, Castle Valley, Utah, which is located just outside of Moab. In between the March 2003 U.S. invasion of Iraq and the 2004 presidential elections (the same historical moment in which *U.S. News* published its homage to

U.S. exceptionalism), she wrote a series of essays on questions of space, risk, and democracy (Williams 2004). These essays argued for a populist vision of democracy rooted in deep connections to place and community and, in many ways, echoed historically entrenched notions of wilderness as emblematic of nationalistic values: she even recalled the intimate relationship between open spaces and democratic institutions that patriots since Frederick Jackson Turner have noted.

Williams, however, imagined wilderness as an "open space of democracy" in very different terms than did Turner, or Burnett in his grotesque *Eco-Challenge®* productions. For her, "open space" provides a metaphorical and material public space[26] that might inspire a multicultural democratic practice that requires public involvement but does not require people to agree with, or even necessarily like, each other but nonetheless listen:

> We are nothing but whiners if we are not willing to put our concerns and convictions on the line with a willingness to honestly listen and learn something beyond our own assumptions [. . .]
>
> To commit to the open space of democracy is to begin to make room for conversations that can move us toward a personal diplomacy. By personal diplomacy, I mean a flesh-and-blood encounter with public process . . . It's not altogether pleasant and there is no guarantee as to the outcome [. . .]. (Williams 2004, 22–24)

Williams's work allows me to cautiously consider that a historicized view of wilderness—one that also takes seriously the liveliness of its non-human elements—could make the claims to innocence, "right" of use, and ownership that infuse practices of wilderness travel less plausible.

Although the kind of "wilderness adventure experience" that became widely valued late in the twentieth century was formed through taken-for-granted narratives of the emptiness and innocence of nature and nation, perhaps there remains the possibility for human–nature narratives that do not erase historical complexity or conflict and thus enable the imagination of more than individual self-improvement and enrichment.

Notes

I wish to extend my most sincere thanks to all the members of the Making the Nation research group—particularly to Macarena Gómez-Barris and Herman Gray, as well as to Eric Chesmar, Jen Reck, and Clare Sears for countless helpful conversations and suggestions on this chapter. All errors are, of course, my responsibility.

1. Eco-Challenge®: The Expedition Race™ and its television coverage were Burnett's first foray into television. "Eco-Challenge" is unsurprisingly copyrighted as a brand name, but Burnett also trademarked the term "Expedition Race" prior to the 1999 Eco-Challenge®, held in Morocco. I faithfully include the trademark and copyright symbols when writing the name of the event as a critique of this appropriation of language for the production of wealth.

2. See also Gómez-Barris, Naono, and Musikawong in this volume for useful discussions of the importance of national memory in producing national identities.

3. This "co-ed" innovation has persisted throughout the short history of adventure racing, though not without contention (and, unsurprisingly, it usually means exactly one woman per team; e.g., Kay and Laberge 2004).

4. Fusil was supposed to supply consulting, but Burnett and Fusil clashed over ownership rights, and their relationship was settled, for good, in court.

5. A European colonial narrative, such as *Lawrence of Arabia*, could never be staged on "home" soil, and this is, perhaps, a defining feature of U.S. imperialism and the reason that the United States has for so long been able to cast itself as exceptional and benevolent in its expansion, even while its movement across the continent and beyond certainly qualifies as violent and exploitative as any imperial encroachment (Kaplan 1993; Stoler 2006).

6. Historian Frederick Jackson Turner famously articulated this nostalgia in his 1893 frontier thesis, in which he argued that it was the wilderness—the "free land"—of the American frontier that fundamentally altered the European colonist to create a land and a people truly new and unique by forcing the colonist to adapt, and he worried that this unique national quality was being lost (Turner 1986, 1–38).

7. John Ford westerns shot in Monument Valley and the Moab and Kanab, Utah, area include *Stagecoach* (1939), *My Darling Clementine* (1946), *Fort Apache* (1948), *She Wore a Yellow Ribbon* (1949), *Wagon Master* (1949), *Rio Grande* (1950), *The Searchers* (1956), *Sergeant Rutledge* (1960), and *Cheyenne Autumn* (1964). More recently, films such as *Indiana Jones and the Last Crusade* (Stephen Spielberg, 1989), *Thelma and Louise* (Ridley Scott, 1991) and *City Slickers II: The Legend of Curly's Gold* (Paul Weiland, 1994) were shot in the region.

8. The rugged, contemplative masculinity of the "Marlboro Man" image was updated in 1992 when an "extreme" version—the Marlboro Adventure Team (MAT)—was launched in U.S. and international markets.

9. This phrase in the heading to this section is used by Bette Stanton as the title of her Moab film history. She attributes it to John Wayne, as part of a longer quote: "TV you can make on the backlot, but for the big screen, for the real outdoor dramas, you have to do it where God put the West [...] and there is no better

example of this than around Moab [one of the largest, and most visited, towns of
the region]" (Stanton and Canyonlands Natural History Association 2003, 1).

Because of the relative lack of human development in the region, the
International Dark-Sky Association recently named Natural Bridges National
Monument in southeastern Utah the first International Dark Sky Park (see Inter-
national Dark-Sky Association n.d.).

10. It was in a slot canyon in southeastern Utah where climber Aaron Ralston
was trapped in 2003 when a boulder pinned his forearm to the side of the canyon
wall. After surviving five days in that situation, and knowing that no one would
happen by, he chose to use his dull multitool knife to sever the lower portion of
his right arm, rather than die of dehydration (Ralston 2004).

11. Arches was made into a national monument in 1929 by Herbert Hoover,
and Richard Nixon made it a national park in 1971; Canyonlands was made a
national park by Lyndon Johnson in 1964.

12. Abbey's two most influential works in this regard are *Desert Solitaire: A
Season in the Wilderness* (1968) and *The Monkey Wrench Gang* (1975). *The Monkey
Wrench Gang* is a novel about four ecologically minded and socially disgruntled
characters who sabotaged development projects, including the Glenn Canyon
Dam. The novel is credited with inspiring the formation of a radical contingent
of environmental activists, and with coining the verb term "to monkey wrench,"
meaning to sabotage.

13. Telephone interview with founding member of SUWA, November 28,
2005. I conducted interviews with members and employees of SUWA, employees
of the BLM, independent environmental advocates, former mine employees, and
tourism advocates in southern Utah, in person and by telephone, from 2004 to
2005. All interviews were conducted in confidentiality, and the names are with-
held by mutual agreement.

14. The 1964 Wilderness Act defines wilderness as "an area where the earth and
its community of life are untrammeled by man, where man himself is a visitor
who does not remain [. . .] an area of underdeveloped Federal land retaining its
primeval character and influence, without permanent improvements or human
habitation, which is protected and managed so as to preserve its natural conditions and which (1) generally appears to have been affected primarily by the forces
of nature [. . .] (2) has outstanding opportunities for solitude or a primitive and
unconfined type of recreation; (3) has at least five thousand acres of land [. . .]
(4) may also contain ecological, geological, or other features of scientific, educational, scenic, or historical value" (Wilderness Act 1964).

15. Telephone interview with former mine employee, November 27, 2005.

16. Slickrock was the name given to Navajo Sandstone by white settlers whose
metal-shoed horses and metal-rimmed wagon wheels slipped on the smooth
rock surfaces. Rubber, however, sticks to the sandstone and motorcyclists and

mountain bikers found an amazing outdoor playground on the distinctive geological formations. The Slickrock Trail, just east of the town of Moab, is among the most well-known mountain-biking destinations in the world.

17. Interview conducted in southern Utah, November 20, 2004.

18. Ibid.

19. After the broadcast, MTV asked Burnett to ensure that all competitors would be between eighteen and twenty-five years old in future broadcasts, but future broadcasts on MTV never happened because Burnett moved the race to The Discovery Channel in 1996.

20. Interview conducted in Price, Utah, December 23, 2004.

21. Ibid.

22. Ibid.

23. In mountain climbing, "anchors" are metal bolts drilled or hammered into rock in order to fix the rappel ropes, enabling them to bear the weight of the athletes using them. A Tyrolean Traverse is a mountaineering maneuver that entails traveling between two high points on ropes stretched tight between them.

24. It was only the beginning for Burnett's television productions, as well as for adventure racing in the United States. The brouhaha over *Eco-Challenge's®* permit continues to resonate for race directors who want to stage races virtually anywhere in the United States, as they continue to encounter environmental opposition. Directors I spoke with have come up with various ways to address these problems. For example, a director in Texas avoids public lands altogether and stages his races on the abundant private ranch land after obtaining permission from landowners. A race director in California, on the other hand, hired an environmental lawyer and conducted studies to demonstrate the low level of impact adventure races have on the environment. She also suggested that her race organization was planning to present their results to Congress in order to get the permitting process simplified and standardized.

25. In interviews conducted from 2003 to 2005 in Salt Lake City, Utah, Mountain View, California, and South Lake Tahoe, California, I was told by two separate American adventure-race directors and a former *Eco-Challenge®* production employee that permitting hassles were the reason Burnett stopped holding the race in the United States.

26. Williams's notion of open space is somewhat similar to Habermas's articulation of the public sphere (Habermas 1989; Kellner n.d.). However, unlike Habermas, Williams does not assume the fairness or democracy of the public sphere but recognizes that if it is to work as a space of democracy, then it will take conscious effort to ensure the inclusion of a diverse array of voices.

Works Cited

Abbey, Edward. 1968. *Desert Solitaire: A Season in the Wilderness.* New York: McGraw-Hill.

———. 1975. *The Monkey Wrench Gang.* Philadelphia: Lippincott, Williams, and Wilkins.

Aikin, Roger Cushing. 2000. "Paintings of Manifest Destiny: Mapping the Nation." *American Art* 14 (3): 78–89.

Anderson, Benedict. 1991. *Imagined Communities: Reflections on the Origin and Spread of Nationalism.* Rev. and extended ed. London: Verso.

Banet-Weiser, Sarah. 1999. *The Most Beautiful Girl in the World: Beauty Pageants and National Identity.* Berkeley: University of California Press.

Barnes, Barbara. 2009. "'Everybody Wants to Pioneer Something Out Here': Contested Meanings of Landscape and Adventure in the American Southwest." *Journal of Sport and Social Issues* 33 (3): 230–56.

Barone, Michael. 2004. "A Place Like No Other." *U.S. News and World Report,* June 28, 38–39.

Barringer, Tim. 2002. "The Course of Empires: Landscape and Identity in America and Britain, 1820–1880." In *American Sublime: Landscape Painting in the United States 1820–1880,* ed. Andrew Wilton and Tim Barringer, 38–65. Princeton, N.J.: Princeton University Press.

Bederman, Gail. 1995. *Manliness and Civilization: A Cultural History of Gender and Race in the United States, 1880–1917.* Chicago: University of Chicago Press.

Berlant, Lauren Gail. 1991. *The Anatomy of National Fantasy: Hawthorne, Utopia, and Everyday Life.* Chicago: University of Chicago Press.

———. 1997. *The Queen of America Goes to Washington City: Essays on Sex and Citizenship.* Durham, N.C.: Duke University Press.

Burnett, Mark. 1994. Competitor communication, October. Records available through the Federal Bureau of Land Management.

———. 2001. *Dare to Succeed: How to Survive and Thrive in the Game of Life.* New York: Hyperion.

———. 2005. *Jump In! Even If You Don't Know How to Swim.* New York: Ballantine Books.

Byrnes, Patrick, and Mike Sears. 1995. *Eco-Challenge: Utah.* 50 minutes. MTV.

Clifford, Frank. 1995. "Fears Grow over Wilderness Race." *Los Angeles Times,* January 23, A3, A19.

Cole, C. L. 1996. "American Jordon: P.L.A.Y., Consensus, and Punishment. *Sociology of Sport Journal* 13 (4): 366–97.

Cronon, William. 1996. "The Trouble with Wilderness: Or, Getting Back to the Wrong Nature." In *Uncommon Ground: Rethinking the Human Place in Nature,* ed. William Cronon, 69–90. New York: W. W. Norton & Co.

Delaney, Robert W. 1974. *The Southern Ute People*. Ed. John I. Griffin. Phoenix, Ariz.: Indian Tribal Series.

Doanne, Mary Ann. 1990. "Information, Crisis, Catastrophe." In *Logics of Television: Essays in Cultural Criticism*, ed. Patricia Melloncamp, 222–39. Bloomington: Indiana University Press.

Dugard, Martin. 2000. *Surviving the Most Difficult Race on Earth*. Duluth, Minn.: Ragged Mountain Press.

Eley, Geoff, and Ronald Gigor Suny. 1996. "Introduction: From the Moment of Social History to the Work of Cultural Representation." In *Becoming National*, ed. Geoff Eley and Ronald Gigor Suny, 3–37. New York: Oxford University Press.

Feuer, Jane. 1983. "The Concept of Live Television: Ontology as Ideology." In *Regarding Television*, ed. E. Ann Kaplan, 12–21. Frederick, Md.: University Publications of America.

Firmage, Richard, A. 1996. *A History of Grand County*. Ed. Allan Kent Powell and Craig Fuller. Salt Lake City: Utah State Historical Society.

Foucault, Michel. 1970. *The Order of Things: An Archeology of the Human Sciences*. New York: Vintage.

———. 1972. *The Archeology of Language and the Discourse on Language*. Trans. A. M. Sheridan Smith. New York: Pantheon.

———. 1997. *"Society Must Be Defended": Lectures at the Collège De France, 1975–1976*. Trans. David Macey. New York: Picador.

Fusil, Gerard. 2001. "Gerard Fusil, in His Own Words. . . ." In *The Complete Guide to Adventure Racing*, ed. Don Mann and Kara Schaad, 15. New York: Hatherleigh Press.

Gorrell, Mike. 1994. "Critics Fear 300-Mile Race Could Scar Environment." *The Salt Lake Tribune*, December 2, D1, D4.

Gray, Herman. 2005. *Cultural Moves: African Americans and the Politics of Representation*. Berkeley: University of California Press.

Habermas, Jürgen. 1989. *The Structural Transformation of the Public Sphere: An Inquiry into a Category of Bourgeois Society, Studies in Contemporary German Social Thought*. Cambridge, Mass.: MIT Press.

Haraway, Donna Jeanne. 1989. *Primate Visions: Gender, Race, and Nature in the World of Modern Science*. New York: Routledge.

Hausladen, Gary. 2003. *Western Places, American Myths: How We Think about the West*. Reno: University of Nevada Press.

Haynes, Roslynn. 2003. "From Habitat to Wilderness: Tasmania's Role in the Politicising of Place." In *Disputed Territories: Land, Culture and Identity in Settler Societies*, ed. David Trigger and Gareth Griffiths, 81–107. Hong Kong: Hong Kong University Press.

International Dark-Sky Association. n.d. "International Dark Sky Parks." http://www.darksky.org/mc/page.do?sitePageId=59827 (accessed May 4, 2010).

Kaplan, Amy. 1993. "'Left Alone with America': The Absence of Empire in the Study of American Culture." In *Cultures of United States Imperialism*, ed. Amy Kaplan and Donald E. Pease, 3–21. Durham, N.C.: Duke University Press.

———. 2002. *The Anarchy of Empire in the Making of U.S. Culture*. Cambridge, Mass.: Harvard University Press.

Kay, Joanne, and Suzanne Laberge. 2004. "'Mandatory Equipment': Women in Adventure Racing." In *Understanding Lifestyle Sports: Consumption, Identity and Difference*, ed. B. Wheaton, 154–74. London: Routledge.

Kellner, Douglas. n.d. "Habermas, the Public Sphere, and Democracy: A Critical Intervention." http://www.gseis.ucla.edu/faculty/kellner/2009_essays.html (accessed May 4, 2010).

Lean, David (Dir.). 1962. *Lawrence of Arabia*, DVD. Burbank, CA: Columbia Tristar Home Video, 2001.

———. 1984. *A Passage to India*, VHS. Burbank, CA: RCA/Columbia Pictures Home Video, 1985.

Limerick, Patricia Nelson. 1987. *The Legacy of Conquest: The Unbroken Past of the American West*. New York: Norton.

Martin, Emily. 1994. *Flexible Bodies: Tracking Immunity in American Culture from the Days of Polio to the Age of Aids*. Boston: Beacon Press.

Matsumoto, Valerie J., and Blake Allmendinger, ed. 1999. *Over the Edge: Remapping the American West*. Berkeley: University of California Press.

McClintock, Anne. 1995. *Imperial Leather: Race, Gender, and Sexuality in the Colonial Conquest*. New York: Routledge.

Nash, Roderick. 2001. *Wilderness and the American Mind*. 4th ed. New Haven, Conn.: Yale University Press.

Neumann, Mark. 2002. "Making the Scene: The Poetics and Performances of Displacement at the Grand Canyon." In *Tourism: Between Place and Performance*, ed. Simon Colman and Mike Crang, 38–53. New York: Berghahn Books.

Ong, Aihwa. 2005. "(Re)Articulations of Citizenship." *PS, political science & politics* 38 (4): 697–99.

Paterson, Derek, and Steve Gurney. 1999. *Adventure Racing Guide to Survival: Techniques, Planning and Skills*. N.p.: Sporting Endeavors.

Porter, Eliot, and David Ross Brower. 1963. *The Place No One Knew: Glen Canyon on the Colorado*. San Francisco: Sierra Club.

Pratt, Mary Louise. 1992. *Imperial Eyes: Travel Writing and Transculturation*. New York: Routledge.

Price, Patricia L. 2004. *Dry Place: Landscapes of Belonging and Exclusion*. Minneapolis: University of Minnesota Press.

Ralston, Aaron. 2004. *Between a Rock and a Hard Place*. New York: Atria Books.

Ringholz, Raye Carleson. 2002. *Uranium Frenzy: Saga of the Nuclear West*. Rev. and expanded ed. Logan: Utah State University Press.

Roosevelt, Theodore. 1888. "Frontier Types." *Century Illustrated Magazine* 36 (6): 831–44.

———. 1890. "'Professionalism' in Sports." *North American Review* 151:187–91.

———. 1899. *The Strenuous Life.* New York: The Century Co.

Rose, Nikolas. 1999. *Powers of Freedom: Reframing Political Thought.* Cambridge: Cambridge University Press.

Roush, Jon. 1995. "Freedom and Responsibility: What We Can Learn from the Wise Use Movement." In *Let the People Judge: Wise Use and the Property Rights Movement,* ed. John Echeverria and Raymond Booth Eby, 1–10. Washington, D.C.: Island Press.

Said, Edward W. 1994. *Orientalism.* New York: Vintage Books.

Sears, John F. 1989. *Sacred Places: American Tourist Attractions in the Nineteenth Century.* Amherst: University of Massachusetts Press.

Shaffer, Marguerite S. 2001. *See America First: Tourism and National Identity, 1880–1940.* Washington, D.C.: Smithsonian Institution Press.

Shohat, Ella, and Robert Stam. 1994. *Unthinking Eurocentrism: Multiculturalism and the Media.* London: Routledge.

Southern Utah Wilderness Alliance (SUWA). 1995. "Eco-Circus." *Southern Utah Wilderness Alliance Newsletter* 12 (Spring): 12.

Spence, Mark David. 1999. *Dispossessing the Wilderness: Indian Removal and the Making of the National Park.* New York: Oxford University Press.

Stanton, Bette L., and Canyonlands Natural History Association. 2003. *Where God Put the West: Movie Making in the Desert: A Moab-Monument Valley Movie History.* 2nd ed. Moab, Utah: Canyonlands Natural History Association.

Stiles, Jim. 1999. "The Most Tumultuous Decade." *Canyon Country Zephyr,* April–May, 19–24.

Stoler, Ann Laura. 1995. *Race and the Education of Desire: Foucault's History of Sexuality and the Colonial Order of Things.* Durham, N.C.: Duke University Press.

———. 2006. "Tense and Tender Ties: The Politics of Comparison in North American History and (Post)Colonial Studies." In *Haunted by Empire: Geographies of Intimacy in North America History,* ed. Ann Laura Stoler, 23–67. Durham, N.C.: Duke University Press.

Sturken, Marita. 1997. *Tangled Memories: The Vietnam War, the AIDS Epidemic, and the Politics of Remembering.* Berkeley: University of California Press.

Thoreau, Henry David. 1862. "Walking." In *Essays: English and American,* 28. The Harvard Classics. New York: P. F. Collier & Son, 1909–14. *Bartleby.com.* http://www.bartleby.com/28/15.html (accessed May 4, 2010).

Tsing, Anna Lowenhaupt. 2001. "Inside the Economy of Appearances." In *Globalization,* ed. A. Appadurai, 155–88. Durham, N.C.: Duke University Press.

Tuan, Yi-Fu. 1974. *Topophilia: A Study of Environmental Perception, Attitudes, and Values.* Englewood Cliffs, N.J.: Prentice Hall.

Turner, Frederick Jackson. 1986. "The Significance of the Frontier in American History." In *The Frontier in American History*, 1–38. Tucson: University of Arizona Press.

Viehman, John. 1995. "A Choice, Not a Challenge: Does an Endurance Race Belong in the Backcountry?" *Backpacker*, April, 7–8.

White, Richard, Patricia Nelson Limerick, and James R. Grossman. 1994. *The Frontier in American Culture: An Exhibition at the Newberry Library, August 26, 1994–January 7, 1995.* Berkeley: University of California Press.

Weigle, Marta. 1992. "Exposition and Meditation: Mary Colter, Erna Fergusson, and the Santa Fe/Harvey Popularization of the Native Southwest, 1902–1940." *Frontiers: A Journal of Women's Studies* 12 (3): 117–50.

Wilderness Act. 1964. Public Law 88-577. *16 U.S. Code 1131–1136.* § 1.

Williams, Florence. 1994. "A Passive Town in Utah Awaits Its Fate." In *Discovered Country: Tourism and Survival in the American West,* ed. Scott Norris, 40–44. Albuquerque, N.Mex: Stone Ladder Press.

Williams, Raymond. 1974. *Television: Technology and Cultural Form.* New York: Schocken Books.

Williams, Terry Tempest. 2004. *The Open Space of Democracy.* Great Barrington, Mass.: Orion Society.

· III ·

Managing and Reconciling Memory

CHAPTER 8

Drinking the Nation and Making Masculinity

Tequila, Pancho Villa, and the U.S. Media

Marie Sarita Gaytán

I N THE INTRODUCTION TO *Heaven, Earth, Tequila: Un viaje al cora-zón de México* (A trip to the heart of Mexico), author Douglas Menuez declares, "Tequila makes a man confess even the most profound reaches of his machismo" (2005, 1). Like other coffee table books on the subject, its striking photographs and fawning prose associate tequila with idealized aspects of manhood and describe it as a central element of Mexico's spiritual landscape. An award-winning writer and journalist, Menuez explains that although the book "started as a quest to explore the mysterious traditions from which tequila was born [. . .] it offers the reader something more—the intense pride and passion of the Mexican people [. . .]" (1). Visualizing Mexico's "national drink" through a nostalgic and timeless lens, the author's perspective is only one of many that are produced, circulated, and consumed within global popular culture. For instance, in contrast to inspiring notions of collectivity and patriotism, in the United States, tequila is more likely to conjure images of wild parties, excessive drinking, and heavy hangovers. Reflecting its close ties to intemperance and abandon, posters, T-shirts, and bumper stickers proclaim, "One tequila, two tequila, three tequila, floor!" and "Lick it, slam it, suck it!" Television and film also commemorate tequila's role in narratives of overindulgence and pleasure, as reality programming like *Girls Gone Wild* and *The Real Cancun* document its centrality in the highly sexualized exploits of spring-break revelry. While on the surface it may appear that these representations have little in common, I argue that they emerge from interrelated struggles that together shape and are shaped by the formation of national and social identities.

In this chapter, I analyze tequila as a contested terrain and unfinished signifier of Mexican identity by looking at historical relations within and between Mexico and the United States. Focusing on the years preceding and following the Mexican Revolution, I pay close attention to how structures of feeling (Williams 1975) operate across geopolitical borders. To this end, I consider the connections that link material culture and knowledge production by situating commodities as vital to the transmission of emotions and allegiances. By examining the trajectories of commodities and their consumption through a transnational perspective, I seek to add a critical piece to our understanding about the everyday production of identity, national belonging, and oppositional discourse. Therefore, instead of promoting the notion that there is something inherently special about tequila, I use it as an optic through which to observe how different struggles spill over onto traditional media spaces and play out in commercial, economic, and political realms. Because Mexicans experience themselves "as national through public sphere accounts of what is important about them," I engage cultural symbols and ordinary forms of communication that people use to express connections to one another (Berlant 1997, 10). National icons such as the charro (Mexican cowboy) and Pancho Villa, figures that, at first glance, seem to have only ancillary relationships to tequila, provide traces of its association with processes of racialization and resistance on both sides of the border. As a means of exploring these unexpected intersections, I examine song lyrics, tequila labels, and newspaper articles—multiple archives from varying time periods that shed light on the continuous interactions between material objects and social relations. With this in mind, I ask the following questions: How did tequila become so closely associated with expressions of Mexican commensality in Mexico? Why is it often related to notions of indulgence and vice in the United States? How do these social conditions together structure meanings about Mexican masculinity and national identity across borders?

Negotiating Mexican Nationalism

Early twentieth-century Mexico was marked by widespread concern regarding the progress of the nation. While the vast majority of the populace continued to suffer at the hands of Porfirio Díaz's dictatorial reign, politicians sought to implement innovative measures to support his regime and promote fiscal development. Central to these discussions were the ideas of positivist writers such as Herbert Spencer and Charles Darwin. Relying on the strict application of scientific method, positivists maintained that societies, much like animal species, were subject to the laws of evolution. According to this formulation, only "those societies that adapted to their historical circumstances, human resources, and material necessities survived and progressed" (Benjamin and Ocasio-Melendez 1984, 328). *Científicos* (positivist public intellectuals) such as Justo Sierra published works that praised President Díaz's positivist path and called for the continued incorporation of European scientific principles and models of economic expansion. For writers such as Sierra, what Mexico needed, and found in Díaz, "was a strong and just ruler to build the economic foundation necessary for the true realization of liberty" (329).[1] The concept of race was central to the administration's quest for prosperity. Specifically, the mestizo, "the product of two races, two cultures, and two histories," was promoted as "the great unifier of ethnic, ideological, and class contradictions" (329). Positioning himself as representing the interests of *all* Mexicans, Porfirio Díaz heralded the mestizo as the prototype of Mexican progress. In reality, however, Indians and the rural masses were seen and treated as obstacles to modernization.

In the years following the Mexican Revolution, public intellectuals such as José Vasconcelos and artists like Diego Rivera, David Siqueiros, José Clemente Orozco, and Frida Kahlo sought to break free from the domination of European standards that characterized life under the dictatorship of Porfirio Díaz (a period known as the *Porfiriato*). Among the various intellectuals that contributed to the development of a more-inclusive collective conscience and the advancement of a renewed Mexican national identity was noted Mexican anthropologist Manuel Gamio. Interested in creating a Mexican nation based on a model of cultural integration, Gamio sought not to exclude indigenous cultures from the new approach to nationalism, but rather, like many anthropologists of that era, to promote social policy that would assimilate them into "mainstream" Mexican society.

The state-sponsored *indigenismo* movement endorsed by Gamio set out to create a more inclusive national identity. This controversial approach was criticized and praised—criticized because of its assimilative focus that promoted mestizo identity over indigenous identity—praised because it recognized and extolled Indian arts, crafts, and architecture. As Dawson (1998) described it, the movement "not only celebrated the ancient Indian past as the source of the Mexican nation, but also connected living Indians to that past, and acclaimed them for the first time as an integral part of the [. . .] nation" (280). However, in the end, Gamio's effort to create "a powerful patria and a coherent, defined nationality" failed to incorporate modern Indian social, political, or economic contributions (Gamio 1960, 177). As historian David Brading explained, "The all-important fact that contemporary Indians in Mexico preserved in their daily lives the essential configuration of pre-Hispanic civilization was not for Gamio a cause for national exaltation . . . but rather embodied an obstacle to *mestizaje*, and signified economic backwardness and cultural stagnation" (1988, 83). Although Gamio's approach had elements of equality, it was unable to break free from the traditional liberal ideology that Indians obstructed efforts aimed at forging a homogenous Mexican identity.

Manuel Gamio's attempt to establish a collective conscience that commemorated Mexico's indigenous past, while entangled in ideological inconsistencies pertaining to the indigenous present, reflected a major shift in Mexican nationalist thought. Widely regarded as "backward" under the Díaz regime, indigenous contributions were now celebrated in art, literature, music, and other aspects of Mexican cultural life. The concepts of *mestizaje* and *indigenismo* were commonly used by government officials to promote a new Mexican nationalism rooted in the idea of spiritual and racial homogeneity—a *raza cósmica* (cosmic race; Vasconcelos 1997) that would allow mestizos to "build a future society based on Latin civilizations" (González 2004, 143). The phrase of *"lo mexicano,"* a notion of self-awareness in which beliefs about racial equality were embedded into the foundation of nationalism, became equally popular during the postrevolutionary period. More broadly, *lo mexicano* was seen as an "authentic" expression of Mexican character that reflected the rise of a shared understanding that "transcend[ed] the nationalistic-cosmopolitan conflict in Mexican history" (Schmidt 1978, 165). Novelists were among the many intellectuals that aligned themselves with new literary forms that highlighted Mexico's revitalized nationalism. Often, story lines featured peasants and Indians as protagonists and emphasized their newly valued place in the nation.

Such is the case with Jaliscan-born writer Mariano Azuela's (1915) famous novel about the revolutionary movement, *Los de abajo* (The Underdogs). Considered the "quasi-official text of the revolution" and credited as the "first 'novel of the masses,'" *Los de abajo* is loosely based on Azuela's combat experiences during war (Parra 2005, 23–24). Starting off with honorable intentions, the central character, Demetrio Macías, together with a small band of revolutionaries, becomes corrupted by the war and loses his ideals. Standing in contrast to the literary norms of the *Porfiriato*, the story unromantically illustrates the brutal and self-serving conduct of the army. Described as "the organic intellectual of the revolutionary struggle," Macías is portrayed as having a preference for Mexican-origin products during a time when foreign goods were considered symbols of power and mobility (Parra 2005, 23–24). For instance, in one scene the narrator notes, "To champagne that sparkles and foams as the beaded bubbles burst at the brim of the glass, Demetrio preferred the native tequila, limpid and fiery" (84). Tim Mitchell (2004) explains that Demetrio Macías's partiality for tequila over champagne revealed "his purity of heart and st[ood] the Porfirian taste system on its head" (11). In the pages that follow, Macías's troops boast of the cruelty they inflict as they make their way through the houses and haciendas of the rich. Commenting on their plunder, Azuela writes, "Bottles of tequila, dishes of cut glass, bowls, porcelains, and vases lay scattered" (1963, 93). Littering the home of a wealthy family with tequila bottles suggests a figurative and literal assault against the upper classes, who favored cut glass, porcelains, and vases—affluent furnishings that were most likely imported. More important, however, it demonstrates how, as an emergent cultural symbol, tequila visually enabled the lower classes to convey their allegiance to the nation and to express their sentiments about pervading class inequalities. Therefore, tequila symbolically provided a means through which members of the lower classes could assert new national identities, marking their transition from disrespected citizens to acknowledged citizens.

Despite the emergence of figures, symbols, and expressions that were seen as embodying Mexican values and the new national identity, no one ideology or faction dominated the social or political sphere (Benjamin 2000). For example, while the *indigenismo* movement gained steadfast momentum, it never achieved complete hegemony. *Hispanistas*, or intellectuals and politicians who maintained that Spanish attributes (e.g., Catholic doctrines and the colonial system) were the "authentic genesis of the national spirit," continued to powerfully challenge *indigenistas* (Orozco 1998, 51). Fredrick Pike describes *hispanismo* as resting "on the conviction that through the course of history Spaniards have developed a life style and culture, a set of characteristics, of traditions and value judgments that render them distinct from other peoples" (1971, 307). In particular, they held that the population that best represented the ideals of *hispanismo* came from the tequila-producing region of Los Altos, in the state of Jalisco. As Orozco explains, "This proposition was bolstered through the creation and propagation of a region creation myth [. . .] in which racial and cultural contact between the Spaniards that colonized the region and Indians that inhabited it is minimized, controlled, and or excised" (Orozco 1998, 52). Rooted in the conviction that the Los Altos region was divinely inspired because of its spatial segregation from indigenous populations and supposed European genetic purity (a result of the effects of the Mixtón War [1540–42]), the myth of Alteño exceptionalism affirmed the region's symbolism as "a source of national redemption" amid the "racial dilemma" of postrevolutionary efforts to construct a homogeneous national identity (Orozco 1998, 53). According to Orozco, *hispanista* claims regarding the Los Altos region's ability to represent an "appropriate" Mexican identity failed to achieve widespread popular acceptance in the period immediately following the revolution. Specifically, he maintains that is was not until the advent of the Mexican movie and music industries (1930s–1950s) that Alteño exceptionalism, uniquely embodied as the image of the charro (Mexican cowboy), became fully integrated in the Mexican popular imaginary. While the Mexican media of this era contributed considerably to the production and diffusion of this image, anthropologist Olga Nájera-Ramírez's research on the charro and Mexican nationalism proposes that it was during the *Porfiriato* (1876–1911) that the charro emerged as an "invincible national hero" and "became thoroughly integrated with the ideas of manhood, nationhood, and power" (1994, 4). Thus, this suggests that elements of *hispanismo*, in general, and Alteño exceptionalism, in particular, were in circulation not only before the revolution but were also among the ideological discourses that survived and flourished in spite of it. In other words, while *indigenismo* did indeed become a popular force, we cannot dismiss the ongoing influence of *hispanismo* in the formation of Mexican nationalism during this period of time.

Cultural symbols (original and recycled) became increasingly important in the effort to reconstruct the image and psyche of the postrevolutionary period. As noted cultural theorist Carlos Monsiváis put it, "This was the great moment of Mexican nationalism, and in both natural and induced ways as many emblems and signals of national identity as possible were sought to parade" (1999, 15). Although Mexico had a long history of articulating its early history through female symbols (i.e., La Malinche and the Virgin of Guadalupe),[2] after the revolution, this phenomenon shifted, and male figures became more visible in order to accommodate the patriarchal impulses of modernization (Limón 1990). The momentum of modernity operated within the scope of a masculine agenda, or "national fantasy," in which male icons mapped the country's "glorious" past onto its "coherent" present (Berlant 1991). Specifically, the charro became a prototype used for "packaging and representing Mexican culture for public consumption both inside and outside of Mexico" (Nájera-Ramírez 1994, 6). According to Nájera-Ramírez, representations of the charro aligned with "the post-revolutionary romantic nationalist efforts to identify and promote traditional customs perceived as uniquely Mexican and to foster a sense of Mexican national unity and democratic ideals" (1994, 6).

Predating the professionalization of American rodeo, charros performed regularly on both sides of the border (Sands 1993). The establishment of charro associations (in Mexico and the American Southwest) and the promotion of *charrería* in American acts such as "Buffalo Bill's Wild West Show" helped standardize public perceptions of an idealized Mexican manhood. Charro associations outlined strict principles of behavior through an institutionalized code of ethics, stipulating that members were barred from partaking in disorderly conduct while in costume. Drinking and fighting were expressly prohibited because carrying a real gun was part of the charro regalia.[3] With the intention of encouraging responsibility and safety, the code of ethics "sought to protect the status and reputation of the charro as a positive representative of Mexico" (Nájera-Ramírez 1994, 6). Images of *lo mexicano* associated with the charro were also closely linked to romantic portrayals of hacienda life that emphasized traditional social roles (e.g., class, gender, sexuality, and race). While the charro was one example of a particular version of Mexican manliness and a symbol of "good" citizenship that was promoted locally and internationally, another icon also started to emerge during this period—one that stood in opposition to the state's representation of respectable Mexican manhood: the legendary revolutionary rebel General Francisco "Pancho" Villa.

Pancho Villa and the U.S. Media

A hired insurgent and charismatic leader, Pancho Villa exemplifies the legacy, imagery, and mystique associated with the Mexican Revolution. Described as "Mexico's *macho* hero *par excellence*" (Stevens 1965, 850), and the "Mexican Robin Hood" (Womack 2002, 27), Pancho Villa simultaneously represents the embodiment of machismo and a symbol of national pride (De la Mora 2006). Rising from poverty to fight the wealthy while advocating peasants' and workers' rights, Villa's commitment to social change evolved from a number of life experiences and crystallized during his participation in the revolution (Meyers 1991). In the years that followed the end of Porfirio Díaz's thirty-five-year dictatorship, Mexico, marked by a military coup, military regime, and presidential assassination, remained politically unstable. Dismayed by the lack of social progress and the amount of continued government corruption, Villa was concerned that the country's leaders were losing sight of the goals of the revolution. As he saw it, the election of President Venustiano Carranza in Mexico, and the American government's recognition of his presidency, was further evidence of worsening domestic and international political decisions. The final straw, however, occurred when the United States reneged on an arms deal with Villa. In response, on March 9, 1916, Villa led 1,500 troops across the U.S. border, killing seventeen Americans at Columbus, New Mexico. Villa and his army instigated the attack with the intention of severing U.S.–Mexican relations and bringing Carranza down (Katz 1998). However, the plan failed; the United States and Mexico did not break off relations, and Carranza remained in power. President Woodrow Wilson responded to the assault by sending ten thousand troops under the command of General John Pershing to locate Villa and his army. President Carranza also sent troops. Pursued by two different and well-equipped armies, Villa evaded arrest from both. After two U.S. Army expeditions failed to capture Villa, in 1920, the Mexican government accepted his surrender and retired him on a general's salary. In 1923 he was assassinated in Parral, Chihuahua.

By challenging the authority of the U.S. government and the Mexican establishment, Villa embodied resistance to exploitation and injustice on both sides of the border. The image of Pancho Villa contributed to the revitalized Mexican nationalism, one that was "accompanied by sentiments of distrust and inferiority towards foreigners, especially the United States" (Paredes 1967, 83). Immortalized in music and film, Pancho Villa became an emblem of Mexican national identity in Mexico and the United States. Mexican corridos (folk ballads) sung in northern Mexico and in the American Southwest commemorated his determination and ability to outsmart both the U.S. and Mexican armies. Hundreds of corridos were written about Villa, glorifying him as a hero of the common people of Mexico (Brandt 1964). One characteristic of these songs was the depiction of Pancho Villa in relation to alcohol. For example, in Miguel Lira's "Corrido de la muerte de Pancho Villa" (Ballad of the death of Pancho Villa).[4] Villa is described as having visited a cantina on the day of his assassination:

¡Pobre Pancho Villa . . . !
Iba dejando Parral
Saliendo de una cantina,
El valiente general
Autor de La Valentina
"Si porque me ves borracho
Mañana ya no me ves;
Si me han de matar mañana,
Que me maten de una vez . . ."
¡Pobre Pancho Villa . . . !

[Poor Pancho Villa!
As he was leaving Parral
Walking out of a cantina,
The brave general
Composer of La Valentina[5]
"If I look drunk to you it's because
Tomorrow you won't see me again;
If they're going to kill me tomorrow . . .
Let them kill me now once and for all . . ."
Poor Pancho Villa!]

Just above, Villa has a premonition of his death as he walks out of a cantina. In a confrontational tone, he proclaims, perhaps in earshot of his would-be assassins, or perhaps just to himself, "Let them kill me now once and for all . . ." At the end of the stanza, the lyrics remind listeners to lament the revolutionary leader's inevitable demise.

According to the eminent border scholar Américo Paredes, corridos are folk performances that communicate collective ideas and illustrate expressions of resistance. In particular, he maintains that corridos are dialogical responses to the conflict and tension of Anglo–Mexican border relations during the early part of the twentieth century (1963). In other words, many corridos of this time period contested dominant representations, among these, the consistent depiction of Mexican revolutionaries as bandits by the U.S. press (Flores, 1992). Corridos, therefore, often inverted U.S.-based meanings of Mexicans as "lazy, dirty, thieving, devious, conspiratorial, sexually hyperactive, and overly fond of alcohol" such that, depending on the listener, mentioning Pancho Villa's cavalier language and presence at a cantina could be interpreted as a playful appropriation of American stereotypes (Límon 1983, 217).

Movies in the United States and Mexico also documented Villa's rise as a symbol of Mexico's revolution and elevated the public status of army generals, populist figures, and reform-minded groups who participated in the revolutionary movement. Mexican films captured the tumultuous post-revolutionary period and served as a "conduit for a complex of ideas and influences: Mexican music, slang, performers, and folklore were popularized throughout the Hispanic world" (Mora 1989, 3). In the United States, Villa's revolutionary reputation spread with the 1914 release of the film *Gen'l Villa in Battle, Photographed Under Fire, With Extra Scenes Showing the Tragic Story of GEN'L VILLA'S EARLY LIFE*. Depicting the rebellion as "a popular protest against despotic outrages, a struggle by upright Mexican farmers fighting for liberty and justice," the film showed Villa distributing food and clothes to the poor and promising land to his troops (Womack 2002, 27). The American press was fascinated by Villa's image and ran numerous stories both condemning and defending his pursuits. For example, the *Fortnightly Review* described Villa's actions as "a recital of cold-blooded murders, thefts, torturings [*sic*], and atrocities of an even worse description," while the *Nation* magazine described him as "very different from the purely selfish and utterly ignorant cutthroat and robber" (Brandt 1964, 154).

In 1914, Villa signed a deal with American movie producer Harry Aitken to film his battles and to screen the newsreels in the United States, Mexico, and Canada. However, filming real-life attacks proved to be difficult, and the scenes turned out to be a disappointment. A few weeks later, Villa (or his bodyguard) killed a British rancher seeking reimbursement for some lost cattle. Almost immediately, once sympathetic publishers began to portray Villa as "a bandit born" (Womack 2002, 28). Things went from bad to worse when, two years later in 1916, in response to the U.S. government's refusal to deliver weapons that were paid for, Villa attacked the town of Columbus, New Mexico. However, even before his U.S. incursion, Villa's actions provided the American press with an excuse to describe Mexicans as warring tribes and outlaws. For example, an article in the *North American Review* observed, "Mexico is not, in fact, a nation, but a country peopled by many tribes of Indians [. . .] none reaching what we would call civilization" (1914, 33). Often, newspaper articles and cartoons depicted Mexican statesmen and revolutionaries as violent bandits and insatiable drunks. For example, as Figures 8.1 and 8.2 illustrate, representations of male drunkenness not only underscored Mexican irreverence to social order but also fed into and gained momentum from U.S. domestic racism toward blacks, immigrants, and Native Americans prevalent during this period. Drawing on exaggerated racialized images and using labels such as "ignorant" or "savage" enabled the press to easily communicate the ineptitude of Mexicans to the American public by relying on an already established language and symbolism of racial and ethnic inferiority used to disempower other communities of color.

Mexican men, in general, and Pancho Villa, in particular, were prime targets of the U.S. media.[6] Yet, Pancho Villa's image was manipulated to communicate *both* American and Mexican views of the revolution. In other words, public opinion of Villa was also wide ranging in each country. For poor and lower-class Mexicans, Villa symbolized the promise of equality and a future in which the "underdogs" could prevail. For wealthy, land-owning Mexicans, Villa and his revolutionary counterparts were viewed as threats to the status quo. At first celebrated by the United States and then later denigrated, Villa's image caught the attention of the American public whose knowledge of Mexico was limited to "picture postcards, newsreels, silent movies—pictures for excitement, not explanation" (Womack 2002, 27). To be sure, media depictions of Villa "visually reinforced the radical otherness of Mexicans to U.S. whites" (Marez 2004, 215). In one glaring attempt to further accentuate this "radical otherness," a 1914 *New York Times* article went so far as to claim that Pancho Villa was actually "a negro native of Maryland," who, after getting into trouble with the law in Texas, fled across the border, became a bandit under the name of "Rondolz," and joined the Mexican army (*Los Angeles Times* 1914d, 12).

Pancho Villa was reduced to a villain and bandit capable only of destruction—a specter against which American innocence, morality, and masculinity was defined.

In Mexico and the United States, Villa was depicted as the epitome of machismo, an exaggerated stereotype of manliness that appealed to conservative gender, familial, and cultural categories; a type of "symbolic capital" that sustained national and individual identity (Gutmann 1996, 27). However,

Figure 8.1. "*How Long Will It Continue?*" *Editorial cartoon in the* Los Angeles Times, *March 30, 1914. Embodying drunkenness and anarchy, the Mexican man raises his arms in celebration of chaos.*

Figure 8.2. "*A Substitute for Pulque.*" *Editorial cartoon in the* Los Angeles Times, *May 9, 1914. Instead of drinking pulque (an early incarnation of tequila), the darkened Mexican man should consume U.S.* "*mediation tonic.*"

the portrayal of Villa's "macho" attributes was framed differently and served separate purposes in both countries. Instead of having purely negative connotations in Mexico, Villa's macho characteristics stressed codes of courage, honor, and respect. In his excellent analysis of the perceptions of machismo within Mexican and Latino culture, Alfredo Mirandé maintains that there are at least two models of machismo. The first, known as the "compensatory view," is a pejorative conception that emphasizes violence, irresponsibility, and male dominance over women as fundamental to the essence of Mexican male character. The second, described as the "ethical view," directs attention away from outward qualities of physical strength and virility and focuses on "inner ones such as personal integrity, commitment, loyalty, and most importantly, strength of character" (1988, 65). Challenging both the Mexican establishment and the U.S. government, Villa was respected by "common" people and feared by elites. Therefore, similar to the multiple and often-contradictory conceptions of machismo, Villa likewise became associated with characteristics of Mexican manhood that differed within Mexican culture and varied across geopolitical borders. These depictions also had similarities, especially with regard to how they represented Villa in association with alcohol.

In cultural accounts as wide ranging as corridos, American newspaper articles, and Mexican and Hollywood films, Pancho Villa is portrayed in relation to alcohol. The consistent representation of Pancho Villa with alcohol is curious for several reasons. First and foremost, contrary to the popular portrayal, Villa abstained from alcohol. In fact, because of his concern about alcoholism in Mexico, he outlawed alcohol in his home state of Chihuahua and reportedly ordered the death penalty not only for the individuals who violated the ban but also for their horses, dogs, and goats (*San Jose Mercury Herald* 1918). Before his relationship with the U.S. government broke down, Villa publicly expressed his admiration for President Wilson in the form of a toast, but not before adding the following disclaimer: "[. . .] for the first time in my life I am going to propose a toast, and for the first time in my life I am going to drink a toast, and it will be the first time that I ever willingly let liquor pass my lips [. . .]" (Anderson 1998, 60). In the famous 1914 meeting of Villa's army with Emiliano Zapata's army in Mexico City, Villa gagged on sip of brandy when the two generals shared a toast (Cummings 2006). A nondrinker and nonsmoker, the highly self-disciplined Villa, in statements made to American newspapers, often described his enemies as "drunks."

For instance, in an article published in a May 1914 edition of the *San Francisco Examiner*, Villa exclaimed, "I will go back to work as soon as I drive out that drunkard, Huerta. I am only a poor man. I wish only to see my countrymen freed from tyranny. I am a patriot. Yet I am the man they call the Bandit Villa" (Anderson 1998, 65). Ironically, it was Villa, and not Huerta, whose image would be forever associated with alcohol.

Although Pancho Villa abstained from alcohol, his image became and remained intimately linked to tequila on both sides of the border. U.S. newspapers played a major role in forging this association. For example, when British rancher William Benton was assassinated in 1914, the front page headline of the *Los Angeles Times* declared, "Blame Tequila for Execution: Benton Victim of Villa's Lust for Liquor, It is Said" (1914a, 12). The article continued by stating, "[. . .] Gen. Francisco Villa, with four of his cronies, were crazed with marijuana and tequila at the time Villa gave the order to shoot William S. Benton, a British subject and wealthy ranchman [. . .]" (12). Two months later, when Villa had several American media representatives deported from Mexico, the newspaper reported that Villa and his "so-called advisors" were "more or less under the influence of the native tequila" when the events unfolded (*Los Angeles Times* 1914a, 12). A similar image was circulated through other forms of media. For example, well received in the United States and in Europe, the 1934 American motion picture *Viva Villa!*, directed by Jack Conway and starring Wallace Beery as Pancho Villa and Fay Wray as his love interest, famously portrayed Villa as aggressive, drunk, and misogynistic. Curtis Marez, in his research on the early twentieth-century U.S. drug war against Mexican immigrants, provides a compelling analysis of the portrayal of Villa and his army. Describing a particularly vivid scene, Marez observes,

> A prime example of Villa's sexual sadism occurs during the last third of the film when Villa threatens to rape one of his benefactors Teresa, a wealthy Spanish Creole. Villa occupies her hacienda, and his soldiers raid the pantry and fondle the female servants, Sierra (Villa's sidekick) is charged with locating Teresa and bringing her to the revolutionary's darkened room, where he drunkenly tells her, "I only know how to make love one way. If I see an angel I got to make love that way, I got to grab hard." When he pulls her to him for a bruising kiss, Teresa breaks away, produces a gun, and shoots him in the hand. (2003, 178)

In addition to depicting Mexican men as criminal and perverse, the "script grossly underestimated Villa's intelligence, invented episodes that never happened, and oversimplified the complex Mexican Revolution [...]" (Katz 1998, 792).[7] For American readers and viewers of the early twentieth century, representations of Pancho Villa, Mexicans, and the revolution were conflated with the vices of alcohol in general, and often tequila in particular.

The American media's use of tequila as a metaphor for Mexican deviance emerged from and became structured within a range of material and discursive registers related to the changing logic of U.S. national expansion. In particular, heightened tensions regarding the U.S.–Mexican border as an ambiguous territory required a new language to explain the enforcement of stricter regulatory controls between the two countries and rationalize the increase in U.S. intervention in Mexican domestic affairs (Kaplan 2002). Able to project its desires onto Mexico from as early as 1865, the forces of American empire established a context in which U.S. entrepreneurs could justify their efforts to economically and politically control Mexico. As one investor put it, "Pushing American enterprise up to, and within Mexico wherever it can profitably go will give us advantages which force and money would hardly procure. It would give us a peaceful conquest of the country" (Pletcher 1958, 38). However, under the "harmless" guise of "peaceful conquest," extensive foreign investment in northern Mexico spurred an internal demand for labor and resulted in a significant northward migration of hundreds of thousands of displaced Mexicans. When work in mining and railroads slowed down in the early years of the twentieth century, Mexican laborers started to enter the United States in sizable numbers. These demographic shifts did not originate in Mexico; "rather, they emanated from large-scale foreign corporate enterprises operating under the protection of the U.S. government's foreign policy" (Gonzalez and Fernandez 2002, 42). In other words, the rise in Mexican migration to the United States during this period was not simply a result of the devastation of the revolution but was propelled by the economic intrusion of U.S. capital investment. However, instead of focusing these factors, the press blamed Mexicans for criminal activity, decried the rise in immigration, and called for tighter border regulations.

Tequila was a Mexican spirit whose production and reputation began to rise at a time when ideas regarding temperance and nativism were gaining momentum in the U.S. political sphere. Compounding matters, there was growing overlap between prohibition philosophy and anti-immigrant sentiment. As a powerful "symbolic crusade," the temperance movement invoked the language of morality and values that denigrated "one group in opposition to others within the society" (Gusfield 1963, 172). Consequently, in spite of its economically successful connotations in Mexico and its ability to keep up with the pace of modern market demands (i.e., bottling, transport, and bulk export), upon its arrival to the United States, tequila was mobilized as a metaphor to debase Mexicans. For example, an 1899 Los Angeles Times travel article about Guadalajara, described "the native drink" in the following manner: "The very cheapness of this vile stuff, which brings it within the reach of all, is a calamity. American whisky is bad, but this is infinitely worse in the physical and moral degeneracy wrought, especially among the best families. Unless the [Mexican] nation awakes to this awful curse, it will become a nation of decadent manhood" (Shafer 1899, 14).

An 1894 article from *Overland Monthly and Out West* magazine described the mezcal from Tequila as "distilled from the root of a species of agave, and smells and tastes rather like Scotch whisky. It is of a light straw color, and highly intoxicating. As the best quality is made at Tequila, almost all mescal (mezcal) bears that name. Many of the rows and fatal affrays in Mexico are due to over-indulgence in mescal (mezcal)" (Inkersley 1894, 229).

Even scientific publications, including the *American Journal of Pharmacy*, declared that tequila and mezcal were "very powerful in their effects. A Mexican Indian, addicted to their use, can drink a glass of any one [. . .] without effect; two or three glasses will set him demonically crazy" (Harshberger 1896, 591). Thus, journalists, travel writers, and newspaper columnists *produced* images of Mexico and Mexicans for Americans and other English-language readers by symbolically locating Mexican deviance within a Mexican product.

Projecting negative meanings about Mexicans onto material objects at a time when Americans were more likely to read about other cultures than interact with them illustrates the dynamism of consumption in extending the symbolic reach of U.S. imperialism. Elaborating on how justification processes operate in specific historical periods, Mary Louise Pratt contends that the collective works of European travel writers legitimized colonial intervention and expansionism to the general public (1992, 9). For Pratt, "asymmetrical relations of domination and subordination" were and continue to be played out in what she calls "contact zones" (4).

A contact zone is a social space where "disparate cultures meet, clash, and grapple with each other, often in highly asymmetrical relations of domination and subordination [. . .] A 'contact' perspective emphasizes how subjects are constituted in and by their relations to each other" (4–7). The discursive imagining of Mexico through narratives regarding tequila and alcohol operates as a type of contact zone in which U.S. "frontier" ideologies are consumed, extended, and rationalized through the authoritative accounts of journalists, travel writers, and newspaper columnists.

Described as overindulgent, degenerate, and subject to demonic lunacy when consuming their "native" drink, the only solution left for Mexicans and Mexico, it seems, is the aid and intercession of the United States. Therefore, contact zones, as sites of legitimation, also serve as locales where "individual and collective fantasy become nationally embodied" (Berlant 1991, 17) and deviance, as an emotional register, becomes structured as fundamental for understanding difference. However, despite the intensity of particular conditions of inequality, these relations offer the potential for resistance. In the next section, I illustrate how imagery and rhetoric about Pancho Villa and tequila was mobilized for different purposes with disparate political implications on both sides of the border.

Branding Pancho Villa

The U.S. portrayal of Pancho Villa as a macho, tequila-drinking bandit established a racialized metaphor in which notions of masculinity and alcohol consumption were fused together within the broader framework of Mexican national identity. In spite of the stability of this formulation, national identity, as Stuart Hall reminds us, comprises unstable signifiers that appear to represent the nation's "true" character. In his words, national identity "is not a fixed essence at all, lying unchanged outside history and culture [. . .] It has its histories–and histories have their real material, and symbolic effects. The past continues to speak to us [. . .] It is always constructed through memory, fantasy, narrative and myth. Cultural identities are the points of identification, the unstable points of identification or suture, which are made through the discourse of history and culture. Not an essence but a *positioning*" (1989, 211).

The dominant *positioning* of Pancho Villa and Mexicans in relation to alcohol and tequila operated on multiple levels. Specifically, it reflected an ideology of empire that promoted U.S. economic expansion within Mexico

while it supported the increased policing of Mexicans already living in the
United States. In addition, the portrayal of Mexicans as intemperate and
dangerous to the U.S. national well-being through the metaphor of tequila
reproduced the image that alcohol was inherent to the essence of Mexican masculinity—adding yet another negative attribute to conceptions
of Mexican male identity. The U.S. positioning of Pancho Villa simultaneously affirmed long-standing preconceptions of Mexican inferiority and
served as the very basis from which a set of new influential stereotypes
were established. Furthermore, it shaped notions of belonging within the
United States by erecting boundaries that stabilized meanings of "foreign"
and "domestic"—concepts that secured the purity and integrity of U.S.
national identity (Kaplan 2002).

While tequila was becoming closely associated with negative stereotypes of Mexicanness in the United States, in Mexico it was slowly
becoming associated with positive aspects of modernization and economic
success.[8] New technologies in production, such as the replacement of the
inground stone oven with the aboveground brick oven and advancements
in the distillation and bottling process, improved efficiency and output
(Luna Zamora 1991, 80). Greater demand, both locally and internationally, led to an increase in the amount of distilleries and the establishment of
new tequila-producing zones outside of the Tequila region in areas of Jalisco such as Autlán, Los Altos, and Ciudad Guzmán. Overall, the decades
leading up to the revolution saw the accumulation of land and the founding of hacienda estates by local tequila industrialists. With greater wealth,
families such as Sauza, Cuervo, and Oredáin "expanded their businesses
[and] developed [new] mechanisms of production, distribution, and
commercialization [. . .]" (Luna Zamora 1991, 83). Improvements in the
infrastructure, such as the completion of the Ferrocarril Central Mexicano
(the central Mexican railroad) in 1884, facilitated tequila's transport within
the country and into the United States. Thus, the period before the revolution was marked by rural prosperity, which, while not affecting everyone
equally, became crystallized in the Mexican imaginary as an era that symbolized steady fiscal growth in the backdrop of the idyllic countryside.
Mexican cinema of the 1940s would later draw heavily on this nostalgic
imagery with *comedias rancheras* (western comedies) and the portrayal of
provincial charros and life on the *"rancho grande"* (Alfaro 1995, 84).

Even though the development of the tequila industry followed a conventional path toward industrialization, in the decades after the revolution

its modern association began to decline and eventually it became syn-
onymous with working-class masculinity. It is difficult to say exactly why
this phenomenon unfolded. Perhaps it evolved from the changing terms
of consumer culture in Mexico; perhaps it reflected a form of class reap-
propriation that sought to stake its claim to the image of an "authentic"
Mexican spirit; or perhaps it was a combination of these circumstances.
What we do know is that each of these possibilities point to the observation that tequila's shifting meanings were consistently "shaped and
contested at the levels of production and reception by capital interests, the
state, and consumers" (Zolov 1999, 15).

Tequila's working-class connotations also eventually merged with the
image of Pancho Villa. Numerous brands continue to pay tribute to this
enduring association. For example, La Leyenda Tequila 30–30 (The Legend Tequila 30–30), refers to the 30–30 rifle used by Villa and his army,
Los Dorados. Tequila Siete Leguas (Seven Leagues Tequila) is named
after Pancho Villa's horse. Laura Becerril, contributor to *The Tequila
Guide*, describes Siete Leguas as "[. . .] by far Pancho Villa's favorite steed:
whenever it heard the train whistle, it would rear up and neigh [. . .] This
tequila's potency and feistiness render homage to the horse that belonged
to Villa, the Centaur of the North" (1998, 132). Aside from Tequila Pancho
Villa, Viva Villa, Pancho Villa Viejo (old Pancho Villa), and Hijos de Villa
(children of Villa), there is also Tequila Los Arango, which is a reference to
Doroteo Arango, Pancho Villa's given name, and Tequila De Los Dorados,
which "invokes the image of Los Dorados, the notorious and elite armed
guard whose members were handpicked by none other than [. . .] Pancho
Villa" (Becerril 1998, 76). The label displays a bullet hole and a picture of
Villa's troops. Numerous brands, while not referring to Villa directly, utilize images of bandit or revolutionary figures—many brandishing guns,
mustaches, and sombreros. In addition to the names of different tequila
brands, there are dozens of cocktails (many of which are tequila based)
that also draw on Villa's namesake (e.g., The Pancho Villa, The Pancho
Villa Shooter, and The Pancho Villa #2).

Stuart Hall's notion of positioning also lends itself to an analysis of the
link between Pancho Villa, the revolution, and tequila within Mexico. Not
the image promoted by *hispanistas* or *indigenistas*, Pancho Villa emerged
from the revolutionary milieu as an icon of *lo mexicano*—a symbol that
was as subversive as it was problematic, fitting into neither prevailing identity master narrative completely. Instead, meanings and representations of

Pancho Villa were negotiated within and in response to the dominating beliefs of *hispanismo* and *indigenismo* that pervaded the postrevolutionary period. On one hand, the rise of Villa's reputation and association with *lo mexicano* was bolstered by the widespread disillusionment in the capabilities of Mexican leaders to govern the nation in a manner that prioritized local development and the rights of ordinary citizens. On the other hand, Villa's representation as an icon of *lo mexicano* served as a response to the distorted portrayals of Villa and Mexicans by members of the American media and government officials. Different from the sober and polished image of the charro, Pancho Villa stood as an alternative formulation of national belonging. Hence, Pancho Villa's status materialized as a symbol of resistance to the official discourse of the Mexican state and as a rejection of the debased images of Mexicans circulated in U.S. popular culture.

Pancho Villa's image as a gun-slinging, tequila-drinking bandit–hero is a source of romance and independence—qualities easily incorporated into different expressions of social positioning. For instance, as a counterhegemonic cultural symbol, Pancho Villa signified and evoked sentiments of a particular account of Mexican national pride in which expressions of bravery and loyalty were constructed as indelible to the nation's character. While certain negative traits (e.g., drinking, womanizing, and fighting) were promoted and mythologized in Mexican corridos and films, Pancho Villa, a national hero who died a violent death much like the estimated two million Mexicans killed during the revolution, became more known for his martyr-like qualities and less associated with the abusive traits embellished by the media. With justifiable goals, honorable intentions, and the ability to relate to the experiences of less privileged Mexicans, Pancho Villa's complicated life and brutal death tempered his disreputable attributes.

Initially used to debase Villa by the U.S. media, and already in a solid position to represent Mexico's commitment to modernity by the beginning of the revolution, tequila became associated with an oppositional consciousness not necessarily motivated by unity but by the momentum for social change in the face of decades of corruption and inequality. The relationship between tequila and Pancho Villa was inevitable because their representations were shaped by and emerged within similar historical situations rooted in cross-border conflicts—struggles in which their images were simultaneously mobilized to racialize Mexicans as foreign "others," dangerous to the well-being of American innocence and Anglo manhood. As commodities, tequila and Pancho Villa brought together various components of *lo mexicano* that appealed to the rejuvenated national identity. Thus, the production and consumption of the image of tequila and Pancho Villa "serve[d] both the economic interests of the producers and the cultural interests of the consumers while not completely separating the two" (Fiske 1989, 25).

Conclusion

The period during and following the revolution was pivotal in bolstering tequila's reputation as Mexico's national spirit. Amid widespread social transformation, new symbols were mobilized by the state to promote a united national identity. Struggles between conflicting groups (liberals and conservatives) and their ideologies (*indigenismo* and *hispanismo*) regarding how to modernize Mexico followed "the dominant European conviction that a state is the expression of a people with a common culture and the same language and is produced by having a common history" (Batalla 2002, 30). With an emphasis on unity and no true commitment to equality, both *indigenistas* and *hispanistas* sought to establish a homogeneous national identity whose past traditions would serve as a base from which to stimulate modern development. To be sure, the new Mexican revolutionary state was "eager to perpetuate notions of *Mexicanidad* rooted in an 'authentic' mestizo rural culture of which it was the legitimate custodian and beneficiary" (Joseph and Henderson 2002, 2).

At the same time that tequila appealed to liberals and conservatives concerned with modernity and focused on establishing a unified (and acceptable) image of the nation, tequila also became associated with notions of *lo mexicano* that stood in contrast to the positivist trajectory of the Mexican elite. The embodiment of machismo, Pancho Villa emerged as a symbol of the revolution on both sides of the U.S.–Mexican border. Challenging the Mexican establishment and the American government, Pancho Villa was simultaneously depicted as a villain and hero whose attributes became incorporated into divergent conceptions of Mexican masculinity. Even though he abstained from alcohol, Pancho Villa's macho characteristics were narrated through alcohol, in general, and tequila, in particular. In the United States, Pancho Villa's macho, tequila-drinking image established a racialized metaphor that fused notions of Mexican manhood and alcohol consumption with dysfunctional notions of Mexican national identity that justified U.S. expansionist ideology and validated the increased policing not only of the border but also of Mexicans living within the United States. In Mexico, Villa's portrayal in popular culture emphasized laudable aspects of machismo that elevated his status as an icon of resistance who stood up to the Mexican and American governments. A romantic symbol of the revolution, Pancho Villa and his close association with tequila together embody and reflect commemorative aspects of Mexican nationalism, which, for some aficionados, illustrate the "the intense pride and passion of the Mexican people [...]" (Menuez 2005, 1).

In contrast to these celebratory representations, alcohol prohibition (1920–33) in the United States further pathologized Mexicans and Mexico as dangerous to American innocence by "enhanc[ing] the prestige of the victors (non-drinkers) and degrad[ing] the culture of the losers (drinkers)" (Gusfield 1963, 5). Despite attempts by prohibitionists to restrict American travel to Mexico in order to purchase alcohol, tourism continued to increase. The act of crossing the border into Mexico signaled one's predilection for illicit activities that included alcohol, drugs, gambling, and prostitution. As a site of vice that contrasted with the "virtuous" laws of the United States, Mexico was depicted as risky, unruly, and immoral—a place where forbidden behavior was seen as customary and, perhaps, even expected. From a historic perspective, Mexico has been portrayed as a location where "inappropriate" behavior is the norm. Consequently, it comes as little surprise that, a century later, Mexico is one of the primary destinations for American spring-break revelers who, known for indulging in excessive drinking, seek out new and exciting forms of pleasure. Visiting places like Cancún, where "nothing happens in moderation," new generations of Americans, much like the U.S. media from years past, reproduce symbolically, through consumption, particular metaphors of domination whereby Mexico is imagined as site of intemperance (Leinwand 2003).

As a social practice that illustrates people's commitment to the nation and communicates expressions of national belonging, consumption remains a complicated and insufficiently understood process (Banet-Weiser 2007; Gray 2005). Furthermore, it poses elusive challenges to scholars interested in empirically capturing lesser-known linkages between the political, economic, and affective circumstances that influence common perceptions of "others." Sociologists interested in critically engaging with politics related to structures of feeling (Williams 1975) should pay greater attention to connecting the social, cultural, and emotional contexts that not only naturalize particular national attributes but also reinforce hegemonic constructions of difference and normality. Tracing the multiple representations of tequila in a particular historical moment across borders, this chapter sheds light on the conditions that simultaneously structure seemingly divergent meanings of Mexican social identities.

Notes

1. Despite its inclusive undertones, the definition of *mestizaje* excluded people of African descent whose presence was well documented in the work force.

2. Both the Virgin of Guadalupe and La Malinche figure prominently in explanations of "traditional" gender norms and narratives of national identity in Mexico. Chicana feminists have challenged these master narratives on the grounds that such frameworks limit women's representations, arguing that The Virgin of Guadalupe and La Malinche can also signify the struggle for indigenous rights, expressions of resistance, and women's empowerment (Anzaldúa 1987; Pérez 1999; Romero and Harris 2005).

3. While real life charros were prohibited from drinking, charros in Mexican *comedia ranchera* (western comedy) films of the 1940s and 1950s were frequently depicted drinking alcohol, most often tequila.

4. Traditional ballad attributed to Miguel Lira (see María y Campos 1962). English translation by the author.

5. La Valentina is the name of popular corrido said to be written by Pancho Villa.

6. Historian Elliott Young (2004), in his work on the revolution and the Texas–Mexican border, illustrates how the U.S. press also defiled Catarino Garza, a well-known Mexican journalist and political activist, as a bandit.

7. *Viva Villa!* was one of many Hollywood films to transform "the image of Villa from ally to blood-thirsty and impetuous Number One enemy and hence manipulate public opinion to suit the economic and political interests of the United States" (De la Mora 2006, 9).

8. Here, I am referring to the time period before the onset of the 1910 revolution. Tequila production decreased during the revolution and the Cristero War (1926–29; Luna Zamora 1991).

Works Cited

Alfaro, Alfonso. 1995. "Tequila and Its Signs: In Praise of the Country Gentleman." In *El tequila: Arte traditicional de México* (Tequila: traditional art of Mexico) ed. Alberto Ruy Sánchez Lacy, 83–85. México D. F.: Artes de México.

Anderson, Mark. 1998. "What's to Be Done with 'Em? Images of Mexican Cultural Backwardness, Racial Limitations, and Moral Decrepitude in the United States Press, 1913–1915." *Mexican Studies/Estudios Mexicanos* 4 (1): 23–70.

Anzaldúa, Gloria. 1987. *Borderlands/La Frontera: The New Mestiza*. San Francisco: Aunt Lute Books.

Azuela, Mariano. 1963. *The Underdogs*. New York: Penguin Books.

Banet-Weiser, Sarah. 2007. *Kids Rule!: Nickelodeon and Consumer Citizenship*. Durham, N.C.: Duke University Press.

Barr, Andrew. 1999. *Drink: A Social History of America*. New York: Carroll and Graff Publishers.

Becerril, Laura. 1998. "Tequila Brands from A to Z." In *Guía del Tequila* (The Tequila guide), ed. Alberto Ruy Sánchez Lacy, 60–141, México D. F.: Artes de México.

Benjamin, Thomas. 2000. *La Revolución: Mexico's Great Revolution as Memory, Myth, and History*. Austin: University of Texas Press.

———. and Marcial Ocasio-Melendez. 1984. "Organizing the Memory of Modern Mexico: Porfirian Historiography in Perspective, 1880s–1980s." *Hispanic American Historical Review* 64 (2): 323–64.

Berlant, Lauren. 1991. *The Anatomy of National Fantasy: Hawthorne, Utopia, and Everyday Life*. Chicago: University of Chicago Press.

———. 1997. *The Queen of America Goes to Washington City: Essays on Sex and Citizenship*. Durham, N.C.: Duke University Press.

Brading, David A. 1988. "Manuel Gamio and Official Indigenismo in Mexico." *Bulletin of Latin American Research* 7 (1): 75–89.

Brandt, Nancy. 1964. "Pancho Villa: The Making of a Modern Legend." *Americas* 21 (2): 146–62.

Cummings, Joe. 2006. "Francisco Pancho Villa." *Mexconnect*, January 1. http://www.mexconnect.com/mex_/travel/jcummings/jcpanchovilla.html (accessed April 29, 2007).

Dawson, Alexander. 1998. "From Models for the Nation to Model Citizens: Indigenismo and the 'Revindication' of the Mexican Indian, 1920–1940." *Journal of Latin American Studies* 30 (2): 279–308.

De la Mora, Sergio. 2006. *Cinemachismo: Masculinities and Sexuality in Mexican Film*. Austin: University of Texas Press.

Fiske, John. 1989. *Reading the Popular*. Boston: Unwin Hyman.

Flores, Richard. 1992. "The Corrido and the Emergence of Texas–Mexican Social Identity." *Journal of American Folklore* 105 (416): 166–82.

Gamio, Manuel. 1960. *Forjando patria* (Forging a fatherland). México D. F.: Editorial Porrúa, S. A. (Orig. pub. 1916.)

Gonzalez, Gil, and Raúl Fernandez. 2002. "Empire and the Origins of Twentieth-Century Migration from Mexico to the United States." *Pacific Historical Review* 71 (1): 19–57.

González, Roberto. 2004. "From Indigenismo to Zapatismo: Theory and Practice in Mexican Anthropology." *Human Organization* 63 (2): 127–36.

Gray, Herman. 2005. *Cultural Moves: African Americans and the Politics of Representation.* Berkeley: University of California Press.

Gusfield, Joseph. 1963. *Symbolic Crusade: Status Politics and the American Temperance Movement.* Urbana: University of Illinois Press.

Gutmann, Matthew. 1996. *The Meanings of Macho: Being a Man in Mexico City.* Berkeley: University of California Press.

Hall, Stuart. 1989. "Cultural Identity and Cinematic Representation." *Framework* 36:68–81.

Harshberger, John. 1896. "A Botanical Excursion to Mexico." *American Journal of Pharmacy* (November): 588–92.

Inkersley, Arthur. 1894. "Pulque, the National Drink of Mexico." *Overland Monthly and Out West Magazine* 24 (141): 255–59.

Joseph, Gilbert, and Timothy Henderson. 2002. "Introduction." In *The Mexico Reader: History, Culture, Politics,* ed. Gilbert Joseph and Timothy Henderson, 1–8. Durham, N.C.: Duke University Press.

Kaplan, Amy. 2002. *The Anarchy of Empire in the Making of U.S. Culture.* Cambridge, Mass.: Harvard University Press.

Katz, Friedrich. 1998. *The Life and Times of Pancho Villa.* Stanford, Calif.: Stanford University Press.

Limón, José. 1983. "Folklore, Social Conflict, and the United States–Mexican Border." In *Handbook of American Folklore,* ed. Richard Dorson, 216–26. Bloomington: University of Indiana Press.

———. 1990. "La Llorona, the Third Legend of Greater Mexico: Cultural Symbols, Women, and the Political Unconscious." In *Between Borders: Essays on Mexicana/Chicana History,* ed. Adelaida R. Del Castillo, 399–432. Encino, Calif.: Floricanto Press.

Leiwand, Donna. 2003. "Alcohol-Soaked Spring Break Lures Students Abroad." *USA Today,* January 5.

Los Angeles Times. 1914a. "Blame Tequila for Execution." February 24.

———. 1914b. "How Long Will It Continue?" March 30.

———. 1914c."A Substitute for Pulque." May 9.

———. 1914d."Villa a Negro, Soldier Says." February 25, I2.

Luna Zamora, Rogelio 1991. *La historia del tequila, de sus regiones y sus hombres* (The history of tequila, its regions, and its men). México, D. F.: Conaculta.

Marez, Curtis. 2003. "Subaltern Soundtracks: Mexican Immigrants and the Making of Hollywood Cinema." *Aztlán: A Journal of Chicano Studies* 29 (1): 57–82.

———. 2004. *Drug Wars: The Political Economy of Narcotics.* Minneapolis: University of Minnesota Press.

María y Campos, Armando de. 1962. *La Revolución Mexicana a través de los corridos populares* (The Mexican Revolution through popular corridos). México,

D. F.: Biblioteca del Instituto Nacional de Estudios Históricos de la Revolución Mexicana.

Menuez, Douglas. 2005. *Heaven, Earth, Tequila: Un viaje al corazón de Mexico* (A trip to the heart of Mexico). N.p.: Perseus Distribution Services.

Meyers, William. 1991. "Pancho Villa and the Multinationals: United States Mining Interests in Villista Mexico, 1913–1915." *Journal of Latin American Studies* 23 (2): 339–63.

Mirandé, Alfredo. 1988. "Qué Gacho es ser Macho: It's a Drag to Be a Macho Man." *Aztlán: A Journal of Chicano Studies* 17 (2): 63–89.

Mitchell, Tim. 2004. *Intoxicated Identities: Alcohol's Power in Mexican History and Culture*. New York: Routledge.

Mora, Carl. 1989. *Mexican Cinema: Reflections of a Society: 1896–1988*. Berkeley: University of California Press.

Nájera-Ramírez, Olga. 1994. "Engendering Nationalism: Identity, Discourse, and the Mexican Charro." *Anthropological Quarterly* 67 (1): 1–14.

Orozco, José. 1998. *"Esos Altos de Jalisco!": Emigration and the Idea of Alteño Exceptionalism, 1926–1952*. PhD diss., Harvard University.

Paredes, Américo. 1963. "The Ancestry of Mexico's Corridos: A Matter of Definition." *Journal of American Folklore* 76 (301): 231–35.

———. 1967. "Mexico, Machismo, and the U.S." *Journal of the Folklore Institute* 8 (1): 17–37.

Parra, Max. 2005. *Writing Pancho Villa's Revolution: Rebels in the Literary Imagination of Mexico*. Austin: University of Texas Press.

Pérez, Laura Elisa. 1999. "El desorden, Nationalism, and Chicana/o Aesthetics." In *Between Woman and Nation: Nationalisms, Transnational Feminisms, and the State*, ed. Caren Kaplan, Norma Alarcón, and Minoo Moallem, 19–46. Durham. N.C.: Duke University Press.

Pike, Fredrick B. 1971. "Making the Hispanic World Safe from Democracy: Spanish Liberals and Hispanismo." *Review of Politics* 33 (3): 307–22.

Pletcher, David. 1958. *Rails, Mines, and Progress: Seven American Promoters in Mexico, 1867–1911*. Ithaca, N.Y.: Cornell University Press.

Pratt, Mary Louise. 1992. *Imperial Eyes: Travel Writing and Transculturation*. London: Routledge.

Romero, Ronaldo, and Amanda Nolacea Harris, ed. 2005. *Feminism, Nation, and Myth: La Malinche*. Houston, Tex.: Arte Público Press.

Sandos, James, A. 1984. "Northern Separatism during the Mexican Revolution: An Inquiry into the Role of Drug Trafficking, 1910–1920." *Americas* 41 (2): 191–214.

Sands, Kathleen. 1993. *Charreria Mexicana: An Equestrian Folk Tradition*. Tucson: University of Arizona Press.

San Jose Mercury Herald. 1918. "Near Prohibition Ordered in Mexico." May 11, 9.

Schmidt, Henry. 1978. *The Roots of Lo Mexicano: Self and Society in Mexican Thought.* College Station: Texas A & M University Press.

Shafer, A. C. "Guadalajara." *Los Angeles Times*, November 19, 1899, 14.

Stevens, Evelyn. 1965. "Mexican Machismo: Politics and Value Orientations." *Western Political Quarterly* 18 (4): 848–57.

Vasconcelos, José. 1997. *The Cosmic Race/La raza cósmica.* Baltimore, Md.: The Johns Hopkins University Press.

Williams, Raymond. 1975. *The Long Revolution.* Westport, Conn.: Greenwood.

Womack, John, Jr. 2002. "Pancho Villa: A Revolutionary Life." *Journal of the Historical Society* 11 (1): 21–42.

Young, Elliott. 2004. *Catarino Garza's Revolution on the Texas–Mexico Border.* Durham, N.C.: Duke University Press.

Zolov, Eric. 1999. *Refried Elvis: The Rise of the Mexican Counterculture.* Berkeley: University of California Press.

CHAPTER 9

Reinscribing Memory through the Other 9/11

Macarena Gómez-Barris

But how transformative was September 11? Would it become an iconic historical event, marking a transition in the history of the United States and of the world? Or was it instead best understood as an aspect of preexisting historical trajectories?

—Mary Dudziak, *September 11 in History*

I T IS IMPOSSIBLE TO EXPIATE THE NUMBERS 9/11, numbers that seamlessly insert me within the southern hemisphere in a direct time and place: Chile, September 11, 1973. The return to a date with high personal and political stakes is exacted through a series of unexperienced yet entirely recognizable moments. Through others' documentation and witnessing, I am returned to the original point of political disaster. The sounds of the bombing of La Moneda presidential palace are omnipresent in an audioscape of terror that leaves its trace. Too young to remember that fated day, I experienced the moments of political terror only through particular documentaries of state violence,[1] personal stories, and black-and-white still photographs, which have left their indelible imprint wherein September 11, 1973, forms a memory repertoire of sensorial political experiences.

As Susana Kaiser documents regarding the aftermath of political violence in Argentina, the experience of the second generation that were not "direct victims" of the repression (differentiated from, for instance, the case of children of the *desaparecidos*, those who were disappeared by the military) is a gray zone of memory construction that is often mediated through the lived experience of the witness generation (2005, 13). Kaiser suggests how this postmemory generation defines the "relevance and weight that the dictatorship has for them in creating a lieux de mémoire of this past" (12). Indeed, for members of this witness generation, the route into feeling and attempting to ascertain immediacy and a sense of "reality" of historical experience may travel through productions of memory that operate within the cultural terrain. Thus, the long list of names of those who were disappeared, fading in songs by Godwana and Moyenei Váldes or the etchings on houses in Santiago that publicly marked the home of a torturer, as they have for others of the gray zone generation, have provided the backdrop to my persistent search for memories that evoked the shadowy past.

In the way that authoritarianism is for many South American second-generation "gray zoners"—a fuzzy memoryscape—Chile has often represented for me a frustrated search. In part, my search has been for forms of horizontal sociality and conviviality that may or may not have existed in an earlier moment, enlivened as it was by mass social and cultural movements only to be truncated by fundamentalist neoliberalism. Despite the weight of the social trace and the legacy of authoritarianism, were these heterotopic state–led and social movement–led visions possible to materialize? To address this question, one is led to narrativize the history of peaceful, electoral revolution by framing it through its contradictions: For instance, were the literacy campaigns that my mother was involved in positive attempts to right historical injustice? Or, did they otherwise represent a homogenizing form of civic socialization that expressed the worse kind of paternalistic, liberal fantasies? Perhaps one could measure the success of such large-scale social policies and movements on a more intimate scale: how did the campaign come to matter through the affective exchanges between those that possessed literacy and those without such forms of possession? In terms of overarching historical questions, who was left out of, estranged by, and even coerced by the utopic socialist imaginary?[2]

If the Chilean nation occupies an ever-moving picture of historical contrasts in my mind, then "the United States" as a signifier of dominance frames my feelings of alienation and estrangement, particularly because it was situated in familial socialization as the locus and root of all significant global troubles. Sitting around the dinner table with a group of Chilean political exiles, my mother would guide the conversation. In very concrete ways, the United States came to signify all that was wrong in the world during the 1980s (and beyond), ruled as it was by Reaganomics, neoliberal authoritarian regimes, and very real and "hot" wars in regions like Central America, despite cold war rhetoric of preventive armament. In these intimate landscapes, I became educated and began to learn a language for how empire erased the trace of former social worlds, not yet fully realized. This bounded terrain between intimacy and occupation is my first entry point into how state violence elucidates the workings and debris of empire and the expansion of global power: a personal obsession with dates, an endless reckoning through collection and analysis of stories about September 11, 1973, and the U.S. role in what soon became a deadly project of counterrevolution.

My second entry point into the expansion of U.S. global power and the comparison between two 9/11s operates in broader strokes, stating an obvious point for the critic, namely, that the U.S. racial state[3] uses terror, whether in representational or material formats, as a main weapon to secure a global hegemony that is never fully realizable. Part of the capitalist impetus is structured through the logic of fortification of the U.S. penal experiment, a war on the poor with racial differentials. The U.S. racial state operates through an organized, bureaucratic, rational, and flexible suite of practices that enable punishment upon certain kinds of bodies.[4]

Does an analysis that intermeshes two historically significant dates capture such forms of state terror and intervention? What is the historical coincidence that sets the stage for later condescension of specific forms of economic, political, cultural, and social hegemony, and coercion? In other words, what is unveiled, hidden, managed, and made salient by putting together the historical memory of September 11, 1973, with that of post–September 11, 2001?

Bringing the memory of Chile's 9/11 into the foreground of a discussion about the aftermath of 9/11 in the United States can produce an instance of what Tzvetan Todorov calls exemplary memory, where the past and its lessons are principles in the struggle toward present-day social justice (1995). In this case, the persistent effects of torture, the negotiation of the identity of exile, and, more generally, the aftermath of violence from Chile's authoritarianism all work as important past reminders in the context of an aggressive post-9/11 response by the United States. As such, circulating within the United States, there is specific work that Chilean memory politics can do to call attention to the logics of empire and its war, following Dudziak, not by a new historical configuration, but by making visible, through relational connections, how foreign policy enacts state violence with lasting consequences. The use of exemplary memory also functions on a symbolic level: Chile's political and economic experiment with socialism in 1973 was a global symbol of how democratic revolution can be suddenly thwarted by powerful interests, in this case with the backing and support of the U.S. government and the Central Intelligence Agency (CIA). The bombing of La Moneda palace was the beginning of the end of

a national socialist dream. And, like the wars in Southeast Asia, the bombings marked a critical historical crossroads with global consequences. As
Eric Hershberg and Kevin Moore argue, "September 11 brought home
with renewed force the importance of the United States as a symbol. The
World Trade Center and the Pentagon represented more than American
economic and military dominance. They also symbolized the global economic, military, and cultural ascendancy of the West, and the comparative
marginalization of much of the rest of the world" (2002, 3).

Many commentators have suggested the uncanny coincidence of Chile's
military coup on September 11, 1973, and the terrorist attack in New York
exactly twenty-eight years later on September 11, 2001. Even so, the former
date was vastly overshadowed by the latter, in part because of Latin America's marginal geopolitical position vis-à-vis the project of U.S. hegemony,
including global media coverage, the level of impact of the event, and the
perhaps immeasurable magnitude and rippling effect of the disaster. Best-
selling novelist Isabel Allende and literary scholar and playwright Ariel
Dorfman, both Chilean born and currently living in the United States,
repeatedly made the controversial point in U.S. public arenas that the coincidence was a form of historical karma, which was a polite way of saying what
others later suggested as the "chickens coming home to roost."[5] Their common project, especially in the aftermath of September 11, 2001, has been to
wrestle national consciousness from the throes of U.S. public amnesia about
its role in Chile's military takeover and subsequent political violence. Moreover, both authors pointed to how U.S. nationalism worked to exclude the
immigrant experience not only through contemporary immigration policy
at the structural level but also through the lack of U.S. accountability in Central American civil wars and South American dictatorships, which continue
to haunt the lives of hundreds and thousands of Latin Americans.

In the sections that follow, I discuss how Allende and Dorfman's cultural production operates to instantiate historical memory about empire
within the U.S. public, with different strategies and to different effect.
My point here is to ask, how does state violence in Chile—and more
importantly, the lessons learned from the aftermath of collective violence
imposed from above—illuminate the ways that U.S. hegemony is constituted through memory of the September 11, 2001, case? *My Invented
Country* (2003) evokes Allende's memories and perspectives on Chile's
national experience of social protest, class struggle, and, later, the military
coup and the subsequent human rights abuses committed by the Pinochet

regime. Allende renders the story of Chile in ways that make the U.S. state accountable to the historical record. Similarly, for several decades after his famous *How to Read Donald Duck: Imperialist Ideology in the Disney Comic* with Armand Mattelart (1971), Ariel Dorfman made intellectual and cultural work that continued to make the issue of U.S. involvement in Southern Cone authoritarianism, especially in Chile, central to his mission. How do these efforts to remember and represent this history prompt opportunities for exemplary memory in the U.S. public arena?

Reading Dorfman on Torture

In order for torture to be used as a weapon in "the war on terror," it had to be accompanied by a vast discursive regime where particular narratives were mobilized to prop up the material practice of torture in sites not always hidden from public view. Before the public's eyes, and through the endless machinations and chatter of government officials and media pundits, torture was transformed from an internationally illegal practice into a plausible strategy for extracting information to secure the nation. In one reiterating narrative, torture and its practice was the product of a "few bad apples" rather than the logical extension of a highly ideological and organized state security system. Another overarching story has been to deny the U.S. role in torture around the world prior to the post-9/11 scenario, or what Gary Wills calls "original sinlessness."[6] For instance, throughout the 2008 U.S. presidential race and campaign, John McCain perpetuated the narrative of U.S. innocence by alluding to his experience as a prisoner of war in Hanoi. As a form of testimonial, McCain's story was already embedded within the public discourse prior to the presidential campaign as the following quote intimates: "Many of my comrades were subjected to very cruel, very inhumane and degrading treatment, a few of them unto death. But every one of us—every single one of us—knew and took great strength from the belief that we were different from our enemies, that we were better than them, that we, if the roles were reversed, would not disgrace ourselves by committing or approving such mistreatment of them" (2005). As Naomi Klein has commented, this discursive inclusion is a feat of "stunning historical distortion. By the time McCain was taken captive, the CIA had already launched the Phoenix program," where more than forty interrogation centers were operating in South Vietnam, twenty thousand were killed, and thousands more tortured (Klein quoted by McCoy 2006). By evacuating, individuating, and poorly contextualizing the historical record of an earlier era, testimonials of original sinlessness drove a discursive agenda that distorted the memory of U.S. foreign involvement and produced the kind of historical amnesia presumed by the story of U.S. innocence.

Dorfman's position in the U.S. media has been at times to interrupt and to otherwise critique the very idea of a "torture debate," using his own experience with torture survivors as the basis for his political and literary intervention. In an editorial that appeared in the *Washington Post*, ironically framed by the phrase "The Torture Debate," Dorfman describes his reaction to seeing a torture survivor as they both sought refuge in the Argentine embassy in the weeks following the Chilean military coup. He writes, "That is what stays with me—that he was cold under the balmy afternoon sun of Santiago de Chile, trembling as though he would never be warm again, as though the electric current was still coursing through him. Still possessed, somehow still inhabited by his captors, still imprisoned in that cell in the National Stadium, his hands disobeying the orders from his brain to quell the shuddering, his body unable to forget what had been done to it just as, nearly 33 years later, I, too, cannot banish that devastated life from my memory" (2006).

In this passage, Dorfman's figure of "devastated life" recalls the Agambian category of *homo sacer*, or "bare life," which is based on Roman law; *homo sacer* refers to one that has few political rights in front of the state sovereign, despite the fact of biological life. More resonantly, in rendering torture and its effects, the image of a life that has been devastated by state terror is a central trope of the over two-thousand-page Valech Report (or the *National Commission on Political Imprisonment and Torture Report*; Valech 2004).[7] The testimonials of more than thirty thousand torture victims of the Pinochet authoritarian regime populate the memoryscape of the period. The genre of testimonial making has become the key domain that mediates the long distance between torture survivors' suffering and the legal apparatus. What Dorfman's poetic and pointed commentary makes visible is the degree to which torture is a relevantly new object of interest in the United States, despite the formidable role the nation has played in globalizing the phenomenon, especially during the cold war. Dorfman's editorial explains how, for the past thirty years, Chilean human rights workers, cultural activists, lawyers, psychologists, and sociologists have been at the forefront of an international effort that addresses both the complex contextual terrain that creates torture and its persistent effects

As a way of introducing Dorfman's audiovisual labor, let me return to the question of how the post-9/11 discursive regime makes historical memory absent through the presumption of American innocence. As Vishay Prashad put it in the immediate aftermath of the collapsing of the twin towers in New York and his subsequent discussion of American Innocence,

> The genocide of the Amerindians, the slavery of peoples from Africa, the widespread disruption of anti-colonialism in the name of anti-communism—this is the legacy that is lost by America's innocent amnesia [. . .] Our remembrance of things past is not geared toward a justification of the innocent amnesia will not allow us to see why such a thing happened, indeed to render those who did those acts outside understanding. Such an attitude means we can do little to combat such vast acts of terror, since we can then only take recourse in some manner of prayers that the irrational madness does not strike again. (2001)

In this quote, Prashad refers to how innocence functions as a proxy for amnesiac constructions of history, which, in the presence of contemporary events, disavow the possibility for contextual and historical engagement. One of my main arguments in this chapter is that, for Chileans that witnessed the prior 9/11, this disavowal is structurally an impossibility because of the historical articulation of U.S. events with the other 9/11.

In *Innocence*, a Point of View (POV) American Shadows short, Ariel Dorfman describes his take on the events of September 11, 2001: "One of the first things I thought after the second plane hit was not again, not another September 11th. Not again death and violence coming from the sky." The four-minute film is a meditation on what I and the 9/11 collective have elsewhere referred to as "Two 9/11s in a Lifetime," the experience of having suffered September 11, 1973, and reliving that national tragedy as an exile to and resident of the United States in 2001 (Gómez-Barris 2005). Dorfman's film, much like San Francisco–based filmmaker Ariel López's films, uses visual and audio montage to invoke both national tragedies simultaneously. For instance, in the background we hear General Pinochet's voice on the day of September 11 declaring both a state of emergency and martial law. On screen is the evacuated site of the World Trade Center after September 11, 2001. Dorfman asks,

I wonder how many of the visitors to the September 11 site in New York know of other catastrophes. Other catastrophes that happen over and over again in the world? I wonder if they know about my September 11th. *Mi once de septiembre.* My September 11th of 1973. I wonder if they know that the terrorists that tortured and killed my friends were trained by the United States, backed by the United States. I wonder what happens when you're not willing to face the pain of the rest of the world, the pain you may have inflicted on the world. Because the day that that terror finally strikes you, you find yourself unable to understand what's happening to your life. You plead your innocence. Your false sense of innocence. (Dorfman 2004)

In this short documentary, Dorfman refers to the School of the Americas, now evasively called the Western Hemisphere Institute for Security Cooperation officially, and unofficially the School of Assassins. Broadly speaking, the base is the site of U.S. and Latin American military training on torture that provided the personnel support for various social and dirty wars, including military dictatorships, civil wars, and the contemporary U.S.-backed "war on drugs" in Colombia, Bolivia, and Peru. Without explicitly naming the infamous site, which has graduated more than sixty thousand hemispheric military personal since its inception in 1946, Dorfman invokes the bloody history of torture as a strategy of U.S. intervention throughout the region.

By breaking the discourse of American innocence, Dorfman hails a U.S. audience that perhaps can reach beyond nationalist-oriented notions of citizenship and patriotism and think instead in humanitarian terms, beyond identification with a specifically American subject of 9/11 trauma:

We should use this occasion to understand all of the victims of history, and all of the survivors of history and not to turn this into the only one. These are not the only victims here these are not the only dead. Still standing in front of the trade center, and then making a visual bridge to footage of planes on September 11, 1973, dropping bombs on La Moneda Palace. Crises allow you to think and rethink yourself. And you can go in two directions. You can become very conservative and patriotic and allow the fear to turn you into a monster of vengeance. Or it can make you understand that what happened to you happens to everyone all the time all around the world. And therefore you can build from that something different. (Dorfman 2004)

The return to the earlier 9/11 is meant to frame Dorfman's as a veteran perspective on crisis that both sees beyond immediate political disasters and is already inscribed by other historical political and social traumas. In this way, Dorfman locates himself, his generation, and presumably the majority of the global population as always outside of the discourse of American innocence, a position that enables a linkage between historical memory, atrocity, and self-awareness through an alternate rendering of September 11, 2001, in opposition to neoconservative official narratives. In direct address, Dorfman also touches on the topic of vengeance as a conservative political tool. In fact, the discourse of patriotism and vengeance has been used in countless historical examples as a weapon of the powerful against the politically weak (i.e., the domino theory, social wars against criminality, and so forth).

Another issue that has resonance and relevance in the context of human rights is the attempted extradition of former dictator Augusto Pinochet, or what is commonly referred to as the Pinochet case. For Dorfman, this example provides a platform from which to analyze and denounce the Bush administration's undoing of international human rights' standards, allowing Dorfman to illustrate how September 11 was a form of limiting sovereignty for those that have been targeted as the new enemy of the United States (in much the same way "dissident" and "subversive" served to label those involved in social efforts during the cold war era). Centrally in *Exorcising Terror* (2002), Dorfman explains the Lords' decisions by providing context for the reader in ways that could be applied to the present day. For instance, he uses transcripts of the hearings mixed in with his own commentary to elucidate points about how international law expects high standards of conduct:

Lord Nicholls explains that: international law has made plain that certain types of conduct, including torture and hostage-taking, are not acceptable conduct on the part of anyone. This applies as much to heads of state, or even more so, as it does to everyone else. The contrary conclusion would make a mockery of international law. Lord Steyn stated that "The development of international law since the Second World War justifies the conclusion that by the time of the 1973 coup d'état and certainly since, international law condemned genocide, torture, hostage-taking and crimes against humanity (during an armed conflict or in peace time) as international crimes deserving of punishment." (Dorfman 2002, 71)

Dorfman draws attention to the Lords' discussion of international law at a time when international law was indeed under great duress by the practices of torture, war, and invasion by the Bush' administration. Pinochet was head of state and began a war on terror in the name of insurgents. Dorfman's effort is to make visible the comparisons between state violence in the Southern Cone and the contemporary U.S. global war on terror in terms of their parallel subversion of international laws and agreements.

Though Chile was a pivotal country for political battles during the cold war turmoil, representing in Henry Kissinger's eyes "the irresponsibility of its own citizens," as a story of counterrevolution it often resides outside the purview of centers of power, even while there are important linkages to this history through U.S. foreign policy and economic globalization.[8] Though the global news story, especially after Pinochet's London arrest in 1998, put the issues of state terror, disappearance, and Pinochet as terrible dictator squarely within the purview of U.S. public attention, the role of the United States was often disarticulated from a discussion of the historical period and its effects. Thus, by invoking the other 9/11 in a U.S. context, Dorfman interrupts dominant historical narratives.

The Other 9/11

Bringing forward this other 9/11 as Dorfman and Allende do into the public sphere (as many exiles also do, though their efforts are less noticed) does the work of what Lisa Yoneyama describes as the useful ways that memory can point out the constructedness of national and global histories (1999). By writing on the indelible traces and articulations of memory in Hiroshima, Yoneyama shows us how Hiroshima's decimation and its memory have been, as she succinctly puts it, "secured within the global narrative of the universal history of humanity" (13). Similarly, the narrative of Chile as an economic miracle and "democratic" government was secured through global and national political arenas that eclipse the complexity of memory formations, writing out of the historical archive (often in large swaths of black pen in unreadable CIA documents) those that suffered in their bodies and minds the political heat of the cold war and its long shadow.

As sociologist Elizabeth Jelin, Susan Kaufman, and their collaborators have noted in their fieldwork on memory archives (2006), dates are important historical indexes that anchor present-day struggles over memory. Like September 11, 2001, the 9/11 of 1973 was in Chile for many years an occasion for triumphant military parades and, from the margins, a chance to commemorate the tragedy of Allende's death through protest by throwing Molotov cocktails at the police. Of course, currently Pinochet and his family have all but been discredited, while Allende has in many ways been vindicated, especially during Michelle Bachelet's presidency, which often made reference to the social damage committed by Pinochet's legacy.

In the public domain, there is also an ever-expanding rich cultural and activist production that commemorates September 11, 1973, including special issues of Nelly Richard's *Revista de Crítica Literaria*, the commemorations of the thirtieth anniversary of Salvador Allende's death, and other important sites of memory's excavation. In the United States, as a central form of exilic identification, there are important efforts by Chilean exiles to keep this history alive, including the San Francisco Bay Area collective "Two 9/11s in a Lifetime," which had one event and exhibit on memory politics in 2003 and then another exhibit this year. Other important efforts are Cecilia Vicuña's poetry and visual artwork, the video work of Ariel López and Hector Salgado, the distribution of Canadian National Film Board documentaries, such as Marilú Mallet's *Unfinished Diary,* and the circulation of Patricio Guzmán's films *Obstinate Memory, The Pinochet Case,* and *Salvador Allende.* But these are often lesser-known efforts and cultural projects, some of which circulate regionally, while others have national and global attention though outside of the U.S. mainstream mediascape.

Situating Allende

Both Ariel Dorfman and Isabel Allende function within that ambiguous category that sometimes dubs them as public intellectuals, a nomenclature that is almost a point in contradiction given that the public sphere has been privatized in terms of intellectual participation (Somers 1997). In the few years after September 11, 2001, Dorfman and Allende seemed to have continuous access to major national media outlets, like the *Washington Post*, National Public Radio (NPR), the Public Broadcasting Service (PBS), the *New York Times*, and so forth. Among a host of other public voices, they became the voices of the South in the North about the "torture question," state violence, the excesses of a military state, and, in the case of Isabel Allende, the question of belonging to the U.S. nation through her newfound status as immigrant rather than exile. From the perspective of hegemonic historical amnesia, in telling the story of 9/11, Allende and Dorfman foreground the role and consequences of the 1973 U.S. military intervention in Salvador Allende's unfulfilled social project.

In Chile, prior to the military coup, for my mother and grandmother's generations Isabel Allende was most known for her column in *Paula*, a fashion magazine with hardy journalistic pieces. It was there that Isabel Allende had a large following among working-class and middle-class women. Allende's writings were often viewed as saucy, outlandish, and even feminist, as female family members and relatives have relayed their joy and interest in reading her columns. In many ways, she articulated things about heterosexual desire and its effects that were considered taboo in the days prior to the feminist movement in Chile, including abortion, divorce, women's pleasure, and extramarital sex. It was not until the 1980s, during the dictatorship period, which had a close connection to the human rights movement, that a visible feminist movement had political clout in Chile. As Isabel Allende has said in interviews, it was the early development of her literary personality as ironic and embellished in *Paula* that helped her voicing in the later best-selling work.

All ten of Isabel Allende's books (genres of fiction, memoir, auto-biography, and part cookbook, part pop erotic) have been on the U.S. national best-sellers' list. Isabel Allende's commercial success has been enhanced by how she has been configured by the media, by Harper Collins, her publisher, and as a multicultural author. At the same time that the multicultural debates in public intellectual spheres were taking place in the United States, in the United Kingdom, and more broadly around the world (in places like Canada, France, and Australia), Isabel Allende was enjoying best-selling status, with her books on multicultural food, multicultural history, and, with the latest memoir, on her yearning for "belonging" to the nation state. Her work depends on the post–civil rights era, where claims for recognition are rearticulated in the dominant media and political-racial landscape into multiculturalism (Dávila 2001). The terrain of multiculturalism seemed to simultaneously see a widening of space for certain texts, authors, and alliances, producing a backlash among what Roger Hewitt would say were disparate but related phenomena. This backlash included responses in local and national communities to policies on immigration, community relations, and racism. In the United States, this attack on multiculturalism was a backlash to the increasingly high profile of the ideas of equal opportunity—the "level" playing field. Undoubtedly, Allende benefited from the widening terrain that put questions of race, even in the liberal coding of multiculturalism, at the center of political discourses and practices.

Immigrant Subjects

In the post-9/11 landscape of surveillance and in ever widening discourses about national security, forms of governance have become increasingly organized around the deportation of immigrants in order to make the United States "a safer place." In 2004, the U.S. Department of Homeland Security (DHS) and Immigration and Customs Enforcement (ICE) supported the National Intelligence Reform and Terrorism Prevention Act of 2004, which mandates the creation of forty thousand new beds and barracks for immigrants at four undisclosed locations over the next five years. As the ICE Web site states, "Strengthening the nation's capacity to detain and remove criminal and other deportable aliens is a key component of the comprehensive strategy to deter illegal immigration and protect public safety. Detention and removal of illegal aliens is a priority of U.S. Immigration and Customs Enforcement (ICE). This commitment has been backed by significant resources devoted to detention and removal efforts" (U.S. Immigration and Customs Enforcement 2010). I do not cite the ICE Web site for its subtlety. The language and strategy of "removal" hearkens back to the U.S. period of forced removal of native populations at the end of the eighteenth century, making direct links between neocolonial rule and the establishment of the U.S. nation. In the post-9/11 era, the tortured subject and the immigrant subject share a governmentally produced ontology that stretches back through time to the native captive of successive removal periods. These subjectivities are those at once banished and excluded from the "rights" structures of the nation.

One way the captive has been normalized within current regimes of state power is through the "detainee," which includes the immigrant, the tortured subject, "the alien" (as the ICE Web site names), and the foreigner. Much of the movement of the state to deregulate and dismantle human rights, in turn normalizing contemporary configurations of state power, has been precisely by naming torture, or cruel treatment and punishment of state prisoners, as a debate rather than a strict violation of international accords and first-generation security rights. How does historical memory operate in this overdetermined discursive terrain?

One significant axis of Isabel Allende's memoir is to locate it memory public discussions regarding successive waves of anti-immigrant developments. That is, what is notable is her move from a primary identification with "exile" to an identification in the United States with the category, or term, "immigrant." Indeed, it is clear in the opening of *My Invented Country* that she has made this shift in her identity, a shift that corresponds to the aftermath of September 11, 2001, attack in New York:

> Until only a short time ago, if someone had asked me where I'm from, I would have answered, without much thought, nowhere; or Latin America; or, maybe, in my heart I'm Chilean. Today, however, I say I'm an American, not simply because that's what my passport verifies, or because that word includes all of America from north to south, or because my husband, my son, my grandchildren, most of my friends, my books, and my home are in northern California; but because a terrorist attack destroyed the twin towers of the World Trade Center and starting with that instant, many things have changed. We can't be neutral in moments of crisis. I realize today that I am one person in the multicolored population of North America, just as before I was Chilean. I no longer feel that I am an alien in the United States. (Allende 2003, xi)

The obvious point in this passage, other passages like this in the book, and comments made in forums like an interview with Bill Moyers, interviews on NPR, and book presentations at Barnes and Noble is that precisely at the time that Isabel Allende no longer feels alien, so many groups are cast as "alien" to the nation. In other words, there is a renouncement of critical engagement in the politics of post-9/11 by saying "I now belong" precisely when so many others now do not belong (or continue to not belong) in the hegemonic conception of the nation. Another reading here is her contradictory and confused invocation of the term "American," at once including the hemisphere and then immediately casting it away when she references North America and the United States. On another level, Isabel Allende moves away from the identity of exile at a moment when this identity can be the source of contestatory politics.

Edward Said talked about the condition of exile as "strangely compelling to think about but terrible to experience. It is the unhealable rift forced between a human being and a native place, between the self and its true home: its essential sadness can never be surmounted" (1994, 137). For Chileans who experienced state terror, the insurmountable sadness of forced exile is often multifaceted, including the loss of dear friends and family members, the psychological pain and physical memory of torture, the loss of a social dream, and so on. It is not surprising then that, *after exile*, longing, mourning, and political critique would be predominant ways of feeling and acting in the social world. Because of the protracted character of the Chilean dictatorship (1973–90), the truncated road to social justice, and the inability to work through trauma that these conditions produced, many first-generation exiles still hold onto the memory of the past as a way to make an identity for themselves in the present. Thus, "ex-political prisoner" and "tortured" are primary identities for many Chilean exiles, even some thirty years later. And, as I have talked about elsewhere, these primary identities motivate political standings, critiques, and activism for exiles living in the United States, even among a second generation. Bharati Mukherjee describes this connection between the condition of exile and politics: "Exile lacks the grandeur, the majesty, of expatriation. The expatriate, at least, is validated by a host culture, which extends the hospitality, and he often returns it in civic dutifulness. But the exile is a petitioner. He brings with him the guilty reminders of suffering, his stay is provisional and easily revoked, and he is often consigned to the underworld of ethnic intrigue, outside the purview of the law or of the press. If expatriation is the route of cool detachment, exile is for some that of furious engagement" (1999, 218).

Mukherjee's move to understand exile as "reminders" to the host nation and as the foundation for "furious engagement" evokes the potential sources and makings of a politics of and in exile for more than one generation of exiles. On the one hand, Allende renounces the critical space that an identification with exile puts into motion. On the other, her engagement in her memoir with memory, trauma, and the collapsing of time can be read as continuing to deal with the substantive issues with which Chilean exiles deal. In other words, if one reads her memoir, one cannot help but notice that those things that shape the exile continue to persist: memory, longing, fantasy or frozen memory, repetition of the nightmare, and nostalgia. In fact, Allende sees nostalgia as an important departure for the book, as she notes, "At the end of my brief talk, a hand was raised in the audience and a young man asked me what role nostalgia played in my novels. For a moment I was silent. Nostalgia . . . according to the dictionary, nostalgia is 'a bittersweet longing for things, persons, or situations of the past. The condition of being homesick.' The question took my breath away because until that instant I'd never realized that I write as a constant exercise in longing" (Allende 2003, xi).

This affective landscape on which she consistently returns points to the disjunctures of the exilic position but moreover to an affective desire for an official stance vis-à-vis the nation-state that trumps a critical political perspective and identification. For instance, there is a construction of innocence as a voice and positionality in front of questions of exilic identification, as when Allende says, "I'd never realized that I write as a constant exercise in longing," that seems forced for a U.S. audience that does not have access to the multiple determinations and double confluence of exile that someone like Allende has experienced.[9] In many places in the book, there are references to rootedness, rootlessness, a loss of home, and a desire to belong that are somehow written into an official construction of nation, a point to which I will return briefly. There is a way to say that this book that invents Chile as a country of her past and longing is precisely the invented Chile of the exiled imagination—in fact, in many passages she relays how she is always negotiating her past views of the country with how it really is today and that it is difficult for her to accept the present. In the literature on trauma and exile, this would be abstracted as instances of frozen memory.

Themes in her work—themes of rupture, repetitions, and "having to start over and stitch a life for herself multiple times"—are consonant with the collective experience of trauma that many Chileans faced in the aftermath of dictatorship. As Isabel Allende states, "When I watched the collapse of the towers, I had a sense of having lived a nearly identical nightmare. By a blood-chilling coincidence—historic karma—the commandeered airplanes struck their U.S. targets on a Tuesday, September 11, exactly the same day of the week and month—and at almost the same time in the morning—of the 1973 military coup in Chile, a terrorist act orchestrated by the CIA against a democracy" (2003, xii). The images of burning buildings, some, flames, and panic are similar in both settings. As many Chileans, and especially those living in the U.S. have commented, this connection between two dates, two geographical experiences, and two experiences of traumatic memory, was instantaneous. As they (we) saw the images on television, there was an instantaneous connection to that other 9/11, what is called in the literature on collective trauma, a collapsing of time-sense—the past immerses itself in the present. In this sense, the writer's experience is consonant and convergent with an exilic landscape of memories and social trauma, rather than a move away from it.

The repetition of her Chilean story and of "inventing the country" in the frame of the United States, I would suggest, is also an expression of reinstatement of personhood. Annie Coombes says that in traumatic contexts, the act of making can become an insurance against forgetting and thus against the loss of personhood by reinstating—particularly in the case of whimsical manufactures—the capacity for fantasy (2003, 9). In working against the psychologized accounts of fantasy, then, creation and invention provides a set of possibilities for "working through" the past.

The distinct problem that Allende produces through an "invented country" is best understood through Amy Kaplan's eloquent reading of the new terminology of the post-9/11, particularly in the renarrativization of "homeland," and all the symbolic architecture that is constructed around it. She says,

> At a time when the rights of so-called aliens and immigrants have been attacked and abrogated by the USA Patriot Act, when they can be detained indefinitely incommunicado and deported in the name of homeland security, the notion of homeland itself contributes to making the life of immigrants terribly insecure [...] it does this by continually redrawing those boundaries everywhere throughout the nation, between Americans who can somehow claim the United States as their native land, their birthright, and immigrants and those who look to homelands elsewhere who can be rendered inexorably foreign. This distinction takes on a decidedly racialized cast through the identification of the homeland with a sense of racial purity and ethnic homogeneity that even naturalization and citizenship cannot erase. (Kaplan 2003, 61)

The foreboding concept of homeland in the present eerily invokes the Third Reich but moreover demands the smoothing out of heterogeneous subject positions beyond what the security nation is able to contain in its sweep toward the categorization of detainee, or terrorist, for that matter. Inevitably a politicized stance from the position of exile would be rendered "foreign" if incorporation, rather than critical distance, was not its main objective. Moving from a politics of memory and identification where exile is central provides a way to attenuate Allende's position; Allende's real rejection of the term "exile" is an attempt to leave the past behind, perhaps as a working through of the rifts that trauma produces. Unfortunately, in the context of the United States, in narrating her individual working through and distancing herself from the category of exile, she ends up reproducing conservative discourses on immigration, race, nation, and sexuality. For instance, on immigration she discusses, "When I compare my experience as an exile with my current situation as an immigrant, I can see how different my state of mind is. In the former instance, you are forced to leave, whether you're escaping or expelled and you feel like a victim who has lost half her life; in the latter it's your own decision, you are moving toward an adventure, master of your fate. The exile looks toward the past, licking his wounds, the immigrant looks toward the future, ready to take advantage of the opportunities within his reach" (2003, 174).

I read in this passage a desire to move past the exile condition, as a way to work through the tiring repetition of the traumatic past, in Dominick LaCapra's reinterpretation of Freud's categories of "acting out" and "working through." LaCapra reworks these categories to think of the collectivity, and so "acting out," instead of Freudian melancholy, is actually dehistoricized nostalgia and political mythmaking (2001). "Working through" is aligned with cultural practices that allow for historicization, mourning, and transformative memory work. I would suggest that the way Isabel Allende's memoir has discursively played out in the U.S. public sphere is that it is supposed to do the work of "working through."

Unfortunately, in making this conclusion, she is no longer exile and instead considers herself an immigrant able to eschew the structural racialization and material effects of this condition. In such an incorporative move, Isabel Allende forecloses the possibilities of what Ella Shohat terms the "prospects of critical community affiliations" (1998, 52). Allende forecloses the possibility of exile identity as the source of political action and connection between communities. This is precisely the opportunity that Dorfman's work opens up by suggesting comparative points of historical continuity. It is important to note here that many first-generation Chileans, one-and-a-half generation, and second-generation persons living in the United States continue to identify as exiles as a source for furious political engagement, critical interventions, and community affiliation.

Conclusion

To evoke a historical space outside of U.S. exceptionalism and innocence, I have been concerned with historical reminders of political violence exacted upon subaltern populations as a continuity, rather than rupture, with the past. One way to establish lineages of power is by discussing the coercion and punishment of bodies in the context of 9/11 and its aftermath, namely through torture (see Avery F. Gordon, chapter 2, this volume); another way to address how the rhetoric of the racial state creates yet another scene for the proliferation of violence is through the discursive production of difference, or, for instance, to question practices of the state that have long been internationally banned (i.e., "the torture debate"). Scholars such as Susan Buck-Morss and Jürgen Habermas put into play a Benjaminian dialectics of history to rethink conventional historiography and the reconstruction of memory as a future-oriented project with a radical orientation toward the past, much in the same way that I referred to Todorov's notion of exemplary memory (1995). In fact, the importance of much of Isabel Allende and Ariel Dorfman's public intellectual work and discourse, especially in the immediate aftermath of the events of September 11, 2001, was to interrupt the narrative of U.S. innocence and the multifold justifications for torture, unlawful detention, the war in Iraq, and the Bush administration's narratives about external threats to national security, including the persistent construction of immigrants crossing the U.S.–Mexico border as a terrorist threat.

Certain forms of commemoration of September 11, 2001, provide a platform and justification for state coercion. In contradistinction, the 9/11 from the south, when analyzed from the perspective of empire, provides a point of contestation to these dominant memory formats. The question of memory, "invention," identity, and exile within the recent documentary work and circulation of Isabel Allende and Dorfman's proposal on the subject of torture and American innocence at the very least makes present a struggle over historical memory that is valuable for the ongoing constitution of more just social narrations about the past toward a potential better future.

Notes

1. Patricio Guzmán's films, as I have written elsewhere (2007), are especially poignant on the bombing, including *The Battle of Chile* (1978) and *Obstinate Memory* (1997). Marilú Mallet's film *They Danced Alone* (2003) uses slide images of the

scene of September 11, 1973, from documentary footage and still photographs. See also Ariel Herrera (2003).

2. This is a topic that Josefina Saldaña-Portillo takes up with success through an analysis of the developmentalist discourse and masculinist revolutionary imaginaries of Latin American political Left ideologies (2003).

3. Here I am referring to Goldberg's elaborated definition of the modern nation as being deeply racial in its character "from the moment of its emergence [. . .] at precisely the time rapidly emergent and expanding social mobilities produced increasingly heterogeneous societies globally, [the] social order was challenged to maintain homogeneity increasingly and assertively" (2002, 11). For a discussion of racial states that emerge out of naturalism and historicism, or what Goldberg describes as two "seemingly mutually exclusive" but historically coexistent traditions (74), see chapter 4 of this volume.

4. Specifically, in the aftermath of the attacks on the World Trade Center, Arab Americans have been the target of differential treatment, which has produced "premature death." Ruthie Gilmore discusses racism in the prison industrial complex and, more broadly, in precisely this way as the "state sanctioned or extralegal production and exploitation of group-differentiated vulnerability to premature death" (2007, 247).

5. Journalist Christopher Hitchens gave his opinion early on about this formulation, saying, "Loose talk about chickens coming home to roost is the moral equivalent of the hateful garbage emitted by Falwell and Robertson, and exhibits about the same intellectual content. Indiscriminate murder is not a judgment, even obliquely, on the victims or their way of life, or ours" (2001).

6. See Gary Wills chapter "Original Sinlessness" in his book on American myths and Reagan's legacies (1987, 449–60).

7. This 2004 report was commissioned by Ricardo Lagos's administration and headed by Sergio Valech to document the testimonials of Chilean survivors. Though it did not have wide circulation, it was a momentous marker, acknowledging what had been the invisible subjects of political violence in the nation.

8. For detailed discussions of the history of Richard Nixon, Henry Kissinger, and U.S. state involvement in supporting the military coup in Chile, see Peter Kornbluh's *The Pinochet File: A Declassified Dossier on Atrocity and Accountability*.

9. Isabel Allende was technically not a political exile, though this matters little. She left Chile for Venezuela with her husband prior to the military coup, and then when the military dictatorship occurred there in 1974, she left for the United States.

Works Cited

Allende, Isabel. 2003. *My Invented Country: A Memoir*. New York: HarperCollins.

Coombes, Annie. 2003. *History after Apartheid: Visual Culture and Public Memory in a Democratic South Africa*. Durham, N.C.: Duke University Press.

Dávila, Arlene. 2001. *Latinos, Inc.: The Marketing and Making of a People*. Berkeley: University of California Press.

Dorfman, Ariel. 2002. *Exorcising Terror: The Incredible Unending Trial of General Augusto Pinochet*. New York: Seven Stories Press.

———. 2005. *Innocence*. American Shadows Series. New York: POV.

———. 2006. "The Torture Debate: Are We Really So Fearful?" *Washington Post*, September 24. http://www.washingtonpost.com/wp-dyn/content/article/2006/09/22/AR2006092201303.html (accessed May 6, 2010).

———. and Armand Mattelart. 1971. *How to Read Donald Duck: Imperialist Ideology in the Disney Comic*. New York: International General.

Dudziak, Mary, ed. 2003. *September 11 in History: A Watershed Moment*. Durham, N.C.: Duke University Press.

Gilmore, Ruthie. 2007. *Golden Gulag: Prisons, Surplus, Crisis, and Opposition in Globalizing California*. Berkeley: University of California Press

Goldberg, David Theo. 2002. *The Racial State*. Malden, Mass.: Blackwell.

Gómez-Barris, Macarena. 2005. "Two 9/11s in a Lifetime: Chilean Displacement, Art and Terror." *Latino Studies* 3 (1): 97–112.

Herrera, Ariel. 2003. *Two 9/11s in a Lifetime*. San Francisco: Video Independent Production.

Hershberg, Eric, and Kevin W. Moore. 2002. *Critical Views of September 11: Analyses from Around the World*. New York: The New Press.

Hitchens, Christopher. 2001. "Against Rationalization." *The Nation*, October 8. http://www.thenation.com/doc/20011008/hitchens (accessed May 10, 2008).

Jelin, Elizabeth, and Susana G. Kaufman. 2006. *Subjetividad y figuras de la memoria*. Mexico City: Siglo XXI.

Kaplan, Amy. 2003. "Homeland Insecurities, Transformations of Language and Space." In *September 11 in History: A Watershed Moment*, ed. Mary Dudziak, 55–69. Durham, N.C.: Duke University Press.

Kaiser, Susana. 2005. *Postmemories of Terror: A New Generation Copes with the Legacy of the Dirty War*. London: Palgrave Macmillan.

Kornbluh, Peter. 2003. *The Pinochet File: A Declassified Dossier on Atrocity and Accountability*. New York: The New Press.

LaCapra, Dominick. 2001. *Writing History, Writing Trauma*. Baltimore: The John Hopkins University Press.

McCain, John. 2005. "Torture's Terrible Toll." *Newsweek*, November 21. http://www.newsweek.com/id/51200/page/1 (accessed May 30, 2008).

McCoy, Alfred W. 2006. *A Question of Torture: CIA Interrogation, from the Cold War to the War on Terror.* New York: Metropolitan Books.

Mukherjee, Bharati. 1999. "Imagining Homelands." In *Letters of Transit: Reflections on Exile, Identity, Language and Loss,* ed. André Aciman, 65–87. New York: The New Press.

Prashad, Vishay. 2001. "Hitchens' Call for Blood, American Innocence." *Counterpunch.org,* September 24. http://www.counterpunch.org/prashad3.html (accessed May 14, 2008).

Said, Edward. 1994. *The Politics of Dispossession: The Struggle for Palestinian Self-Determination.* New York: First Vintage Books.

Saldaña-Portillo, María Josefina. 2003. *The Revolutionary Imagination in the Americas and the Age of Development.* Durham, N.C.: Duke University Press.

Shohat, Ella, and Robert Stam, eds. 1998. *Talking Visions: Multicultural Feminism in a Transnational Age.* Cambridge: MIT Press.

Somers, Margaret R. 1997. "Fear and Loathing of the Public Sphere and the Privatization of Citizenship: How to Deconstruct a Knowledge Culture." Center for Research on Social Organization Working Paper #5, *Transformations: Comparative Study of Transformations,* March. http://hdl.handle.net/2027.42/51319.

Todorov, Tzvetan. 1995. *Les abus de la mémoire.* Paris: Arléa.

U.S. Immigration and Customs Enforcement. 2010. "Immigration Detention Facilities," April 13. http://www.ice.gov/pi/dro/facilities.htm (accessed May 7, 2010).

Valech, Sergio. 2004. *National Commission on Political Imprisonment and Torture Report.* Santiago: Ministerio del Interior.

Wills, Gary. 1987. *Reagan's America: Innocents at Home.* New York: Doubleday.

Yoneyama, Lisa. 1999. *Hiroshima Traces: Time, Space, and the Dialectics of Memory.* Berkeley: University of California Press..

CHAPTER 10

Between Celebration and Mourning

Political Violence in Thailand in the 1970s

Sudarat Musikawong

Those of October 6 do not have material body to this day. The two [October] events are like siblings. We have happiness and suffering together [...] October 14 emphasizing freedom, rights, and democracy [...] October 6, a socialist justice and anti-imperialism. Thai society and those who have power are trying to separate them, as different, and making October 6 homeless, without a physical body.

—Thirayuth Boonmee, keynote commemoration address
at Thammasat University

O CTOBER 14, 1973, WAS THE FIRST TIME IN THAILAND that a popular uprising of more than five hundred thousand demonstrators in the nation's capital of Bangkok successfully ousted a military regime. Only three years after the October 14 uprising, on October 6, 1976, inside the gates of Thammasat University, four to five thousand students and supporters protested against the return of former dictator General Thanom Kittikachorn. That Wednesday morning, Thai military, police, and right-wing civilian vigilante groups shot rocket-propelled grenades, bullets, and antitank missiles into the campus. The assault escalated to shootings and students being rounded up to be to be beaten, hanged, sexually mutilated, and burned. According to official records, forty-three people were killed and more than three thousand people were arrested after the massacre. The October 14 uprising and the October 6 massacre have become two of the most contentious events in Thai contemporary social movements. While the October

14 uprising has become a celebrated national event in Thai democracy, the October 6 massacre has become a deeply painful memory for the generation that experienced it, whether victims or perpetrators. Until public commemoration activities some twenty years later, Thailand was plagued by a lack of public articulation for these tumultuous events that redefined a generation.

Thailand in the 1970s can be understood in the context of an Asian version of the American 1960s: a period in which new forms of political subjectivity; critiques of capitalism and imperialism in politics; activism; and cultural production were at their height (Connery 2006, 545). Ji Ungpakorn argues that the eventual defeat of the left in 1970s Thailand disarmed contemporary people's movements. The October generation that emerged either became key members in Thaksin Shinawatra's Thai Rak Thai party; abandoned party politics and opted for direct action as local anarchists, ultimately refusing to participate in electoral and party politics; or adopted free-market logic and neoliberalism as the ruling idea of the day (Ungpakorn 2006). While several Asian contexts reveal the lasting impact of the Left's defeat, one cannot turn simply to official political participation in elections and political parties to understand the cultural shifts and social significance occasioned by the struggles over remembering and forgetting state violence in Thailand.

During my fieldwork in Bangkok in 2003, I met Eam, a woman in her twenties studying women's studies at Chiangmai University. She had been interested in the October 6 massacre of the student activists since she was in high school; the massacre was not taught or spoken about at school, but Eam had an uncle who was part of the student movement in the northern provinces. She told me that, in 1999, she had found a photograph of a young woman's violated body when she was reading one of her uncle's books about the massacre. Every October 6 since then, Eam lights incense, prays that the young woman's soul found peace, and wonders: What was her name? Who was she? Why did this happen? When I first came across this image, I was struck by the same questions and a similar sense of loss for a young woman I did not know. Hers was a case of state violence, but her political activism against the government made her unavailable for incorporation into stories of female sacrifice for national progress. Under conservative nationalist constructions, women could be active agents of national history, but only in the fight against invading foreigners, like that of Burmese in the legend of sixteenth-century Queen Suriyothai.

What happens when the state seeks to monopolize the commemorations of national tragedies, enlisting loss as social practice and eliciting national subjects to celebrate the state's glory? Here, loss operates in double inscription: loss evokes the trauma of state violence by becoming the ground for celebratory practices ensuring the repair and maintenance of Thai state nationalism (nation, religion, monarchy), and loss is transformed into mourning practices by nonstate actors (relatives in coalition with activists), reminding the public of the violence caused by the state and challenging the state's transformation of loss as celebration of nation. In this ethnographic account, I observed this loose coalition of nonstate actors who call themselves unofficially, the people's contingent (*fai prachachon*) and insist on mourning practices that challenge the call for celebration from the state (i.e., parliament, prime minister's administration, politicians). *Fai prachachon* literally translates to "the side of the people" and is what many relatives in coalition with activists would refer to themselves as, which is in contrast to the side of government (*fai ratthaban*).

While loss appears overdetermined with state mastery, I posit that the excess of tragedy and atrocity of state violence fosters unruly commemorative practices that reveal uncontainable loss. No state commemoration can manage the meaning of loss as experienced and practiced by communities, activists, and relatives of those killed. With regard to episodes of political violence as practiced on women's bodies (an unmentionable aspect of state violence in the 1970s), the strategies against the state's monopoly over history and nation reside in a politics of loss and the insistence against complete obliteration of this loss from public memory. Ultimately, in contrast with state-prescribed notions of the subject, multiple subjectivities emerge through the unruly and uncontainable social practice of commemoration. The commemoration itself can be thought of as a social practice that links past to present as a public act; it gives a sense of performative, temporal continuity from a past self to a present self. In the national context, this self can be the subject (both constituted by the state and self-made; Ong 1996).

According to Jeffrey Olick, "new regimes seek ways to 'settle' the residues of their predecessors, while established systems face a rise in historical consciousness and increasingly pursue a 'politics of regret'" (1999, 333). This politics of regret over past injustices is the contested ground, a moment of opportunity prior to the settling of hegemonic meaning. The contest may take several forms, but I turn to commemoration as a social practice that demonstrates how space and subjectivity are imbued with meaning through social actors who decide whether to either participate in state celebration or forget the challenges against dictatorship and capitalism, which were indicative of the radical Left social movements of the 1970s. For Thailand and the experience of political violence in the 1970s, a contest materialized between a politics celebrating democracy already achieved and a politics of mourning over incommensurable loss of life and a Left political subject observable through the social practice of commemoration. Unlike the monument and the archive, the continual unfolding of commemorative acts, of which I provide an ethnographic account, demonstrate an instability before meaning is settled. In Thailand, ideologies of the political Right are rooted in the power of the sovereign monarch, the military and police elite, and the Buddhist Sangha order over life. Royalist nationalism, as the ideology of the political Right, emerged as a hegemonic expression committed to neoliberalism and a rising tide of cultural conservatism.

This is a story of how state entities like the Thai parliament and the Thaksin Shinawatra administration enlisted royalist notions of national subjectivity in their commemoration prescriptions. In spite of, and because of, this prescription, activists have struggled to reclaim a Left political subject. The contest over Thai political subjectivity is waged between two distinct factions. On one hand, activists seek to give voice to a marginalized "Left subject," one that mourns past political violence, calls attention to the state's monopoly on violence, and connects past social injustices with the present condition. On the other, factions of parliament and their allies elevate a democratic "royalist subject" that celebrates traumatic pasts by transforming tragedy to heroic sacrifice. Ultimately, while the contest was "won" in hegemonic terms by the more-conservative factions, the instability over who owns the meaning of the subjectivity of a Thai Left and oppositional movements give reason to believe that trigger events and social practices rooted in a people's commemoration of past state crimes may loosen the grasp over such meaning that state entities and royalism currently enjoy.

Often, the nation lays claim to subjects by requiring the ultimate sacrifice: life (Anderson 1991). As Rebecca Scott in chapter 6 of this volume suggests, Appalachia reclaims its belonging to the U.S. nation through notions of self-sacrifice in relation to military service. But not all lives that sacrificed for the nation are claimed through military service. Some thirty years after the October 14 uprising, the lives of demonstrators lost due to state violence were reclaimed as an act of national sacrifice against military rule and were symbolically rearticulated by the conservative factions as expressions of loyalty to the nation, religion, and monarchy. "Royalism," be it from the political Right or the Left, maintains and reinvents the royalist subject as loyal to the nation-state, its religion, and its king. My use of the "Thai Left subject" refers to a subjectivity rooted in the Communist Party of Thailand (CPT), and student, labor, and farmers' movements from the 1970s, including Marxist–Maoist political alliances. After the CPT struggle was abandoned following an amnesty in 1982, the history of the Left was systematically eliminated, and thousands on the political left, were killed, went into exile, or abandoned their political convictions.

For the royal family, parliament, and various government administrations, national commemorations can define the terms of "proper" Thai citizenship, whereby subjects must remain loyal to the ideological pillars of national identity (nation, religion [Buddhism], and monarchy). The reference to the three pillars of identity originated in the early twentieth century, when King Vajiravudh (1910–25) fashioned Thai nationalism according to the British model of king, church, and country (Vella and Vella 1978). During the fascist years in the 1940s and the military rule by Field Marshall Phibun Songkram and his Minister of Culture Luang Vichit Watakan in the 1950s, the protection of "nation, religion, and monarchy" resurfaced to punish political opponents, criminalize the Left, and legitimize Thailand's several coup d'états. The current King Bhumibol Adulyadej plays an integral role in Thailand's politics and remains a powerful cultural icon. As such, military regimes and civilian administrations in the 1990s, as well as nationalist groups today, have increasingly laid claim to protecting "nation, religion, monarchy." "Nation, religion, monarchy" maintains the impression that Thailand is under threat from outside (ancient Burma and its present-day migrants, 1970s communist Laos, Cambodia, Vietnam, and China) and within (Muslim insurgents in the south, radical labor, farmer–villagers, ethnic minorities, and the Left disrupting political and economic stability).

During the 1940s, the discourse of the protection of "nation, religion, monarchy" was used to legitimate and advocate state sponsored violence against the political Left, a fact relevant to my concerns. However, the mantra's reusability not only points to its function for a conservative nationalism but also demonstrates how it must be continually celebrated and maintained against the challenges posed by commemorations from "the people" that enlist mourning as critical practice. In Thailand, systematic state violence against the Left dates back to the extrajudicial killings of the 1940s, the executions, the banning of books, and forced exile; the October 14 uprising and the October 6 massacre were a continuation of state violence against the Left in Thailand. The Village Scouts, one of the right-wing groups attacking the students during the October 6 massacre, employed ritual practices that fused the symbol of the royal with that of family, "engendering a kind of euphoria," loving the king through the core of one's being (Bowie 1997, 282–83).

The contrast between mourning and celebration are hardly accidental. The conflict brings to light opposing political investments that enlist emotion as their governing sentiment. The tensions between the state and a people's contingent in organizing the commemoration activities of both the October 14 uprising and the October 6 massacre mirror the tensions behind the recovery of a political Left that had lost its ground to that of royalism after the defeat of the Communist Party of Thailand (CPT). The commemorations were foregrounded by two major trigger events: the popular uprising against General Suchinda's coup (known as Black May 1992) and the 1997 Asian financial crisis. These trigger events enabled a revival in progressive political sentiment and gave social capital to commemorating the October 14 uprising via a rearticulation of nationalism. This is not the only instance in which the recognition of the Thai Left was brokered by a conservative nationalism. According to Rosalind Morris (2003, 49), when CPT poet and Marxist revolutionary Atsani Phonlajan's body was returned for funeral services many years after his death, immediately after the Asian financial crisis in 1997, nationalism was used to reclaim his body, erasing his radical Left politics. Here, repatriation became a nationalist act that reclaimed his body and denied his intention of expatriation and political exile in Laos, a neighboring socialist country. Quite differently, in 2006 a popular military coup used "nation, religion, monarchy" against the elected government of Thaksin Shinawatra. The Thaksin administration was not deposed because of its gross human rights violations during the war on drugs in the provinces or its imposing martial law in the south, but rather, Thaksin was deemed unacceptable because he was accused of advocating for a republic, threatening monarchal power (Chokchaimadon 2006). These events together are symptomatic of a crisis over a viable political Thai subject (contested between the Thai Left and conservative nationalism). The contested subjectivities that I focus on are not exceptional for their instability; however, they illustrate the state's recurring attempts to capture and garner the narrative of national history and identity by enlisting specific notions of valued subjectivity, experience, and emotions. Herein lies the challenge of demonstrating temporal moments when personal and collective grief is recast through commemorative acts.

Two iconic events of state violence against the Left and the reformist social movements are the October 14 national uprising (that ousted the military regime) and the October 6 massacre against the student movement. (The latter event marked the exodus of the Left into armed revolution with the Communist Party of Thailand). The cultural memories associated with the October 14 uprising and the October 6 massacre are articulated as conflict between royalist nationalism and the Thai Left, both struggling to define the contemporary Thai political subject. One way in which subjectivity is defined is through the contest over the national past. The state uses public commemorations to tame and shape citizens into loyal subjects that are obedient to the state, Buddhism, and the monarchy. This is an instance in which the discourse of the nation slips into an equivalence; "the state religion" is Buddhism, and monarchy with absolute royalism.

However, national memories, as practiced through commemorative acts regarding trauma, are often unmanageable and potentially disruptive to a coherent story about the greatness of nation and the state project of making "the good citizen." Embedded in each commemorative act are temporal connections between past and present. The commemorative act becomes an affective engagement, the very grounds on which to contest and define what and who are viable political subjects. Commemorative acts become sites where subjects are enlisted into state-sanctioned nationalist projects or recruited into a collective social memory that demands social justice. Commemorations are pliable locations where state entities and politicians celebrate the martyred past, transforming political violence into a national narrative about democracy in contrast to social acts that mourn and reckon with atrocities and injustices. Other articulations of loss operate simultaneously alongside state celebrations and popular mourning practices among the people. Thongchai Winichakul suggests that the trauma of state violence at its first articulation, even in commemoration practices, becomes unspeakable, silenced, and full of ambivalence. Together these social practices demonstrate how loss can be a productive material practice making claim for past deep moral and social wrongs (2002a, 258–66). Loss can be understood as "ruptures of experience, witnessing, history, and truth are a starting point for political activism and transformation [. . .] loss moves from epistemological structures of unknowability to the politics of mourning" (Eng and Kazanjian 2003, 10). I argue that politics can be located in the disruptive possibilities of commemorations that illuminate subjugated social memories expressed through popular practices and a politics of loss. These social practices create the discursive space for a Thai national subject, revealing that the relationship between citizen and the state is one forged from violence. Indeed, the state can assert its power by reconfiguring loss to make both citizen subjects and colonial subjects disposable, as Akiko Naono shows regarding Japan's postwar "endurance doctrine" (this volume). Ultimately, the state can use policy (both juridical and cultural) to maneuver a politics of loss that eradicates people, denying humanity to some while granting it to others.

While constructive for considerations of state projects, the political stakes over the rearticulation of past political violence requires at least three levels of analysis. First, I consider how affective engagements show *how* the practice of memory (commemorations in this case) enlists public sympathies. Second, focusing on nonstate entities, such as the people's movement or the relatives of those killed, reveals how mourning victims as a public act challenges the state celebration of martyred heroes. In the settling of meaning through public commemorations that redefine the narrative "history" of particular public spaces, the state is, at the moment, outmaneuvered by a people's contingent employing mourning and royalism. At each commemorative opportunity, the social practice of loss, popular contingents lay claim to a viable alternative subject, connecting the victims of previous state violence with contemporary social injustice. Last, while my analysis remains hopeful that the renewal of a 1970s Left political subject would revitalize critical perspectives on contemporary social injustices rooted in economic globalization and American imperialism, even the mourning of the Left political subject is problematic.

In an attempt to rescue the Left political subject, one must not forget the gendered terms of state violence enacted upon women victims during the October 6 massacre. The Left and student-activist generation from the 1970s continue to erase gendered and sexual violence enacted on young women activists. Using Avery Gordon's (1997) concept of haunting, I interrogate the absent presence of female victims of sexual violence without resorting to further erasure, dehumanization, or condemnation to the role of victim. When faced with the irreconcilable past, Gordon suggests that one can think about haunting as a "social thing," a trace of a deep, past social wrong that bears its mark on society while remaining invisible to empirical modes of inquiry. She who is without name and biography becomes a social figure reminding us that the commemoration of what is visible in the commemoration practice, even with clear articulations in contest between celebration and mourning, is incomplete.

The Unruliness of Commemorating October

From the mid-1970s until the late 1990s, the student movement was demonized by Thai society as communists and antiroyalists. Government officials who identified themselves as the "October generation" were determined to rewrite themselves as democratic, friendly to the state and capital, and ideologically aligned to "nation, religion, and monarchy." They did so through commemorative acts. The October generation of politicians eliminated the radical elements from the student movement, including memories about the coalition between students, labor activists, and farmers involved in land reform and labor strikes. The scale of strikes brought the country to a standstill. In 1974 there were 358 strikes and 241 strikes in 1975 (Yingworaphan 1977, 15).

Ironically, celebrating the October 14 uprising also meant forgetting the key activists in the student, labor, farmer, and socialist movements who were assassinated in the 1970s. From 1974 to 1975, there were at least twenty-one assassinations of members of the Farmers Federation of Thailand alone (Morell and Chai-anan 1981, 225).This rewriting of events through omission signals an emptying out of the semantics of the "1970s student movement–October Generation." Doing so suggests that neoliberalism and royalism had successfully established relative hegemony over critiques of capital, as well as critiques of governmental and monarchal power. As Kobena Mercer offers, an erasure of the recent past often plays an integral role in emptying the ground for an emergence of new "collective identities [. . .] embedded in systemic relations of class, party and nation-state" (1994, 289). But even more so, as Mercer so aptly points out, the emptying of the meaning of the 1960s and 1970s social movements as a worldwide generational ethos of Left political investments led to a deradicalization based on, at best, benign liberal democratic movements and, at worst, co-optation by the political Right, a demonstration that no one has a monopoly over oppositional subjectivity (Mercer 1994, 290).

Organizing for the thirtieth anniversary of the October 14 uprising in 2003 began early in the year. During the summer, parliament, with a 30-million-baht (a bit less than US$8 million) budget, organized commemorative activities in Bangkok and throughout the provinces. Parliament's efforts to celebrate the October 14 uprising literally demonstrates the state's participation in what Larry Grossberg calls an "economy of affect." The economy of affect refers to how neoliberalism established an alliance with neoconservatism through affective political strategies, which restructured and transformed the lived geographies of the everyday. A conservative political project of "empassioned apathy," which constructed an "organized cynicism or nihilism," eliminated alternative visions, and left one disinvested and depoliticized. Here capitalism transforms not only politics but also subjectivity and the terms in which one interpellates oneself in relation to one's labor as valued bourgeois subject or national citizen (Grossberg 2000, 60, 62). In Thailand, millions of baht are literally invested into generating concerts, democracy celebrations in provincial towns, school projects, and "democracy student camps" that were designed to resignify national history and to depoliticize victims of state violence into heroic martyrs sacrificed for present-day democracy.

Officials like Somsak Prisananthakul, vice chair of the House of Representatives of the Chart Thai Party expressed concern that the heroics of October 14 as an event that signaled modern Thai democracy would be forgotten. He insisted that "[w]hether it be pictures of the millions of people gathered at democracy monument, people running from gunfire from soldiers and the helicopter, or people swimming and running to Jitlada asking *for Royal protection, the King's television announcement calling it a Day of Tragedy . . . All these pictures are in the memories that resonate in our hearts awakened to the spirit of democracy when we commemorate (raleuk)* [. . .]" (2003, 6, emphasis added).

Somsak's rendering "remembers" that the October 14 uprising was a national protest involving millions against the Thanom Kittikajorn military rule; however, by evoking the King's narrative of tragedy, Somsak connects the student movement to royalist democracy. For Somsak, institutionalizing October 14 into a language of Thai citizenship imagines a student movement born of heroic sacrifice, democracy, and royalism, but not of radicalism. His insistence that democracy be remembered was made possible by forgetting radicalism. The initiatives to celebrate the uprising are operations in statecraft that forge a Thai subject born out of a deradicalized student movement.

Despite such concerted acts of forgetting, parliament's millions of baht invested in planning state-sponsored commemorations did not guarantee such a monopoly over meaning. While parliament activities emphasized the celebration and embrace of a national history of democracy, the people's contingent of popular commemorations challenged such celebrations by practicing a politics of mourning that connected the October 14 uprising to local contemporary politics. Their politics of mourning included concerns for relatives' and survivors' redress (*Bangkok Post* 2001) and the "People's Parliament" for land reform and self-determination over natural resources. In 2001, relatives of victims of October 14 receive 4,600 baht per month (approximately US$121), the disabled receive medical assistance and 7,000 baht per month (approximately US$184), and 110 families each received a lump sum of 50,000 baht or US$1,300 (*Matichon* 2003a). Symposiums often focused on the significance of the past in relation to today's possibilities for Thai democratic social movements. In 2003, parliament spent US$7.5 million to organize commemorations separate from that of the people's contingent (Chongkittavorn 2003). While parliament organized activities throughout the country, the people's organizers focused their major activities in Bangkok.

The people's contingent activities included a concert by various bands performing political folk songs, a series of ten-foot freestanding canvases by activist artists, and vendors selling old student activist literature from the 1970s, videos of Black May 1992, and photographic reproductions of the both October events. They planned to use Sanam Luang ("Royal Grounds") for a public stage, a large open field near the Grand Palace and Thammasat University, the main site of the violence during the October 6 massacre (Organizing Committee for October 14 Day of Democracy 2003). However, in October 2003, the Thaksin Shinawatra administration was planning for the Asian Pacific Economic Cooperation (APEC) summit. APEC was to facilitate free-trade talks across regions and to establish Thailand as the central trading hub for Southeast Asia as the effects of the Asian financial crisis wore off. In late September, Bangkok Governor Samak Soonthoraweit rejected the people's contingents' requests to use the Sanam Luang public grounds, arguing that the city was preparing for APEC, beautifying its major streets, and growing new grass on Sanam Luang. While the people's contingent stood their ground and organized activities on October 12 through 14, the city refused to supply electricity and toilets for Sanam Luang on October 14, 2003. In the 1970s, Governor

Samak was known for his vocal antistudent radio programs broadcast on the army station. Samak was accused of instigating the violence against the students through his program on military radio during his early political career in parliament. However, Samak has always denied that allegation (Kongrut 2003). During these years, Samak was part of the civilian political right-wing movement, which included a coalition of staunch royalists, the police and military housewives' association, politicians, paramilitary groups, and right-wing monks like Kittivuttho. Monk Kittivuttho is most famous for giving an interview condoning the killing of communists:

> CHATURAS: Is it wrong to kill the leftist or communists?
> MONK KITTIVUTTHO: I believe it is the right thing to do. Even
>   though Thais are Buddhists, we do not consider this action
>   as murder. Anyone who is trying to destroy our nation, our
>   religion, and our monarchy is not a good person. We must focus
>   on the fact that we are killing demons. This is every Thai's duty.
>   (*Chaturas* 1976)

While the cold war, anticommunist sentiments subsided, tensions still exist between those on the political Right and a newer generation of activists reviving a sense of the left in the 1970s. An October generation, who came of age at the height of the 1970s student movement, has emerged as a strong yet conflicted public voice in politics and among public intellectuals. Public opinion support for celebrating the significance of October 14 as the Day of Democracy indicates that the 1970s student movement has gained uncritical acceptance. A poll results showed 71.6 percent of those surveyed believed the celebrations should proceed, against 7.1 percent who did not (Kaewmorakot and Kitchutrakul 2003; *Matichon* 2003a, 2003c). Surichai Wangaew, the chair of the people's contingent, asserted the importance of the demonstration against Samak's ban on Sanam Luang to reject the comparative importance of the APEC meetings over that of remembering October 14 (*Matichon* 2003b). In contrast, parliament Vice Chair Somsak Prisananthakul avoided Samak's ban on Sanam Luang altogether by holding parliament commemorations inside Thammasat and at the Parliament House (*Matichon* 2003a). The people's contingent chose to protest the ban on Sanam Luang. While I was in Thailand, I attended a rally just two days prior to the major commemorations. What follows is a description of the events that took place on October 12 through 14, 2003.

At that time, a people's contingent organized a rally at Sanam Luang and a march to the October 14 Memorial to protest Governor Samak's ban on the use of public space.

Sanam Luang as Public Space and People's Place

I arrived at Sanam Luang early in the morning on October 12. By then, about a hundred people were already gathered, and artists were setting up large, protest art on freestanding canvases.

In Figure 10.1, a caricature of Samak is depicted in the artwork saying, "Arrest all the poor of Thailand and put them in jail, they shame us. APEC will applaud us that our country truly has a Dinosaur governing our brilliant country." One of the organizing artists featured in the photograph is Vasan Sitthikeit, an artist–activist who came of age during the mid-1970s. While the press's cameras and reporters swarmed around taking pictures, the vocal members of the people's contingent, consisting mainly of the artists and the organizers, spoke against Samak's act of making Sanam Luang

Figure 10.1. Protest against Governor Samak Soonthoraweit at Sanam Luang fairgrounds in Bangkok, October 12, 2003. Photograph by the author.

into a show for foreigners during APEC rather than respecting October's history rooted in democracy. But theirs was not a celebration. The people's contingent marched in silent and solemn protest to the October 14 Memorial, and away from the contested field. I recognized some of the demonstrators as being from a homeless organization; in particular, there was one very vocal "Uncle," who was one of the main organizers for the Makasan Homeless Association.

I served as a translator for an international humanitarian group who had visited the Makasan Homeless Association a few months prior. I had not expected the homeless group to be one of those participating in the people's contingent coalition. We recognized each other and exchanged greetings. As the protest procession began, we walked together. As a member of the homeless movement, Uncle understood his own subjectivity in a nexus of personal memories about October 14 connected to notions of democratic rights. He recalled that, as a monk at Wat Mahathat temple in Bangkok, he witnessed the excessive use of force during the October 14 uprising, and he understood the political position of those like Samak, who were opposed to the commemorations, as right-wing. Uncle insisted that to demonstrate became for him a "sacred human right" to "not hide" the collective participation in the October 14 uprising. He also wanted to counter the attempt to erase the events from public consciousness.[1]

I asked this Uncle about the homeless near Sanam Luang who were being rounded up for the APEC beautification policy and transported to provincial job-training camps or deported if they could not prove citizenship. At that time, the deported homeless population in Bangkok was portrayed in the newspapers as Cambodian non-Thai citizens (*Nation* 2003). He explained, "It is wrong to round up the poor and the homeless, we are people that work, too. It is wrong. What if your son or daughter was rounded up? They think they have rights, in the way that we *do not* have rights. Any activity demanding rights and human rights the homeless group would come out and join in. The homeless need to be in coalition with others, including those doing the October activities."

Scholars such as Don Mitchell suggest that the private sector and state efforts to curb public spaces that include the homeless transform public spaces of debate and rallies into open spaces void of political participation (1995, 121). Similarly, the displacement of the commemorative activities, homeless Thais, and the other nationals from the public space of Sanam Luang indicates state imperatives in maintaining order, the apolitical open space of grass fields, and acceptable celebrations that reinforce royalism while disavowing dissent. This is not so different than Barbara Barnes's (this volume) suggestion that empty spaces of the American Southwest erase histories of conquest and Native massacre and maintain a semblance of American innocence. Samak's empty space of Sanam Luang is a metaphoric and literal intent to erase traumatic histories and people's struggles. In these ways, space and time can be emptied of meaning, leading to the discursive battles over the narrative of national history and how social relations between state, citizen, and noncitizen will be defined, all discursive operations that have material consequences.

In the weeks before APEC, Bangkok city officials implemented several projects to beautify the city, such as repaving streets, planting and trimming trees, installing new telephone booths advertising, "Welcome APEC," practicing the ceremonial activities for the APEC dignitaries, and getting rid of the homeless. Locations such as Sanam Luang became a space fought over by the Bangkok governor and the former student activists of the 1970s. It was also a symbolic space fashioned by the Thai state's performative positioning in the global economy, clearing undesirable people from public view. The homeless and others who live and work at Sanam Luang were portrayed as foreign Cambodians or citizens that lacked proper technical training.

Even as those within the people's contingent claimed that commemorating October bolstered recognition of democracy in Thailand, the commemoration was seen as challenging the nation's attempt to secure a position in the global economy simply because it detracted from preparations for APEC. The practice of alliances between the homeless and the people's contingent organizing the commemorations called attention to the stifling of human rights, including the right to free speech and self-determination. However, the case of the homeless organization's protest against APEC suggested opposition against global capital and revealed how the people's contingent protest against Samak (but not APEC) reworked the meaning of the October events in terms of a neoliberal democracy supportive of global capital.

These competing political stakes demonstrate how Sanam Luang as space and place are both highly contested and socially constructed. For David Harvey (1990), concepts of space change according to new material practices of social production, which include not only capitalist production and colonial production but also that of subversive movements. The contest over Sanam Luang shows how material practices of protest discursively reconfigure these royal grounds from governmental controlled space to that of a "people's place" embedded with the social memories connected to the 1970s' student and radical Left movements. It also illustrates that these processes do not necessarily guarantee the transfer of radical politics. As Gupta and Ferguson (1992, 7–8, 11) suggest, space is hierarchically connected by social forces and is therefore understood as being about the places and people associated with it. In this regard, parliament's strategic use of the leased and sanctioned private space of the university and Parliament House, rather than public space, not only signals that celebrating October 14 cannot challenge government in taming the more radical histories of October but also shows that commemorating October can be contained physically. The meaning of October 14 is made into an idea of democracy tied to parliament and amenable to global capital. The following discussion (based on my ethnographic observations) sharply contrasts the people's contingent's insistence that Thai society mourns the loss of lives and ideals against parliament's imperative to celebrate that loss as nationalist heroic sacrifice.

Retracing the Marches and Rallies

On October 14, 2003, both parliament and the people's contingent were coordinating early morning marches to retrace the demonstrations on October 14, 1973. They occupied separate spaces and expressed different politics and emotions. That day, I marched with the people's contingent. Compared to the parliament's march with thousands in attendance, the people's contingent only drew several hundred marchers. The emotions apparent on the marchers' faces contrasted with parliament's celebration. The relatives and survivors of 1973 wore faces that relived mourning and physical disability. Dressed in black and dark colors, they marched with one wheelchair disabled man. They carried framed portrait photos of those killed. The activists in that march (the People's Parliament, the Makasan Homeless Association, members from the Assembly of the Poor, various and labor organizations) expressed a militant demand for the expansion of economic rights. Student groups and former student activist from the 1970s all marched in silence, wearing stern solemn faces. There were no chants, songs, or expressions of anger. Here and there, recognizable faces of those of whom I came to know nodded or gave a brief smile.

The people's contingent began its march inside Thammasat at the bodhi tree, where thirty years earlier, five hundred thousand people had assembled on October 13, 1973. We crossed Sanam Luang and joined with the parliament marchers. Then we started down Rachadomnoen Avenue. However, where the people's contingent's march led to Dusit Park and back to the October 14 Memorial, the parliament marchers proceeded from Sanam Luang to the Parliament House to attend a religious tribute and speeches by parliament members. These two contingents were joined at the finale: the ceremonies at the October 14 Memorial. Outside Thammasat at Sanam Luang, at least twenty tour buses parked and unloaded marchers wearing yellow T-shirts with the parliament's logo for "October 14, Day of Democracy." These were the marchers that the parliament bused to the event.

In contrast to the solemn mood of the relatives, artists, and activist groups, the marchers arriving on buses recruited by parliament were smiling, talking, wearing bright yellow T-shirts, and waving small Thai flags given to them by parliament.[2] I was curious about who these marchers were. There seemed to be at least a thousand. I discovered that a contingent of the parliament marchers was once here on Rachadomnoen Avenue thirty years ago. The mood was cheerful, uplifting, but their consent to march did not guarantee that a celebration of the October 14 uprising would unfold precisely as planned by parliament. This act of commemoration did not guarantee that embodied social memory would be uniform. Parliament could sponsor buses of marchers, but it could not control the meaning and significance of the commemorative reenactment. The parliament marchers demonstrated a relative autonomy that inscribed one's biography into the October 14 uprising without attributing the meaning of the social movement as "belonging" to parliament or the Thai state.

Midroute, I met a group of ten women, perhaps in their fifties. I asked one woman why she and her group of women friends, from the central provinces about fifty miles from Bangkok, decided to march. She replied that she and her group of friends were working in the textile factories of Bangkok on October 14 and that she had vivid memories of participating in the demonstrations. She had not returned to Bangkok since the 1970s and wanted to take part in the "celebrations," recognizing the importance of October 14. They were part of a contingent recruited from villages by parliament and bussed in to partake in the October commemoration activities. Although parliament sponsored this group of marchers financially and symbolically (e.g., by having them wear the parliament T-shirt), participating in the march did not necessarily mean that they subscribed to the state's version of events. Their participation in the state ritual did not translate to an embodiment of the state's intent, as Paul Connerton's concept of *embodied social memory* might suggest (1989, 102). For the group of women who I met marching down Rachadomnoen Avenue, the experience of marching was about reliving the past and remembering what they witnessed on October 14 as active and informed subjects.

The morning activities ended at the October 14 Memorial with a heavily attended keynote address. All participants from the march poured onto the streets at the memorial. Special rooms and speakers were set up but could not facilitate an audience in the thousands. The keynote speaker was former lead student organizer Seksan Prasertkul. In Thailand, he is well known as an iconic figure in the October 14 uprising. His speech stressed that, as a social movement, the October 14 event could not enact systemic change. The coalition of labor, farmers, and students was not equipped to deal with the systemic exploitation and inequality that was in place in Thailand. He conflated the October 14 events with the student movement. However, Seksan linked the story of struggles against exploitation during the 1970s with that of contemporary struggles. He urged that the work, spirit, and the fight for justice of the 1970s should not end. In light of economic globalization, coupled with the rise of business interests in parliament and the prime minister's office, he reminded audiences of the widening gap between rich and poor. According to Seksan, by the 2001 elections, 92 percent of politicians in office were from an elite background of bureaucracy and business.[3] In contrast to Parliament Member Somsak, Seksan's agents of history were not those who were killed but those who are living, that is, those who could make a difference in the present. In his keynote, the struggle for social economic equality began with October 14, 1973, and continues with these contemporary struggles.

While the narratives between all the speakers may differ, all spoke at the October 14 Memorial. Most significantly, the October memorial for that morning was a public space for multiple and competing narratives. However, accounts by and about women in the movement were notably absent. The problem with the story of heroes and victims of state violence is that few want to discuss what happened to women. As a consequence, the narratives of Left political movements and victims of state violence were eclipsed by a de facto male subject within the people's contingent and at the Parliament House. Women were welcome to participate in the march, but they rarely participated as central figures. The explicit participation by the state to celebrate the October 14 uprising was possible because of the publicly known support that the royal family gave to those injured and the royal cremation ceremony for the "heroes of the October 14 uprising." Therefore, recognition over the October 14 uprising takes place because of its appearance as a historical royalist public condolence. Royalism becomes a hegemonic formation of the male and female loyal–royal subject that is employed by both the neoliberal state and within the "October generation." In sharp contrast, mainstream politicians and state officials avoided the commemoration activities honoring the dead of the October 6 massacre.

In the next section, I focus on the events of the October 6 massacre and argue that gender unravels the logic of royalism, unsettles the de facto male subjectivity prevalent in the Left, and highlights the logic of a masculinity in both left-wing and right-wing groups. I maintain that masculinity obscures not only gendered violence and violation during the massacre but also the memories that privilege the radical Left hero. With these considerations, how can research and writing about events of state violence reconstitute personhood in lieu of women as core social actors in social movements?

It Happened during the October 6 Massacre

Analyzing interviews and personal accounts about the October 6 massacre demands self-reflexivity, a care toward context, and writing "with" the subject. By this, I mean writing from the position of those one studies with the intent to reconstitute their subjectivity. Trinh Minh-ha's (1994) proposes that *speaking nearby* is an indirect language that does not distance or objectify the subject; rather, it comes very close to the subject without claiming to speak for it: "In other words, a speaking that does not objectify does not point to an object as if it is distant from the speaking subject or absent from the speaking place [. . .] To say therefore that one prefers not to speak about but rather to speak nearby is a great challenge. Because actually, this is not just a technique or a statement to be made verbally. It is an attitude in life, a way of positioning oneself in relation to the world" (Minh-ha 1994, 218).

Implementing, Minh-ha's notion of speaking nearby is a difficult task. How does one humanize representations of victims? Simply finding the

trace of the atrocity was difficult. In 1977, the government shut down the free
press and produced propaganda sanitizing the October 6 massacre. During
those days, aside from cheap paperbacks and handouts, radio was one of the
most cost-effective and immediate medium accessible to the Left. The Communist Party of Thailand's (CPT) station, Voice of the People of Thailand,
became an alternative source for accessing the details of the sexual violence
against women (Naew Tautan Padetkan Hang Chat 1977).

A young woman working in the factories interviewed by CPT radio
recalled, "I remember that day. It was two o'clock in the morning and
thought how can I go to work when I should join the student protest." She
recounted how the bullets began to sound like rain. Inside a temporary
medic room at the university, she watched a member of Krathing Daeng
force a girl to undress and crawl across the broken glass bleeding. She
recounted how two young women were ordered to take off their clothes
and were then raped (Naew Tautan Padetkan Hang Chat 1977, 30–44).
Cases of rape were not officially documented by the state.

While cases of rape went undocumented, there was photographed
documentation on a case of the sexual violation of a young woman's
already-deceased body. Occasionally, this photograph was reproduced in
underground books and pamphlets in the 1980s. Additionally, an image
of young women being forced to take off their shirts and lie face down
on the football field is another photograph that circulated since the 1970s
(Cheunthai 1988; *Athit* 1978). However, while the image is present, other
less-visible forms of violence, such as the beatings, hangings, and burnings,
likewise marginalize the occurrence of sexual violence against women.
Rather than remaining solely as evidence of extreme state violence, thirty
years later, these acts of gendered violation overpoweringly evoke shame
for both the women and their families. When I asked an organizer of the
relatives' group of the October 6 massacre why sexual violation was not
publicly discussed, she asked me, "Whose mother or father would want to
even know that aside from being killed, their daughter was raped?"[4]

The October generation, the women who experienced sexual violence and shame, and those who encounter the photograph of this young
woman who was so violated cannot forget the veracity of the image but
cannot remember her name, her biography, her greater significance.
Ironically, perhaps her greater significance is found in the inability to
remember how she was killed. Forgetting sexual violence against women
activists teaches us that in the fight to remember state violence against

the Left, the most buried memories are gendered and sexualized. The force of the trauma of sexual violation makes an already horrible massacre even more unspeakable.

The unnamed young woman in the photograph is a trace that signifies a continued *haunting*. In the work of Avery Gordon,

> If haunting describes how that which appears to be not there is often a seething presence, acting on and often meddling with taken-for-granted realities, the ghost is just the sign, or the empirical evidence if you like, that tells you a haunting is taking place. The ghost is not simply a dead or missing person, but a social figure, and investigating it can lead to that dense site where history and subjectivity make social life [...] Being haunted draws us affectively, sometimes against our will and always a bit magically, into the structure of feeling of a reality we come to experience, not as cold knowledge, but as a transformative recognition. (1997, 8)

As Gordon suggests, we must treat the reappearance and insistence against erasure of the ghost (the young woman) as a haunting. She who is without name and biography is a social figure that reminds us that the commemoration (both celebration and mourning) of what is visible is still incomplete. The rape of the young woman's dead body reveals the degree to which dehumanization can take on gendered terms. While young men were hung and burned among tires, women, dead or alive, were sexually violated in the name of national security and protecting the three pillars of the Thai establishment. If October 6 was already an event made silent, the acts of sexual violence made it something even more marginal. Yet, sexual violence and the rape of a young woman's dead body are just a few of the consequences of making an enemy "other" out of the student movement, constructing them as un-Thai.

The twenty-fifth anniversary of October 6 took place in 2001. The Fact-finding and Witness Interviewing Committee (subsequently referred to as the fact-finding committee) released their findings in two books by a former student leader-turned-academic, Thirayuth Boonmee (2001), and proposed that Sanam Luang house a memorial for October 6. The year 2001 would also mark the opening of the October 14 Memorial. While the activities memorializing October 6 pointed to the survivor's need for public acceptance and recognition, with Prime Minister Thaksin as the guest of honor opening the October 14 Memorial, it would seem that October 14 secured a physical place and recognition by the state.

The activities and speeches of the morning of October 6, 2001, once again reveal contested narratives about the past. I was in attendance at the opening of the October 6 massacre memorial at Thammasat University. I was among many journalists, students, members of the October Generation, and relatives of those killed. In the very important person (VIP) area, Chamlong Srimuang, a 1970s military officer in the counterinsurgency who later became an ascetic monk and politician, and several other state officials presided over the opening of the October 6 memorial and participated in the press release of the fact-finding committee's final report. When I turned to ask a *Bangkok Post* newspaper journalist about her thoughts, she said that he was perhaps asking for forgiveness, and she emphasized that we need to forgive Chamlong. While state representatives did not have speaking roles, their presence offered the possibility of co-opting October 6 into a narrative of prodemocracy, premature forgiveness, or worse yet, complacency. While the October 14 uprising could be tamed and co-opted by state narratives into the progress of national democracy, October 6's trauma could not be tamed.

The conflicting public art surrounding the physical space at Thammasat wavered between militancy, bloody massacre, and prodemocratic event. The masters of ceremonies' scripts focused on poetic readings demanding that commemorations be in line with the official theme for that year: "to clear history and to pass on a legacy of spirit" and to search for a true account of those missing from October 6. The fact-finding committee demanded that October 6 be recognized as a state crime and not a violent accident.[5] Despite this, nobody spoke about the cases of sexual violence and violation committed during the massacre. As a result, in the recounting of these narratives, the Leftist subject was de facto codified as a male. Still, questions remain about the identity of the young women activists. Why were they so violated and forgotten?

During the 1970s, young female student and labor activists campaigned against beauty pageants, the exploitation of sex workers by U.S. soldiers, and the exploitative conditions of textile factory work. Their involvement in politics was punished on gendered terms when, in fact, they were sexually violated. Gendered violation demonstrated through police orders to remove women's shirts and the sexual violence committed against the young woman who was already killed were dehumanizing acts fueled by police and paramilitary caught in the fervor of protecting nation, religion, and monar-chy. At least two decades after the massacre, while the commemoration by the people's contingent serves to remember the victims of state violence, the marginalization of sexual violation of women more specifically produces a masculine radical Left subject as the subject of 1970s national history. Spe-cifically, commemorations erase the female victim and ignore how state violence, when enacted in its extremities, operates through the deep viola-tion of gendered bodies in addition to the decimation of the political Left or the ethnic un-Thai body (whether real or imagined).

At the twentieth anniversary of the October 6 massacre in 1996, the popular *Feature Magazine* published an interview with Siemkieng, mother of Poranee Julakrin, a young woman that was killed. She was one of the four young women killed during the massacre, but I would caution against suggesting that she was sexually violated after her death. The point, how-ever, is to "reconstitute" her personhood.[6] In the archives, I found whatever scant evidence of sexual violence I could, but it was in the commemora-tive act published by a popular magazine that those killed, like Poranee, became young people full of inspiration and unfulfilled dreams. Here, I draw from a published interview excerpt in which Poranee's mother, Mrs. Siemkieng Julakrin describes her memories of the October 6 massacre:

> "Poranee was a student at the District of Banbeung since she was in high school. Soon she took the entrance exam for the univer-sity. She was a kid who was a good student. She wanted to be an accountant. She was so lucky to get admitted into the accounting department at the prestigious national university, Thammasat. She told me with such pride, 'I will earn my degree when I am 22 and I will be done before I am 24. I will be an excellent student so that you can be proud of me, mom.' Back then, nobody in our neigh-borhood had ever gone to university [. . .] we were all so proud."
>
> "Father knew about the news on October 6 when he came back from work. He came into the house pale-faced. [He said] he was going to Bangkok. Father went to look for her at Tham-masat, but could not find her. Finally, he went to Pautek-teung, [a Chinese charitable organization that performs burial rites for the unidentified dead]."
>
> "Father and our relatives did not allow me to see her [the way they found her]. I only saw her face at the services. Later there was

a friend of hers who was a Bangkok police officer who told me [. . .]
he saw her when she got shot. She fell and was beaten with the rifle
handle, breaking her legs and arms. Why did they have to be so
violent? She was just a young small girl, just one person."

"Some neighbors said that they had heard that my daughter was
a communist. I would answer, regardless if she is communist, she
comes home and helps with the housework. Some said she was
Vietnamese. How is she Vietnamese, she is from [our] Ban Beung
district, she is our child! After the funeral service, there were
policemen who came to search the house. At that time we were so
heartbroken, we simply let them do their search. They said this is a
communist house. When they found a Chinese book belonging to
Poranee's uncle they took it. After that, there was nothing."

Poranee's mother's shaking voice told of her unbearable pain.
"[. . .] why did they beat her to that extent? I have cried for over
twenty years, nobody has claimed responsibility. My one daughter,
gone without anything to show for it [. . .] I don't know who to
talk to, who to go and make demands to, and nobody asks about it,
nobody." (*Sarakadee* 1996, 136)

After the massacre, the conservative government and, later, military
coups maintained a system of impunity and silence so that even families seeking an explanation had nowhere to turn. Nobody asked until the
twentieth anniversary brought the October 6 massacre back into public
discourse. In fact, by 2003, so many journalists sought Poranee's mother
for interviews that the family now refuses to be interviewed because in
each retelling, it forces her to relive these deep painful memories.

This chapter shows the national political subject at times entrenched in
conflict and at other times negotiated through affective engagements that
rearticulate past political violence. The state prescribes celebration of the
October 14 uprising as a narrative of national democratic progress. Such
celebratory practices taps into the desire of victims for recognition but
hides and obfuscates the mourning practices that insists that Thai subjects
are forged through a relationship of violence, one in which the state enacts
upon its deviant citizens, in the making of an enemy "other" through political, gendered, and ethnic alterity.

Pierre Nora (1989) asserts that "[t]he passage from memory to history has required every social group to redefine its identity through the

revitalization of its own history," connecting past national self with that of the present (Nora 1989, 15). John Gillis (1995) argues that societies are experiencing a cultural shift from when we once worshiped "the sacred" to a moment when nations worship themselves through commemorations and the symbolic rituals of their pasts. While those studying commemorations and other "sites of memory" demonstrate the shift from the sacred to the nation, what is loss in the process? One may argue that these sites serve to solidify the idea of nation or state projects writing national history through the guise of patriotic duty and sacrifice. Social practice and unrelenting opposition, as in the case of those insisting on remembering the October 6 massacre and the traces of gendered violence against women, may represent in Foucauldian terms an "insurrection of subjugated knowledges" (Foucault 1980, 81–83). Here, a refusal to be incorporated into state-sanctioned national history and also an insistence to not be forgotten create a space for oppositional memory. The gendered violence against young women activists cannot be commemorated by the state. Unlike the October 14 uprising, the deep shame and atrocity of the October 6 massacre as a whole cannot be rearticulated into a story of redemption for the sake of national sacrifice. The mourning practices make clear that the loss was unnecessary, but the state celebrations claim that the losses were necessary. Mourning practices, albeit not always successfully, shift the narrative of loss out of redemption and victory to that of the longing for healing and historical justice through recognition. More so, the project of recognition, reconstituting, and humanizing survivors and the dead is an important counterproject to the overdetermined claim that victims of state violence can be sacrificed for nationalism.

Forging a Politics out of an Uprising and a Massacre

Each year, the Bangkok public commemorations have become more like annual rituals recognizing October. Yet the realization of turning the trauma of state violence into comprehensible narratives of celebration or mourning is contingent on the particulars of social practice embarked by the state and nonstate actors. While parliament, as one entity of the state, embarked on inscribing celebration onto the bodies of thousands of bussed-in demonstrators (marching in uniform, parliament-sponsored, yellow-shirt unison), my ethnographic observations revealed that participants were unfaithful subjects who made their own social meanings even as they participated in state-sponsored activities. The protests against the governor's prohibition of the use of public space for the October commemorations demonstrated a tacit refusal of APEC capitalism and the good economically productive citizen. The refusal is rooted in the demand for a people's right to live without state inflicted violence and state monopoly over history.

Methodologically, studying the force of trauma had involved a combination of being embedded in the society affected by the events by observing various commemorative planning committees, participating in the protests, witnessing the commemorative acts, and finding traces in the archives. In the double inscription of celebration and mourning, the radical Left hero omits the gendered nature of state violence. Attention to the gendered experience of state violence after the event turns celebration–mourning into a project of recovery by attempting to *reconstitute* the dead and the victims of state violence through testimony of their loved ones as social figures that challenge the ethics of commemorations and the reconstitution of their "humanity."

On the twenty-fifth anniversary of the October 6 massacre, in light of the lack of formal justice, Thirayth Boonmee, public intellectual and former student activist of the October generation, called for reconciliation through the building of a public memorial at Sanam Luang to recognize those killed in the massacre. He went as far as to state that "the problem of social history is in the interpretation and in finding value in October 6, which is more important than to sentence those who had done wrong."[7] Some, like the journalist I spoke to, find forgiving these violent events, but not forgetting, a political necessity (Satha-Anand 2000). The commemorative memories about the October uprising and massacre are still constituted by competing public discourse about vengeance, heroism, mourning, recognition and reconciliation, and forgiveness, which are inextricably bound by the contest over the Thai subject. Clearly, the 2003 parliament sponsorship for Thais to celebrate the October 14 uprising meant that politicians competed for the democratic cultural capital infused in the uprising, but the incomprehensibility of the October 6 massacre has left deep consequences rooted in an unspoken precedence that legitimates state violence and grants impunity.

The meaning of the events of October 14, 1973, and October 6, 1976, is a litmus test for the treatment of future of state crimes against the state's own peoples. In light of some events after the 1970s, it is clear that state violence in Thailand was not successfully condemned. Amnesty was issued to the military of all ranks after the Black May 1992 beatings and killings of demonstrators. Under the Thaksin administration, the 2004 Takbai massacre against Muslim protestors and the 2003 rampant extrajudiciary killings in the "war on drugs" in response to the increase of amphetamine black markets in Asia demonstrated that impunity for state officials and state violence is still a serious problem in Thailand. While Prime Minister Thaksin was ousted by a military coup in 2006 under popular pressure for incriminating evidence of Thaksin's own conflicts of interest and corruption in his administration, no one has been brought to justice for any of the state crimes committed under Thaksin's elected government. With the king's alleged support for the military coup and the coup's immediate popularity among ordinary Thais, it is clear that two generations of marginalizing the Thai Left contribute to a social amnesia about military dictatorship and any opposition against right nationalist loyalties to nation, religion, and monarchy. In other words, official states accountability for the violence has not taken place in a fashion that suggests justice has or will be administered.

The people's contingent's refusal to collaborate with parliament signaled that, for community based groups, parliament's gestures were inadequate. The people's contingent used mourning of both the forgotten radical politics behind the October 14 uprising and grieved the human loss from the October 6 massacre to advocate for the recognition that the Thailand that one knows of today is styled from past political violence and public trauma. Yet, problematically, the people's contingent continued to marginalize the issue of sexual violation committed against women on October 6, 1976, securing the Octobers as a masculinist discourse. However, the commemorations demonstrate that when justice for past crimes cannot be attained, cultural practices like acts of commemoration remain as traces in the social world that create a viable politicized citizen not subject to the prescriptions of the state. At a discursive level, if October 14, 1973, becomes about celebrating the path to neoroyalist democracy, then October 6, 1976, harbors the grief and tragedy of cold war violence. The October 6 massacre becomes the lingering ethical lesson that must be made into a national public trauma to unsettle the state's monopoly on violence and national history. No matter how often the state attempts to inscribe the citizen through bodily acts of state-sponsored marches or to clear public spaces eradicating disobedient and undesirable subjects that challenge its impunity and forgetting, every commemoration must be seized as an opportunity to call attention to social haunting and responsibility. How else will society bear witness to past political violence and reckon with it?

Notes

I would like to thank the editors, Herman Gray and Macarena Gómez-Barris, for their insightful editorial comments, the reviewers, other contributors in this volume, Hjorleifur Jonsson, Sarita Gaytán, and Nacho Cordova for suggesting the double inscription of loss. This research was completed through the support of the University of California Pacific Rim Research Grant, the Australian National University Henry Luce Fellowship, and the Center for Asian Studies at Willamette University. All translations from Thai to English are my own and I bear the responsibility for any unintended mistranslations.

1. Historians Somsak Jeamterasakul makes a similar claim. Personal exchange, author's field notes, Bangkok, Thailand, October 4, 2004.

2. In Thailand, as in many mainland Southeast Asian countries, the familiar reference to others even when not of blood relation, is dependent on age and kinship: aunt, uncle, grandfather, grandmother, younger or elder sibling. Author's field video log, Bangkok, Thailand, October 12, 2003.

3. In 2003, the significance of the yellow shirt suggesting the hyperroyalist movement that contributed to ousting Thaksin in 2006 was not yet universally understood. It is unclear whether or not the choice of yellow had solidified into royalist significance at that point.

4. Author's field notes, Bangkok, Thailand, October 14, 2003

5. Author's field notes, Bangkok, Thailand, October 6, 2003.

6. Author's field notes, Bangkok, Thailand, October 6, 2001.

7. One of the most powerful public art pieces by the 20th Anniversary of October 6 Committee (official title) was the portrait of Jarupong Thongsin at Thammasat University. Hundreds of mailed-in postcards depicted a larger-than-life portrait of Jarupong Thongsin, a nineteen-year-old Thammasat student killed during the October 6 massacre. These pieces of his face were given out to his friends and family. Their task was to send back their postcard through the mail. Once assembled all the pieces literally "reconstituted" and reassembled his humanity. I attribute the idea of "reconstitution" to a lecture given by Thongchai Winichakul on this project (Winichakul 2002b).

Works Cited

Anderson, Benedict. 1991. *Imagined Communities: Reflections on the Origin and Spread of Nationalism.* Rev. and extended ed. London: Verso.

Athit. 1978. "Kadee hok tula lob rauy prawatisat leud" (The October 6 court case: erasing the bloody history).

Bangkok Post. 2001. "Transparency Slur Rocks Relatives' Foundation." October 14, 1.

Boonmee, Thirayuth. 2001. Keynote for the 25th Anniversary of October 6, 1976, author's field notes, Thammasat University, Bangkok, Thailand, October 6.

Bowie, Katherine. 1997. *Rituals of National Loyalty: An Anthropology of the State and Village Scout Movement in Thailand.* New York: Columbia University Press.

Chaturas. 1976. "Samphat kab pra Kittivuttho" (Interview with Monk Kittivuttho). June 29, 28–32.

Chokchaimadon, Weerayut. 2006. "Thaksin Clearly Wanted Republic, Critics Charge." *Nation,* May 25. http://www.nationmultimedia.com/option/print.php?newsid=30004843.

Chongkittavorn, Kavi. 2003. "Regional Perspective: Voices Raised to Commemorate October 14." *Nation,* August 11. http://www.nationmultimedia.com/option/print.php?newsid=83607 (accessed May 1, 2010).

Connerton, Paul. 1989. *How Societies Remember.* New York: Cambridge University Press.

Connery, Chris. 2006. "Editorial Introduction the Asian Sixties: An Unfinished Project." *Inter-cultural Studies* 7 (4): 545–53.

Eng, David L., and David Kazanjian. 2003. *Loss: The Politics of Mourning.* Berkeley: University of California Press.

Foucault, Michel. 1980. "Two Lectures." In *Power/Knowledge: Selected Interviews and Other Writings 1972–1977,* ed. Colin Gordon, 78–108. New York: Pantheon Books.

Gillis, John. 1995. "Memory and Identity: The History of a Relationship." In *Commemorations: The Politics of National Identity,* ed. John Gillis, 3–26. Princeton, N.J.: Princeton University Press.

Gordon, Avery. 1997. *Ghostly Matters: Haunting and the Sociological Imagination.* Minneapolis: University of Minnesota Press.

Grossberg, Larry. 2000. "The Figure of Subalternity and the Neoliberal Future." *Nepantla: Views from the South* 1 (1): 59–89.

Gupta, Akhil, and James Ferguson. 1992. "Beyond 'Culture': Space, Identity, and the Politics of Difference." *Cultural Anthropology* 7 (1): 6–23.

Harvey, David. 1990. "Between Space and Time: Reflections in the Geographical Imagination." *Annals of Association of American Geography* 80 (3): 418–34.

Kaewmorakot, Napanisa, and Oraphan Kitchutrakul. 2003. "Oct. 14 Organizers Vow to Defy Ban." *Nation,* October 2.

Kongrut, Anchalee. 2003. "City Hall Will Not Sink 30th Anniversary: Organizers Defy Ban on Sanam Luang." *Bangkok Post,* September 29. http://www.bangkokpost.com/News/29Sept2003_news06.html (accessed October 1, 2003).

Matichon. 2003a. "14 tula" (14 October). October 11, 1.

————. 2003b. "Radom chat thok sapha prachachon yok song 4–5 tulakom nai chalong 30 pii 4 tula" (Mustering the discussion in the people's parliament makes 4–5 October celebration of 30 years October 14). September 30, 15.

————. 2003c. "Samak top to" (Samak slams the table). October 7, 1.

Mercer, Kobena. 1994. *Welcome to the Jungle: New Positions in Black Cultural Studies*. New York: Routledge.

Minh-ha, Trinh T. 1994. "Speaking Nearby: Interview by Nancy Chen." In *Visualizing Theory: Selected Essays from Visual Anthropology Review, 1990–1994*, ed. Lucien Taylor, 433–51. New York: Routledge.

Mitchell, Don. 1995. "The End of Public Space?: People's Park, Definitions of the Public, and Democracy." *Annals of Association of American Geographers* 85 (1): 108–33.

Morell, David, and Samudavanija Chai-anan. 1981. *Political Conflict in Thailand: Reform, Reaction, Revolution*. Cambridge, Mass.: Oelgeschlager Gunn & Hain.

Morris, Rosalind. 2003. "Returning the Body without Haunting: Mourning 'Nai Phi' and the End of Revolution in Thailand." In *Loss: The Politics of Mourning*, ed. David Eng and David Kazanjian, 29–58. Berkeley: University of California Press.

Naew Tautan Padetkan Hang Chat (National United Front Against Dictatorship). 1977. "Voice of the People of Thailand: Reprinted Broadcast." In *Hok tula leud: Peudpeuy riey raeid kankauacheyakam kaung chon chan pokkraung la samunborivan garanee buk thumriey naksuksa yang pa theun thi mahawithiyalay thammasat 6 tulakom 2519* (October 6 blood: Exposing the details of crimes by the state and their henchmen, the case of the barbaric attack on the students), 30–44. Bangkok: Naew Tautan Padetkan Hang Chat (National United Front Against Dictatorship).

Nation. 2003. "Illegals Rounded Up ahead of Apec Meeting." June 28. http://www.nationmultimedia.com/option/print.php?newsid=81132 (accessed May 1, 2010).

Nora, Pierre. 1989. "Between Memory and History: Les Lieux De Mémoire." *Representations* 26:7–24.

Olick, Jeffrey K. 1999. "Collective Memory: The Two Cultures." *Sociological Theory* 17 (3): 333–48.

Ong, Aihwa. 1996. "Cultural Citizenship as Subject-Making: Immigrants Negotiate Racial and Cultural Boundaries in the United States." *Current Anthropology* 37 (5): 737–51.

Organizing Committee for October 14 Day of Democracy (Kanna kumakan jad gan 14 tulawan prachatipatai). 2003. *Kitjakum gnanchalong kropraub 30 pi 14 tula, 14 tula wun prachatipatai* (Activities celebrating the anniversary of 30 years October 14, October 14, day of democracy). Bangkok: The National Assembly of Thailand.

Prisananthakul, Somsak. 2003. "4 tula wan prachatipatai kau pieng tae ya pan leuy pai dung sai lom" (October 14 day of democracy, asking only that it not pass like the wind). *Matichon*, July 1, 6.

Sarakadee (Feature Magazine). 1996. "Rwum leud neu chat thai" (Together blood, flesh, Thai nation). Special Issue.

Satha-Anand, Chaiwat. 2000. "Forgiveness in Southeast Asia: Political Necessity and Sacred Justifications." Keynote address, 17th Annual Berkeley Conference on Southeast Asian Studies, Center for Southeast Asian Studies, University of California at Berkeley, February 12–13.

Winichakul, Thongchai. 2002a. "Remembering/Silencing the Traumatic Past: The Ambivalent Memories of the October 1976 Massacre in Bangkok." In *Cultural Crisis and Social Memory: Modernity and Identity in Thailand and Laos*, ed. Shigeharu Tanabe and Charles Keyes, 243–83. Honolulu: University of Hawai'i Press.

———. 2002b. Southeast Asian Studies Summer Institute lecture series, University of Wisconsin at Madison, July 25.

Ungpakorn, Ji. 2006. "The Impact of the Thai 'Sixties' on the People's Movement Today." *Inter-cultural Studies* 7 (4): 570–88.

Vella, Walter F., and Dorothy B. Vella. 1978. *Chaiyo! King Vajiravudh and the Development of Thai Nationalism*. Honolulu: University of Hawai'i Press.

Yingworaphan, Suwit. 1977. "Kan borihan raengngan nai prathet thai" (Labor administration in Thailand). Mimeograph. Bangkok: Department of Labor.

Traces in Social Worlds

Sarah Banet-Weiser

S OCIAL TRACES CAN TAKE MANY FORMS, and the concept itself is difficult to put your hands on: what, really, are the materials that make up culture, representation, and identity? For me, to think of traces often means to think of the materiality of the trace—to think about what it is, what it was, and what its possibilities are. Social landscapes emptied and filled with new meaning, memories refashioned in the "name" of unity, and identities crafted as stand-ins for violence—all leave a trace of not only what they "are" in current manifestation but also what they could be, what they might have been, and what they have been historically. Traces are also found in cultural objects—artifacts from consumer culture, signs at a protest, and new media practices.

This volume, both simply and complexly, offers a sort of definition of the social trace by focusing on the trace as a search for processes and relations of making meaning in cultural forms that are not always engaged in hegemonic struggles over power but rather embedded in forms of attachment and identification. This collection offers a rich variety of voices that illustrate how culture as a means of tracing the meanings and operations of social forces is a conduit through which intellectual conversations from different quarters, fields, and disciplines might be undertaken about questions of attachment and belonging and about questions of the individual and their intersections with the social world. It also represents a series of conversations within the discipline of sociology, conversations about how sociology has been expanded, refined, and enhanced by interdisciplinary formations such as media studies, feminist studies, ethnic studies, and others.[1] These spaces of interdisciplinarity are within what Raymond Williams called structures of feeling—that which is "felt" and "sensed" about a particular time and place—where attachments are performed and enacted and traces of past social formations and future possibilities reside (1978).

Importantly, these spaces of affect are the context for struggle and contradiction over the articulation and formation of identities.

As Williams argued, structures of feeling, the intangibles of an era, explain the quality of life, and because they are intangible, they are difficult to explain with any kind of concrete description and are not, in any formal sense, "learned." When attempting to excavate meaning from culture, then, we need to recognize emotion, attachment, and affect—the often "irreducible realm of cultural expression" that are often difficult to trace. We need to, in other words, not forget the feeling of a space, a culture, and an identity.

The chapters in this volume situate affect not only as an interdisciplinary idea or a concept but also as a cultural practice and a political project. These practices and projects are often found, as the editors of this volume suggest, in the social traces within culture; the traces of identification and attachment are within that irreducible realm of cultural expression. Indeed, interdisciplinarity is not simply a forced union between two bodies of knowledge—it is itself a "social trace"—it is a mark, or a visible appearance, of what is left when the thing itself no longer exists; it represents what traditional disciplines limit and what they enable. Quite literally, the kind of interdisciplinarity reflected in this volume represents what the editors identify as the intersections and ambivalences of culture, representation, and power, and, as with all intersections, moving through them requires boundaries—the concept of "crossing" implies a boundary designed to inhibit transgression. Transgressions rely, in other words, on barriers for the formation of their identity. The chapters in this volume do not necessarily provide a blueprint or a map for how best to struggle over barriers within culture and power for the simple reason that there is no one way to parse out these cultural negotiations. But they do offer us a crucial point of entry into a cultural conversation that is profoundly about interdisciplinarity, meaning making, and identity. The social traces of culture discussed in this volume challenge naturalized meanings about identity, belonging, the nation, the center, and the margins. The chapters also ask us to engage in a project that creates new definitions for these meanings, one that searches spaces within culture where affect, emotion, and desire are not understood as peripheral or even invisible to identity making but rather form the core of this process.

Many of the chapters deal in some way with a form of commercial culture—media representations, advertising, or individual consumption habits. Commercial culture also often functions as a palimpsest—and it is precisely in the incomplete erasure, the legibility of history, that we can find social traces that exploit and make productive these contradictions. In other words, it is clear that commercial cultures have long been important sites of cultural conflict and sites of negotiation within and between the normalization of particular social relations and critiques of such normalization. These negotiations are heightened within global culture with the increase in the circulation of politics, ideologies, relations, and ideas—an increase that creates a kind of "convergence" of culture while enabling the production of multinational cultures, hybrids, and diasporic communities. Thus, traces can be found within articulations of nationalist sensibility, for in order for shared identities to become national consciousness, these identities are shaped and motivated by feeling or affect. But social traces are not just about a kind of nationalist belonging; rather, they are also often found as articulations of a sense of attachment to social relations—region, space, and place. And social traces are often found in unexpected places, as the chapters in this volume demonstrate. Often, it is within these spaces of contradiction where we can examine how particular forms of cultural knowledge create attachment, affect, and feelings of belonging.

When we examine social traces, we are examining the traces of social processes, transformations, and products alongside more ephemeral or performative expressions and attachments. To explore a social trace is not, as the editors of this volume remind us, about necessarily creating new forms of knowledge but rather about exploring how particular forms of knowledge create us and how we know, feel, attach, and belong. It is about how we make, and are made by, social worlds—both real and imagined, both the visible and the invisible.

Rather than a singular focus on a literal site of attachment, struggle, and opposition, the concept of social traces opens up new possibilities for theorizing culture and carves out imaginative spaces for understanding the coproduction of the individual and the social world. The chapters in this volume offer a look at some of these social traces and, importantly, sketch out for us the relationship of individuals to social worlds on a variety of different cultural terrains. Just as important, however, is the notion that these contributions provide points of entry—from a range of cultural locations—to a reimagining not only of identities, power, and representation but also of the promise and possibility of interdisciplinary work.

Again, it is not a blueprint or a simple recipe for resistance that is discussed here; rather, it is the beginnings of a new kind of cultural conversation, one that recognizes feeling, affect, belonging, and attachment and commits to the role of culture as a set of practices and struggles for meaning. As the contributors to this volume remind us, the space of culture is productive for mapping out the processes of connecting subjects to cultural projects, and it is within this space—the space of interdisciplinarity—where the production of and contests over meanings take place.

Note

1. I am grateful to Travers Scott for his helpful insights and conversations about the nature of the social trace and interdisciplinarity.

Work Cited

Williams, Raymond. 1978. *Marxism and Literature*. Oxford: Oxford University Press.

Contributors

SARAH BANET-WEISER is an associate professor at the University of Southern California Annenberg School of Communication. She is the author of *Nickelodeon, Kids Rule! Nickelodeon and Consumer Citizenship* and the coeditor (with Cynthia Chris and Anthony Freitas) of *Cable Visions: Television beyond Broadcasting*. Her forthcoming book is called *Authentic TM: Political Possibility in a Brand Culture*.

BARBARA A. BARNES teaches in the gender and women's studies department at the University of California, Berkeley. Her current work explores how adventure narratives of human bodies within "wilderness" landscapes in television and film enable the production of normalized national identities and feelings of belonging and exclusion. She has been published in the *Journal of Sport and Social Issues*, the *Journal of the American Studies Association of Texas*, and *Quest*.

MARIE SARITA GAYTÁN is currently a postdoctoral fellow in Latino studies at New York University. Her research interests include race and ethnicity, consumption, identity, and material culture, and her work has been published in the *Journal of Contemporary Ethnography*, *Gastronomica*, and *Food, Culture, and Society*.

MACARENA GÓMEZ-BARRIS is an associate professor of sociology and American studies and ethnicity at the University of Southern California, where she teaches classes in the sociology of violence, Latina/o and Latin American studies, and transnationalism. She is the author of *Where Memory Dwells: Culture and Violence in Chile*, and her work has been published in *Latino Studies, Television and New Media, Sociological Forum, Contra Corrientes, Culture and Religion*, and the *Journal of Tourism and Cultural Change*.

AVERY F. GORDON is professor of sociology and law and society at the University of California, Santa Barbara and visiting faculty at the Centre for Research Architecture, Goldsmiths College, University of London. She is the author of *Keeping Good Time: Reflections on Knowledge, Power, and People, Ghostly Matters: Haunting and the Sociological Imagination*, and the coeditor of *Mapping Multiculturalism and Body Politics*, among other works. She is cohost of the weekly radio program *No Alibis* on KCSB 91.9 FM Santa Barbara. She is currently writing about captivity, war, and utopia.

HERMAN GRAY is the author of *Watching Race* (Minnesota, 2004) and *Cultural Moves* (2005). Gray has held positions as professor of sociology and media studies at the University of California, Santa Cruz, and at the Annenberg School for Communication at the University of Southern California.

TANYA MCNEILL is a visiting lecturer in the Women's and Gender Studies Department at Wellesley College. Her chapter in this collection is drawn from her dissertation, "States of Ambivalence: Familial and National (Be)longings." Her research interests include affect, the production of knowledge about the family, childhood and gender, and the regulation of gender, race, and sexuality.

SUDARAT MUSIKAWONG is assistant professor of sociology at Siena College. Her publications include "Art for October: Thai Cold War State Violence in Trauma Art" in *positions: East Asia Cultures Critique*, "Working Practices in Thai Independent Film Production and Distribution" for *Inter-Asia Cultural Studies*, and "Mourning State Celebrations" in *Identities, Global Studies in Culture and Power*, forthcoming. Currently she is working on two projects: one on the formation of Thai homeland politics through Thai Internet and satellite television and another on the denial of citizenship of Thai migrants who face labor trafficking (with the Thai Community Development Center in Los Angeles).

AKIKO NAONO is an associate professor at the Graduate School of Social and Cultural Studies at the Kyushu University, Japan. She was a postdoctoral fellow at the Japan Society for the Promotion of Science, a visiting research fellow at the Hiroshima Peace Institute, and the founder and project director of the Nuclear History Institute at American University in Washington, D.C. She has written on politics of memory, trauma, and the testimony of Hiroshima and is the author of *"Genbaku no e" to deau* (Encountering the drawings of the atomic bomb survivors) and *Hiroshima/America: Genbakuten wo megutte* (Hiroshima/America: On the atomic bomb exhibit), which won the 1997 Award of the Japan Peace and Cooperative Journalism Fund.

REBECCA R. SCOTT is an assistant professor of sociology at the University of Missouri. She is the author of *Removing Mountains: Extracting Nature and Identity in the Appalachian Coalfields* (Minnesota, 2010). Her research interests include environmental inequality and cultural studies.

Index

www.ingramcontent.com/pod-product-compliance
Lightning Source LLC
Chambersburg PA
CBHW020825270326
41928CB00006B/438